Interna

Library of Technology

A SERIES OF TEXTBOOKS FOR PERSONS ENGAGED IN ENGINEER-
ING PROFESSIONS, TRADES, AND VOCATIONAL OCCUPATIONS
OR FOR THOSE WHO DESIRE INFORMATION CONCERN-
ING THEM. FULLY ILLUSTRATED

STENCIL AND BLOCK-PRINT DESIGNING
LEATHER- AND METAL-WORK DESIGNING
CHINA-DECORATION DESIGNING
TILE AND PARQUETRY DESIGNING
LINOLEUM AND OILCLOTH DESIGNING
CARPET AND RUG DESIGNING
WALLPAPER DESIGNING
STAINED- AND LEADED-GLASS DESIGNING
SELLING DESIGNS AND OBTAINING A
POSITION

PREFACE

The volumes of the International Library of Technology are made up of Instruction Papers, or Sections, comprising the various courses of instruction for students of the International Correspondence Schools. The original manuscripts are prepared by persons thoroughly qualified both technically and by experience to write with authority, and in many cases they are regularly employed elsewhere in practical work as experts. The manuscripts are then carefully edited to make them suitable for correspondence instruction. The Instruction Papers are written clearly and in the simplest language possible, so as to make them readily understood by all students. Necessary technical expressions are clearly explained when introduced.

The great majority of our students wish to prepare themselves for advancement in their vocations or to qualify for more congenial occupations. Usually they are employed and able to devote only a few hours a day to study. Therefore every effort must be made to give them practical and accurate information in clear and concise form and to make this information include all of the essentials but none of the nonessentials. To make the text clear, illustrations are used freely. These illustrations are especially made by our own Illustrating Department in order to adapt them fully to the requirements of the text.

In the table of contents that immediately follows are given the titles of the Sections included in this volume, and under each title are listed the main topics discussed. At the end of the volume will be found a complete index, so that any subject treated can be quickly found.

INTERNATIONAL TEXTBOOK COMPANY

CONTENTS

STENCIL AND BLOCK-PRINT DESIGNING   *Section*   *Page*

Purpose 13   1
Stencils and Stenciling 13   3
Making and Using Stencils 13   3
The Stencil and Materials Required 13   3
Stenciling on Fabrics 13   11
Stenciling on Wood and Other Materials 13   22
Stenciling Decorations on Walls 13   24
Designing Stencils 13   26
Planning the Design 13   26
Sources of Ideas for Designs 13   30
Drawing the Design 13   43
Block Prints and Printing 13   52
Making and Using Print Blocks 13   52
The Print Blocks and Materials Required 13   52
Block Printing on Fabrics 13   56
Designing Print Blocks 13   58
Planning the Design 13   58
Sources of Ideas for Designs 13   59
Drawing the Design 13   59
Stencil and Block-Print Designing Exercises 13   62

LEATHER- AND METAL-WORK DESIGNING

Purpose 14   1
Leather Work 14   2
Tooling, Cutting, and Coloring Leather 14   2
Classes of Leather Suitable for Tooling 14   2
Tools Required for Leather Work 14   3
Plain Tooled or Engraved Leather Work 14   5

v

LEATHER- AND METAL-WORK DESIGNING
—*Continued*   *Section*   *Page*

Repoussé, or Embossed, Leather Work.... 14   8
Cut-Leather Work With Tooled Background 14   10
Cut-Out Leather Work Over Silk........ 14   11
Burnt-Leather Work, or Pyrography...... 14.   14
Colored Leather Work 14   16
Designing Leather Work 14   19
Planning the Design................... 14   19
Sources of Ideas for Designs........... 14   22
Drawing the Design................... 14   23
Examples of Tooled and Cut-Leather Work 14   28
Metal Work 14   30
Tooling and Piercing Metal............. 14   30
Classes of Sheet Metal Suitable for Tooling 14   30
Tools Required for Metal Work......... 14   31
Outline Chasing 14   35
Repoussé Work 14   36
Piercing and Sawing 14   37
Etching With Acids................... 14   39
Bending and Construction Work......... 14   40
Coloring and Finishing................ 14   42
Designing Metal Work................. 14   43
Planning the Design................... 14   43
Sources of Ideas for Designs........... 14   45
Drawing the Design................... 14   45
Examples of Tooled Metal.............. 14   50
Leather- and Metal-Work Designing Exer-
    cises 14   52

CHINA-DECORATION DESIGNING

Purpose 15   1
China Decoration 15   2
Classes of Decorated Chinaware......... 15   2
Painting on China..................... 15   4
Chinaware and Materials Required........ 15   4
Methods of Working................... 15   18
Tinting and Grounding................. 15   19

	Section	Page
CHINA-DECORATION DESIGNING—*Continued*		
Transferring the Design to the China	15	21
Painting the Design	15	24
Gold Painting on China	15	25
Luster Painting on China	15	29
Firing the China	15	31
The Kiln and Its Use	15	31
The Process of Firing	15	34
Designing Decoration for China	15	36
Planning the Design	15	36
Sources of Ideas for Designs	15	41
Color Schemes and Coloring for China	15	50
Drawing and Painting the Design	15	60
Examples of Decorated China	15	74
China-Decoration Designing Exercises	15	79
TILE AND PARQUETRY DESIGNING		
Purpose	16	1
Tiles	16	3
Classification of Tiles	16	3
Encaustic Floor Tiles	16	4
Manufacture and Use	16	4
Designing	16	6
Mosaic Floor Tiles	16	8
Manufacture and Use	16	8
Designing	16	16
Wall and Hearth Tiles	16	22
Manufacture and Use	16	22
Designing	16	25
Faience Tiles	16	27
Manufacture and Use	16	27
Designing	16	28
Parquetry	16	32
Classification of Hardwood Floors	16	32
Parquetry Flooring	16	33
Manufacture and Use	16	33
Designing	16	36
Tile and Parquetry Designing Exercises	16	40

CONTENTS

Linoleum and Oilcloth Designing	Section	Page
Purpose	17	1
Linoleum	17	2 .
Classification of Linoleum	17	2
Cork Tiling	17	3
Manufacture and Use	17	3
Designing Cork Tiling	17	4
Typical Designs for Cork Tiling	17	6
Inlaid Linoleum	17	10
Manufacture and Use	17	10
Designing Inlaid Linoleum	17	12
Typical Designs for Inlaid Linoleum	17	12
Printed Linoleum	17	20
Manufacture, Use, and Designing	17	20
Oilcloth	17	22
Classification of Oilcloth	17	22
Floor Oilcloth	17	23
Manufacture	17	23
Printing Floor Oilcloth	17	23
Designing Floor Oilcloth	17	27
Typical Floor-Oilcloth Designs	17	39
Table Oilcloth	17	43
Manufacture	17	43
Printing Table Oilcloth	17	44
Designing Table Oilcloth	17	44
Typical Designs for Table Oilcloth	17	46
Wall Oilcloth	17	52
Manufacture	17	52
Printing Wall Oilcloth	17	53
Designing Wall Oilcloth	17	53
Typical Designs for Wall Oilcloth	17	56
Linoleum and Oilcloth Designing Exercises	17	59
Carpet and Rug Designing		
Purpose	18	1
Carpets	18	3
Classification of Carpets	18	3
Brussels Carpet	18	6

CONTENTS

ix

	Section	Page
CARPET AND RUG DESIGNING—*Continued*		
Manufacture	18	6
Designing	18	13
Typical Example	18	32
Wilton Carpet	18	33
Manufacture	18	33
Designing	18	35
Typical Example	18	36
Ingrain, or Kidderminster, Carpet	18	38
Manufacture	18	38
Designing	18	40
Typical Example	18	42
Axminster Carpet	18	44
Manufacture	18	44
Designing	18	46
Typical Example	18	49
Tapestry Carpets	18	50
Manufacture	18	50
Designing	18	53
Typical Example	18	54
Rugs	18	55
Classification of Rugs	18	55
Oriental Rugs	18	56
Modern Machine-Made Rugs	18	60
Carpet and Rug Designing Exercises	18	66
WALLPAPER DESIGNING		
Purpose	19	1
Wallpapers	19	2
Manufacture	19	2
Designing	19	9
Planning the Design	19	9
Drawing the Design	19	16
Typical Examples of Wallpapers	19	22
Specimen Wallpaper Patterns	19	22
Specimen Arrangements of Wall Surfaces	19	59
Necessity for Various Arrangements	19	64
Wallpaper-Designing Exercises	19	65

CONTENTS

	Section	Page
STAINED- AND LEADED-GLASS DESIGNING		
Purpose	20	1
Evolution of Stained and Leaded Glass....	20	2
Stained- and Leaded-Glass Windows....∴.	20	9
Manufacture	20	9
Materials	20	9
Making Working Drawings and Patterns..	20	13
Cutting the Glass	20	17
Painting the Glass	20	23
Firing the Glass	20	32
Leading Up, or Glazing, the Window	20	34
Finishing the Window and Fixing in Place	20	39
Designing	20	41
General Principles of Leaded-Glass Designing	20	41
Preparing the Sketches	20	46
Preparing the Cartoon	20	62
Stained- and Leaded-Glass Designing Exercises	20	65
SELLING DESIGNS AND OBTAINING A POSITION		
Selling Designs	21	4
Where and How to Sell Designs	21	4
Field of Handicrafts Designing	21	4
Field of Industrial Designing	21	13
Prices Paid for Designs	21	23
Typical Experiences in Selling Designs....	21	25
Obtaining a Position	21	28
Where and How to Obtain a Position	21	28
Choosing the Proper Field	21	28
Reaching Manufacturers and Designers....	21	31
The Personal Interview	21	33
Why Applicant is Sometimes Rejected	21	38
Salaries Paid to Designers	21	40
Typical Experiences in Obtaining Positions	21	42
Practical Application of Training	21	46
Importance of Individual Effort	21	46
Final Word of Advice	21	47

STENCIL AND BLOCK-PRINT DESIGNING

PURPOSE

1. In the broad field of artistic designing, to be applied to practical utilitarian purposes, there are two general classifications, *handicrafts designing* and *industrial designing*.

Handicrafts designing is that division of design work where the designer is also the artisan or workman who will carry out his own designs in the actual material. Many persons are so situated, or so inclined, that they prefer to apply their artistic training to the designing of handicrafts work. Such work may be done for the designer and artisan's own pleasure, to decorate his home, etc., or for the purpose of preparing specially designed handicrafts articles for sale to discerning purchasers. The commercial side of the handicrafts art must be left to each individual.

Industrial designing is the general term used to cover a wide range of design work for commercial purposes, such as designing for tiles, parquetry, linoleum, carpets, wallpapers, stained glass, interior decorations, etc., where the designer, either as salaried employe or as a free-lance artist, makes drawings and designs for fabrics and objects that are manufactured by other hands.

2. Choice of Line of Handicrafts Work.—Some of the lines of handicrafts work that may be engaged in are stencil work and block printing, tooled metal and leather work, handwrought and enameled jewelry, etc. Various considerations and circumstances enter when the designer is endeavoring to

§ 13

choose a line of handicrafts work. Temperament and personal inclination are perhaps the most influencing elements. Some persons' nerves will not stand the filing, sawing, and hammering of metal, and such persons therefore will not want to choose wrought-metal work, and will do well to take up stenciling and block-printing of fabrics. Other persons, although well trained in design and color, may feel that they are naturally weak on color schemes, and such would do well to avoid stencil work, and take up wrought metal and tooled leather.

Of course other considerations, also, enter; such as available time; money; familiarity or lack of familiarity with certain tools, materials, pigments, and fabrics; local conditions and opportunities, etc. A very practical method of making a choice is to select the line that seems most suitable, to make a design for some simple object or piece of handicrafts in that line, secure the necessary materials, and then carry out the work in that material.

As lines of handicrafts work with which to make the start there could hardly be more suitable ones than stencil and block printing, which will be discussed in this Section.

3. Scope of Training in This Section.—The purpose of these Sections on designing for various lines of handicrafts work is to furnish a training that will enable a person to *design* properly for various lines, rather than to train him step by step to make the articles or objects of handicrafts work. It will, however, be necessary to describe fully the actual operations of hand decoration of fabrics, articles, etc., in order that the technical limitations of pigments, fabrics, and other materials will be known, so that it will be possible intelligently to design decorative patterns that can be properly carried out in the material for which they are intended. That such knowledge of materials and processes is necessary will be developed as the work proceeds.

It must be clearly understood, however, that the instruction that will be furnished will be confined to the artistic designing end of the art, rather than to the technical execution. For this reason, that which the student submits to the Schools for criticism will be in the line of small-scale sketches in color of the complete decorated fabric or article, and full-size working drawings of the pattern used for the fabric or article being decorated or made.

This present Section will give training in the processes of making and using stencils and blocks for decorating fabrics, wall surfaces, etc., and in making designs for such stencils and block prints.

_____

STENCILS AND STENCILING

_____

MAKING AND USING STENCILS

_____

THE STENCIL AND MATERIALS REQUIRED

4. The Principle of the Stencil.—The stencil in its simplest form is simply a flat piece of thin metal, heavy cardboard, or paper, from which there has been cut out the shape of the design or pattern to be painted on the fabric. The stencil is placed over the proper portion of the fabric or surface to be decorated and, by means of pigment and a brush or dyes and an atomizer, paint or dye is spread or blown onto the stencil, going through the cut-out openings onto the fabric and thus forming the pattern. This simple principle and its working out, however, require more detailed explanation.

5. Drawing and Cutting the Stencil.—After a satisfactory design has been made for the stenciled decoration of an article, fabric, or wall surface, the full-size drawing for the section to be cut as a stencil should be made, preferably on heavy tracing paper. It is then ready to transfer to the stencil board, and be cut. The stencil "board" may be a thin sheet of brass, but this material is rather expensive to cut in the desired patterns. A cheaper and more convenient material to use is thin cardboard or heavy paper, thoroughly oiled or waxed, so as to not absorb the paint or dye during the process of stenciling. Sheet celluloid is sometimes used. The stencil board should be cut to a size 2 or 3 inches larger on all sides than the space occupied by the design itself; this margin is needed for proper handling of the stencil when doing the stenciling.

The design, the proper making of which will be described in detail later, is transferred to the stencil board as follows: Lay the piece of stencil board on a drawing board or table, place over it a sheet of carbon transfer paper with the blackened face downwards, and over this place the paper with the design on it, and fasten all three sheets tightly together to the drawing board by four thumbtacks. With a 6H pencil, or a pointed stylus, go over the lines of the design, being sure that every one is gone over carefully; lift the drawing paper and the carbon paper, and the design will be found to be drawn in outline on the stencil board.

The three stages of the stencil are shown in Figs. 1, 2, and 3, which are drawn at about half size. In Fig. 1 is shown the stencil design after it has been carefully drawn on the drawing paper or tracing paper. In Fig. 2 is shown the sheet of stencil board with the design or pattern transferred onto it in outline, ready to cut, as described later. In Fig. 3 is shown the same stencil board with the parts (that in the figure show white) cut away, ready for placing over the fabric and painting the stencil.

Stencil knives, designed purposely for cutting stencils, can be bought, but an ordinary pocket knife, with the blade ground down as shown at about half size in Fig. 4, and well sharpened to a point will do just as well.

To cut the stencil, the stencil board or paper, with the design drawn upon it, is laid on a sheet of glass, and the indicated parts are cut out with the knife point. By the use of the glass for a cutting board, the under side of the cut edges will be sharp and clean cut. The surface of the glass, being very smooth and polished, will not dull the point or edge of the knife if care is taken to not press harder than is required merely to cut through the paper or board. An oilstone or whetstone should be kept close at hand so that the knife may be kept perfectly sharp. It will also be of advantage to have at hand a pair of small sharp scissors to cut out corners or small angles.

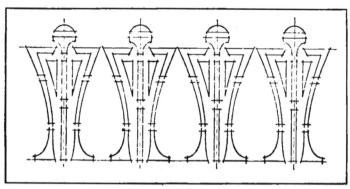

Fig. 1

Fig. 2

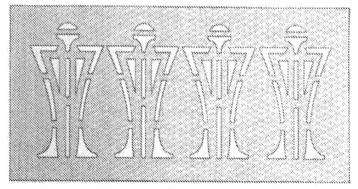

Fig. 3

The method of holding the knife when cutting the stencil is clearly shown in Fig. 5, the knife being almost perpendicular

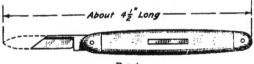

FIG. 4

to the stencil, and the cutting being done with the point of the blade.   The stencil is held in place by the left hand.

6. Ties.—From the nature of the cut-out pattern of a stencil it is evident that certain portions of the design are of such shape that, if cut out entirely, the intervening background would fall away and thus ruin the stencil and the pattern.   For

FIG. 5

instance, in Fig. 3, if the long angular strokes to the left and right of the central vertical line or stroke were cut out entirely from the stencil board, part of the background would fall away. To prevent this, and to make the cut-out pieces of the design of only such shape and size as can be conveniently worked with and as will not make the stencil insecure, parts of the stencil board about $\frac{1}{16}$ inch to $\frac{1}{4}$ inch wide are left uncut, as shown in Fig. 3, to serve as bridges, or ties, to connect the uncut portions. Considerable skill is needed in arranging for these ties, so that they will be strong enough to serve the purpose and at the same time be so placed and drawn as not to interfere with the lines of the design. However, as this is a feature that must be considered by the designer when planning the pattern, a detailed discussion of this point will be reserved until designing is discussed.

The chief point to be emphasized now is that, when cutting the stencil, these ties must not be cut through, but only such portions as are to form the pattern are to be cut out. When a stencil has been cut from specially prepared waxed or oiled stencil board, no further preparation is needed, and it is ready for use. If, however, it has been cut from ordinary heavy paper or thin cardboard, it should then be coated with paraffin, shellac, or oil. Small chips or shavings of paraffin may be sprinkled over the surface of the stencil and melted by a hot iron passed over the surface; the stencil is then allowed to cool. A shellac coating may be applied with a flat brush; and if oil is used it may be put on with a rag.

7. Paints and Dyes.—The general classes of mediums that may be used for stenciling are water colors, oil colors, and dyes. Water colors, while giving beautiful effects, cannot be permanent; that is, the fabric so decorated will not stand washing; so this medium may be eliminated. Of the remaining two mediums, oil color and dyes, the one to be used in any special case depends upon the character, weave, surface, etc. of the fabric to which it is to be applied. Burlap, canvas, denim, crash, linen, madras, muslin, cheese cloth, etc. can safely be stenciled with either paints or dyes and good effects will result. But since dyes do not cover and stiffen the surface of the material being stenciled, it is best to use dyes for delicate materials such as chiffon, satin, velvet, ooze leather, etc. On extremely heavy materials, or on the sides of walls, oil paint in the form of ordinary house paint may be used.

The oil paints used for the finer forms of stenciling come in tubes, as shown about half-size by the one on the left in Fig. 6. These oil colors may be thinned by turpentine or may be mixed with a special stencil medium containing a "size." This medium, as well as the Chinese white, is sold in tubes about twice the size of those shown at the right in Fig. 6. When the stencil liquid, or medium, is used with oil color, it is used in the proportion of eight or nine parts of the color to one part of the stencil liquid. A palette knife may be used to mix the paint

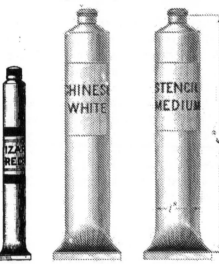

thoroughly, either on a flat glass slab or on a wooden palette. The method of applying the oil colors will be described later.

The dyes used for stenciling come in jars, specially prepared for the purpose. These can be obtained at any local paint or wallpaper store, or through these dealers. If the dyes or other materials cannot be so

Fig. 6

obtained, the names of dealers will be recommended upon inquiry to the Schools.

8. Brushes.—For doing stenciling, special kinds of brushes are required in which the hairs are stiff and the handles fairly stout, because the color is "pounced" onto the stencil and through the openings, rather than painted on in strokes, as is usually done in regular oil painting. In Fig. 7 are shown stencil brushes of various sizes and kinds. The heavy ones of various sizes and with short handles are used for the larger masses and forms of the stencil pattern, while thinner ones with long handles, like that on the right in the illustration, are used for painting in smaller details.

9. A Specimen Equipment of Materials.—It is convenient to have all the materials in compact form, easily acces-

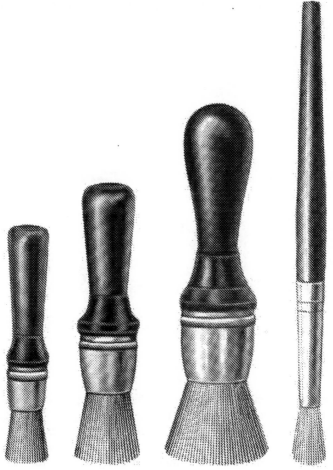

FIG. 7

sible, as in the box form shown in Fig. 8. In the open lid is shown a wooden palette for mixing the oil colors. In the back portion of the box, on the left, are shown fourteen tubes of oil colors containing such pigments as vermilion, red, brown-pink, burnt sienna, yellow lake, orange chrome, chrome yellow, dark green, sap green, cobalt blue, Prussian blue, Egyptian brown, and jet black. This is a very complete equipment of colors; a much more limited range is quite sufficient for the beginner, but the colors shown and listed will all be required

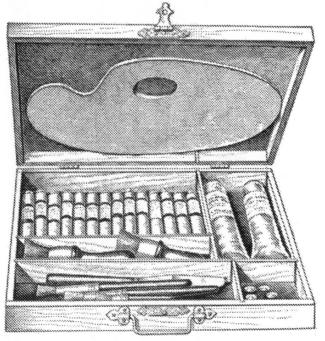

Fig. 8

when the stencil worker gets into high-grade practical work. In the small compartment on the right at the rear, the large tube on the left contains white, a body color much needed for mixture and blending with other colors, and the other large tube contains the stencil medium previously referred to. The compartments in the front of the box contain stencil brushes of various sizes, palette knife, and thumbtacks. Equipments of this kind, some less elaborate and others more complete, can be obtained through any local dealer in paints, wallpapers, etc., or from wholesale dealers in paints, varnishes, etc., whose advertisements can be seen in current magazines or architectural and building journals. These equipments are very moderate in price, and each person engaging in stencil work should provide himself with one that is suited to his needs.

STENCILING ON FABRICS

10. Suitable Fabrics and Surfaces for Stenciling. Satisfactory stencil work can be done on any kind of fabric or surface, from the very open-weave and absorbent surface of cheese cloth, scrim, or spiderweb material to the hard, smooth, unyielding surface of plaster, wood, or marble. However, the medium employed must be adapted to the material to be used. For instance, thick oil colors would be very unsuitable for cheese cloth or scrim, but would do very well for heavy materials or the hard surface of walls; and dyes would not be suitable at all for wall stenciling, but are just the thing for thin delicate materials, if properly treated.

It is assumed that the student understands sufficiently well the natures of the various materials to know what materials are best suited to certain uses. But different materials take certain classes of pigments with different degrees of success. Cheese cloth, scrim, cotton, madras, etc. make very suitable draperies for doors and windows, and if care is exercised in the stenciling give excellent results. For such delicate fabrics, and also for mull, China silk, chiffon, etc., the best results are secured by using a little gum arabic dissolved in the dye, which is then applied to the material while it is tightly stretched over a white blotter.

Very suitable materials for draperies, table covers, etc., are crash, at about 20 or 30 cents per yard, and so-called "monks' cloth," which is three or four times as expensive but which gives excellent results when stenciled. Dyes may be used on these materials, but a greater variety can be secured with oil colors.

For special purposes, such as table covers, mats, etc., leather, silk, etc. may sometimes be employed. The effects of colors and dyes on these materials, however, are very uncertain and it is best to make tests first to find how the colors work.   This recommendation applies also to all classes of materials.

11.   Preparing the Fabric for Stenciling.—When a fabric is to be stenciled, the material must be laid out in a certain way to secure good results.   A flat table top, large drawing board, or whatever is used, should first be covered with large white blotters, or at least with sheets of absorbent paper, such as several layers of newspapers.   Then the fabric should be laid smoothly over these blotters.   If the material is quite heavy, such as crash or monks' cloth, it will stay in position without special adjustment; but if thin, such as scrim, China silk, etc., the material should be tightly stretched and fastened with thumbtacks at the edges.

If the design is to consist of a border that is a running repeat, or of an all-over repeating pattern, its general placing must be measured off and blocked out on the fabric, the center lines and repeat lines being established and indicated with guide lines of charcoal, if on light-colored material, and of tailors' chalk, if on dark colored material.   It is only by first marking these guide lines that the stencil can be placed at the proper positions.

12.   Stenciling With Brush and Pigment.—If the design is to be stenciled on the fabric with oil colors, the desired colors should first be squeezed out in little piles on a glass slab or on the wooden palette.   If a simple color scheme is being carried out, only a few colors will be needed; this matter, however, must be left to the judgment of the individual worker. If the material to be stenciled is light in color, the oil colors squeezed out must be thinned somewhat with turpentine or with the special stencil medium; but if the material is darker in color than the pigment that is to be applied, then the oil color must be mixed with Chinese white or stencil white, pigment to give it body, so that it will show distinctly on the dark background.

It must be remembered that ordinary oil paint will not do for the absorbent surface of the ordinary fabrics, for the oil in the pigment will cause it to run beyond the desired edges and thus blur the outlines. The specially prepared stencil colors must be employed and then mixed with the stencil medium (which contains gum). The idea is that the oil must first be evaporated from the ordinary oil paint and the resulting pigment then be properly moistened and mixed with the stencil medium, or gum size.

A mixture of 1 pint of turpentine, 1 ounce of acetic acid, and 1 ounce of oil of wintergreen makes a good preparation to use with oil paint. Thus the paint can be made fairly thin and not merely painted on the surface, but scrubbed in with the brush, with the result that the color will be solid and pure but the fabric will not be unduly stiffened.

As shown in Fig. 7, stencil brushes are short and round, with stiff bristles. It is well to have one for each color used in the design, so that there will be no delay, confusion, or mistakes. Dip the brush into the color so as to get the bristles well charged with the pigment. This thin color will have been mixed in a china cup or dish, quite thin, and the surplus color can be wiped off on the edge of the cup. Then test strokes should be made on a piece of paper or a scrap of linen, etc., to see whether the color is thick enough and of the proper hue. Such preliminary stroke trials, as well as trials with the stencil itself, should be made before work on the final fabric is begun. One method of testing for the proper amount of color in the brush is to draw the brush across the palm of the hand; then, if a mark of color results, more surplus color should be removed from the brush by means of an absorbent rag.

Having determined the proper thickness and amount of oil color, place the stencil in the proper position, holding it down with the left hand, and fasten loose portions down with pins driven in vertically; then grasp the brush so that it is vertical, holding it close to the bristles. Now work the color well into the fabric that shows through the stencil holes by rubbing the brush back and forth or with a circular motion. The idea is to scrub the color in by rubbing, and not to paint it on in strokes as one would paint on paper or canvas. It is important that all edges of the stencil openings, especially parts of a finely detailed pattern, should be kept in close contact with the fabric by means of pins driven in vertically wherever needed, as previously described. The purpose is to keep the color from running or soaking under the edges of the stencil and thus spoiling the sharpness of the pattern. If the stencil has been well coated on both sides with wax or shellac, such seeping of color is not so liable to happen; but the edges should always be secured with pins.

Little diamond-shaped holes should be cut on the vertical and horizontal limiting lines of the stencil design, so that, when one

Fig. 9

section has been painted and the stencil is to be lifted and placed in its next position, these holes may be made to register on the vertical and horizontal guide lines previously marked in charcoal or chalk on the fabric. If the design is to be in only one solid color on a toned background, or if several colors have been painted through the one stencil, the pins may be pulled out and the stencil may now be carefully lifted from the fabric, the bottom wiped free of any color that may have run under the edges, and it can then be placed in its new position. However, if the stencil is to produce a multicolor design by means of separate stencils these may now be put in place and stenciled.

Fig. 9 shows in a graphic manner just how the brush is held, how the stencil is kept in place, and the general method of working when doing the stenciling.

The foregoing methods are followed also when stenciling with dyes. These dyes come already prepared in bottles or

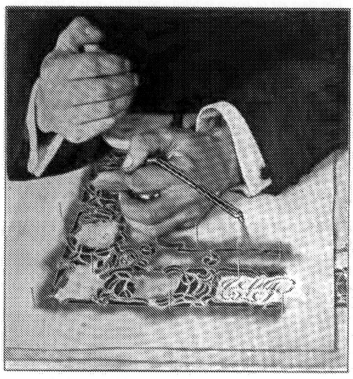

Fig. 10

jars, and can be used direct in that form, or mixed if directions to that effect require it.

13. Stenciling With Atomizer and Dyes.—Another method of stenciling with dyes, other than that of applying them with a brush, is to blow the dye onto the stencil, and thus through the holes onto the fabric, by means of an atomizer. An ordinary blowpipe atomizer such as is used for spraying fixatif onto a charcoal drawing may be used for the purpose, but of course should be used carefully and cleaned often. The safest method is to use an atomizer consisting of a glass jar or bottle and rubber tube and bulb, such as is used for spraying medicinal solutions, and that can be obtained in any drug store.

The glass jar or bottle is filled about half or two-thirds full with the dye, which is then sprayed in the usual way onto the stencil laid horizontally on the material, as shown in Fig. 10. A strong advantage of this method is that colors may be graded from light to dark, or the different colors may be blended.

If it is desired to have the design in dark colors on a light background, the stencil is cut and placed on the fabric and the dye is blown onto the stencil and through the holes onto the fabric. Of course, trials or tests should first be made on separate sheets of paper or on pieces of muslin, crash, etc., to see how the dye works and how the colors look on the material.

But, frequently, a more effective stenciled design will result if the design can be made in a light pattern on a dark background. The method by which this can be accomplished with dyes is as follows: The cut stencil is laid upon the fabric as before, and then a thin layer of library paste or flour paste is painted over the open spaces and thus onto the fabric. If salt is added to the flour when the flour paste is cooked, the best results are secured. After covering all the spaces in the cut stencil with the paste, the stencil is then lifted; and there will then appear on the fabric a pattern consisting of a thin film of paste. This paste acts as a resist, and is so called because it resists the dye and prevents any sprayed-on color from touching the fabric where the paste-film design covers it. The dye of the desired color is then sprayed over the fabric, on which is the pattern, in a flat tone, and the paste prevents the dye from touching the fabric where it is laid. Then the fabric is made wet with cold water and the paste is easily scraped or washed off, the result being that a light design is shown on a dark background.

A convenient plan is to have a number of glass atomizer cups, one for each color, and when it is desired to change from one color to another it is only necessary to remove the metal and rubber attachment from the top of one glass cup and fit it onto the cup containing the desired color and spray that color in the usual manner.

14. If there are to be several colors in the scheme, there must be a separate stencil for each color used. In making these several cut stencils there must be a preliminary drawing, then a tracing, and then the several stencils traced off from their respective portions of the original drawing. The full tracing and the two, three, or four sheets of stencil board are laid flat upon one another, and diamond-shaped guide holes are cut at the four corners, as previously described. These guide holes are cut right through the tracing and the sheets of stencil board, and can then be made to fit over one another as the tracings from the original design are successively made on the stencil sheets. By keeping the holes properly registered the stencils applying the different colors can be made to coincide exactly and thus produce the desired color scheme.

In Figs. 11, 12, 13, and 14 are shown the separate cut stencils that are necessary to produce a stencil print in several colors. Fig. 11 represents a section of a border on a circular table cover, this border being composed of brown stems, blue ribbons, green leaves, purple grapes, and orange-colored fruit. Figs. 12, 13, and 14 represent the cut stencils used to produce the various colors, the white open parts in each stencil being the cut-out portions through which the painting is done. With Fig. 12 the green leaves are stenciled; with Fig. 13, the brown stems, the blue ribbons, and the purple grapes; and with Fig. 14, the orange-colored fruit. At the guide-line intersections in each stencil the diamond-shaped slots are made, and if these are always made to come at the proper place on the guide lines on the fabric, the stencils for the various colors will always register.

15. Stenciling With Acids.—The method, already described, of stenciling a pattern so that the design shows light on a dark background requires that the background of the small portion covered by the design must be darkened, and the pattern itself comes out no lighter than the body color of the fabric. More artistic results are secured, by stenciling with acids.

289—3

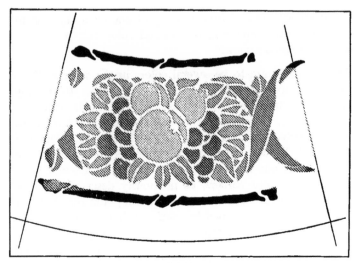

FIG. 11

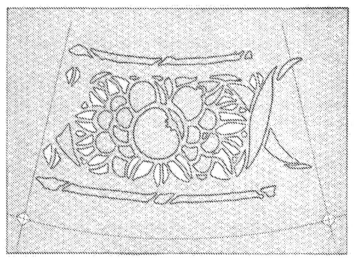

FIG. 12

18

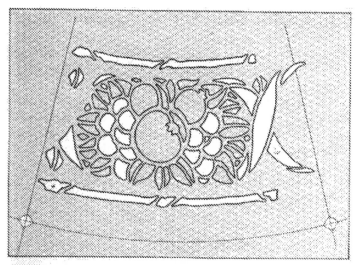

FIG. 13

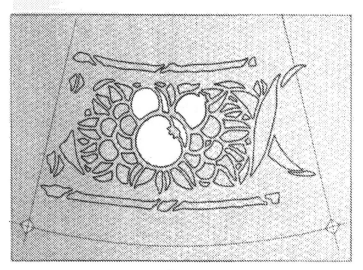

FIG. 14

The process of stenciling fabrics with acids is not a difficult one. The fluid or mixture that is used consists of 1 ounce of tartaric acid, 40 grains of gum, and 1 ounce of water. This may be secured at any drug store for 15 or 20 cents, and may be mixed by the druggist or by the designer doing the work. The stencil and the fabric, with blotting paper under it, are laid in place as before. The liquid, which is colorless, resembling water, may be applied to the stencil openings with the brush, as before described, care being taken that there is not too much fluid on the brush, so that it will not run under the edges of the stencil. When the stencil is lifted there will be no apparent difference in color at first; the fabric will appear as before except that where the pattern was stenciled it will look damp or wet. The fabric should then be hung up to dry.

After it is dry, the stenciled fabric should be placed in a basin or tub containing a bleaching solution. A suitable mixture for such a solution is 1 gallon of water in which there has been dissolved 1 pound of chloride of lime, which should not cost more than 15 or 20 cents per pound. The fabric needs to be immersed only a few minutes in the solution; and when lifted out the parts that were stenciled with the acid solution will be found to have been bleached out to a paler hue of the body color of the fabric. The longer the fabric is left in the solution the paler become the bleached portions. Just how much bleaching is done, that is, just how long the fabric is to be left in the solution, must be determined by the personal taste of the designer. Upon these varying degrees of bleaching depend the artistic results that can be secured.

While such a bleaching solution will not hurt one's hands, the fabric may be handled with two short wooden sticks if desired.

After removing the fabric from the bleaching solution, it should be dipped in a bath of soap and water. If then boiled the design will be more distinct. After the treated fabric is thoroughly dry it should be pressed, on the back, with a warm iron.

By experiments with various kinds and colors of fabrics some surprising and beautiful effects can be obtained. If the above process were tried on a piece of rough silk of a yellow-green color, it would be found that the design would come out in a rich cream color, and the body color of the silk itself (the background) would become of a coppery hue. A dark brown tapestry cloth, of a rough weave, brought out the acid-stenciled pattern in a light écru on a coppery-brown background. On a green denim so stenciled, the design became a cream color and the body of the fabric a blue-green. Many other instances could be described; but the results that can be secured with different materials and different amounts of bleaching can best be discovered by actually making the experiments.

16. Stenciling in the Japanese Method.—The most artistic stencil work is that done by the Japanese. In fact it is thought by some that the Japanese were the originators of the stencil form of decoration in its best effects, although the stencil can be traced back to Greece, Rome, and even to Egypt.

The characteristic of the Japanese stencil work is the absence of crude stiff forms connected by awkward and glaring ties, or bridges, the designs being of the non-repeat variety, mostly conventionally pictorial. Cherry blossom designs; trees with filmy foliage, with a large moon showing through; fish and wave effects with airy bubbles floating about; these and similar schemes can all be arranged for stencil-work decoration.

The secret by which such filmy effects can be secured is that the stencil is drawn with all the freedom desired and cut in the usual manner, the connecting ties and bridges being allowed to remain so as to hold the paper stencil together. Then the stencil is laid face upward, and over its face is lightly pasted some light-weight mosquito netting, or similar open-weave fabric. (The Japanese used thin silk.) The ties, or bridges, may then be cut away. This open-weave fabric then holds the parts of the cut stencil in place without any ties, or bridges, being necessary. The stencil with its pasted-on netting may then be laid on the fabric, and the stenciling done as before described, using oil paints or dyes, and applying them with brushes or atomizer as desired. The paint or dye will not be blocked or marred by the meshes of the netting, but will soak through or around the strands of the meshes and make a flat solid tone wherever there are cut-out portions on the stencil board.

17. Stenciling Combined With Embroidery.—Stenciling on fabrics to be used for various purposes, such as curtains, table covers, pillow tops, etc., is sometimes accented and given an added richness and charm by combining with it embroidery of various kinds. While it is not the purpose here to give a training in embroidery, those who are already skilled in doing embroidery work can produce artistic results by using embroidery combined with stenciling.

For instance, a stenciled design in broad bold tones or colors may first be made to decorate the fabric, and then, either in outline or in appliqué, embroidery may be added to the forms in the design. For instance, a design for a certain purpose, such as a table cover, may be stenciled on white silk, representing a pine-cone motif, the leaves being green and the cones in rich brown. Both the brown and green may be stenciled, and then the brown parts of the pine cones may be emphasized by embroidering them in rich brown embroidery silk. This gives a contrast and snap to the color scheme that would be otherwise impossible. Another example would be a brown linen stenciled in a conventional oriental scheme of greens and blues, both the green and blue being outlined and emphasized by embroidery stitches.

In a treatise such as this only the general directions for doing such work can be given. It is only by making experiments with various kinds of stenciled patterns and then touching them up with the proper kinds of embroidery stitches that various effects can be secured.

STENCILING ON WOOD AND OTHER MATERIALS

18. Character of Stencils, Pigments, Dyes, Etc. for Wood.—Stencil decoration may be applied to many other materials in addition to woven fabrics. Aside from stenciling on walls, which will be discussed separately, this system of decoration may be used for articles made of wood, leather, metal, etc.

The cut stencil itself, the pigments, brushes, etc., and the method of applying the pigment to form the pattern, differ in no way from the materials and processes employed in stenciling on woven fabrics. Judgment must be used, of course, in deciding what kind of oil pigment or dye is best to use for woods of various kinds, for leather, for metal, etc. For wood, almost any of the pigments or dyes previously discussed may be used; oil paints thinned with turpentine, dyes, water colors, etc., may all be used successfully, depending on the hardness or softness of the wood grain. On leather, the best effects are gotten by the use of dyes, for they will least interfere with the texture or grain of the leather. In the case of stenciling on metal, water colors and dyes are useless, and specially prepared oil paints, with a considerable amount of size and dryer in them, applied thick, must be used to get the proper results.

19. Wood, Leather, Metal, and Other Articles for Stenciling.—The decorative process of wood-burning, or pyrography, has been used for so many years that one can obtain in art stores, department stores, stationery stores, etc. useful articles made of wood in the natural finish, ready for pyrography decoration. These articles are sometimes stamped with patterns, usually poorly designed, and all that is necessary is to remove this stamping by sandpapering, after which the surface is ready for decorating with stenciled designs. Among the articles suitable for such decorative work are serving trays, book ends, picture frames, glove boxes, jewel cases, clocks, etc. If such articles are not sold by local stores, lists and catalogs may be obtained from dealers in the larger cities; or in many cases a person interested may be sufficiently skilled with the saw, hammer, glue pot, and sandpaper to make such simple articles himself.

The uses of leather, for articles to be stenciled, are manifold; table covers, table mats, book covers, etc., made of light colored ooze leather or even of heavier leather, can be stenciled very effectively with dyes.

In metal, brass or copper may be employed for cigar trays, desk sets, plaques, etc., in which to get artistic results, oil pigments or enamel paint stenciling may be combined with the tooling of these materials, which will be discussed separately.

STENCILING DECORATIONS ON WALLS

20. Home Stencil-Decoration of Walls.—The stencil method of decoration gives the home lover or housewife the opportunity of having individual and distinctive decoration in the home. There are many people of discernment whose purses will not allow them to purchase wallpapers beyond the grade of such papers as are quite gaudy, covered by highly colored all-over patterns. They prefer simple schemes of wall decoration relieved by touches of decorative motifs at ceiling line, door and window trim, baseboards, etc.; but to secure this effect by using specially designed wallpapers, or by having a professional painter or decorator do the work, is usually beyond the purse of the average home owner or housewife. Here the stencil form of decoration comes in and offers a solution.

21. Stencils and Other Materials, and Methods of Working.—Perhaps the simplest plan is to begin by covering the walls and ceiling with flat washes of distemper color. This material can be obtained in powdered form by the pound from any paint or wallpaper store, and when mixed with water, according to directions that accompany the powdered colors, can be applied easily with a wide brush. Perhaps one of the male members of the household, or a painter friend, will coat the walls and ceilings with oil colors of the desired tints. Whether the walls have been covered with water colors (distemper) or oil colors, they can be readily stenciled upon in the appropriate medium. Still another way to get the solid-color background desired is to have the paper hanger cover the walls with a solid-tone ingrain, oatmeal, cartridge, or grasscloth paper, in brown, green, buff, écru, or whatever color is desired; and this can then be stenciled on.

The stencils for doing this work are made on the same principle as stencils for fabrics, except that it is advisable to use paper or cardboard of somewhat heavier quality than that used for fabrics, because the sheets of stencil paper or board will sometimes be quite large. The stencil should be coated with wax or shellac, as before described, unless cut from a specially prepared stencil board. Usually the designs may be stenciled in distemper color, unless the body of the wall has been painted in oil colors.

22. Preliminary Sketch Design.—Before the stencil designs can be applied to the walls there should be a complete layout in the form of a more or less detailed sketch design to show how the decorative work will look. This sketch design may be a perspective sketch showing the completed interior, or may show simply flat elevations of walls to indicate where the stenciling is to be placed, how large it is to be, what the color scheme is to be, etc.

The designing of such a plan, and of the stencil itself, will be taken up when Designing is discussed.

23. Professional Stencil Decoration of Walls.—Professional stencil decoration in no wise differs in principle from other stencil decoration. Such work is done by decorators when frescoing and decorating churches, bank buildings, theaters, and even private residences. Such decorative work with stencils must of course be made on a much larger scale than the work previously discussed, because the wall surfaces to be covered are much larger and at a greater distance from the spectator than in the case of fabric stenciling or home stencil decoration. The stencil board is usually a heavy tough paper or board, or even tar paper, or metal. These stencils must be heavy, for they are given very rough usage, and require to be used many times in duplicating a pattern around the walls of a large auditorium.

The designer who associates himself with professional decorators doing such work for churches, theaters, etc., will find that the customs and little professional tricks of the trade differ with each decorator or firm of decorators; and he must be ready to adapt himself to these individual practices.

His value as a worker in stencil decoration whether it be for fabric stenciling, home wall decoration, or professional wall decoration, will be governed largely by his ability to *design* satisfactorily decorative schemes and to make the individual cut stencils to carry them out, rather than by his ability to do the actual painting on the walls, although the two must go together. The important matter of designing for decorative work with stencils will now be considered.

DESIGNING STENCILS

PLANNING THE DESIGN

24. Consideration of Purpose for Which Stencil Is to be Used.—In designing for stencil decoration one does not simply design "a stencil," either in motif or complete repeat, and then expect it to fit in anywhere and upon any fabric or object. He must first of all consider the particular fabric or object upon which the stencil decoration is to be placed. It is evident that a finely detailed, graceful stencil pattern suitable for the border of a scrim window curtain would not be suitable at all for the fresco decoration of a church wall, where the decoration would be seen at a great distance. Likewise, the bold stencil pattern suitable for the wall decoration of a bank or public building would be wholly unsuitable for a table cover, sofa-pillow top, etc.

25. Consideration of Medium and Method of Painting.—There must also be considered whether the stencil is to be painted in oil colors with a stencil brush, whether it is to be blown on by dyes from an atomizer, whether it is to be done in the Japanese method, or perhaps by some other system of stenciling.

If the stencil decoration is to be placed on a fabric of a coarse weave by means of oil pigments and stencil brushes, the pattern must be bold, the forms simple, and the ties, or bridges, good and strong. A delicate stencil consisting of intricate forms would not stand the wear and tear of repeated usage on rough goods.

In Fig. 15 is reproduced on a small scale a stencil that was 18 inches in diameter and of bold masses suitable for a rough fabric. Even though the reproduction is greatly reduced from the original, the boldness of treatment is evident.

If, however, the stencil is being made by means of dyes and an atomizer, great delicacy of form may be allowed in the

FIG. 15

design, although this delicacy should not be carried to such excess as to be inappropriate for stencil work.

In Fig. 16 is shown a stencil pattern of a more elaborate and delicate character, such as could very well be used on a delicate fabric by means of blowing it on with dyes and an atomizer.

26. Consideration of Necessity for Ties, or Bridges. The designer of a stencil pattern must always bear in mind that the solid portions of the stencil board, that is, those portions remaining uncut and surrounding the open spaces, must be connected by ties, or bridges.

The best plan is first to make the design for the required space without feeling any restrictions, just as if one were going

FIG. 16

to paint the design onto water color paper with all the freedom that brushes and pigments will permit. When the design is completed in that shape, it can then be translated into sections or spaces representing the parts that are to be cut out, and the breaks and ties, or bridges, can then be put in at the proper spaces. Considerable skill is required in planning these breaks and ties, which comes only with experience.   However, there is a wrong or awkward way of doing this and there is a right way.

In Fig. 17, for instance, an example of the wrong or awkward way, the breaks and the ties as shown are mechanically satis-

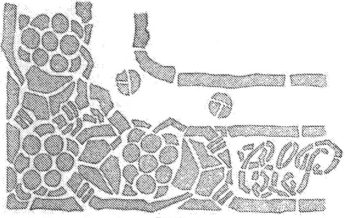

FIG. 17

factory, that is, they would keep the various portions of the stencil from falling apart while it is being used; but they are

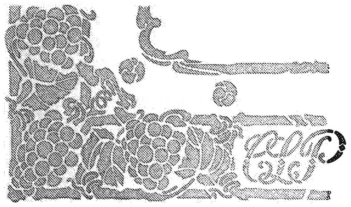

FIG. 18

crude and awkward, there being no reason why they should cut the graceful stem and leaf forms so sharply at an angle.   In

Fig. 18, an example of the right way, this defect has been corrected; and, while the breaks and ties would be just as effective in preserving the unity of the stencil, the graceful manner in which they have been made to follow and blend in with the general directions of the leading lines of the design causes them to appear as component parts of the design rather than something that interferes with it.

This principle of breaks and ties should be studied carefully, as it is an important consideration in making a design and drawing for a stencil.   ————————

SOURCES OF IDEAS FOR DESIGNS

27. Necessity for Original Designs for Stencil Work. There is a wide difference between artistic stenciling designed and executed by the well-trained designer, and the child's-play stenciling that results when one secures stencil patterns put out by paint manufacturers and other commercial concerns and tries to do stencil decoration with them.   It is well known that the stiff and inartistic patterns of "Noah's Ark" trees, block forms, etc., furnished to the undiscriminating by some cut-stencil supply houses, are in large measure responsible for some of the atrocities that are perpetrated as "art stencils."   The effect of these commercial patterns is not only to discourage individual and original design on the part of the beginner in stencil decoration, but also to lower the artistic standard of any original patterns or motifs he may attempt to design.   He at once feels that there are certain limitations of design, of material, and of color, beyond which he dare not go.   The result, too often, is that he produces table covers, pillow tops, and por-tieres of heavy, rough, inappropriate gray crash or monks' cloth, decorated with block-like forms or impossible floral growths in cold blues or muddy, opaque greens, and appears to be satisfied with these creations.   Far too rarely is the attempt made to use the subtle surfaces and textures of silk, of velvet, or even of leather, and to grade and blend the colors in har-monious schemes.   Stencil work of this latter kind is perfectly practicable, and just as easy of execution as the very crude and childish efforts produced by stock stencils.

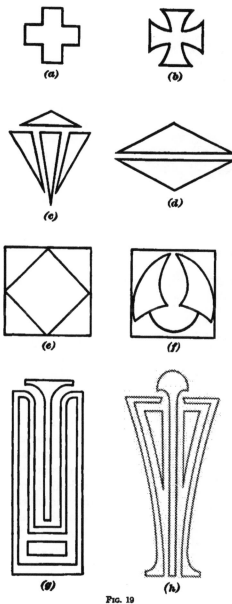

(a)

(b)

(c)

(d)

(e)

(f)

(g)

(h)

Fig. 19

The harmful effect of these machine-made stencil patterns is far reaching, and the plea is therefore made for originality in designing the stencil pattern, instead of blindly accepting what some dealer may force upon us. When it comes to home decoration, whether for the walls or for the furnishings, we can get no better inspiration than that furnished by arbitrary forms, by plant forms, and by historic styles.

28. Designs From Arbitrary Motifs.—In the Sections on *Design Motifs, Design Composition*, and *Space Filling*, the methods of devising and using arbitrary motifs, such as triangles, squares, diamonds, circles, etc., were fully explained. To translate such decorative motifs, in line or mass, into stencil forms is very simple.

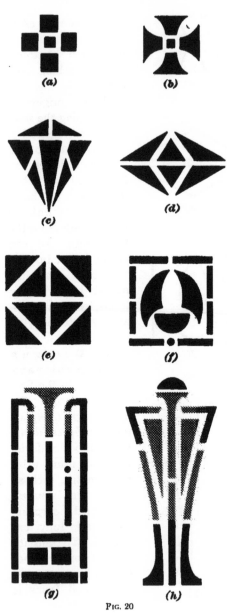

(a)

(b)

(c)

(d)

(e)

(f)

(g)

(h)

Fig. 20

In Fig. 19 is shown a collection of some of these arbitrary motifs, drawn in outline, while in Fig. 20 is shown a collection of stencils made from the same forms. A careful comparative inspection will reveal that the transposing into stencil form of each arbitrary motif does not require a great deal of work. Of course, the proper placing of ties has to be looked after; outlined shapes have to be made into masses; thin lines must be transposed into heavy strokes broken by ties, etc. Otherwise, little redrawing is required.

29. Designs From Plant-Form Motifs.—The preparation of decorative motifs evolved from plant forms and other natural growths has been discussed in a previous Section. When reducing these to forms suitable for stenciling it must be

(a)   (b)

(c)   (d)

(e)   (f)

F<small>IG</small>. 21

63

289—4

(a)   *(b)*

(c)   *(d)*

(e)   *(f)*

Fig. 22

remembered that they must be used as masses rather than lines, and the transpositions must be carefully planned.

In Fig. 21 are shown a number of typical conventionalized plant-form motifs; while in Fig. 22 these same motifs have been transposed into stencil forms composed of black masses separated by ties. A careful comparative study of the two sets of motifs will reveal just how the transpositions into masses have been made. Such transpositions are not easy to make; they require considerable thought and skill in drawing; and one desiring to make original stencils will find it greatly to his advantage to select some other conventionalized plant-form motifs and practice making stencil forms therefrom.

30. Designs From Historic Motifs.—To avoid a quite common modern tendency to use meaningless twisted and contorted forms for stencil work, it is well to consider what has already been done by peoples of the past, and to select our decorative motifs from historic and period styles. In speaking of a historic style, as has already been pointed out, there is meant that style of decoration that was characteristic of a nation or people during the entire length of its existence; thus, the Egyptian style or the Greek style is spoken of. By the term **period style** there is meant that style of decoration that was dependent upon the characteristics of the particular periods of a certain historic style; thus, there is the Louis XIV period of the French Renaissance style, and the Elizabethan period of the English Renaissance style. The styles and periods are, of course, not sharply divided like sections on a map, but blend into one another like the hues of a water-color painting. There are always transitional periods, and usually each period is strongly influenced by the one that went before.

The characteristics of historic and period styles have been quite fully treated in preceding Sections, and further details can be obtained by visiting historical museums. But it will be convenient for the stencil decorator to have, in concrete form, illustrations of the typical decorative motifs in each of the styles and periods of the past. In Figs. 23, 24, 25, and 26 are shown illustrations of these typical motifs, and the stencil forms

EGYPTIAN

GREEK

ROMAN

POMPEIAN

BYZANTINE

ROMANESQUE

SARACENIC

MOORISH

ARABIAN

Fig. 23

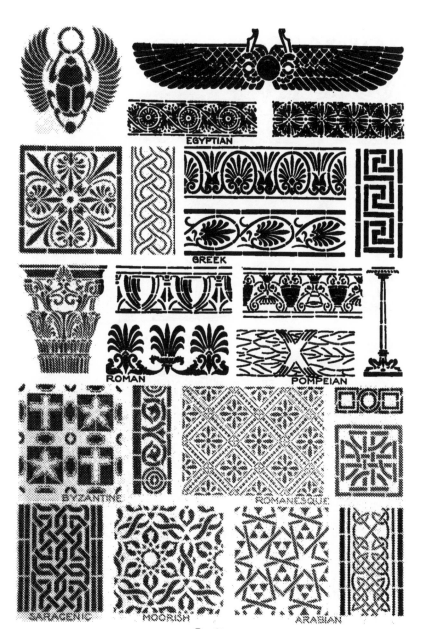

EGYPTIAN

GREEK

ROMAN

POMPEIAN

BYZANTINE

ROMANESQUE

SARACENIC

MOORISH

ARABIAN

FIG. 24

GOTHIC

ITALIAN RENAISSANCE

FRENCH RENAISSANCE

GERMAN AND ENGLISH RENAISSANCE

AMERICAN COLONIAL

MODERN

L'ART NOUVEAU

SECESSION

FIG 25

GOTHIC

ITALIAN RENAISSANCE

FRENCH RENAISSANCE

GERMAN AND ENGLISH RENAISSANCE AMERICAN COLONIAL

MODERN L'ART NOUVEAU

FIG. 26

made from these motifs, from the time of the old Egyptian decorators up to the present day. They are indicated with sufficient clearness for any one to select what motif may be wanted for a particular position or purpose, and to enlarge and reduplicate this motif into an all-over pattern or running band ornament, as will be described later.

31. Converting a Historic Motif Into a Stencil Pattern.—To convert any historic motif into a pattern that will make a successful working stencil will not be particularly difficult if practice has been secured in making stencils from arbitrary motifs and plant-form motifs.

The stencil forms in Figs. 24 and 26 show in graphic form, and more clearly than can be revealed by words, just how each historic motif shown in Figs. 23 and 25 is converted into a pattern for a cut stencil.

These historic motifs and their corresponding stencil forms are shown on a rather small scale in the illustrations, and to be

FIG. 27

usable in a practical way they must be enlarged to the desired size. The method by which this is done is as follows: Take, for example, the first stencil form in Fig. 26, the Gothic all-over pattern. To enlarge this to serve as a stencil for an all-over repeating pattern on the interior walls of a church auditorium, for example, one must first determine the size to which it is to be enlarged. A suitable size for one of the repeats in this case would be about 8 inches square. The small figure at the top left corner of Fig. 26 should then be crossed by horizontal lines and vertical lines so as to divide it into six squares in height and six squares in width. One of the repeats; that is, the portion covered by one complete "kite" formation and its contents—as can readily be seen—will include only four squares in height by four squares in width, and it is only this one repeat that needs to be enlarged, as shown by the portion ruled with cross lines, shown in Fig. 27. Since the repeat is to be enlarged to 8 inches square, an 8-inch square should be laid out as shown on reduced scale in Fig. 28 and divided, by horizontal lines and vertical lines, into four squares high and four squares wide, as shown. The details of the decorative forms for the stencil can then be drawn in freehand in the same relation to the cross lines as the decorative features on the small-scale figure bear to the cross lines there.

For those interested in doing such "converting" for themselves, the first thing to consider is that outlined patterns must frequently be reduced to mass or silhouette patterns, as shown in the case of the panels of Italian Renaissance ornament in the illustration. In such a case the original design in lines should be enlarged as above described, and then, with charcoal or soft pencil, the masses may be blocked in. The rest of the operation becomes simply a matter of proper stencil cutting and of leaving generous allowances for strong ties.

8 inches

Fig. 28

32. Suitability of Historic Styles to Certain Rooms. Any one with a knowledge of the historic motifs can convert them into stencil patterns and decorate any or all of the rooms of his own house in a style that is historically correct. The reading of standard works on period decoration is helpful, it is true, but these works unfortunately overwhelm the reader with their richness of detail, and give the impression that period decoration is only for those with large means, and that those in modest homes might as well give up the ambition to have certain rooms decorated as they want them, unless they have plenty of money to spend. But the abandonment of such

desires is not necessary.   If, for example, it is desired to have
the walls of a library or den decorated to conform to Craftsman or Mission furniture already bought for these rooms, this
can be done by selecting L'Art Nouveau, or Gothic stencil
motifs therefor, and then with the proper solid-color ingrain wallpaper or wall tinting as a background, the frieze, all-over
pattern, or paneling, as may suit best, may be applied.   And
such decoration—inexpensive and comparatively easy to supply
—will furnish the designer and owner with satisfaction because
it suits him.

The earlier historic styles—the Egyptian, the Roman, the
Pompeian, the Byzantine, the Romanesque, and the Saracenic
—furnished inspiration for the Gothic, the Renaissance, and
even the Modern styles; but these earlier styles can hardly be
transplanted bodily for home decoration.   The styles particularly adapted for modern life may be said to be those prevailing
in Italy since 1500, in France since Louis XIV, and in England
since the Italian influence in that country.   General suggestions,
therefore, as to styles appropriate for decorating in stencils
various rooms in the house may be offered as follows:

Hallway, Reception Room, Parlor.—(*a*)   The American
Colonial style of the Elizabethan period of the English Renais-
sance.   (*b*) The Louis XIV or Louis XVI periods of the French
Renaissance.

Dining Room.—(*a*) English Gothic.   (*b*) Jacobean period of
the English Renaissance.   (*c*) Craftsman or L'Art Nouveau
styles of the Modern.

Library.—(*a*) Craftsman or L'Art Nouveau styles of the
Modern.   (*b*) English Gothic.   (*c*) Adaptation of the Greek.

Living Room.—(*a*) Modernized arrangement of French
Renaissance motifs.   (*b*) Free use of L'Art Nouveau motifs
of Modern.

Sleeping Room.—(*a*) Francis I or Louis XIV periods of the
French Renaissance.   (*b*) American Colonial style of Elizabethan period of the English Renaissance.   (*c*) Modernized
arrangement of Greek or Pompeian.

Bathroom.—(*a*) Motifs from the Greek.   (*b*) Motifs from the
French Renaissance.

There should be a conformity of the wall decoration to the architectural style of the house. Thus, if the house be built on classic lines, that is, Greek, or with Colonial suggestions, the hallway would be appropriately decorated in the American Colonial style, although this need not be considered a binding rule.

DRAWING THE DESIGN

33.   Making the Scaled Sketch Design in Colors. To secure the best results when designing stencil work, it is well for the designer to make a small sketch, preferably scaled, in colors, so as to give himself (or perhaps the person for whom the article is being stenciled) an idea as to how the finished stencil decoration is to look.   If, for instance, a table cover is to be stenciled with some carefully designed decoration, a little perspective sketch may be made, showing the table with the decorated cover on it, and the lamp, books, bric-a-brac, etc., in their proper places, the sketch having the proper colors suggested.   If found necessary, another sketch may be made, also in colors, showing the design "on the flat," exactly as it would look when completely stenciled, except very much smaller than the table cover itself.

It is evident that, to make such a preliminary sketch in color, the designer must have a clear idea of exactly what kind of a design he wants to use.   If he wants to stencil a rectangular table cover he should arrange to have the ends that hang over the table contain most of the decoration, in a band, or border, with perhaps a narrow strip border along each long side.   If the table cover is square, the entire four sides may contain a continuous running border with the corners of the field emphasized by additional ornament.   If the square cover is to be used on a round table so that the corners of the cover hang down, then the corners are usually decorated.

If it is a sofa pillow that is to be decorated with stencil, the same general principles apply as in the case of table covers, with the addition that a central spot of ornament is often used.

In the case of window or door draperies, the stenciled design is usually run, in the form of a border, down the inside edges of the two curtains, and along the bottom, the bottom border usually being heavier than the side border.

For decorations of walls, the small border around wainscoting and wood trim, and the wide border at the top of the side wall, are generally used, although all-over patterns of spots and other decorative motifs are suitable.

The small perspective sketch itself may be made on drawing paper or on water color paper in pencil, pen-and-ink, or with

FIG. 29

water colors. Such a preliminary sketch, made in a broad pencil treatment, is shown in Fig. 29, which shows the appearance of the finished stenciled cover when placed on the table in use. In Fig. 30 is shown the *flat* drawing showing how the decoration is to be arranged within the available space on the cover. Such a drawing is not intended to be a finished drawing, but simply a layout, or a blocking out of the proposed table cover. The margin lines, or limits of the goods, are

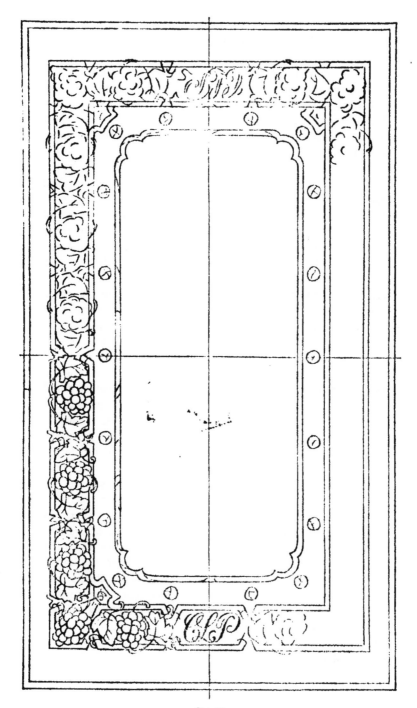

Fig. 30

laid out, to scale, the size that the cover is to be, then the
lines of the border are drawn in all around.   Then horizontal
and vertical center lines divide the design into four corners.
The proposed treatment is roughly sketched in around most
of the margin, and one-fourth is finished in detailed drawing,
as shown.

34. Making the Full-Size Drawing.—Let it be assumed
that the sketch of the table cover as designed in Fig. 30 is
satisfactory, and is to be laid out full size.   This size must of
course be influenced by the size of the table for which the cover
is made.   If the cover is to be a table runner, it should be narrower than the smaller width of the table, a considerable area
of the table top being allowed to show on each side of the cover
as it crosses the table transversely.   The length of the cover
should be such as to allow it to hang over the sides of
the table so as to come down about one-third to one-half the
distance to the floor.   Let it be assumed that the size of
the cover is 30 inches long by 14 inches wide; this size should
then be laid out and the general design should be sketched in
roughly with charcoal or soft lead pencil on a sheet of detail
paper (not necessarily stencil paper, for it will afterwards be
transferred to the stencil paper).   The sketch, as shown in
Fig. 30, should be used as a guide.   Then the details of the
ornament, such as that of a running border, should be platted
in accurately.   In the case of the design in Fig. 30, only one-
fourth of it need be drawn in carefully in the full-size outline
sketch; that is, one corner and the running decoration extending
halfway across one end and halfway up one side as shown in
Fig. 31, which is a reduction of the full-size original drawing
on detail paper.   Next, calculation should be made as to the
exact number of repeats that will go accurately in the halves
of the bottom border and the side border.   When this is then
done all that need be drawn finally for the stencil board is the
corner ornament and several repeats of the running border.
These are shown in solid black on the reproduction of the original
drawing, Fig. 31, so that there can be readily seen just how much
cut-stencil work need be done.

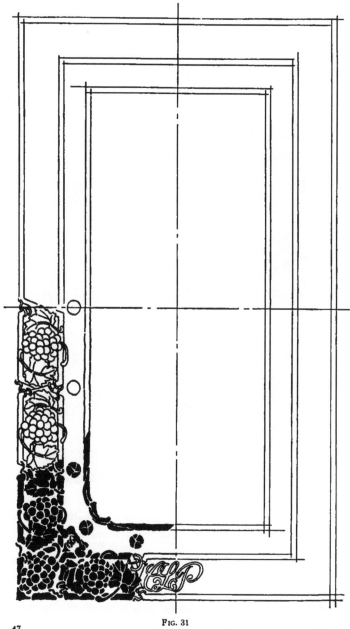

FIG. 31

When the stenciling is done on the fabric, horizontal and vertical guide lines are laid out in chalk on the fabric, corresponding to the pencil guide lines on the original drawing. Little diamond-shaped sections are then cut out from the stencil, at the intersections of these guide lines, to be after-

FIG. 32

wards placed at corresponding places on the chalk guide lines on the fabric, thus securing proper register and correct repeats.

35. Tracing and Cutting the Stencil.—The portions of the original drawing that are to be used for the stencil, that is, those shown in solid black masses in Fig. 31, are then traced off and transferred, by means of carbon paper, to the stencil board; and the stencil is then cut as previously described.

If the stencil is a simple one, it may be printed in two or three colors without there being any necessity of cutting more than the one stencil. However, when the forms are small and intricate, and the pattern is to be stenciled in two or three colors, it is well to cut a stencil for each color; for if it is attempted to paint or blow all the colors through the same stencil onto the fabric beneath, there is a tendency for the colors to overlap, or run into one another, so as to interfere and make a poor piece of work.

For example, to stencil such a design as shown in various forms in Figs. 29, 30, and 31, where the stems are to be orange-brown, the leaves and tendrils green, and the grapes purple, two separate cut stencils are advisable, as shown (on a greatly reduced scale) in Figs. 32 and 33. The cut stencil shown in Fig. 32 is used for painting the brown-orange stems and tendrils and the green leaves; for, if proper care is used, these separate details, in the separate colors indicated, can be painted from the same cut stencil without the colors running. A separate cut stencil, such as that shown in Fig. 33, is required to paint the purple grapes, since there will need to be a blending of reds, blues, red-

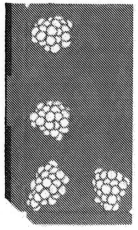

Fig. 33

purple, blue-purple, etc., in painting these grapes, in order to express the proper variegated effect.

The cut stencil shown in Fig. 32 is the one being used in Figs. 9 and 10, where are shown the operations of stenciling with brush and with atomizer.

36. Appearance of Completed Stencil-Print.—After all the stenciling has been done, in the manner described, the various repeats of the border having been accurately judged, and guide lines laid out and stenciling done to conform to these guide lines, the finished result will appear as shown in Fig. 34,

FIG. 34

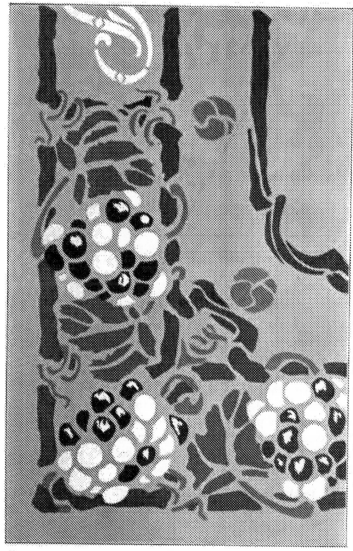

Fig. 35

which is a reproduction on a very small scale, the cover itself being about 30 inches long by 14 inches wide.

Fig. 35, showing a small section of one corner of the completely stenciled fabric, is introduced to show the full size of the stencil, and just how the details of a somewhat elaborate stencil will appear. The white and black on the grapes represent purple varying in values and hues; the dark value of the stems represents orange-brown; and the somewhat lighter value on the leaves represents green. The beginner, however, will not want to attempt as his first work anything quite so elaborate as this; but, rather, will start with a stencil such as those shown in Figs. 3, 15, and 20.

_____

BLOCK PRINTS AND PRINTING

_____

MAKING AND USING PRINT BLOCKS

_____

THE PRINT BLOCKS AND MATERIALS REQUIRED

37. The Principle of the Print Block.—In its final result the effect of block printing is not unlike that of stenciling, but the process is quite different. The printing or stamping of the design or pattern is done by hand by means of wooden blocks, upon which the design has been carved in raised relief. The surface of the block is dipped into pigment or dye, and then the block is pressed onto the desired place on the fabric. The process is exactly the same, in principle, as that of printing impressions from printers' type onto a sheet of paper, except that it is done by hand.

38. Designing and Cutting the Print Block.—When once the design has been made, which will be discussed in detail later, it is ready to trace and then transfer (by means of carbon paper) to the surface of the wooden block.

The print block should be anywhere from $\frac{1}{2}$ inch to $1\frac{1}{2}$ inches thick, and made of wood having a close fine grain so that the pigment used will not sink into the surface of the wood, but will remain on top as a suitable printing medium.   Therefore, an open-grain wood like pine is unsuitable.   Oak, maple, basswood, etc. are all excellent woods for print blocks.   Boxwood is perhaps the best of all, but hard to get sometimes.   The surface should be planed so as to be perfectly level.

When the design has been transferred to the surface, and has been strengthened with pencil, it may be cut out with a sharp pocket knife, or with carving tools.   Some persons can accomplish marvelous results with a sharp pocket knife, but many persons will find that a set of small carving tools will be an aid

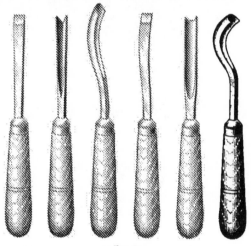

Fig. 36

in producing satisfactory wood blocks.   A set of six carving tools consists of three chisels, one straight edged, one slant edged, and one curved; and one straight gouge and two curved ones.   Such an outfit of carving tools can be procured from, or through, one's local hardware merchant, or from a supply house specializing in tools for craftsmen, the names of which concerns will be suggested upon request.   A set of six tools suitable for this work is shown in Fig. 36.

Before starting to carve the block it should be fastened securely flat upon a table, so that both hands are free to do the carving.   This can be done by first fastening (with screws or brads) a cleat firmly upon the table, then pressing the wood block tightly against it, and fastening another cleat against the wood block, thus keeping it firmly in position, as shown in Figs. 37 and 38. If the carving is done simply with a sharp pocket knife, as shown in Fig. 34, the long straight or curved lines should be cut first by slanting the cutting edge of the knife blade inwards toward and under the background; that is, the surface that is going to be cut away. When all sides of such a

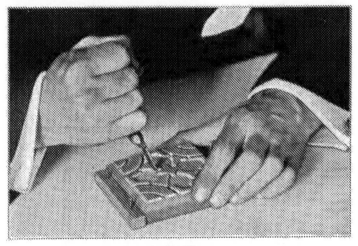

Fig. 37

section have been outlined with such inclined cuts, it can then be gouged out by the edge or point of the knife blade.

If, however, the carving of the block is being done by carving tools, as shown in Fig. 38, the straight-edged chisel is first used to carve into the wood vertically along the lines of the design, and then the background is cut out with a gouge of the proper size and shape. Small chips should be cut away, and no attempt should be made to work rapidly or to cut away large chips. Let the design, the part that is to do the printing, stand up about $\frac{1}{4}$ inch in raised relief. In cutting out curved lines in a design, the proper way is to first block them out roughly with a straight chisel, and then to soften off the contours with a chisel of the proper curve.

39. The Jig-Saw Method of Making Blocks.—If it is desired to produce print blocks somewhat more intricate and elaborate than those usually carved out of solid blocks, the jig-saw method may be employed. By this method, the design is traced on a ¼-inch board and then is sawed out on a scroll-saw or jig saw. Hand jig saws can be obtained through any hardware merchant, and are simple to operate; or the sawing may be done at any planing mill, wood-working establishment, or cabinet shop. After the parts of the design have been sawed

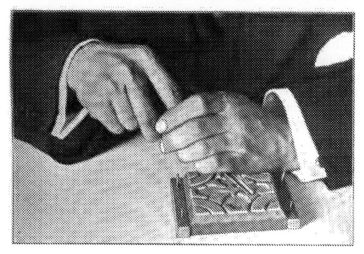

Fig. 38

out of the thin wood, another tracing of the design is made on a solid wood block and the parts of the sawed-out design are then glued thereon in their proper positions.

40. The Color Pad.—The print blocks for block printing are supplied with pigment from a color pad upon which the block is first pressed. Such a color pad is made of eight to twelve thicknesses of coarse muslin or cheese cloth cut somewhat larger all around than the size of the print block, and tacked around the edges to a small board easily handled. The color is put upon this color pad in the manner to be described later.

41. Colors, Paints, and Dyes.—Almost any kind of pigment may be used for block printing; even house paint, which has the advantage of being already mixed, is suitable. However, for small articles where not a great quantity of pigment is required, the tube oil colors and dyes, such as described for stencils and stenciling, will best serve the purpose. Experiments will have to be made to see just how much the oil pigment will have to be thinned by turpentine to be suitable for printing. Dyes may be used as they come in the tubes.

The pigment should be spread over the color pad by means of a brush, sponge, or rag, but not so freely that it will flow off or drip off if the pad is inverted. The muslin or cheese cloth must be allowed to receive just enough color so that part of it may be transferred to the surface of the print block. The condition of the pad must be repeatedly tested before the actual printing operation is started. It is well, usually, to remove the surplus pigment from the surface of the color pad by inverting the pad and pressing it down lightly upon a piece of heavy cloth.

BLOCK PRINTING ON FABRICS

42. Suitable Fabrics for Block Printing.—The most suitable fabrics for block printing can be found only by experimenting. In general, the best fabrics are those of open weave without a dressed surface; linen, cheese cloth, muslin, crash, burlap, etc. are the best. The fabric should not be too coarse in its weave, although sometimes this defect may be overcome by extra pressure upon the block when it is applied.

43. Applying the Blocks to the Fabric.—The test as to whether or not the block has been properly made and the pigment properly spread upon the color pad comes when the printing or stamping process is undertaken.

First of all, the fabric on which the design is to be printed must be spread upon a smooth level surface. The general layout of the main structural lines of the pattern or decoration must first be blocked out, as in the case of stencil work, by means of chalk or charcoal guide lines so that there will be no doubt as to where the blocks are to be placed for printing.

Next, the wood block is held in the palm of the hand, or firmly by the finger tips, and pressed down on the color pad so that the side of the block with the pattern in relief receives a thin coating of pigment. Sometimes, in the case of special work, the pigment is applied to the printing block by means of a camel's-hair brush. The block is then carefully placed in proper position on the fabric, by means of the chalk or charcoal guide lines, and firmly pressed down upon the fabric. If the weave of the fabric is unusually coarse, considerable extra pres-

Fig. 39

sure must be exerted; it may even be necessary to hammer on the back of the block with a mallet. The block should then be lifted, dipped again upon the color pad, and successive impressions made at their proper places until the design is completed.

Fig. 39 shows the operation of doing the block printing; the proper method of placing the block in position and exerting the proper pressure. In this case a border formed of repeats of a square design with a rosette pattern is being produced. Parallel guide lines, and also repeat lines, should be laid off accurately on the fabric, so that the designer and craftsman doing the work may know just where to place the block before exerting the pressure for printing.

DESIGNING PRINT BLOCKS

PLANNING THE DESIGN

44. Consideration of Purpose for Which Print Is to be Used.—Just as in the case of stencil designing, the designer of block-printed articles must consider the particular purpose for which the design is made. There must not be simply a design for a block-printed pattern which may be repeated indefinitely as a vagrant fancy may dictate; the first thought must be, for what kind of an article is the block printing to be done—for a heavy coarse-fabric table cloth on which a bold strong design may be used; or for a window curtain of delicate material requiring a delicate pattern? Having decided this point, the design of the proposed decoration of the entire article (table cover, pillow top, curtain, etc.) must be sketched out; after which are designed the individual blocks, which, by repeated printings, are to compose the design.

45. Considerations of Limitations of Wood Cutting. The design for the wood block must be frankly one that can be freely executed in wood. Delicate tracery, fretwork, tendrils, and finely detailed lines are even more out of place in wood blocks than they are in stencil work. It is true these delicate details could be carved by a skilled wood carver, but such work would be simply an unsuccessful attempt to imitate in a hard unyielding material what would most appropriately be portrayed by the brush on paper or canvass. The patterns on the carved wood blocks should therefore be kept simple and bold.

The pattern to be block-printed may be composed of more than one block; as a pattern composed of a conventionalized red rose with a background of a few conventionalized green leaves and brown stems.   There would thus be required three separate wood blocks for this pattern, if the dipping-on-color-pad process were used.   However, the design may be printed with a single block, if—instead of the color-pad process—the colors are supplied to the pattern face of the block by painting them onto the block with a brush.

46. Designs From Arbitrary, Plant-Form, and Historic Motifs.—Designs for printing blocks must of necessity be original, for they are fortunately not supplied by commercial houses.

Much of what has already been said concerning the transposing of certain arbitrary, plant-form, and historic motifs into work-able stencil patterns will apply to the designing of patterns for print blocks.   In case of the blocks, however, the matter of bridges, or ties, need not be considered, but the effort may simply be made to keep the design strong and bold in its masses.

Great latitude is allowed the designer for the evolution of interesting patterns for these blocks.   The designer need not feel that—because the limits of the design are the four sides of a square—he must therefore produce a design that is stiffly geometric, like the forms on cheap-grade oilcloth patterns.   There need be no such restrictions for one who has had the practice in artistic conventionalization of floral forms that has been given in foregoing Sections, for it should be sufficient to enable him to get up interesting patterns.

DRAWING THE DESIGN

47. Making the Scaled Sketch Design in Colors.   The most successful work in block printing can be done if the designer first makes a small-scale sketch in colors showing how the entire block-printed article will look when completed.   It is not sufficient to design and cut a square block of convenient size and apply it to the article at random, trusting to luck that the finished article will be a success.

The small sketch may be in pictorial perspective form; if of a curtain, the curtain may be shown hanging in place at a doorway or window with its body color and the color of the block-printed decoration fully portrayed, after the same manner as the preliminary sketch for stencil work.   Similarly, such a preliminary sketch should be made if the proposed block-print decorated article is a sofa pillow, a table cover, a shirtwaist front, etc.

48. Making, Tracing, and Transferring Full-Size Design.—After the preliminary sketch has been made it

FIG. 40

becomes a simple matter to draw the full-size design for the individual block.   It is made in outline on any kind of detail paper, and is then traced onto tracing paper, and, by means of carbon transfer paper, or by blocking over with soft lead pencil the back of the tracing, the outlines of the design may then be traced onto the wood.   The block is then ready for carving in the manner already described.   It is not necessary in this case to show reproductions of preliminary or finished drawings for the blocks; these would be comparatively simple. In Fig. 40, however, there is shown, full size, a reproduction of the wooden block with which the border of rosette forms shown in Fig. 39 is being printed. When examining Fig. 40 it must be remembered that the white lines are the high lights, the black lines the shadows, the deep gray values the sunken parts (that do not print), and the very light gray values the raised parts (that do the printing). A careful inspection of Fig. 40 will show clearly just how a wooden block is cut in relief.

Fig. 41

Fig. 41 is a reproduction, direct from the fabric itself, of a print made on scrim or cheese cloth, from the block shown in Fig. 40.

STENCIL AND BLOCK-PRINT DESIGNING EXERCISES

GENERAL INFORMATION

49. Required Work in Stencil and Block-Print Designing.—As already stated, it must be clearly understood that the training given in this Section is a training in *designing* for stencil and block-print work. It is true that the text directions will enable any one to actually cut the stencils and the wood blocks and produce decorative patterns with them, but the required work to be prepared and submitted to the Schools is work in designing the patterns and individual prints, and not the final stenciled or block-printed article.

Therefore, the required drawings to be submitted will be in the form of drawing plates, as before, all work consisting of original designs for the purpose specified.

50. Character of the Drawing Plates.—There will be four drawing plates, each about 10 inches wide and 15 inches high, depending upon the kind of paper used. Ordinary cold-pressed white drawing paper will be satisfactory, although Whatman's paper, commonly known as water color paper, will be most suitable because of the color work required on the small-scale sketches.

These plates are to be sent to the Schools one by one for examination; and, while the first plate is being examined and returned, the student will be working on the following plate; and so on throughout all the plates.

On each plate the sketch in the upper $10'' \times 7\frac{1}{2}''$ rectangle should be carefully drawn, and rendered in water colors. The full-size detail of the stencil, or block print, in the lower $10'' \times 7\frac{1}{2}''$ rectangle, may be colored if desired so as to show just how the design would look on the material.

PLATE 1

51. Exercise A, Plate 1.—In the upper 10″×7½″ rectangle of the plate arranged vertically make original drawings or colored renderings of three sets of motifs suitable for stencils or block prints; one set from arbitrary design motifs, another set from plant-form design motifs; and a third set from historic design motifs. The scale on which they are drawn must depend on the number used, the size of space devoted to each set, etc. The arrangement of these motifs within the 10″ ×7½″ rectangle is left to the taste and judgment of the student.

52. Exercise B, Plate 1.—In the lower 10″×7½″ rectangle of the plate, make a full-size drawing in silhouette form of any selected one of the plant-form motifs designed for Exercise A. The drawing should be made as though it were going to be traced and transferred direct to the stencil board or wood block. If the design is intended for a stencil, all ties, or bridges, must be carefully included in the drawing; or, if the design is for a wood block, it must be so made that it can be properly cut.

53. Final Work on Plate 1.—Letter or write the title, Plate 1: Stencil and Block-Print Designing, at the top of the sheet, and on the back place class letters and number, name and address, and date of completing the plate. Roll the plate, place in the mailing tube, and send to the Schools for examination. Then proceed with Plate 2.

PLATE 2

54. Exercise A, Plate 2.—In the upper 10″×7½″ rectangle of the plate make a pictorial color sketch showing a sofa pillow decorated by an original stencil design and properly arranged on a couch or sofa. The sketch is to be as pictorial as possible, showing clearly just how the proposed pillow will appear when completely stenciled and in use.

55. Exercise B, Plate 2.—In the lower 10″×7½″ rectangle of the plate make a full-size drawing in silhouette form of the stencil that, by means of repeated stencilings, would produce the stencil-pattern decoration designed for Exercise A.

56. Final Work on Plate 2.—Letter or write the title, Plate 2: Stencil and Block-Print Designing, at the top of the sheet, and on the back place class letters and number, name and address, and date of completing the plate. Roll the plate, place in the mailing tube, and send to the Schools for exami- nation. Then proceed with Plate 3.

PLATE 3

57. Exercise A, Plate 3.—In the upper 10"×7½" rectangle of the plate make a color sketch showing a set of portieres, or curtains, hanging in a double doorway (as between living room and dining room), decorated by an original stencil design. Make the sketch pictorial, showing how the curtains will appear when fully decorated by the stencil designs or patterns and hung in place in the doorway.

58. Exercise B, Plate 3.—In the lower 10"×7½" rectangle of the plate make a full-size drawing in silhouette form of the stencil that, by means of repeated stencilings, would produce the stencil-pattern decoration designed for Exercise A.

59. Final Work on Plate 3.—Letter or write the title, Plate 3: Stencil and Block-Print Designing, at the top of the sheet, and on the back place class letters and number, name and address, and date of completing the plate. Roll the plate, place in the mailing tube, and send to the Schools for examination. If all uncompleted work on previous plates has been completed, proceed next with Plate 4.

PLATE 4

60. Exercise A, Plate 4.—In the upper 10"×7½" rectangle of the plate make a color sketch showing any selected article (table cover, pillow top, canvas book cover, etc.), decorated by an original block-print design and placed in its proper surroundings. Make the sketch pictorial, showing exactly how the article will appear when fully decorated by the block-print pattern.

61. Exercise B, Plate 4.—In the lower $10'' \times 7\frac{1}{2}''$ rectangle of the plate make a full-size drawing in silhouette form of the print-block pattern that, by means of repeated and properly placed impressions would produce the block-print decoration designed for Exercise A.

62. Final Work on Plate 4.—Letter or write the title, Plate 4: Stencil and Block-Print Designing, at the top of the sheet, and on the back place class letters and number, name and address, and date of completing the plate. Roll the plate, place in the mailing tube, and send to the Schools for examination.

If any redrawn work on any of the plates of this Section has been called for, and has not yet been completed, it should be satisfactorily finished at this time. After all the required work on the plates of this Section has been completed, the work of the next Section should be taken up at once.

LEATHER- AND METAL-WORK DESIGNING

PURPOSE

1. Characteristics of Leather and Metal Handicrafts.
One whose efforts at designing for handicrafts work have been
confined to stenciling and block-printing on fabrics will find that
leather and metal work offer certain differences in manipulation
of materials, and therefore in design. In the case of stenciling
and block-printing on fabrics, etc., the decoration is simply
painted *onto* the surface; no manipulation of materials is required.
In working with leather and metal, however, the materials themselves must be altered—either pounded or cut—in such a manner
as to produce the decorated article. This feature introduces
new points in designing that require special consideration.

2. Scope of Training in This Section.—Emphasis must
be placed upon the fact that the training given in these Sections on handicrafts work is a training in *designing* for the
various lines of handicrafts work discussed, and not an actual
training in the making of the decorated article, such as might
be given in a manual training school. While the actual processes of manipulating the leather and the metal will of course
be described in order to enable one to design intelligently for
this work, the training furnished does not require the production
of leather or metal articles. The work to be done will consist of
designs drawn out on paper for the various purposes specified.

This present Section treats of the processes of decorating, by
hand, leather and metal so as to make artistic and useful articles
and of making designs for such leather and metal work.

§ 14

LEATHER WORK

TOOLING, CUTTING, AND COLORING LEATHER

CLASSES OF LEATHER SUITABLE FOR TOOLING

3. Names of Leathers.—Leathers suitable for decorative work in tooling, burning, or carving, may be had under the following names: Russia calfskin, russet cowhide, horse leather, sheepskin and goatskin (the latter two specially finished or tanned for the purpose). There are other skins of finer texture, such as lambskin, goose skin, vellum, etc., to be had, but they need not now be discussed.

4. Leathers Suitable for Various Purposes.—Decision must first be made as to what article is going to be made, before one can select a suitable kind of leather. For a large article that will be subjected to much wear, such as a large table cover, a chair back, etc., a heavy leather must be selected; such as cowhide or calfskin. For medium-sized articles, sheepskin or goatskin is the most appropriate leather. For still smaller articles, and for delicately bound books, particularly delicate leather is required, such as lambskin.

Leather can always be bought from a dealer who specializes in leather for the trade. If there is no such dealer at hand, the leather may doubtless be purchased from the local shoemaker, or from some individual or firm that he may recommend. Further, leathers, as also all other necessary supplies for crafts workers, may be secured from firms that specialize on craftsman's materials, the names of which firms can be obtained from the advertising pages of art magazines, or upon request will be furnished by the Schools. The leathers may be purchased by the whole hide, or even by the half hide or quarter hide. Frequently it is charged for by the foot, and the crafts worker must be on the alert to see that he gets the quantity for which he is paying. He must also reject hides or pieces that have an excess quantity of holes or wrinkles. Leather should not be folded, but should either be kept flat or rolled around a wooden cylinder or a cardboard tube. When necessary to cut the leather skin into smaller pieces, it should be laid flat on a sheet of glass, marked with a lead pencil, and the cutting done with a sharp knife.

TOOLS REQUIRED FOR LEATHER WORK

5. Simple Assortment of Tools.—Very satisfactory decorative leather work for various purposes can be done with a simple assortment of tools, some of them home-made. First there must be a pointed tracer of metal or hardwood to transfer the pattern of the design to the moist leather. An orange-wood stick, such as used in manicure sets, and to be secured for a few cents at a drug store, will be suitable for this purpose. Then the little knife for carving must be had. A pocket knife with a long thin blade sharpened at an angle on the end will serve this purpose. The tool used to open the leather along the cut lines and to model the leather, as described later, is made for that purpose and must be purchased. A light hammer is also part of the equipment. The little tools for stamping backgrounds may be home-made, being large nails with a shaft $\frac{1}{8}$ inch in diameter, the stamping head flat, and scored with cross lines put on with a file, and smoothed with emery. There should also be a flat board for laying out the work at first, a sheet of glass, and a marble slab for finally working the leather.

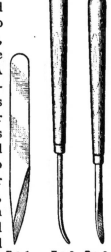

FIG. 1   FIG. 2   FIG. 3

6. A Full Selection of Special Tools.—For those workers who do not have the desire or ability to get up a home-made set of tools, the following complete list of professional leather-working tools is given, the illustrations thereof, in Figs. 1 to 8, being considerably reduced in size:

A shoemaker's paring knife, for cutting the leather; shown in Fig. 1.

A polished steel tracing tool with wooden handle, for transferring the design from the layout on the drawing paper onto the leather; shown in Fig. 2.

A polished steel undercutting tool with wooden handle, for

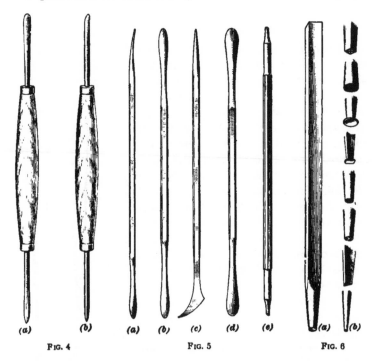

<table>
<tr><td>(a)</td><td>(b)</td><td>(a)</td><td>(b)</td><td>(c)</td><td>(d)</td><td>(e)</td><td>(a)</td><td>(b)</td></tr>
<tr><td colspan="2">Fig. 4</td><td colspan="5">Fig. 5</td><td colspan="2">Fig. 6</td></tr>
</table>

turning back the edges of the cut leather and partly modeling; shown in Fig. 3.

Double-ended steel modeling and burnishing tools with cork or wooden handles, for pressing and modeling backgrounds and ornaments on the leather; two of these are shown in Fig. 4 (a) and (b).

Special polished steel or bone modeling tools for finer work, and of special shapes, as shown in Fig. 5 (a), (b), (c), (d), and (e).

Steel chasing and pearling irons of various patterns for stamping backgrounds and details of small-scale decorative devices, as shown in Fig. 6; a complete tool is shown in (a), and eight varieties of patterns for the tips of the tools in (b).

A chiseling hammer, the use of which will be described later, as shown in Fig. 7.

Roulette wheels, one of which is shown in Fig. 8.

All necessary tools can be secured for a few dollars at most.

There should also be the drawing board, sheet of glass, marble slab, etc., as already described.

Complete outfits of leather-working tools, colors, and other materials, put up in boxes or cases, may be had all the way

Fig. 7

Fig. 8

from $20 or $25 per outfit down to $5 per outfit. If such outfits of tools cannot be obtained from the local hardware dealer, the names of firms supplying them can be gotten from the advertising pages of art magazines, or will be given upon application to the Schools

---

PLAIN TOOLED OR ENGRAVED LEATHER WORK

7. Classes of Decorative Leather Work.—There are scores of ways in which leather may be manipulated with tools, knives, and colors to secure various decorative effects, depending upon the purpose for which the piece of leather is to be used; as for a chair back or seat, a table cover or mat, a book cover, a desk set, etc. However, only the chief classes of such work will be considered here; namely, those that are most frequently employed and fairly simple to handle.

The principal forms of leather manipulation for decorative purposes are plain tooled or engraved leather; repoussé, or

embossed, leather; cut leather with tooled or stamped background; cut-out leather work over silk or other fabric; burnt
leather work; and colored (stained or painted) leather work.

The simplest method of illustrating these different methods
of leather manipulation is to select a standard design, fairly
simple, and to show how this same design appears when worked
up in leather in the different methods described. The strap-
work design, of the German Renaissance motif, so treated, is
shown in its various methods of handling in Figs. 9, 10, 11,
and 12.

8. Preparing the Leather.—First of all the leather must
be moistened by steeping it for a few minutes in tepid water.
The amount of wetting required depends upon the thickness
or weight of the leather.

The piece of leather must then be mounted upon or stretched
over the drawing board, the leather being large enough to
extend over the edges of the board. Small drawing boards
may be obtained at any art store or art supply house, if the
leather work is being done for small articles. First fasten one
end of the piece of leather over the edge of the board by means
of thumbtacks or other tacks. Then stretch the leather and
tack the opposite end securely over the other end of the board.
Then fasten one side of the leather, stretch, and then fasten the
other side. The tacks should be $\frac{1}{2}$ inch to 1 inch apart, never
farther apart. In this way the moistened leather will be
smoothly stretched. After it has been stretched, the leather
should be allowed to rest for a few hours.

These directions apply to light-weight thin leathers, and this
method of mounting allows somewhat deeper and more distinct impressions to be made than any other system of mounting. However, for very heavy leathers, the mere wetting and
stretching over a sheet of plate glass or a marble slab, sometimes assisted by clamps and other fasteners at the edges, will
be sufficient to mount the leather properly for tooling.

9. Transferring the Design to the Leather.—Let it
be assumed that the design for the leather work has been properly made, say a pattern such as shown in Fig. 9. There are

various methods of transferring the design to the moistened leather. The drawing of the pattern, made on heavy paper or even muslin, is laid over the moist leather and then, with a tracing wheel on which are pricking points, the lines of the pattern are gone over in such a way as to press the pricking points through the paper onto, but not into, the surface of the leather.

A more common way of transferring is to use a steel tracing tool such as shown in Fig. 2, and with it to go over the lines of the design, pressing down upon the paper until the impression is made upon the moist leather underneath.

The paper is then removed from the leather and the lines of the design—whether made by pricked points or by the impressions from the steel tracing tool —are then strengthened with a sharp-pointed soft pencil or crayon, so that the lines may be clearer for subsequent tooling.

10. Tooling the Outlines. When the traced lines of the design have been clearly defined, the lines may be gone over with a tracing tool, or the roulette shown in Fig. 8, direct on the leather, and the lines made

FIG. 9

clearer and deeper. If any difficulty is experienced in making clear distinct grooves in certain kinds of leather, the lines may first be gone over with a sharp penknife so as to cut through the polished surface of the leather, but no farther, and then this line may be gone over with the roulette or the steel tracing or engraving tool, the result being a clear, distinct outline.

The leather may be slightly moistened with a sponge at any time during the process of working, if there is a tendency for it to become dry.

A careful inspection of Fig. 9 will show, on a considerably reduced scale, the appearance of a specimen of leather simply tooled or engraved in lines. The cross-section drawing at the bottom shows that the surface of the leather is practically on a level all over, the background being just as high as the strap-work decoration, the latter being outlined by means of grooves or scorings below the general surface of the leather. The illustration shows what general effects are secured and also the results produced by the action of the tools.

REPOUSSÉ, OR EMBOSSED, LEATHER WORK

11. Preparing the Leather and Transferring the Design.—First, the leather must be soaked in water for several minutes. Then several thicknesses of damp linen are laid flat upon a drawing board, to serve as a sort of cushion, and over them the moistened leather is stretched. The tracing paper, upon which the design has been carefully drawn in outline, is then laid over the moist leather and, by means of the tracing tool, the outlines are transferred to the leather; the tracing paper is then removed and the design gone over and strengthened by means of the point of the tracing tool.

To build up the backing to produce the embossed effect, one should be familiar with modeling wax and modeling. To acquire such familiarity is not difficult, for the modeling wax may be purchased by quarter, half, or full pound for a small amount. Or, one of the toy modeling outfits made for children may be purchased and the slight practice work may be done with it in accordance with the directions in the booklet of instructions accompanying the outfit. Such simple practice work will enable any one to build up the backing required.

The leather is taken from the moist linen cushion, where the outlines of the design were tooled on, and is laid face downwards on a sheet of glass. The back, or reverse side, of the leather will then be upwards, and the scoring or tooling lines of the design will then appear raised on this reverse side of the leather and will stand up in little ridges. It now remains to place the modeling wax on this reverse side of the leather at the places where it is desired to have the details of the final design or pattern stand up in relief. The wax, of course, should be placed thick on the leather where it is desired to have the design in high relief, and thinner where the design is to be in low relief, the edges of the wax blending gradually and evenly down to the surface level of the leather.

To reverse the leather with its backings of modeling wax, another sheet of glass is placed over the wax backing, and the two sheets of glass, with the leather and wax between and kept pressed together by the hands, are then reversed and laid flat, and the top sheet is lifted off, thus revealing the upper or right side of the leather, upon which the pattern is to appear.

12. Tooling or Modeling the Leather.—The modeling or tooling process may now be carried on, bone tools being used where no great depth of line is required, and steel tools for deep lines; for steel tools can be given

FIG. 10

the necessary heat. The pliable wax underneath the leather enables the worker to do whatever he wishes with the leather, tooling it lightly or deeply at will. Finally, a thin coat of glue or dextrine is brushed over the back of the leather and backings, thus imparting firmness and rigidity to the work.

Fig. 10 shows, on a scale considerably reduced from the original, a simple example of repoussé, or embossed, work.

The same German Renaissance strapwork pattern has been selected as was treated in simple outline tooling or engraving in Fig. 9. An examination of the illustration, particularly the cross-section view shown at the bottom, will show that the surface of the leather is no longer of one even plane throughout, but the portions representing the strapwork are raised above the surface; that is, embossed, while the background remains the regular surface of the leather, and thus by contrast appears sunken.

Though the pattern shown in Fig. 10 is a very simple one, the wax backing enables the worker to accomplish the modeling of the most intricate and elaborate patterns, if desired. It is well, however, to confine oneself to effects of low relief, and comparatively simple patterns.

CUT-LEATHER WORK WITH TOOLED BACKGROUND

13. Preparing the Leather and the Design.—The process of producing cut-leather work with a tooled background does not differ greatly from the manipulation of simple tooled or engraved leather in outline, although several new features need consideration.

The leather is soaked and drained as before, stretched upon a drawing board, and allowed to stand several hours. The design, previously drawn in outline on tracing paper, may then be transferred to the moist leather as previously described.

14. Tooling the Leather.—After the design or pattern is transferred to the leather, it is well to accentuate or strengthen it with a pointed engraving tool. Next, with a very sharp knife all the outlines should be cut, great care being taken to cut only through the smooth surface and not entirely through the leather. When all the edges have been cleanly cut with the knife the background is ready for tooling.

With one or two tools similar to those shown in Fig. 6 (a) and (b), or even with a heavy nail the head of which has been scored by cross markings with a file, the background may now be tooled or chased with any desired all-over pattern.

The pearling or chasing tool should be held perpendicularly to the leather and then struck sharply with a hammer to make the desired scoring. By moving the tool about over the entire background, an irregular all-over pattern may be produced. A round-headed tool will do for the general surface of the background, but where it is necessary to get into angles and corners the tool with the triangular-shaped head should be employed.

Fig. 11 shows, very much reduced from the original, the appearance of the German Renaissance strapwork design, previously illustrated in other methods of leather manipulation, cut and tooled as described. The cross-section of the leather as shown at the bottom of the illustration shows clearly that the edges of the strapwork in the design are clean cut and that the straps remain as the regular surface of the leather. The background surface, however, is depressed below the general level due to the hammerings of the pearling or chasing irons. Thus, the strapwork stands up in re-

Fig. 11

lief, with sharp edges, while the background is depressed and scored with a pattern of more or less irregular markings.

CUT-OUT LEATHER WORK OVER SILK

15. Preparing the Leather and the Design.—For cut-out leather work it is not particularly necessary to moisten the leather first. The tracing-paper design may be placed over the leather laid flat upon a sheet of glass and transferred in the usual way. It is well to strengthen the outlines of the design with a sharp-pointed soft lead pencil so as to accentuate them to make them more distinct for cutting.

16. Cutting the Leather.—The best tool to use for cutting out the background in a cut-leather pattern is an ordinary pocketknife with one of the smaller blades ground down to a point, and the edge and point made very sharp. If the leather is always cut over a sheet of glass, and the knife is kept sharp, good clean-cut edges can always be made.

In cutting the leather, each worker will discover for himself little tricks of handling that will enable him to secure the best results. The leather should be held firmly in contact with the glass by means of pressure from the left hand. Then, grasped by the right hand, the cutting knife is held almost perpendicular to the leather, perhaps slightly inclined, and in all cases is drawn toward the worker, the fingers of the left hand being placed close to the portions of leather being cut and pulling the leather slightly in the opposite direction. As the cutting process continues the leather is gradually swung around on the glass so that all lines to be cut extend toward the worker. Sharp corners or angles should be cut out by starting the cutting at the corner, thus insuring a clean cut. With a little practice in cutting leather the worker can easily tell when his knife has gone through the comparatively tough leather and is sliding along the smooth surface of the glass; and he will not then keep pressing any harder than is absolutely necessary to continue cutting through the leather in front of the knife. If he presses too hard when once the leather has been cut through, he is likely to turn the edge of the knife blade and render it useless for cutting.

The smaller portions in a design should always be cut out first, the large and more open ones being reserved until the last, so as to keep the leather as firm as possible up to the end of the cutting process.

17. Mounting the Cut-Out Leather Over Silk, Etc. Let it be supposed that the leather is of a golden-brown hue, and is to be mounted over orange or yellow silk. First, a piece of leather the same size as that which has been cut-is-secured, turned face downwards, and on the back is glued (by putting glue only around the outside edges) a piece of heavy silk the same size. Then the cut-out leather is turned face downwards and little strokes of glue are brushed lightly onto the leather over its entire back surface, or simply touched here and there along the straps or sections of leather. Then the piece of leather with the silk glued to it is picked up, reversed, and placed silk side downwards on the glued side of the cut-out leather. Then the entire work is again reversed so that the cut-out leather is proper face upwards and the silk shows through the holes properly. Then a sheet of glass should be laid over the face of the leather to assure the contact of leather with silk until the glue dries. Great care must be taken that the glued leather and silk are not pressed so firmly together that the glue oozes out. A slight pressure is sufficient.

Fig. 12

The illustration in Fig. 12 shows clearly, but considerably reduced in size, the appearance of a finished piece of work after the leather has been cut out and mounted over the silk. The cross-section drawing placed at the bottom of the illustration indicates the various surface levels and the arrangement of cut leather, silk, and leather backing.

BURNT-LEATHER WORK, OR PYROGRAPHY

18. The Leather and the Design.—The purpose here is not to teach pyrography, but merely to mention this process in passing, so that the young handicrafts designer may know how to make designs for such work. Further, a special outfit is required for burnt-leather work, or pyrography, and such outfits are always accompanied by booklets of directions for use, so that detailed directions here are unnecessary.

The outfit selected may be one that has a hand bulb or bellows, or one that has a foot bellows. The latter is more convenient because it allows both hands to be free to hold the leather

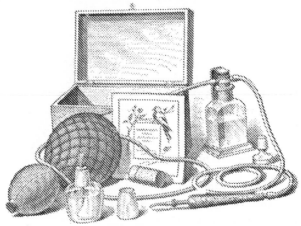

Fig. 13

and to operate the burning point, which is made of platinum placed at the end of a cork handle. A simple outfit for such work is shown in Fig. 13. The principle upon which the work is done is that by squeezing the bulb the flame is fanned so that the platinum point can be heated to a very high temperature. This point is then moved back and forth over the leather to produce the desired pattern or design. The effects can be secured in line only; no even gradations, as in wash work, can be made. However, such gradations on decorated leather are not wanted, for they would be out of place there.

By the use of closely placed parallel lines, or by cross-hatching, as in pen-and-ink work, effects of modeling can be produced.

No special preliminary treatment need be given the leather before working on it with the hot point, although the leather should be tightly stretched over a flat surface. If the leather is dark in color, or of a deep tone, the general lines of the design should be placed thereon with chalk. In doing this the design or pattern is first made on tracing paper as before described, and the reverse side of the tracing paper is then gone over with heavy parallel strokes with a piece of white chalk. The surplus chalk is then shaken off from the sheet of tracing paper, which is then laid, chalk side down, upon the leather. With a 4H pencil, or a sharp steel tracing tool, the design is now gone over, and when the tracing paper is lifted it will be found that the design or pattern appears on the leather in white chalk lines.

If the leather is light in color, such as cream-colored, or light brown, the transferring of the design may be done as previously described for transferring onto drawing paper, no chalk being necessary. The use of light-colored leathers will give opportunity to make copies, in burnt-leather work, of very elaborate subjects, even those that are pictorial, but it is best for the novice to start with bold simple patterns.

19. Burning the Leather.—The operation of the pyrography outfit is soon learned by following the directions in the book of instructions accompanying it. Further, the salesman at the shop where the outfit is purchased is usually ready to demonstrate how to use it.

When once the mechanical features of holding the handle, using the lamp flame, regulating the bulb pressure, etc., are mastered, it only remains for the worker to experiment on separate scraps of leather to determine how much or how little pressure is needed on the platinum point to produce lines of various weights, and cross-hatchings of different values, etc. The worker who has had some experience in pyrography on wood must bear in mind that leather is a more delicate substance, and must slide the point along lightly, otherwise he may burn a hole through the leather.

It is not necessary to show any specimens of burnt-leather work. As practice work, the same German Renaissance strap-work pattern may be used as was used for other methods of leather decoration. Fig. 11, although employed for another purpose, will give an idea as to how this particular pattern would appear when treated by pyrography. The straps could be portrayed by simple outlines, as shown, and the background could be made darker by means of carefully drawn horizontal and vertical lines producing cross-hatching, or by dots in a stipple effect.

————

COLORED LEATHER WORK

20. Spattering or Air-Brush Work in Colors.—The burnt-leather work previously described may be supplemented by, or may be used as an aid or accessory to, colored work on leather. One form of this color work is the application of transparent water colors or tapestry dyes to the leather by the spattering process, by means of an atomizer, or by the now commonly used air brush. The pattern or design may be so drawn that the decoration itself is to be in colors, the natural color of the leather serving as the background; or it may be arranged so that the background itself is to be in color and the decoration show as the natural color of the leather itself. Another plan will show the design in one color on a background of a contrasting color; but it is best to utilize as far as possible the naturally beautiful color of the leather itself.

In any event, some sort of a mask, shield, or stencil should be cut. Let it be assumed that the German Renaissance pattern previously shown in Figs. 9 to 12 is to be used. The pattern is then drawn on regular stencil paper or board, or on heavy manilla paper afterwards to be waxed, and then, with a sharp-pointed knife, the desired portions are cut out. The mask or shield is then placed over the leather in such position that the design will come in its proper place, and the coloring may then be done.

The coloring may be in flat values or in graded values. A liberal supply of transparent wash or tapestry dye should be available, and may first be applied with a camel's-hair or sable brush. When dry, a second colored coating may be spattered on by dipping a tooth brush in the color and drawing it across a comb or a match, thus allowing the bristles to fly forwards and throw a fine spray of color onto those parts of the leather not covered by the mask or shield.

Another method is to put the transparent water color, properly diluted, or the tapestry dye, in an ordinary atomizer and spray it onto the leather.

Still another method is to blow the color through an air brush; this method, however, requires considerable practice before skill is obtained, but with this instrument beautiful effects in color can be secured. When the coloring process is concluded the mask or shield is removed.

If desired, the leather may then be stretched over a drawing board, fastened with thumbtacks, and the colored areas touched up and intensified by pyrography work as previously explained.

21. Painting and Varnishing Leather.—Unusually attractive effects in colored leather are secured by painting and varnishing the leather. A special kind of varnish, known as flexible varnish, the kind that is employed for patent leather, is required for this work. The proper procedure is to first place a coat of oil paint, or a thin coat of this varnish, over the areas to be colored, and then allow it to dry. If, when dry, it is not quite smooth it should be hand-polished with a very fine sandpaper, after which the color should be applied carefully. After the color has dried thoroughly it should be varnished.

The effect of old ivory, or of old stamped parchment, is secured in a very interesting manner. The leather is first given a coat of flexible varnish. Then it is given a coat of white oil color with a little yellow mixed with it, thus giving it an ivory tone. Next the painted leather surface is tooled with gravers, etc., as previously described, after which, with Vandyke brown and a fine brush, the fine lines and dots of tooling can be filled in or painted. This is then given one or two coats of varnish, after which the effect will be that of old tooled leather or parchment.

22. Using Corrosive Liquids on Leather.—The corrosive liquids used for this work are weak solutions of certain acids, which should be purchased from art dealers or supply houses. The liquid usually employed is colorless, and if used skilfully will impart a beautiful deep brown tone to the natural leather color in the spots where it is applied. The leather having been fastened flat to the drawing board by means of thumb-tacks, the corrosive liquid is then applied with brush or sponge. Two flat china dishes or trays should be kept close at hand; one to receive the corrosive liquid, and the other a mixture of the corrosive liquid and water. There are then three distinct operations in applying the liquid: first, using a red-sable water-color brush, spread the full-strength corrosive liquid over the space to be treated; next, dip the brush in the mixture of cor-rosive liquid and water, and thus blend the already applied corrosive and the diluted mixture; and, third, using clear water in the brush, go over the space again for a final blending. Remove the surplus liquid or moisture with a clean white blotter.

If a mottled effect, rather than an even tone or value, is desired, a sponge fastened to the end of a pencil or stick should be used, and the liquid daubed on at places here and there over the surface, care being observed to not let the sponge rest for any length of time on the leather.

23. Gilding Leather.—There are two main forms of gilding employed for the decoration of leather: one with bronze or gold powders or paints; and the other with gold leaf. In the former case, the gold paint or powder is simply mixed with a good gum size, and applied with a fine brush, just as are ordinary water-color paints. Varnish over the final result will help to preserve the work.

The most permanent, and in every way most artistic, results are secured by the use of pure gold leaf. This gold leaf can be had commercially in little books of 24 leaves each, so arranged for convenience in handling. First, the portions to receive the gold leaf must be properly treated. The surface should be painted over with the white of an egg applied with a brush, or with gold *size*. Before the size is dry, and while just suf-ficiently tacky to receive the gold, a sheet, or sheets, of gold leaf is applied with a palette knife or spatula, and then smoothed over with a special gilder's brush, the superfluous gold leaf then being removed.

The process of using gold leaf on leather is a somewhat complicated one, requiring certain special tools and materials, and considerable skill and dexterity, but the general outline here given is sufficiently comprehensive for the present purpose.

DESIGNING LEATHER WORK

PLANNING THE DESIGN

24. Articles Suitable for Decorative Leather Work. The handicrafts worker studying the theory and practice of design as applicable to leather should understand that one does not tool, cut, burn, etch, or otherwise decoratively treat leather merely for the purpose of altering its surface. The purpose is to produce some article that will be beautiful as well as useful.

Some of the simplest forms of useful articles that can be made appropriately in decorated leather are: mats of various shapes and sizes for tables, such as mats for portable lamps, for vases, for cigar trays or ash receivers; bookcovers or jackets to fit loosely over a volume and to serve as a carrying case; pocketbooks with sides decorated; hand bags; wallets; etc. The list can readily be extended by the versatile craftsman. It might be said that table mats, book jackets, pocketbooks, hand bags, wallets, etc., would be just as useful if made of plain leather undecorated. This is true; but they would not then be beautiful, and the craftsman as well as the uninitiated layman knows that an article that is both useful and beautiful is far more to be desired than one that is merely useful.

25. Consideration of Article to Be Made.—In making a design for any decorated leather work the first consideration should be the character of the article to which it is to be applied, and the design should be laid out accordingly. For instance, if the design is for a table mat, it must be considered that the lamp, vase, ash tray, etc., will stand in the center of the mat; therefore, usually, the decoration is placed in a border around the

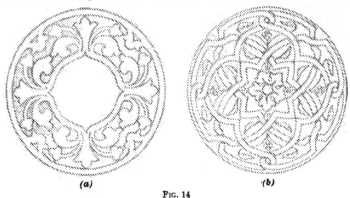

(a)   (b)

FIG. 14

margin of the mat, as shown in Fig. 14 (a). Some designers are accustomed to make such designs grow in radiating lines from a central spot, as in Fig. 14 (b); but this is hardly appropriate

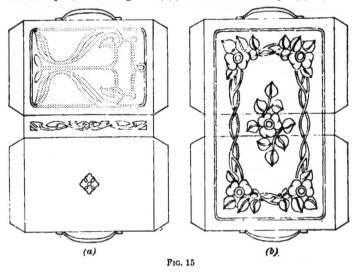

(a)   (b)

FIG. 15

except for small mats that are not in steady use, but are shifted around constantly. Likewise, if the decorative work is for a leather book-carrying case, or jacket, each portion of the deco-ration should be contained within a panel of the front, back edge, or back, as shown in Fig. 15 (a), and not be scattered indis-criminately over the entire large rectangle of leather as in (b), which would be considered poor design, because, when the case is in use, the pattern appears incomplete or cut off.

Thus every article for which decorative leather work is to be done must be studied with care to determine just the amount and character of decorative work to be used upon it, and how this decoration should be distributed.

26. Consideration of Kind of Leather Treatment. There must also be taken into account by the designer, before commencing to draw his design, the method by which the leather is to be tooled, burned, cut, etched, etc.; otherwise, a design that could very well be carried out in one of the methods of treatment might be wholly unsuited to another method. It is true that the same design, the German Renaissance strap-work, was used in Figs. 9, 10, 11, and 12, each one treated in a different method; but this is an extremely simple design, not too difficult for any process, and was introduced purposely to bring out more clearly the characteristics of each process.

If a design is being made for an article that is to be plain tooled or engraved, a considerable degree of elaborateness may be used, for the tooling consists simply of dots, strokes, and continuous outlines, and the supply of gravers and stamping tools available is large. Therefore, other considerations allow-ing it, the designer may prepare designs or patterns with a great degree of intricacy if he so desires. In the case of repoussé, or embossed, leather, however, the designer must get his effects, not with multitudes of intricate dots, strokes, and lines, but with masses, as already described. The masses to be raised or embossed must be simple and bold, so that the underlying wax modeling can be done, and must be so arranged that the margins will blend down softly into the background shapes. In the case of partly-cut leather work with pressed-down and stamped background, the designer must also think and design in masses and contoured shapes rather than in lines. In doing cut-out leather work over silk, many of the same points must be considered by the designer of leather work as are considered by the stencil designer. While there is not always the same necessity for ties that there is in the case of stencil work, yet the work must be tied together, as can be well understood when it is considered that the background shapes of the design are entirely cut away. In the case of burnt-leather work, or pyrography, and even in the case of corrosive-liquid etching work, a great degree of elaborateness may be employed, even pictorial subjects being used if desired. The reason for this is that the pyrographic point can be moved back and forth over the leather with as great freedom as the pencil or pen over drawing paper.

The foregoing general survey of what considerations must enter when making designs for various methods of leather working will give a clear idea of when freedom may be allowed and when certain restrictions enter. However, there is no better method of impressing these restrictions upon the designer than actual experimenting in the various methods of tooling, cutting, burning, etching, etc., on the leather itself.

SOURCES OF IDEAS FOR DESIGNS

27. Importance of Original Designs for Leather Work.—As in the case of stencil work and some of the other crafts, there are always mediocre craftsmen who work in leather and, through lack of appreciation as to what is good in line and form, and through lack of training in design, use over and over again hackneyed decorative forms and awkward straight-line motifs simply because they know no better. Certain stiff and commonplace designs are also put out by supply houses that furnish materials for this craft. These in themselves do no harm; but the beginner in this craft naturally copies these awkward and meaningless motifs and designs and thus wastes time and leather in making tooled-leather articles that are crude in every way.

If the worker in leather intends to go to the trouble of tooling or cutting leather for some article that is to express his or her individuality, it must be individually designed; the motif or design must be original. Further, if the tooled-leather article is being made for sale to some friend or customer, the assumption is that it is to be unique and original in design; otherwise, the friend or customer could purchase an article just as good at a five-and-ten-cent store, or a department store. These are but a few of the many reasons why any article of tooled leather that is to be individual or distinctive must be made from an original design.

28. Designs From Arbitrary, Plant-Form, and Historic Motifs.—In previous Sections training has been given in the methods of originating design motifs based on arbitrary forms, on plant forms, and on historic decorative forms; and the method of applying these motifs to designs made for definite shapes, such as squares, rectangles, triangles, circles, etc., has been shown. In the Section devoted to designing for stencils some additional training was given in adapting these various motifs and designs to suit the peculiar character of the material on which the work was done. This material will all apply with equal appropriateness to the preparation of original designs for tooled-leather work.

Once the shape of the surface to be decorated has been decided on, as, for example, a rectangle for a wallet or a bookcover, a circle for a table mat, etc., it remains simply to apply the principles of space filling, as has already been taught, remembering always that what one draws is to be tooled on leather and not merely drawn with pencil on paper.

DRAWING THE DESIGN

29. Making Preliminary Trial Sketches.—Some craftsmen are accustomed to doing no further preliminary work in the line of designing and drawing than to roughly plot out the full-size pattern or design. The experience of practical designers has shown, however, that it always pays to make a number of preliminary sketches to determine which scheme is most artistic and in every way suitable. These sketches may be roughly blocked out in pencil; not necessarily the full size of the finished article, nor to any specified scale. Suppose, for example, that a design is to be made for a tooled or cut-leather mat for an ash tray. The best plan would be to make several, say four, rough sketches that might be suitable for use on a mat for this purpose, as shown in Fig. 16 (a), (b), (c), and (d). An

(a)

(b)

(c)

(d)

FIG. 16

examination of these preliminary sketches will enable the designer to get a general idea of the faults of certain schemes and the advantages of others, and thus to eliminate faulty arrangements before it is too late and decide on the best design. For instance, the design in Fig. 16 (a), although perfectly satisfactory, from the standpoint of design principles, as a method of filling a circular shape with decoration, would not be entirely suitable when worked up in tooled leather as a mat for an ash tray, because the tray would cover a great part of the decoration and would not stand firmly or evenly on the mat. The arrangement of decoration as shown in the design in (b) might be said to conform to conditions not met by the design in (a), and yet the design in (b) is not entirely suitable to its special purpose, because there is nothing individual or unique about the design, and nothing that makes it appropriate for holding an ash tray. The design in (c) would meet the objections expressed in the case of the design in (b), but would be unsuitable for its purpose because it is placed in the center of the mat and hence covered by the ash tray. The design in (d), however, appears to meet every requirement, as the central space is so decorated by an all-over monogram as to be practically flat to receive the tray, and the design or decoration is placed around the margin in the form of a border, this border consisting of elements or motifs referring specifically to smokers and smoking. An added touch of individuality is given by introducing the initials of the person for whom the mat is made. It is therefore assumed that the sketch in (d) is the one that will be selected.

For some articles for which tooled-leather work is being designed, it is well to make a little preliminary sketch, rendered in pencil only, to show just how the finished article will appear. Suppose, for example, it is desired to make tooled-leather coverings for wooden book-ends, that are to support a row of books on a library table. A penciled perspective showing the book-ends and books actually in place on a section of the table, the selected design being sketched in pictorially, will materially assist the designer in seeing how the finished article will appear.

30. Making the Full-Size Drawing.—Let it be assumed that the crafts worker has selected the design in Fig. 16 (d) for the ash-tray mat to be made in cut leather. The next step is to lay it out full size. The size must be influenced by the kind and shape of ash tray to be used and by the space usually available on a library table. Let it be assumed that the ash receiver

is in the form of an average-size brass or copper bowl, say 4 or
5 inches in diameter. This will then allow the leather mat to
be made 8 inches in diameter, the band of decoration forming
the circular border being about 2 inches wide.

A circle 8 inches in diameter may then be drawn with a compass on ordinary drawing paper (or directly on the tracing
paper), and the design or decoration roughly blocked in, as
previously explained in the methods of blocking out designs.
In detailing the drawing the designer must remember that the

Fig. 17

background of the design is to consist of the leather, and that
the pipes, cigars, smoke, initials, etc., are to be portrayed by
cutting away the leather, and backing up these cut-out parts
with brown silk and cream-colored silk. It will probably be
necessary to introduce cleverly drawn ties at places; but these
should give no trouble to one that has had training in such
work in connection with designing for stencils. Also, in drawing the individual parts of the design, care must be taken to
keep the shapes simple, so that they may be easily cut with the

point of a sharp knife blade. If the designer has any doubt as to whether or not any detail of his design can or can not be cut out of leather, he should trace off that detail onto a scrap of leather and actually cut out that portion of the design for practice work. Several preliminary attempts of this kind will give him a clear idea as to how much or how little elaboration may be included in a design.

When the full-size sketch of the selected design, Fig. 16 (d), has been drawn in detail, in accordance with the directions

Fig. 18

already given, it will appear as shown in Fig. 17, although here it is considerably reduced in size.

31. Tracing and Transferring the Design to the Leather.—If the design has not already been laid out on tracing paper, it should next be traced on tough, transparent tracing paper or tracing cloth with a sharp-pointed pencil. The transfer to the leather may be made with a pointed steel tracing tool, or by means of the carbon-paper transfer method and a 4H or 6H pencil. The transfer must be made with care so that all lines are clean-cut and exact.

The leather is then ready to place upon a sheet of glass for cutting, after the method previously described; the silk and the backing of leather are then glued in place, in the manner described in the early part of this Section.

The finished cut-leather mat for the ash receiver is shown, considerably reduced in size, in Fig. 18. A study of this, and the previous illustrations, will clearly reveal just what problems are met with in cut-leather work and how they must be handled.

The same progressive method of procedure, as just described for making the preliminary sketches, full-size drawings, tracings, etc., must be carried out when designing for any form of tooled- or cut-leather articles.

EXAMPLES OF TOOLED- AND CUT-LEATHER WORK

32. Mention has already been made of various types of articles that may be made in tooled leather, and a visit to a leather-goods store or a department store will show or suggest to the designer many other useful and beautiful articles adapted to be made in that material by the methods that have been described.

For the benefit of the beginner, however, there is presented, in Fig. 19 (a) to (j), a collection of useful leather articles decorated with simple patterns in outline tooling, such as are suitable for first attempts. In (a) and (b) are shown wallets, or bill purses, appropriately decorated with plain line patterns; in (c), (d), (e), and (f) are coin purses with simple but appropriate outline tooling; in (h) and (g) are small mats also in outline tooling; in (i) is a table mat of outline tooling, yet showing the flowers and leaves in mass, because the background of the border is colored or etched with corrosive liquid; and in (j) is a very artistic table mat with line tooling.

These few examples will be sufficient to start the craftsman-designer on the right path. There would be nothing gained for him by showing further examples of tooled-leather designs made by other workers. As previous Sections have taught the

Fig. 19

methods of making original and individual designs for various articles of crafts work, and the technical requirements of tooled-leather work have been explained, it is therefore now only necessary to apply to this particular craft the principles of designing already learned.

METAL WORK

TOOLING AND PIERCING METAL

CLASSES OF SHEET METAL SUITABLE FOR TOOLING

33. Various Forms of Metal in Sheets.—The purpose here is not to discuss metal working in all its forms, but only to present data about simple crafts work in metal with which the handicrafts designer should be familiar. For such handicrafts work as is here treated, only thin sheets of malleable metal are used.

The three main classes of metal sheets that are suitable for the work here described are sheet **copper,** sheet **brass,** and sheet **silver.** Copper is a pure metal itself; brass is an alloy of copper. The silver, of course, would be used only for making the more elaborate or expensive articles, therefore the instructions here given for tooling, piercing, and etching metal will be made to apply only to sheet copper or to sheet brass.

34. Varieties and Thickness of Sheet Copper.—Sheet copper is made by rolling copper between steel rolls, each pass between the rolls making it thinner, till the desired thickness is reached. Hot-rolled sheet copper is heated during the process of rolling; cold-rolled copper is rolled without heating, and is harder, smoother, and more elastic than the hot-rolled, and is the kind that should be used for crafts work such as is here described.

The thickness of metal sheets is designated by a series of gauge numbers, of which there are various systems in use in the trades and industries, and there is considerable variation in the thicknesses represented by the same numbers in the different systems. The gauge that is generally used by craftsmen working in copper, brass, silver, and gold is known as the Brown & Sharpe gauge.

In the Brown & Sharpe gauge system, the number representing the greatest thickness is 0000, which is .46 inch; next in thinness follow 000, 00, and 0 in regular order; then, beginning at No. 1, the numbers run consecutively to No. 40, which represents a thickness of .003144 inch. It should be noted that the larger the number the thinner is the metal sheet.

Suitable gauges of copper sheets for the work here described are No. 18 gauge, which is a little more than .04, or $\frac{1}{16}$, inch thick, and No. 20 gauge, which is a little over .03 inch thick.

There is much sheet copper on the market that is rolled to another gauge called the Birmingham gauge. The numbers in this system represent slightly thicker sheets than the same numbers in the Brown & Sharpe system. Nos. 19 and 21 of Birmingham gauge are, respectively, the nearest equivalents to Nos. 18 and 20 of Brown & Sharpe gauge.

The names of firms from which sheet copper and brass can be purchased can be obtained from the advertising pages of magazines devoted to art and craftsman's work, or will be furnished by the Schools if requested.

TOOLS REQUIRED FOR METAL WORK

35. **A Simple Equipment of Useful Materials and Tools**—As will be fully discussed later, the simple crafts work in metal, for which the handicrafts designer will want to make designs, will comprise work in outline chasing, repoussé, or beaten work, piercing and sawing, and etching with acids. It is possible, of course, to extend the working in metals to the more advanced work of constructing useful articles and objects, such as lamp shades, lanterns, etc.; but such structural work leads the student into the field of manual training or apprentice work to the professional metal worker or jeweler, which is not the purpose of this Section. Therefore, the materials and tools

described here are such as will be suitable for working more or
less on the flat, although they would also be of service to any

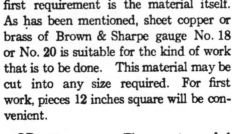

crafts worker who desires to go into work
that is more structural in character.

36. Sheet Copper or Brass.—The
first requirement is the material itself.
As has been mentioned, sheet copper or
brass of Brown & Sharpe gauge No. 18
or No. 20 is suitable for the kind of work
that is to be done. This material may be
cut into any size required. For first
work, pieces 12 inches square will be convenient.

37. Hammer.—The most useful
hammer is what is known as a machinist's
ball-peen hammer, of about ¾-pound

FIG. 20   FIG. 21

weight. Such a hammer is shown in Fig. 20. The flat, hammer portion may be used when hammering or tapping on the
small chisel or tool when doing the outline chasing or tooling,
and the ball-shaped end of the hammer may be used for making

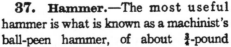

hammer marks on finished work when desired,
or for hammering up rounded surfaces.

**38. Shears to Cut Sheet Copper or
Brass.**—There will also be needed a pair of
tinner's shears, 10 or
12 inches long, for cut-
ting the sheet copper or
brass into pieces of the
required sizes and

FIG. 22   FIG. 23

shapes. Such a pair of shears is shown
in Fig. 21.

39. Small Chisel.—For doing the
necessary scoring or tooling in outline
chasing, a small chisel suitable for work-

FIG. 24

ing on metal will be needed. Such an edged punch, or chisel,
is shown in Fig. 22.

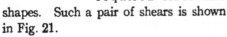

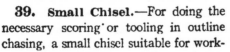

40. Wooden Block.—A wooden block, say 2 in. ×2 in. ×4 in., of fairly hard wood should be secured, on which some of the punching, pounding, or bending can be done. The form of the block is shown in Fig. 23.

41. Base Plate and Lapping Stake.—Special metal-workers' equipment in the shape of a base plate, with separate lapping stake, as

FIG. 25   FIG. 26   FIG. 27

shown in Fig. 24, is needed, for bending over edges of small metal pieces. The lapping stake fits firmly into the base plate,

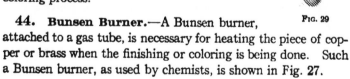

as shown, but can easily be lifted out when it is desired to use another kind of stake in its place.

42. Smoothing Stake.—For certain classes of metal manipulation, where edges are not needed to be sharply bent over but where a smooth gradual bending of a surface must be done, a bending stake such as shown in Fig. 25 must be used This is inserted in the base

FIG. 28

plate illustrated in Fig. 24.

43. Pliers.—Special metal-workers' pliers 5 or 6 inches in length, as illustrated in Fig. 26, will be required for certain classes of metal manipulation, and for holding the metal in the flame of the Bunsen burner in the finishing and coloring process.

44. Bunsen Burner.—A Bunsen burner,   FIG. 29
attached to a gas tube, is necessary for heating the piece of copper or brass when the finishing or coloring is being done. Such a Bunsen burner, as used by chemists, is shown in Fig. 27.

45. Wooden Mallet.—A small wooden hand mallet, such as shown in Fig. 28, having one flat and one round face, will

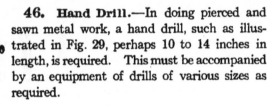

be necessary for lapping and folding edges of metal pieces.

46. Hand Drill.—In doing pierced and sawn metal work, a hand drill, such as illustrated in Fig. 29, perhaps 10 to 14 inches in length, is required. This must be accompanied by an equipment of drills of various sizes as required.

Fig. 30

47. Saw Frame and Saws.—The kind of saw used for craftsman's work in metal consists of what is known as a jeweler's saw frame, and in it are used jeweler's saws. It is illustrated in Fig. 30. The frame most convenient is one about 5 inches deep. The method of using the saw will be discussed later.

48. Punch, or Prick.—A punch, or prick, such as illustrated in Fig. 31, sometimes known as a fine nail set, is needed for certain parts of the piercing and sawing work.

49. Rough-Cast Stake.—A rough-cast stake, polished along the upper slanting, or beveled, edge, as shown in Fig. 32, is needed. This stake fits into the base plate, Fig. 24, just as do the lapping stake and smoothing stake previously described.

Fig. 31

50. Other Materials and Tools Required.—Certain other articles of equipment are required, which can be procured at home or purchased locally very cheaply, as follows:

A piece of ½-inch or ¾-inch wood about 4 inches by 10 inches in size, to be fastened on the edge of the work bench or table and to be used as a sawing board when using the jeweler's hand saw for piercing and sawing metal.

Fig. 32

A small water-color brush for laying out designs for etched metal work, or other classes of decorated metal work; some nitric acid for etching; a small dish or tray to hold the acid; some banana oil; a can of lye; some black asphaltum varnish, or stove-pipe enamel, to use in the etching process; and some turpentine to thin the asphaltum when required.

———

51. Materials and Tools.—One of the simplest forms of tooling metal, and one which is not unlike the system of tooling leather, which has already been described, is known as outline chasing.

Aside from the metal itself, which may be sheet copper or sheet brass of No. 18 or No. 20 gauge, or even heavier, the only tools needed of those already described are the ball-peen hammer and several tooling chisels. These tooling chisels may be purchased, or may be made by the worker from a piece of steel rod, $\frac{3}{16}$ inch or $\frac{1}{4}$ inch square in cross-section and perhaps 4 inches long. The end of one of the tools is filed down to a straight-chisel edge, but not sharp enough to cut the metal, simply rounded off so as to be suitable for making an indentation. Another one of the tracers or chisel tools is filed to a curved edge; that is, an edge that exactly fits a small section of the circumference of a $\frac{3}{4}$-inch or 1-inch circle. With these two tools or tracers, and the small punch previously referred to, the details of practically any design or pattern can be produced.

52. Transferring the Design.—A suitable design having been made—the making of which will be discussed later in this Section under the head of Designing for Metal Work—a tracing is made on tough tracing paper in the usual manner and then placed over the sheet of metal at the proper place. Between the tracing paper and the face of the metal is inserted a sheet of carbon transfer paper with the carbon surface down in contact with the metal. The pattern can then be transferred by going over the lines of the design with a 4H pencil.

53. Tooling, or Outline, Chasing.—To tool the design, the sheet of metal is laid on a board of fairly soft wood, and the lines of the design are followed with the chisel, which is held so that its edge is horizontal and is struck lightly with the flat face of the hammer. The method of doing this is plainly shown in Fig. 33. The beginner may find difficulty in keeping the tracing chisel on the lines of the design, and it will be well, therefore,

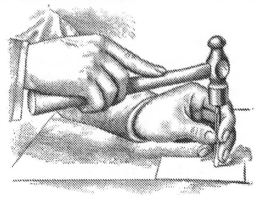

Fig. 33

to practice such tooling first on a piece of cardboard or even on wood, and then on a scrap piece of sheet copper or brass, before actually doing the final work.

A variation of simple chased work is made by cutting out certain portions of the background, and leaving other portions chased in outline. For this cutting out a very sharp-edged chisel is employed so as to cut entirely through the metal. Specimens of simple outline chasing on sheet metal will be shown later, when designing for metal work is discussed.

REPOUSSÉ WORK

54. Materials and Tools.—Repoussé work in metal is an extension of the outline chasing work already discussed. While the simple character of outline chasing enables the work to be done on a sheet of metal laid on a flat board, repoussé work, which is really relief modeling of sheet metal, must be done over some more pliable surface or material. Experience has shown that the best substance for this purpose is chaser's pitch, which is composed of plaster of Paris and Burgundy pitch in equal parts. The pitch is melted, a small lump of tallow is added, and the plaster of Paris is mixed in. The material may then be poured into a small pan such as is used for baking cakes.

55. Transferring the Design, Chasing, and Planishing.—Having prepared a suitable design, the method of doing which will be discussed later, the worker traces it and transfers it to the metal in the same manner as described for outline chasing.

Next the piece of sheet metal, held by means of the pliers, is heated slightly in the flame of the Bunsen burner, but not so hot that it will sink too far into the pitch, and, after having its edges bent down slightly, the metal is laid on the pitch, into which it will sink just far enough to rest in a flat position. The method of holding the hammer and the tracer, or chasing chisel, is practically the same as shown in Fig. 33, for outline chasing, except that the tool is not held perfectly vertical, but its top is tilted slightly. After the outline chasing has been done, a certain amount of relief modeling, or low bas-relief effect, may be secured by what is known as planishing, the tools for this purpose being called planishers. Special planishers of large and of small sizes may be secured as needed, and the backgrounds punched or beaten down with them. The sheet or piece of metal may then be removed from the pitch in which it was embedded, by heating the metal slightly and lifting it out with a piece of wire.

PIERCING AND SAWING

56. Materials and Tools.—Another effective form of surface decoration of sheet copper and brass is that of cutting or sawing out the background, leaving the design or pattern composed of metal filagree work, or vice versa. This work is similar in its effects to the cut-leather work which has already been described; but, on account of the more rigid character of the material in which the work is done, they must be secured by different methods.

The materials and tools needed, in addition to the sheet metal itself, are the prick, or punch, the hand drill, the roughcast stake, the jeweler's saw and saw blades, and the small piece of wood to be attached to the work bench upon which the sawing may be done, all of which have already been described.

57. Transferring the Design, Piercing and Sawing.
The design is transferred to the metal by the process previously explained, and the metal is then ready for piercing and sawing.

Before the actual process is begun, however, the worker must learn how to prepare and use his saw. He must be careful to fit the small delicate saw blade in the saw frame, not only so that the teeth of the saw are toward the outside of the frame, but so that these teeth point downwards toward the handle. The metal parts of the saw frame must be pressed together

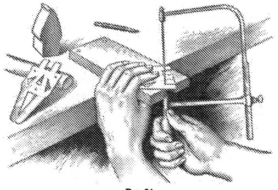

FIG. 34

slightly when the saw blade is inserted, so that, upon being released when the saw is fastened, the frame will spring back and stretch the saw blade tightly, thus preventing the blade from bending or breaking while the work is in progress.

When the work is being done the metal is laid flat on the small sawing board, that has been previously fastened to the work bench, and the saw is moved up and down along the line to be sawn, the saw blade being held vertically, as shown in Fig. 34, and the greatest pressure being exerted when the down stroke is made; because the cutting teeth of the saw then bite through the metal.

When openings are to be sawn out of the center of a piece of metal where it is impossible to get at them from the outside edge of the metal, a hole must be punched, first with the prick, or punch, then drilled with the hand drill large enough for the saw to go through. The saw, of course, must first be unfastened at one end, slipped through the hole, and then tightly fastened again before beginning to saw. A little beeswax placed on the saw blade occasionally will assist the smooth sawing.

If the foregoing points are carefully observed the worker will not experience any particular difficulty in doing sawing and piercing. As he practices, he will find that the process of sawing is easily mastered.

Examples of pierced and sawn work will be shown when designing for metal work is discussed.

<hr/>

ETCHING WITH ACIDS

58. Materials and Tools.—It will have been observed by this time that the processes of decorating metal work are similar, in their results, to some of the processes of decorating leather. Etching metal by means of acids resembles the process already treated of burning leather with the corrosive solution; except that the metal, being a hard, tough material, requires the vigorous treatment of more active acids.

First of all is needed a piece of No. 18-gauge or No. 20-gauge copper, and the tinner's shears to cut it to the desired shape and size for the article to be decorated. Then there must be the asphaltum varnish and the small water-color brush to apply it; the turpentine to thin the varnish; the nitric acid for the etching, and the dish to hold it; the lye, etc.; all as previously described.

59. Transferring the Design, and Etching.—The outlines of the design or pattern should be traced and transferred to the metal by the carbon-paper process previously described. The design for etched work should be such that the details of the ornament or decoration should stand up as the metal itself and the background should be the part that is to be etched or eaten away by acid. The outlines of the design are now such that the design can be painted in silhouette with asphaltum,

directly on the metal.　For this purpose only a little asphaltum
varnish need be used, which may be thinned with turpentine
if required, and it can be worked by means of an ordinary sable
water-color brush.　The design should then be painted in
wherever the metal itself is to show finally; even the margin,
edges, and back of the metal piece must be painted, for every
part not protected by the asphaltum will be attacked by the
acid.　It will take several hours for the asphaltum to dry
thoroughly so that the etching process may be begun.

The etching solution will consist of two-thirds water and one-
third nitric acid, and should be placed in a glass dish of the
proper size to enable the piece of copper or brass to be immersed
therein.　After the metal is placed in the acid it should be left
there for anywhere from a half an hour to two hours, depending
upon the freshness of the acid, and therefore the rapidity of the
etching process. . The rapid etching can be told from the fact
that large bubbles arise to the surface and appreciable fumes
are given off; slow etching is revealed by small bubbles.　Whenever it is desired to hasten the etching, more acid may be poured
into the solution. . After removing the piece of copper from the
etching bath, the asphaltum varnish may be removed by the use
of lye and by scraping and by rubbing with a little turpentine.

BENDING AND CONSTRUCTION WORK

60.　Bending and Curving, and Turning Over Edges.
It is not the purpose of this Section to serve as a treatise on
metal construction work, which most appropriately belongs to
the field of manual training.　However, the worker who has
so far learned to decorate in various ways surfaces of metal
will occasionally desire to bend and twist them in various ways
and into different shapes, to make useful articles, such as corners of desk blotters, curved backs of hand blotters, etc.　This
can be done without difficulty with the equipment of tools
already described.

For instance, if it is required to turn over the two end edges
of a blotter back, the piece of tooled, pierced, or etched metal
should first be hammered down over the smoothing stake fitted

into the base plate, and then placed on the lapping stake and held as shown in Fig. 35, design side upwards, and allowed to project about ¼ inch over the edge of the lapping stake; it is then hammered with the flat end of the wooden mallet until the edge fits down over the side edge of the head of the lapping stake and is at right angles to the main body of the metal. It is possible to bend the ¼-inch edges over farther than at right angles if desired. One method of constructing the blotter is to spring into place under each turned-down end of the decorated metal top a piece of spring brass of the same size as the top, together with several pieces of blotter of the same size.

A similar method is employed in bending down edges of corner pieces for desk blotters, etc., although the edges in these cases are carried entirely around to be parallel (on the opposite side) to the decorated side of the metal.

Fig. 35

61. Hammering Up, Riveting, Solder- ing, Etc.—As previously stated, it is not the purpose of this Section to go into the manual training side of crafts work in metal. The special purpose of this Section and Course is to train in designing for handicrafts work as applied to surface decoration.

However, a few general hints here may be of service to those who have an aptitude and liking for work in sheet metals.

A piece of flat copper or brass may be beaten up, or hammered up (that is, rounded on one face), by placing it face downwards on a block of wood and, using the ball-peen hammer, pounding it with repeated blows until the required amount of swelling has been produced.

For more extended raising of surfaces, as of a plate or bowl, a large vise, a bottom stake and a tee stake, are required, and the article is pounded, with either ball-peen hammer or the mallet, over these or over a wooden block until the desired shape is secured.

When annealing, riveting, and seaming are to be done, in addition to the large vise, a heavy blow-horn stake, to be held in the vise, and a neck hammer must be secured; and, for soldering, a special blowpiping outfit is required. Mention is made of these special materials and tools, not in any attempt to describe these processes, but to indicate the necessity for specialized study and training, and special equipment, if it is desired to go into minor structural work in sheet metals.

COLORING AND FINISHING

62. Finishing the Metal in Colors.—Greatly added beauty in the appearance of crafts work in metal can be secured by the proper process of coloring the work, the processes being chemical or physical.

One simple method is to heat the article in the flame of a gas stove or a Bunsen burner, whereby, depending upon the rapidity or slowness of the process, beautiful purples, irridescent effects, brass effects, deep red, orange, etc., may be secured. Also, by means of various chemical solutions, beautiful shades of browns and reds may be obtained.

63. Finishing the Metal in Various "Dips."—By means of various solutions of combined sulphuric, nitric, and hydrofluoric acid, certain *dips* may be made that will produce satin effects, bright glossy effects, etc. Again, the student must be cautioned about attempting to use these acids without getting the exact proportions and methods of dipping. The information is not included here, because it is needed only by those who are sufficiently interested in the craft to actually make articles in decorated metal.

DESIGNING METAL WORK

PLANNING THE DESIGN

64. Articles Suitable for Decorative Metal Work. Among the many useful articles composed of decorative metal work are belt buckles, tie pins, watch fobs, paper knives, hand-blotter backs, desk-blotter corners, book ends, etc., all in flat or slightly rounded metal. Then, if the craftsman possesses the desire or the ability to proceed into hammering and construction work in metal, the field becomes correspondingly widened, and articles such as plates, bowls, pitchers, lanterns, lamp shades, smokers' sets, etc., can be produced.

65. Consideration of Article to Be Made.—As in the case of other crafts-work designing, consideration must be given, first of all, to the character of the article that will be constructed of the decorated metal. One does not simply make "a design for tooled or pierced metal," but designs a pattern or decoration that will be suitable for the particular article that is to be constructed.

As an example, if a design is being made for a blotter-corner, which is usually of a right-angle-triangle shape, the decoration should follow the principle of designing for triangles, the decoration coming from the corners toward the center, or vice versa. If the design is for a paper cutter, the design should be confined mostly to the handle of the knife, and not occupy any great portion of the blade, which is the cutting part. Or, if it is a plate that is being designed, the decoration should follow the contour of the margin in the form of a border. For book ends, as a further example, the decoration should seem to grow from the base of the article, thus giving an appearance of stability.

As the worker in this craft familiarizes himself with the shapes and uses of other articles to be made in decorated metal, he will understand just how the decorative work must be arranged to be most suitable for the article or object to be made.

66. Consideration of Kind of Metal Treatment.—The particular process to be used in treating the metal will have a considerable influence upon the kind and degree of elaborateness of decoration allowable.

Metal is such a hard, unyielding material that no form of tooling, or piercing, will allow any elaborate degree of decoration. There must be simplicity, restraint, and in many cases a very great degree of conventionalization, employed; although this does not mean that the decoration employed must be stiff or awkward.

Perhaps the greatest degree of elaboration in detail can be allowed in the case of outline chasing. The tools are many and varied, and in the hands of an expert metal worker the most intricate and delicate effects can be secured, such as sprays and wreaths of flowers, leaves, berries, etc. However, the beginner must not attempt any elaborate work, but must confine himself to the simplest forms.

In the case of repoussé, or work raised in bas-relief, on metal, less elaboration is allowed than in the case of outline chasing. . Inasmuch as the decoration is beaten up from the back, or raised, by means of punching or pounding with special tools, allowance must be made for fairly simple shapes, especially by the beginner.

In the case of piercing and sawing, the same general restrictions apply as were applicable to the work of cut stencils or cut-leather work, except that the restrictions in the case of metal are even greater. Inasmuch as the background shapes must be sawed out, they must of necessity be kept quite simple, as the worker will find when he comes to do the actual piercing and sawing.

In the case of etching with acids, the delicacy and elaborateness of the decoration can be influenced by the carefulness and skill of the worker in painting the design onto the metal with the asphaltum varnish. If a fairly fine brush is employed, and the asphaltum flows freely, but is not too thin, very intricate filagree effects can be secured, for the acid will bite into, or etch, the metal only where the asphaltum varnish has not protected the metal. However, the beginner should not attempt too elaborate designs for etching.

67. Importance of Original Designs for Metal Work.
The chief reason for the need of originality in the designs for metal work that is to be made by the craftsman is that the article so made may be distinctive and individual—one that its possessor may feel to be peculiarly suited to himself or herself alone. Otherwise the article might be regarded no more highly than an article of similar use that could be bought at a metal-goods shop and that might have decoration stamped on it in a design that is an exact duplicate of thousands of others.

Further, much of the machine-tooled and machine-pierced metal work is poor in its decorative design, and is flimsy and unsubstantial in construction. The craftsman, therefore, who prepares distinctive and original designs for his tooled metal work is producing articles that are not only more artistic but are also more durable, and therefore more lasting and valuable.

68. Use of the Various Classes of Design Motifs.
There is no need to repeat what has already been discussed regarding the application of well-known arbitrary, plant-form, and historic motifs to metal work. The principles that have already been discussed in the Sections treating of the theory of design and on stencil, block-print, and leather-work designing, apply also to designing for decorative metal work, the important point always being kept well in mind that metal is a more difficult material to work upon than any other so far considered.

----

69. Making Preliminary Trial Sketches.—In designing for decorative metal work, as for other forms of crafts work, the conscientious designer finds it of great advantage to make a number of preliminary trial sketches, so as to decide upon the most suitable design possible for the work upon which he is engaged. These sketches need only be in pencil, and on a small scale, to get proper proportioning and arrangement of parts.

Let it be supposed that such simple articles as a desk set are to be made in tooled or etched metal. There will be the hand-blotter back, the paper knife, the pen rest, the corners for the desk blotter, etc. It might be thought that no particular care or attention need be given to designing such simple articles, but this view is an error. The arrangement of decoration on the paper knife, for instance, might be crowded onto the blade instead of the handle, and in other ways violate principles of good design and of common sense. Errors such as this might never be noticed unless preliminary sketches were made. It would even be well to make a pictorial perspective sketch of the article, or collection of articles, as the desk set, for example, so that not only the designs for the various individual articles may be seen, but also so that the general effect of the correlation of the individual articles in the set may be judged.

70. Making the Full-Size Drawing.—The full-size drawing for each article of the desk set may be laid out on detail paper or directly on tracing paper. The size of the articles in this case depends partly on custom and partly on common sense. Articles of desk sets, as hand blotters, paper knives, desk blotters, etc., can always be seen in jewelry, stationery, or department stores, and a general idea of the appearance and sizes can thus be obtained. These are matters that the crafts-man is expected to investigate for himself, and with which he must become familiar.

In making the full-size drawing, there must always be kept in mind the method of tooling or etching that is to be used in the decoration of the metal. If outline tooling or chasing is to be done, the design must be drawn in bold lines such as can actually be tooled in the copper or the brass. If either saw-piercing or etching with acids is to be the method of treating the metal, the forms used in the design and drawing must be arranged as masses and not as lines; for it must be remembered that it is the decoration that stands out as the metal itself and it is the background that is cut away in saw-piercing work or that is etched to a lower level and different color in the acid-etching process.

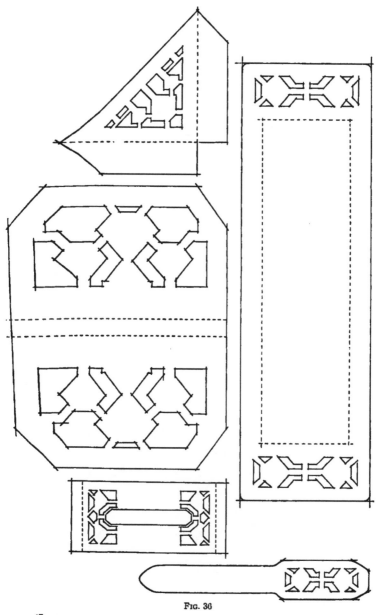

FIG. 36

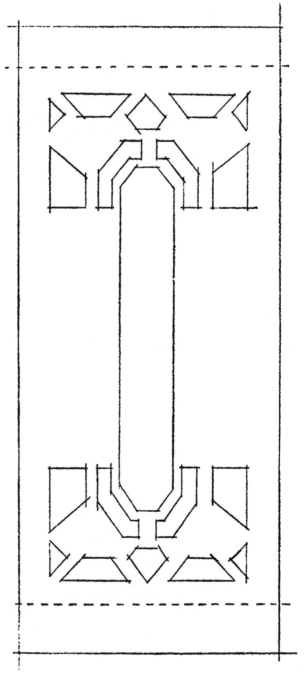

Fig 37

When the various articles of the desk set have been drawn out full size, ready for tracing and transfer, the group will look like that shown in. Fig. 36, which, of course, is very greatly

FIG. 38

reduced in size.   In Fig. 37 is shown the full-size working drawing for the blotter back to give an idea as to the scale and strength of decoration appropriate for such work.

71. Tracing and Transferring the Design to the Metal.—If tne full-size drawings have been made on detail

drawing paper it will be necessary to trace them on tracing
paper, from which they can be transferred to the metal by the
method of carbon transfer pencil and stylus or 4H pencil, as
previously described.

The metal is now ready for tooling, sawing, or etching, as the
case may be, according to the various processes already
described.

The completed articles of the desk set are shown in Fig. 38.
No matter what articles of tooled, sawn, or etched metal are
to be executed, the same progressive methods of making preliminary sketches, full-size drawings, tracings, etc. should be
carried out before any work on the actual metal is started.

EXAMPLES OF TOOLED METAL

72. It is not necessary to discuss the great diversity of
useful articles that can be made in tooled metal. It is assumed
that the young craftsman is interested in the designing of artistic
wrought metal work and therefore is familiar with the various
useful articles that can be made in metal; if he is not, a visit
to any jewelry store or department store will give him ideas
for scores of such articles.

The examples of handicrafts metal work shown in Fig. 38
are some of the simplest forms of these articles, such as would
be suitable for a beginner to attempt; and the work on them is all
done by saw-piercing and bending. It will be observed that
the very severely conventionalized straight-line motifs are
carried out in all the articles. The relative sizes of desk-blotter
corners, book ends, blotter back, paper knife, and pen tray are
clearly indicated, for the illustration was made direct from a
photograph of the articles grouped together.

The beginner doing saw-pierced work ought not to attempt at
first anything more elaborate or complicated than the simple
straight-line work shown in Fig. 38.

73. In Fig. 39 are shown some articles in handicrafts metal
work made by other forms of tooling. In the case of the necklace at the top of the illustration, the work is done largely by

saw-piercing, while the circular button or pin to the left of the necklace is done by etching with acids. The two paper knives, or letter openers, are examples of simple contour sawn work,

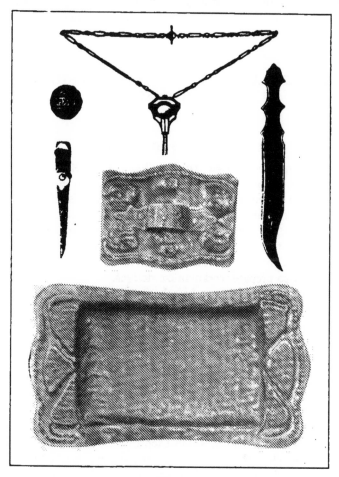

Fig. 39

with bending and riveting. The blotter back, and the pen tray at the bottom of the illustration are hammered, or repoussé, work.

The photographic reproductions of handicrafts work in sheet metal shown in Figs. 38 and 39 are given for the purpose of indicating the results that may be attained with simple designs. As the designer and worker becomes more experienced, more elaborate designs can be worked out.

LEATHER- AND METAL-WORK DESIGNING EXERCISES

GENERAL INFORMATION

74. Required Work in Leather- and Metal-Work Designing.—The work the student is expected to prepare and send in for criticism in this Section is to consist of *designs* for leather and metal work, and not the articles of tooled leather and metal. The material given in this Section on the actual processes of tooling the leather and the metal is included so that the student may have the proper technical knowledge to enable him to prepare workmanlike designs.

The required drawings to be submitted for examination and criticism will therefore be in the form of drawing plates, as in previous Sections, and will consist of original sketches and designs for the purposes specified.

75. Character of the Drawing Plates.—Four drawing plates, each about 10 inches wide and 15 inches high, will be asked for in this Section. On two of these plates are to be original designs for tooled leather work, and on the other two, original designs for tooled metal work. The top portion of each plate, marked Exercise A, will in each case be devoted to preliminary sketches, the lower portion of the plate, marked Exercise B, being devoted to working up the selected scheme to the proper scale.

Whatman's cold-pressed drawing paper, called water-color paper, will be suitable for this work, although the ordinary cold-pressed white drawing paper will do, depending upon the method of rendering employed. The drawings may all be made in pencil outline, or in shaded pencil work if desired; or, if a more pictorial effect is desired in the sketches and the full-size drawings, they may be rendered in washes or in water colors.

The plates should be submitted one by one to the Schools for examination, as in the case of previous subjects.

PLATE 1

76. Exercise A, Plate 1.—In the upper 10″×5″ rectangle of the plate arranged vertically, lay out three sketch designs, each about 2½ inches or 3 inches in diameter, marking them (a), (b), and (c), respectively, for a tooled or cut-leather table mat suitable for holding a lamp. Make these designs in accordance with the principles laid down in this Section, and in every way suitable for leather work. Mark the one selected to be worked up full size.

77. Exercise B, Plate 1.—In the lower 10″×10″ rectangle of the plate arranged vertically, lay out the selected design from those in Exercise A for the tooled or cut-leather mat, making it about 8 inches or 9 inches in diameter. Draw and render all the surface decoration in such a manner that it can actually be executed in the leather, and so that the mat is in every way practical for its purpose.

78. Final Work on Plate 1.—Letter or write the title, Plate 1: Leather- and Metal-Work Designing, at the top of the sheet, and on the back place class letters and number, name, address, and the date of completing the plate. Roll the plate, place in the mailing tube, and send to the Schools for examination. Then proceed with Plate 2.

PLATE 2

79. Exercise A, Plate 2.—In the upper 10″×7½″ rectangle of the plate arranged vertically, lay out four sketch designs, each about 2 in.×3 in., or 2 in.×4 in., marking them (a), (b), (c), and (d), respectively, for a tooled-leather pocket book, wallet, or bill-fold. Design these articles in accordance with the principles already laid down, and so that the decoration will be entirely suitable for tooled-leather work. Mark the one selected to be worked up full size.

80. Exercise B, Plate 2.—In the lower $10'' \times 7\frac{1}{2}''$ rectangle of the plate arranged vertically, lay out the selected design from those in Exercise A for the tooled-leather pocketbook, wallet, or bill-fold, making it about 4 in. $\times$ 6 in., or 4 in. $\times$ 8 in. in size. Draw and render all the surface decoration in such a manner that it can actually be executed in the leather, and is perfectly practical for its purpose.

81. Final Work on Plate 2.—Letter or write the title, Plate 2: Leather- and Metal-Work Designing, at the top of the sheet, and on the back place class letters and number, name, address, and the date of completing the plate. Roll the plate, place in the mailing tube, and send to the Schools for examination. Then proceed with Plate 3.

PLATE 3

82. Exercise A, Plate 3.—In the upper $10'' \times 7\frac{1}{2}''$ rectangle of the plate arranged vertically, lay out two sets of sketch designs, marking the sets (a) and (b), respectively, for a tooled or pierced-metal hand-blotter back, or a pen tray, and two metal desk-blotter corners. Make the sizes of the sketches to suit the allotted spaces. Make the designs of the surface decoration suit the character of the articles, and use only such decoration as can actually be executed in metal. Mark the set selected to be worked up full size.

83. Exercise B, Plate 3.—In the lower $10'' \times 7\frac{1}{2}''$ rectangle of the plate arranged vertically, lay out the selected set, containing the hand-blotter back or the pen tray, and the two desk-blotter corners, making the hand-blotter back (if used), about 3 inches wide by 4 inches high, or the pen tray (if used), about 4 inches wide by 7 inches high, and the desk-blotter corners about $3\frac{1}{2}$ inches each on the shorter edges of the rectangle. Draw and render the decoration so that it can actually be executed in the metal.

84. Final Work on Plate 3.—Letter or write the title, Plate 3: Leather- and Metal-Work Designing, at the top of the sheet, and on the back place class letters and number, name, address, and the date of completing the plate. Roll the plate, place in the mailing tube, and send to the Schools for examination. If all uncompleted work on previous plates has by this time been finished, proceed next with Plate 4.

PLATE 4

85. Exercise A, Plate 4.—In the upper $10''\times7\frac{1}{2}''$ rectangle of the plate arranged vertically, lay out two sets of sketch designs for a pierced-metal necklace, belt-buckle, hat-pin head, or other selected article or articles, marking the sets (a) and (b), respectively. Make the sizes of the sketches to suit the allotted spaces. Design the articles themselves, and the manner of their decoration, so that they can actually be executed in metal. Mark the set selected to be worked up full size.

86. Exercise B, Plate 4.—In the lower $10''\times7\frac{1}{2}''$ rectangle of the plate arranged vertically, lay out the selected design, or set of designs, from the trial sketches in Exercise A. Make the sizes of the full-size drawings conform to the usual sizes of such articles and have the drawing fit well within the $10''\times7\frac{1}{2}''$ space. Draw and render the article, or articles, in such a realistic manner that there will be clearly shown, not only the method of construction, but the character of the decoration, making all ornament so that it can actually be executed in metal.

87. Final Work on Plate 4.—Letter or write the title, Plate 4. Leather- and Metal-Work Designing, at the top of the sheet, and on the back place class letters and number, name, address, and the date of completing the plate. Roll the plate, place in the mailing tube, and send to the Schools for examination.

If any redrawn work on any of the plates of this Section has been called for, and has not yet been completed, it should be satisfactorily finished at this time. After all the required work on the plates of this Section has been completed, the work of the next Section should be taken up at once.

CHINA-DECORATION DESIGNING

INTRODUCTION

1. Status of China Decoration in Commercial Art Work.—The art of decorating china, commonly referred to as china painting, is one that cannot be strictly classified as belonging exclusively either to the field of handicrafts designing or to that of industrial designing. The young artist may decorate china for his or her personal use or to give to friends; and thus may be doing handicrafts work. If the painter of china does this work and does it well, and becomes known as a skilled artist in this line, his or her work will become so well known and in such great demand that a regular clientele can be built up and ready and regular sales of painted china can be made. In this case the work can be said to be industrial designing as well as handicrafts designing.

2. Scope of Training in This Section.—The purpose of this Section on designing for china decoration is to give training in the making of designs that are artistically and technically correct and that are in every way best suited for the particular article they are to decorate. It is not the purpose to give an extended technical treatise on painting and firing china, although those phases of china decoration will be discussed to the extent that the decorative designer needs to know them in order to design intelligently for this form of work. The purpose, rather, will be to concentrate on training the designer, perhaps already a painter of china, to prepare designs of the proper kind for his or her work.

It must also be understood that the work that is to be submitted by the student to the Schools for examination and advice will comprise colored designs and sketches on paper, and *not* the finished and completely decorated article of chinaware, unless very special arrangements are made in individual cases.

CHINA DECORATION

CLASSES OF DECORATED CHINAWARE

3. Methods of Decorating China.—Speaking broadly, it may be said that there are two general methods of decorating chinaware; first, during the process of its manufacture, and, second, after it has been manufactured and put on the market. By the first method, the colored decoration may be placed on the unburned clay or upon the burned clay under the glaze, or it may be incorporated with and applied at the same time as the glaze; by the second method, the decoration may be applied to and burnt into the glaze after the glaze has been made hard by firing. It is chiefly the latter class of work that will be here treated.

4. Under-Glaze Decoration.—The decorating of the unburned clay, under the glaze, may be of several kinds; the decoration may be scratched in, or incised, which is termed *sgraffito* work; it may be painted with diluted clay; or it may be inlaid, the latter being known as *pâte-sur-pâte*. In the cases of the inlaid clay and the overlaid clay, they should be of the same composition as that of the body of the article decorated, otherwise there will be a separation and a spoiling of the work when the object is fired.

When the under-glaze decoration is placed upon the burned china, the work may be done by painting or by printing, both of which processes will be described later.

5. Glaze Decoration.—When the decoration is such that the color is incorporated with and becomes a part of the glaze. some brilliant effects, of a Japanese character and other broad methods of treatment, may be secured. This glaze method of decoration is largely commercial; that is, is done by factories that specialize in this class of work, and therefore need not be discussed in detail here.

6. Over-Glaze Decoration.—Over-glaze decoration, commonly known as china painting, is the class of china decoration that especially interests the beginner. For this work, the articles of chinaware, as plaques, plates, saucers, cups, etc., are secured in their finished form from the manufacturer or dealer; the decoration is painted on with proper pigments and brushes; the articles of china are then fired or baked in a kiln until the pigment has become fused into, and has become a component part of, the china itself; all of which processes will be fully described later.

7. Printing on China.—There are a number of methods of printing the decorative work on china, instead of painting it on by hand; two of these methods are printing from copper plates and printing by lithography. In printing from copper plates, the pattern, design, or picture is engraved on the surface of a smooth copper plate, which is then made quite hot. The color or pigment to be used in the printing is mixed with oil and is also kept quite hot; the copper plate is then inked with this color, and an impression is taken on thin paper. After the superfluous edges of the paper have been trimmed away, the print is pressed upon, and thus transferred to, the surface of the china to be decorated, after which an application of cold water *fixes* it to the china. Then it is fired.

In the lithographic method of printing on china, the patterns or designs are drawn on the lithographic stones, as in ordinary lithography. However, no colored pigments are placed on the lithographic stones, but an impression is taken in varnish on the transfer paper and the proper colors, which are the regular vitrifiable china-painters' colors, are dusted onto this varnish impression. Then the print is pressed upon, and thus transferred to, the surface of the china, and afterwards fired.

8. Transfer Picture, or Decalcomania, China Decoration.—The transfer picture, or decalcomania, for china decoration is in the form of a picture painted or printed, in vitrifiable china colors, on paper; this picture is applied to and transferred to the surface of the china, and then fired in the usual manner.

In one form of these transfers, it is simply necessary to soak them for 10 or 15 minutes in cold water, apply them, with face to the surface of the china, at the proper place, press upon them lightly with a moistened rag or sponge, and after an interval of, say, a quarter of an hour, peel off the paper. The transfer should then be allowed to dry thoroughly, without wrinkles or air bubbles, after which the color work is given the first fire.

In another form of transfer, the picture is first coated with a thin film of transfer varnish, which is allowed to get tacky; the back is then moistened and the transfer is placed face downwards on the china and, by means of a small rubber roller, such as photographers use for mounting prints, is then rolled or flattened onto the china. The surplus paper is then removed by means of a sponge and water, and, after drying, the firing is done.

Some transfers are applied to the china surface with the picture upwards, instead of face down, as just described. In this case the preliminary soaking is done with hot water, and the paper can then be pulled out carefully from under the film holding the picture painted or printed in china colors. After drying, the firing is done as before.

Reference is made to these transfer processes simply that the student may have some knowledge of them. It is of course understood that all designing for patterns for china decoration in connection with this Section is to be original.

PAINTING ON CHINA

CHINAWARE AND MATERIALS REQUIRED

9. Chinaware.—The term chinaware arose from the porcelain originally manufactured in the Chinese empire, but it is now used generally to refer to the soft porcelain made in England, and referred to in America as *bone china*.

The class of porcelain known as bone china is composed of 40 parts of bone ash (largely imported from America), 40 parts of Cornwall stone (found in Cornwall, England), and 20 parts of kaolin (a clay, also found in Cornwall, England). The ware composed of these ingredients is baked in kilns at the very high temperatures ranging from 2,300° to 2,400° F. The result is a pure white ware with a rich glaze, making a most suitable surface for decorating with vitrifiable colors.

Any articles of plain white chinaware, such as plaques, trays, plates, saucers, cups, pitchers, vases, etc., will be suitable for decorating. These may range in quality from the cheapest kind, obtainable in any department store or five-and-ten-cent store, up to the finest grades of china. The cheaper grades are good enough for the beginner's practice work, though certain results cannot always be guaranteed for them in the firing.

The china decorator has the choice of the products of a number of manufacturers of, and dealers in, fine china, who specialize on furnishing articles of chinaware to be decorated. The names of such firms of china manufacturers and dealers can be obtained from local china

FIG. 1

stores, from the advertisements in trade papers dealing with ceramic interests, or will be furnished, upon request, to any student who cannot otherwise obtain them.

10. Pencil Medium.—When a design has been made and is to be copied onto the china (either freehand or by tracing) for the purpose of painting, the first requirement is to prepare the smooth china surface so that it can be drawn on; for such a surface, untreated, will not take pencil marks. The china surface must therefore first be treated with a preparation known as **pencil medium,** which is a liquid sold in vials, at 10 or 15 cents each; this can be applied with a brush or a piece of tissue paper to the surface of the china, where it will dry in a few minutes, after which pencil marks can be freely made on the china.

11. China, or Lithographers', Crayons.—For work that is not too finely detailed, the special use of pencil medium may be dispensed with, and the lines of the design or pattern may be drawn direct on the china by means of wax crayon, which comes in pencil form, with detachable paper wrapping, as shown in Fig. 1. Such a pencil costs about 12 cents. The marks made by such a crayon can be painted over without trouble and any not desired will disappear in the process of firing.

12. Ring Dividers.—Many modern designs, in order to conform to the prevailing trend in ceramic decoration, are of a conventional character, from either arbitrary motifs or conventionalized plant-form motifs, the units of the design repeating uniformly and symmetrically at pleasing intervals around a plate, a cup, a vase, etc. These intervals of repeats must be carefully plotted out by properly spaced construction lines and points. For this spacing of construction lines, the most useful devices are known as **ring dividers**, which are simply circular disks of cardboard, some with circular holes cut out, and others solid. The general appearance and the manner of using these are shown later in Fig. 41. These disks or rings, with the proper divisions

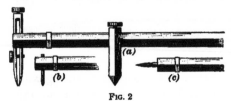

Fig. 2

marked out thereon, can be purchased very cheaply; 10 or 15 cents for a set of three; or quite satisfactory ones can be made by folding a circular piece of paper upon itself any desired number of times, and marking the divisions indicated by the creases when it is unfolded; thus, one fold makes two divisions; a second fold makes four; a third fold, eight; the fourth, sixteen, etc. With the proper construction points and lines located, the details of the design or pattern can then be transferred to the object by tracing, or may be sketched in freehand.

13. Ceramic Gauge and Liner.—The ceramic gauge and liner, as shown in Fig. 2, is a device for plotting out the desired center points on the surface of plates or plaques, and for making bands, edges, etc. It is in the form of a bar divider, and with it circles can be drawn, up to 12 inches in diameter. A piece of adhesive tape, or paper, pasted at the center of the plate, forms a firm place to stand the center pin of the gauge, or even the leg of a pair of compasses, so that it will not slip when circles are drawn.

The marking device is fixed into one end of the bar; it may be a ruling pen to take color, as shown in Fig. 2 (a), or a pencil lead, as in (b), or a small brush, as in (c). The gauge, with an ordinary pencil lead as a marker, may be set to work from the edge of a plate, or bands of color may be drawn or striped thereon by using the pen shown in (a) or the brush shown in (c).

The gauge costs anywhere from 35 cents to 75 cents, depending upon the attachments furnished with it.

There are other devices for plotting construction lines, doing banding, striping, etc.; they are known as dividers, banding wheels, etc., and run into many dollars in cost. They may be purchased from any dealer in china-painters' supplies, but the beginner can very well get along without this more expensive equipment.

14. Outlining Pens and Ink.—In drawing a pattern on china, particularly if it is elaborate, whether plotted freehand or traced and transferred, it is necessary
to make permanent
the lines as one goes

FIG. 3

along, so that they will not be obliterated while the rest of the lines are being drawn. For this purpose a special type of pen, such as shown in Fig. 3, and costing from 6 to 12 cents each, is necessary. This pen is useful not only for the ink outlining of the original drawing on the china, just described, but also for out-lining with color or gold when the actual painting is being done.

A suitable ink for such outlining is specially prepared, costing 12 cents per vial, which will flow well from the pen and attach itself to the surface of the china, and will stand painting over. The ink lines will burn away in the firing.

15. Gelatine Tracing Paper, Graphite Paper, Wax, Etc.—When doing china-decoration work, those designers who are trained in drawing prefer to sketch out their outline designs on the china direct, using the china crayons and working free-hand; yet some designers find it advisable to draw the designs first on paper, then to trace them onto tracing paper and finally transfer them to the surface of the china. While ordinary white transparent tracing paper, costing about 6 cents for an 11″×17″ sheet, would do, yet a better paper is known as *gelatine tracing paper*, which is very thin and transparent, and can be used on curved surfaces. One side of the paper has a matt surface which makes it excellent for drawing. Such paper costs about 17 cents for an 11″×18″ sheet.

The best transfer paper, to place under the tracing paper, is known as *graphite paper*. This is very thin, and makes a tracing of delicate gray lines on the china, which lines disappear in the firing. This graphite paper costs 6 cents for a 10″×15″ sheet.

The best method of attaching the tracing paper and transfer paper to the china and holding it there until the tracing operation has been accomplished, is to use a special kind of wax, known as *tracing-paper wax*. This comes in small boxes, at 12 cents each, and can be used over again a number of times.

16. Pigments.—The pigments used for painting on china differ from ordinary oil paints used for painting on canvas, in that they are vitrifiable; that is, by intense heat they can be fused with, and incorporated into, the surface of the china upon which they are placed.

These pigments for ceramic work are a combination of a metallic oxide with a fusible flux, a flux being a substance that assists materially in the melting and fusing of metallic oxides and in causing them to become incorporated with the china itself or with the glaze. These fluxes are composed of quartz sand, borax, and red lead melted together to form a kind of glass, which is then finely ground. Sometimes the flux and the metallic oxide for the color are melted together and then ground; in other cases they are merely mixed and ground together into powder form.

While it is not the purpose at this point to list in detail the colors of pigments used for painting china, yet it may be pointed out that the main metallic oxides for producing certain colors are as follows: The oxides of iron are used to produce reds and browns; oxides of manganese for dark browns; oxides of nickel and iridium for grays; oxides of copper and chromium for greens; oxide of cobalt for blues; and gold produces a beautiful rose color.

Fig. 4

17. Moist Colors in Tubes.—The prepared pigments for china painting come in two forms: moist colors in tubes, as shown in Fig. 4, and powder colors in vials, as in Fig. 5. Either form may be used, as desired. If the tube colors are fresh, they have the advantage of being practically ready for use, as it is necessary simply to dilute them slightly with spirits of turpentine to which, in some cases, a drop or two of oil of turpentine needs to be added. Some china painters recommend clove oil, and others oil of lavender, for this purpose; but turpentine seems to give the best results on account of its help in drying the colors rapidly.

If tube colors are used, they should be secured as fresh as possible, and then every effort should be made to keep them from becoming hard and dry. They should be kept away from heat as much as possible. If, however, they should in time become dry, which will probably not be in less than a year's time, the tube may be opened at the "wrong" end, and some of the pigment removed and then rubbed down with turpentine on a china palette or dish until it is again of the desired consistency.

Fig. 5

Moist colors in tubes, which come in the form shown in Fig. 4, cost anywhere from 18 cents to 75 cents per tube, the more expensive colors being the reds and the purples. On the average, the price is about 20 cents per tube.

18. Powder Colors in Vials.—There are certain advantages in using powder colors that make them very popular with the beginner as well as with the experienced china decorator.

One reason is that the powder will keep in good condition for an indefinite period, and can always be mixed readily with·the painting oil when needed for use. This process of mixing is a simpler one than that of thinning tube colors with turpentine, and better results are secured in the painting. The proper oils for mixing, grounding, etc., will be described later. These powder colors in vials come in the form shown in Fig. 5, and cost about the same as those in the tubes.

Dealers in china colors list in their catalogs a great number of different kinds of colors. In most cases, the names explain the nature or the particular purpose of each. Some of those most commonly used will be here mentioned.

19. Over-Glaze Colors.—The term over-glaze colors means the china colors that are used in painting over the glossy surface, or glaze, of the china, and the colors themselves when fired are glazed. Dealers list an almost endless variety of colors, hues, shades, tints, etc., but a very good simple selection of colors with which the beginner may start is as follows: Ruby purple; violet; rose; primrose yellow; yellow-red; Albert yellow; banding blue; black; shading green; yellow-green; finishing brown; yellow-brown.

Of course, with progress in the work of china painting a larger and more diversified selection of colors will be desired, and these can easily be selected from any dealer's catalog.

The method of mixing colors with the mixing oils, and of working with them on the china, will be discussed later.

20. Matt Colors.—Certain powder colors, also coming in vials, at about 10 cents per vial, are known as matt colors, because after being fired their surface is not a glaze, but is a *matt* surface; that is, it has a dull sheen. Such matt colors are much used for the painting of handles on cups, pitchers, etc., for contrasting effects with over-glaze colors, and for soft backgrounds.

21. Luster Colors.—For certain kinds of china decoration, as particular conventional effects, luster colors are very widely used. They come in vials, at about 15 cents each, but are in liquid form, not powder. When fired, they come out with

remarkable brilliancy.   The use of luster colors and the method
of working with them will be discussed later.

22.   Gold.—Some of the most effective decoration on
china is done with the use of gold, especially for conventionalized
work; for the combination of the glazed white surface of the
china and the gold banding, edging or other decoration is very
brilliant and effective.

One form of gold, coming in bottles or vials, is known as
liquid bright gold; and, when fired and properly burnished,
it gives a brilliant polished glaze effect, like a piece of highly
polished gold jewelry.
Roman gold is pure gold,
and when burnished and
polished it has a beautiful
luster.   Another form of
gold for china decoration is
known as **matt burnish
gold,** which, when prop-
erly fired and burnished
with the glass brush (to be
described later) finishes
with a beautiful dull matt

Fig. 6

surface or sheen.   Gold is furnished, mounted on a glass or
porcelain slab, and protected, as shown in Fig. 6.

The method of applying, firing, and burnishing golds of
various kinds will be discussed later. '

23.   Oils, Fluxes, and Other Painting Mediums.
For the proper thinning of moist color in tubes, spirits of
turpentine is needed, which can be purchased for a few cents at
any paint or drug store.   But there are also occasionally needed
in this connection such oils as oil of turpentine, oil of cloves, oil
of lavender, balsam copaiba, fat oil, etc., which can be purchased in half-ounce vials or bottles at 20 cents to 25 cents
each, from reputable dealers in china-painters' materials.

For the proper mixing and rubbing down of the powder
colors after being taken from the vials, a certain prepared oil,
known as **painting oil,** is sold in quantities varying from a

half-ounce bottle at 17 cents up to a pint can at $2.25. This oil is free from stickiness, has a pleasant odor, and makes the pigment of just the right consistency for painting.

A special oil for assisting in pouncing on, or dusting on, the ground or flat-color covering desired on the china is called **grounding oil.** One form of this, sold in half-ounce bottles at 17 cents, is black, which, when spread over the china surface to be decorated, appears gray. In this way, when the powder color is dusted or pounced on it is easy to tell when the color is placed evenly. A description of the use of this oil and the method of grounding will be given at the proper time.

Flux, as has been previously explained, is a medium that, combined with the vitrifiable colors, enables them, when fired, to be melted and become incorporated with the china glaze. For the average china colors now put out by reliable makers or dealers it is not necessary to add flux, except when desiring to secure a very thin tint of color on the china. Such flux varies in price from 10 cents to 30 cents per vial, depending upon kind and size.

24. Brushes for China Painting.—There are many and diverse kinds and shapes of brushes used for china painting, the shape and nature depending on the use to which they are to be be put, the manufacturer, etc. Speaking broadly, however, it may be said that there are three general classes of brushes for china-decoration work: *painting and shading brushes, tinting and grounding brushes,* and *stippling brushes.* Typical brushes of these three classes are illustrated in Figs. 7, 8, and 9.

In Fig. 7 are shown some forms of **painting and shading brushes;** that is, the brushes employed for outlining, shading and coloring flowers, figure subjects, conventional decoration, etc., on china. In Fig. 7 (a) is shown a camel's-hair rigger, or liner, used for fine line and outline work. In (b) is shown a camel's-hair liner not quite so long and supple, and not making such a fine line, as the rigger shown in (a). ·In (c), (d), and (e) are shown camel's-hair painting brushes called pointed shaders; that is, brushes used for painting on the colors and shades used to portray the values and modeling of flowers, leaves, figures, decoration, etc. In (*f*) is shown an extra-long shader referred to as a camel's-hair tracer; in (*g*), a camel's-hair square shader; that is, one with the hairs of the brush cut off square; in (*h*), a camel's-hair cut liner for making sharp, even lines; and in (*i*), a round-end camel's hair scroller, used for making evenly curved

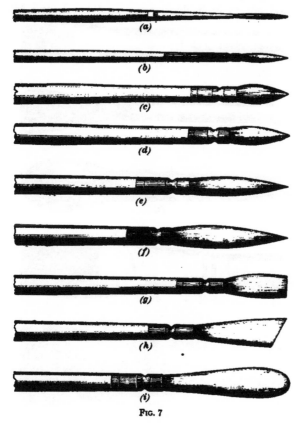

FIG. 7

lines and scrolls in conventional decorative work. Brushes such as these cost from 5 cents to 15 cents each.

In Fig. 8 is shown a group of five brushes that are typical examples of the class known as **tinting** or **grounding brushes;** that is, brushes that are used for putting on flat or graded tints of color, in either naturalistic or conventional china decoration, or for the laying of grounds or backgrounds on the surface of the china, over which, or against which, the painted decoration is to stand forth.   In Fig. 8 (a) is shown a Russian-sable tinting brush, the hairs being short and springy, thus enabling the color to be laid heavily and evenly so as to secure good effects in backgrounds.   In (b), (c), and (d) are

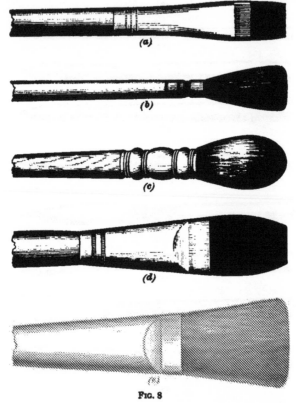

Fig. 8

shown different shapes of camel's-hair tinting and grounding brushes, sometimes used alone for placing the grounds, dusting dry colors over the grounding oil, etc., and sometimes loosely covered with a silk handkerchief to secure the same results.   In (e) is shown an extra large tinting or grounding brush.   Brushes of this kind can be had for from 12 cents to 25 cents each.

In Fig. 9 four specimens are shown of the general class of brushes known as **stippling brushes** or **stipplers**. In (a) is shown a small slanting fitch-hair stippler, in a quill handle; this is particularly useful for fine work like stippling and pouncing gold over matt colors, etc. In (b) is a heavier fitch-hair stippler, square and wired onto a wood handle; and in (c) and (d) are shown slanting and square fitch-hair stipplers,

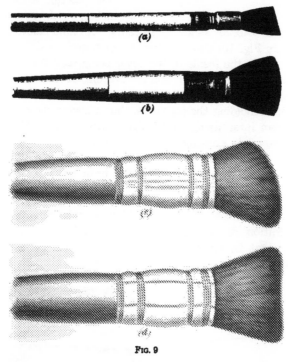

Fig. 9

respectively, on wood handles, for general stippling, such as blending grounds and backgrounds evenly after dusting on, and for other purposes. Such brushes cost from 6 cents to 85 cents each, depending on their size. Still other forms of brushes, for odd and special uses, can be seen in dealers' catalogs.

25. Palette for China Colors.—The palette for china decorators, which differs from the ordinary palette for oil painters doing landscape and figure work, has one compartment for mixing the powder color and the oil and another compart-

ment, properly divided, for placing the various colors, lusters, gold, etc., so that they are ready for use.

It is possible to get a suitable palette, 9 inches × 12 inches, with removable

Fig. 10

opal-glass slab, for as low as 75 cents. A china palette, such as shown in Fig. 10, also sells for 75 cents, and consists of a base and a cover, the inside of the cover being used for mixing the powder color and the oil, and the bottom, or main part, of the palette being divided into shallow compartments or cups, as shown, for holding the pigments, thus allowing the colors to be kept from intermixing, and keeping them fresh. The shallow wells are made slanting, and are used for the gold and for the lusters; the latter should be removed from the vial a few drops at a time and placed on the palette, from which they are then taken up with the brush.

26. Palette Knives.—For thinning moist color from tubes by addition of turpentine, and for rubbing down powder colors; that is, mixing them with the oil, palette knives are necessary. Two styles are shown in Fig. 11; that in (a) is the

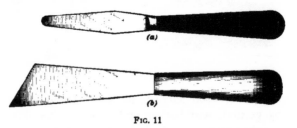

(a)

(b)

Fig. 11

regular straight shape, and that in (b) is the clipped-end palette knife. These sell for from 20 cents to 45 cents each.

27. Steel Erasing Knives.—Erasing knives, with either straight or curved blades, are useful instruments with which to make corrections, straighten up lines, etc.   In Fig. 12 is shown one with a curved blade, to fit concave and convex surfaces; it sells for 35 cents.

There is also an erasing liquid, put up in bottles at 35 cents each, which will remove colors or gold, if mistakes have been

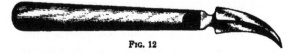

FIG. 12

made and need correcting.   The surface of china so corrected may be painted over again.

28. Dust Needle.—The dust needle, adjustable within a handle of turned bone about 3 inches long, and costing 20 cents, is very useful for removing specks of dust from painted surfaces without spoiling the surrounding field.   Such a needle is shown in Fig. 13.

29. Glass Burnishing Brush.—The most suitable means of burnishing Roman gold after it is fired is the glass

FIG. 13

burnishing brush, such as shown in Fig. 14, made of fibers of fine spun glass bound together as shown.   They may be had in small sizes a few inches long at 10 cents each, up to the large professional size, 8 inches long, at 45 cents.

Gold can also be burnished by rubbing with a wet rag and fine burnishing sand (glass sand) which is sold in 10-cent bottles, or at 48 cents per pound.

30. Arranged Painting Outfits for Beginners.—As an assistance to beginners, who might have difficulty in choosing

FIG. 14

a suitable assortment from the great array of painting materials listed in the dealers' catalogs, beginners' outfits, of various degrees of elaborateness, and selling at moderate prices, have been prepared by manufacturers and dealers. One such outfit, suitable for any beginner, consists of a polished-wood box for holding the materials, a collection of powdered china-decoration colors in vials, such as listed in Art. **19** under Over-Glaze Colors, a box of Roman gold, a bottle of painting oil or medium, a white tile or palette for mixing colors, five brushes (4 shaders and 1 outliner), five handles, set of dividers, palette knife, china crayon, graphite paper, tracing paper, wax for fastening, ink for outlining and painting, etc., the whole being very complete, and costing less than $3.50. More extended and elaborate outfits can be secured, at prices correspondingly higher.

METHODS OF WORKING

31. Proper Position When Working.—The position in which the worker places himself and the tools and materials with which he works has a great influence upon the success of the work in hand. He should be seated on a comfortable chair without arms, before a table that is firm and substantial and so arranged in relation to a window that the light comes over the worker's left shoulder.

32. Disposition of Materials.—The materials with which to do the painting should be arranged on the table in front of the worker; the palette should be on the right with a little jar of turpentine beside it, and near that the bottle of mixing oil or medium, and perhaps a small saucer into which to pour the mixing oil. There should also be two squares of muslin provided, one folded for drying the oil brush and the other for cleaning the palette when necessary.

The pencils, gauge, crayons, brushes, colors, palette knife, and other materials should be placed on the table to the left of the worker, so that they are easily accessible.

TINTING AND GROUNDING

33. Preparing the Colors.—With the worker in the proper position, the materials properly arranged, and the article of chinaware, say a flat plate, cleaned and dried and ready for a coating tint or ground, the colors should now be prepared.

First of all, the palette or mixing slab should be perfectly clean, and dried with the muslin rag. Let it be assumed that the powder color in vials is to be used. Pour out from the vial a small quantity of the desired powder colors, say enough to cover a dime. If the plate is to have a grounding tint of light écru, or ivory, then use two parts of yellow-brown and one part of yellow-green. The mixing oil may be removed from the jar or saucer by means of the brush and placed beside the mound of powder color on the palette; the two are then rubbed down, or mixed, with the palette knife. Or, the clean palette knife may be dipped in the oil, and then the oil and powder color can be rubbed down together to form a mass of the consistency of putty, after which it may be lifted up with a palette knife and placed on a clean palette, or a clean portion of the same palette. The mixed color should be of such consistency that it will stand up in a cohesive mass on the palette. Too much oil mixed with the pigment makes it too thin, so that it runs, in which event more powdered color should be added.

Each color that is needed for the work in hand should be ground or rubbed down in this way, care being taken that the slab is always first wiped perfectly clean with a turpentined rag.

34. Tinting the China Surface.—With the desired colors properly mixed, the problem is now to tint the surface of the plate with a ground tint or color—in this case light ecru, or ivory. The palette knife should be used to take up the required pigments, in this case yellow-brown and yellow-green, and with these should be mixed some of the mixing oil or medium already described, so that the resulting pigment becomes thin enough to flow from the brush when it is drawn along in a stroke. A good brush to use for this purpose is a camel's-hair square shader, such as is shown in Fig. 7 (g).

First dip the brush freely in the oil or medium and rub it around on a spot on the palette, thus working the oil thoroughly into the hairs of the brush; then wipe the brush free of surplus oil. Then fill the brush with the desired color, in this case ivory, and with bold free strokes carefully paint over the entire surface of the plate.

In making such a tint smooth and even, a silk pad, or pounce, is of great assistance. This may be made by tying a piece of silk over a small ball of cotton, or a silk handkerchief over the hairs of a round-headed brush. A little of the oil or medium may be spread in the palm of the hand and the silk pad or pounce then rubbed into it. This oiled pad or pounce should then be lightly touched to, or padded upon, the surface of the plate that has just been painted. The padding, or pouncing, should be done systematically, say in horizontal adjacent rows, and not in a haphazard manner. If properly done, the result will be a beautiful waxy surface to the pounced tint, but if it is shiny or sticky in appearance too much oil has been used. There is no remedy for this fault; the whole coating must be wiped off clean and another attempt made.

Whether or not the painted plate is to be fired by the artist or is to be sent out to be fired, the ground tint should be first carefully dried; either slowly, or hurried by placing it in an oven with the door open.

35. Ground-Laying.—Another form of placing a tint (either solid, or graded and blended) on china is known as **ground-laying, or grounding;** this is accomplished by dusting the powder color over a coat of grounding oil or medium previously applied to the surface of the china. The grounding oil, which is dark in tint, should be well shaken in the bottle, then enough poured out for the work in hand, after which it should be stirred and manipulated with the palette knife to remove air bubbles, etc. The oil should then be applied to the surface of the china with a square shader, as previously explained, with broad free strokes, care being taken that every part of the china surface is covered with the oil. Make several silk pads, or pounces, as previously explained, and tap or pad over the entire surface of the oil just laid until the background becomes a smooth, even tint. Then allow the china with its pounced coat of oil to stand for about half an hour.

The next process is to dust on, or spread on, the powder color over the oiled surface. Powder color from the vials sometimes coheres into lumps caused by the powder being tightly packed. If left unbroken, these lumps would prevent the powder from spreading smoothly and would probably scratch the oil surface; they must therefore be broken up and the powder color passed through a fine sieve. Now to spread the powder color over the oiled surface proceed as follows: On a large plate, place a generous quantity of the powder color and above it hold horizontally, oil-covered side up, the china to be decorated. Drop powder color onto the oil by means of a piece of soft cotton dipped in the powder; the surplus powder will then fall off onto the plate or dish of powder underneath. Use plenty of powder and spread it lightly with a circular motion over the oiled surface. Several successive dustings or powderings should be given until the oiled surface will hold no more. The superfluous powder may now be removed from the oiled surface by means of a soft dry brush. If the background is now dusted with powdered flux, or glaze, a more brilliant effect will be secured in the firing.

The ground-covered plate is now ready for firing.

TRANSFERRING THE DESIGN TO THE CHINA

36. Plotting Out the Construction Lines.—After the plate that has been tinted or covered with a ground color has been properly fired and returned to the china decorator, he must next transfer the design to it, ready for painting.

The process of planning out and making designs of all kinds for china decoration will be discussed later in this Section, for it is only after having an idea of the technical requirements of painting on china, and of firing china, that the artist can prepare suitable ceramic designs.

It being assumed, therefore, for the present, that the design has been planned out, and perhaps drawn or painted on paper, the next step is to transfer the design to the surface of the china. Those who have been trained in drawing and rendering will want to draw the design directly onto the china, without any preliminary tracing. This may be done with the china crayon, or lithographer's crayon; or the china, after being coated with the preparation known as pencil medium, may be drawn upon with an ordinary lead pencil. However, if the design is conventional, with details repeating at regular intervals, as around a border, they must first be plotted out on a basis of definite construction lines.

37. There are several devices that assist in doing this plotting out, among which are the ceramic gauge and the ring dividers. With the ceramic gauge the center of the plate can easily be located, and border lines at any desired positions can be drawn around the margin of the plate. The ring dividers come in three or more sizes and, as their name indicates, consist of flat disks or rings with all necessary divisions marked on their edges. These ring dividers fit over or upon the article of china being decorated, as cups, vases, pictures, plates, etc., and can be fastened in any desired position with wax, and the divisions can then be marked on the china surface with the crayon. The home-made ring divider already described is used in the same way.

In the case of a plate, it is a simple matter to lay it face downwards on the ring divider and, with the crayon, to mark the desired divisions on the edges or on the back of the plate, which divisions can be extended in lines across the front of the plate if necessary. These straight lines, forming segments, can be drawn with an ordinary rule or straightedge, but for deep, bowl-shaped plates there is employed a flexible rule or straightedge that adapts itself to, and allows lines to be drawn upon, the concave surface of the plate. When laying out the divisions on the plate, and calculating the arrangements and repeats of a design that is to be traced, the utmost care must be observed to see that exactness is secured, so that, when traced, the design will come out right on the china.

38. Tracing and Transferring the Design.—The method of drawing the design or study direct on the surface of the china with the crayon pencil has already been referred to. No difficulty will be found in working in this manner on certain classes of naturalistic studies and designs, but certain kinds of conventional designs require great exactness in plotting and in laying out, and it is best to trace and transfer these.

There are several methods of tracing and transferring a design to china. One method is as follows: From the design, that has been carefully plotted, drawn, and perhaps colored, on a separate sheet of paper, make, on gelatine tracing paper, a very careful drawing or tracing of the section to be transferred. Place the tracing paper at the desired place on the surface of the china plate and either hold it very carefully in position or fasten it at the edges of the china with wax, or with slips of gummed paper. Then slip beneath the tracing paper a small piece of graphite paper with the graphite side face downwards, in contact with the china. Now go over the design on the tracing paper with a 4H or 6H pencil, being sure to trace every part of the design. When the tracing paper and the graphite paper are lifted it will be found that the lines of the design appear in gray on the china. At this stage it is best to go over the lines of the tracing with the outlining ink, using a pen or a brush. When outlining with ink or color, a little sugar water introduced will assist the outline in drying so quickly that remaining portions of the design can be readily transferred to their proper positions without rubbing out or spoiling the parts already transferred. Further, this outlining can be painted over, when the time comes, without being disturbed. The advantage of outlining with ink each section as traced is that it makes it permanent; otherwise it would be rubbed, and perhaps obliterated, during the process of tracing the other sections.

Another method of making the transfer is as follows: Make the tracing from the original design, as already described, then turn it over, and, with a fine needle, prick holes close together along the lines of the design. Then reverse the tracing again so that the rough side is up, place it in proper position, and, with a pounce or pad and some powdered charcoal, rub over the holes so that the powdered charcoal will go through them onto the china. Outline with ink as before described to preserve the pounced design, and then proceed to pounce, from the same perforated tracing, the remaining sections of the design.

---

39. Similarity of China Painting to Other Painting. When the design has been outlined on the plate in the manner described, it is ready to be painted. One can really give the beginner very little more in the line of help at this point than to say, Take the brush, fill it with color, and *paint*. Too many beginners in china decoration approach this work with timidity because they think there is some new and untried process connected with painting on china that they have never before attempted. As a matter of fact, for those who have studied and practiced the work of the preceding Sections, there is nothing particularly new to be learned. They have had considerable experience in painting with sable brushes and washes, both in monochrome and in colors, and therefore know how to use a brush to lift colors from a receptacle and apply them to a surface to be decorated. It is true that, for china painting, several different kinds of brushes are needed, the pigments are also somewhat different, being thicker and heavier to work with, and the surface worked upon is smooth and glossy; but these are about the only differences. A few additional general points of advice, however, will be helpful.

Get used to using a brush of good size. For example, when painting a leaf or the petal of a flower, use one of the brushes called a square shader, already referred to, dip it into and rub it around in the color, and then paint the leaf in two or three bold strokes of pure color that flows from the brush and adheres to the china surface, as it will on account of the oil. Do not use haggling little strokes, but work boldly, except of course where fine outlining is done with a small brush, in which case a steady hand and deliberate care are required to do the work well. Do not try to touch up, or patch up, work that has been painted; but paint it correctly with the first strokes, which can be done if thought and care are exercised and preliminary practicing is done. If the color is too thick when working with it, add a little more of the mixing medium.

If necessary to clean up, or true up, the edges of forms or outlines, this may be done with a small pointed piece of wood, such as the pointed end of a brush handle or a toothpick.

If the design, which should be a simple one to start with, is not satisfactory when entirely painted and does not look well, it should be rubbed out or wiped off, and an entirely new painting made. It would be absolutely useless to go to the trouble and expense of firing a poorly painted plate or other article. The repainting will be well worth while for what it teaches in additional practice in painting. When the painting is satisfactory, the plate or other article should then be fired, a process which will be described later in this Section.

40. Firing, Repainting, and Refiring.—After the firing is completed, it will probably be found that certain parts of the painted design will be weak. These should be gone over again, and touched up, in the same way as in the original painting. The solid colors and tinting will also probably need touching up. When this has been done the work should be fired again.

It sometimes occurs, on account of the arrangement and color scheme of a certain pattern or design, that several separate repaintings, followed by refirings, must be done.

GOLD PAINTING ON CHINA

41. Kinds of Gold and the Methods of Using Them. As has already been indicated, the gold for use in china painting comes in two main forms: **Roman gold,** as a moist brown mass or paste on a small glass slab in a small covered box, and **liquid bright gold,** as a brown liquid in a bottle or vial, in reality a diluted solution of pure gold.

The amount of gold to be used on any decorated article must be influenced by the judgment and good taste of the worker, care being taken that the gold is used sparingly, for the overloading of an article of china with gold decoration is an evidence of lack of refinement, as will be pointed out later. It is usually best, on large articles like plates, pitchers, cups, saucers, etc., to confine the gold decoration to bands around the edges, fine spot motifs, and occasionally handles.

Some china decorators claim that the best effects are secured by first using liquid bright gold, then firing the piece, and before the second firing using Roman gold. The liquid bright gold, if used by itself, is rather more gaudy than the artistic decorator would desire, which is another reason for using it in combination with Roman gold. The liquid bright gold can be used direct from the vial or bottle, but the brush should first be wiped free of surplus liquid on the edge of the bottle.

The paste form of gold—that is, Roman gold—is hard and dry, and when working with it a little turpentine, or perhaps oil of lavender, must be used, and when the lump gold is rubbed down with this it will be a brown paste. Sometimes a little of the liquid bright gold added to the paste will soften it if it is very hard.

42. Applying the Gold to the China.—Before applying the gold, the china surface must be quite clean and dry, and the lines of the design must have been properly traced, transferred, and outlined in ink on the surface of the china. In doing gold outlining; that is, painting lines of gold, the rigger or long-pointed outlining brush should be used, and should be drawn slowly and steadily along, the hand being steadied by resting the little finger on the china and sliding it along as the line is painted. Some decorators use a *painting bridge*, which is simply a flat piece of wood raised slightly above the surface of the table, and upon which the hand rests while working. For making lines around the edge of a plate, for instance, a device known as a *banding wheel* is used; the hand with its brushful of gold is held steadily on a fixed platform, the brush being perfectly perpendicular, above a revolving turntable upon which the china plate has been placed. The tip of the brush charged with gold is allowed just to touch the surface of the china; and the turntable with its china plate is spun around, and thus the brush paints a line of gold upon the rim of the plate.

Heavier portions of the design are painted by using the square shader well charged with gold. The square shader should also be used for painting handles of cups, pitchers, etc., and for the entire surface of such small objects as salt cellars, etc.

43. Points to Be Observed in Using Gold.—The Roman gold that has been spoken of is fluxed gold; that is, a gold with which a flux has been previously combined so that, with heat, it will become incorporated with the white glazed china surface upon which it is applied. Such fluxed Roman gold is therefore the proper kind to use on white, unpainted china. It can also be used over matt colors after they have been fired. The unfluxed gold cannot be used successfully on white china, for it will come off; but it can be used over gold or a color that has been fired.

Roman gold must be applied with such strength that the sheen of the china underneath will just be covered. If it is used too heavy it will be quite rough when fired, and if applied too light and thin it will not properly adhere to the china.

Gold may be used for fine outlining, for which purpose a pen is used. A little medium should be mixed with the gold so as to make it flow smoothly from the pen, which can be filled by means of a brush.

Considerable care is needed in preparing and using the gold, medium, turpentine, brushes, etc., for gold work on china. The palette knife and the brushes used for gold must be reserved for gold work alone. It is a good idea to have a separate china palette, with compartments and a cover for the gold, and to put all materials used for this work away in a special box after use, so that they may be kept free from the contamination of dust, or of possible admixture with other materials.

The best medium to use with the gold to get the proper results in smooth painting is oil of lavender. However, if used too thick it will fire out, and if used too thin it will not accomplish its purpose. In filling the brush with the gold the brush should be well charged, and, in painting, it should be drawn slowly along over the surface of the china, so that the gold flows evenly onto the china in a film that entirely covers the china, but does not pile up.

After painting with gold it will be found that brushes have a tendency to become clogged up with gold. The proper method of cleaning them, in order to save gold and preserve the life of the brush, is to shake the brush around in a small jar of alcohol; this will loosen and wash away the particles of gold, which will sink to the bottom of the jar and thus be saved. After enough gold has thus been deposited in the bottom of the jar, the alcohol may be poured off, the gold placed on a glass slab, mixed with Dresden oil, and later used again for certain minor purposes.

After all the gold painting has been done on a certain article it should be kept free from dust, and from handling, and should be allowed to dry thoroughly before being fired, or being sent out to be fired. This drying process may be accomplished by setting the plate or other gold-painted article on an asbestos mat, placing this in an oven, with the door open so as to let the oil fumes escape, and thus drying it until the gold is no longer moist or sticky. In all this handling, the fingers should not be allowed to touch the gold that has been painted on the china, for the oil or grease from.the finger marks will so affect the gold that, when fired, they will plainly show.

44. Firing and Burnishing Gold.—It is now assumed that the process of firing the gold has been completed, although the details of this process will be discussed later in this Section. It is next necessary to burnish the gold in order to bring out its brilliancy and beauty. There are three principal methods employed for such burnishing; the glass brush, burnishing sand, and the agate burnisher.

The glass brush, as has been previously stated, consists of strands of finely spun glass bound together compactly in brush form. When polishing or burnishing is done with this brush, the fine particles of glass come off from the brush, float through the air, and settle on surrounding objects. Therefore, such polishing or burnishing should be done somewhere away from the place where the painting is done (preferably in another room) so that the fine particles of glass do not get into the china colors or the gold. Further, loose gloves should be worn by the worker, so that the glass particles do not enter or irritate the skin. The work of polishing should be done over a newspaper, so that the glass particles may fall upon and be caught by the newspaper, which may afterwards be burned. Great care must be taken that the particles of glass fiber that become detached do not get into the colors or the gold that is to be used for other work, for, upon firing, such painted work will be found to be spoiled.

A second method of burnishing; namely, with burnishing sand, will be found to be simple and effective for the beginner. The sand is a special glass sand, and must be moistened well with water, taken up on a soft rag and rubbed with a circular motion over the parts to be burnished. When rubbing, the pressure should not be great, but the rag should simply rest on the china as the burnishing is being done.

If a brilliant polish is desired, a third method of burnishing is employed; namely, with the agate burnisher. This tool is not easy for the beginner to use, but sureness of touch and handling comes with practice. The agate burnisher hardens the gold, thus improving its wearing qualities, and gives a very high polish.

LUSTER PAINTING ON CHINA

45. Character of Luster Colors.—The purpose of painting with luster colors on china is to secure effects that, when fired, are not only very brilliant, being even more brilliant than the glaze of the china itself, but that also possess a sheen or irridescence; like mother of pearl, for example. The luster colors are of great variety; such as white, ivory, yellow, orange, light "shammy" (chamois), yellow-brown, gray, blue-gray, black, light-green opal, ivory opal, pink opal, mother of pearl, turquoise, apple green, steel blue, irridescent rose, platinum, copper, etc. These luster colors come in stoppered vials, and when in the vials, as well as when painting with them, there is no distinction in the colors; they all look alike.

46. Points to Observe When Painting With Lusters. First of all, the vials must be shaken well, so that all sediment is dissolved. The next important consideration is that new brushes must be used, and it is advisable to use a separate brush for each luster color. The success of luster painting depends upon the cleanliness of the color, during both the painting and the firing. For this reason a brush once used for one luster color must be very carefully cleaned before it is used for another. It first must be wiped clean on a rag and then washed in a little turpentine, then dried again carefully on a rag, then washed in a clean supply of turpentine and dried again on a rag. Then the same process of washing and drying must be repeated, alcohol instead of turpentine being used, and then the brush laid away to dry thoroughly.

The surface of the china must be free from finger marks and be clean in every respect. If wiped with a piece of tissue paper wet with alcohol and then dried, the surface will be best for luster painting. The china should also be of the same temperature as the room where the painting is being done; otherwise the luster will not adhere properly, and will be irregular in tone and color.

The luster colors should be applied in good bold strokes with a square shader. The color must not be put on too thick for the first firing; better effects can be secured by painting a thin coat, firing that, then painting another thin coat and firing that, and so on. While the painting is being done, the air should be free from dust of any kind, so that none may fall upon the luster colors.

Lusters may be padded or dabbed on with a silk dabber, as has already been described for ground-laying and tinting. Lusters are difficult to pad, but if a little oil of lavender is used with the luster color, the lint singed off the silk dabber, and the dabbing process is done promptly and quickly after the luster has been applied, some beautiful effects can be secured. The insides of cups, etc., can be given a beautiful luster if a little luster color is poured into the cup and then spread around with the silk dabber.

When luster colors are purchased from a dealer, he will be glad to furnish a little manual or folder descriptive of color combinations and effects that can be secured with various luster colors.

Although firing will be discussed later in this Section, it may be mentioned here that, before firing, the luster-painted china should be dried slowly in an oven. Then the firing in the kiln should be done slowly at first with the kiln door partly open so that smoke and gases may escape before the kiln gets red hot.

FIRING THE CHINA

THE KILN AND ITS USE

47. The Firing of China.—It should be understood by this time that it is not sufficient simply to paint the design onto the china; for even though it dries, it is not permanent when left in that condition. The china-painters' colors, gold, lusters, etc. are all vitrifiable, and therefore, after being applied, they must be subjected to intense heat, which will cause them to fuse into and become a part of the surface of the china. This heat is secured by firing, or baking, the china in a kiln of special construction.

FIG. 15

The china decorator will find in any large town or city some amateur or professional china decorator possessing a kiln who will fire newly painted china at moderate rates, ranging from 5 cents to 10 cents for small articles like cream jugs, sugar bowls, spoon trays, etc., up through moderate-sized articles like pitchers, cracker jars, chocolate pots, etc., at 20 cents to 30 cents, to very large articles like punch bowls, plaques, fish and meat platters, etc., at 50 cents to $1.50.

However, most conscientious china decorators will want to do their own firing, for which it is necessary to have a suitable kiln.

48. The Charcoal Kiln.—A small inexpensive kiln is known as a charcoal kiln, such as shown in Fig. 15, and consists of an iron firing pot surrounded with firebrick, and a space for the fuel, which may be dry corn cobs instead of charcoal if desired. Such a kiln must be placed on a brick floor, outdoors in a shed or similar place. It will do better firing with less experience than any other kind of kiln, if reasonable care is exercised.

One such kiln 12 inches in diameter and 10 inches deep, inside measurement, costs $15. A similar kiln, 12 inches in diameter and 16 inches deep, inside measurement, costs $20. A third size of charcoal kiln 15 inches in diameter and 16 inches deep, inside measurement, costs $25.

49. The Oil and Gas Kiln.—A kiln of a higher grade, working on a different principle, and accommodating more china, is shown in Fig. 16. This kiln burns kerosene oil as fuel, the oil being placed in the

Fig. 16

can that rests on the bracket at the side of the kiln, as shown in the illustration. Controlled by a valve, the oil is allowed to drip into a funnel at the end of a pipe through which the oil is conveyed to a heavy cast-iron tray underneath the kiln. When in use, the cast-iron tray becomes very hot and the oil becomes converted into gas as it drips into the tray, so that this form of burner really makes gas out of the kerosene, and a very hot flame results from the gas. There is a mica window in the front of the kiln to enable one to watch the progress of the firing. The kiln can be used indoors in the studio, because it has a 6-inch stovepipe that can be connected with the chimney. A kiln such as this, 14 inches long, 12 inches high, and 9 inches wide costs $35; and one 16 inches long, 15 inches high, and 10 inches wide costs $50.

A third style of kiln, of a different type, and more commodious, is shown in Fig. 17. The superior features of this

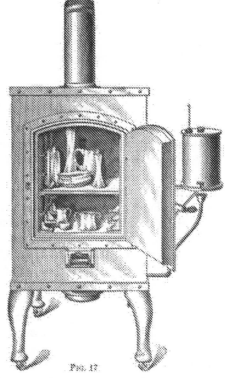

kiln are that the inside walls are all made of straight solid tiles; it is clean and fires with a perfect gloss; is easily stacked full of china; fires in about 2 hours; no bad odor is given off, and no damage or dust occurs. The prices of these kilns range from $48 for a kiln 10 inches wide, 14 inches high, and 15 inches deep, to $175 for a kiln 18 inches wide, 24 inches high, and 36 inches deep. There are also similar kilns the fuel of which is gas.

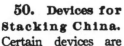

Fig. 17

50. Devices for Stacking China. Certain devices are needed for stacking up the painted china in the kiln, ready for firing, as follows: Asbestos sheets or plattens, 35 cents for a 10″×10″ sheet; asbestos board, 4 cents per square foot; biscuit (unglazed) plates, 9 cents to 12 cents each; triangle straight bars or saddles for stacking, 8 cents to 25 cents; and asbestos cord or twine for tying together stacked china or broken china. Other materials and devices can be secured as needed.

51. Proper Location and Care of Kiln.—Before placing the first article or batch of china in the kiln for firing, the kiln should be dried out thoroughly by means of a little heat in it. Further, to get the best results in firing, the kiln should be so arranged that it has a chimney with a good draft; that is, one whose outdoor exit is high, and not restricted by any narrow space. If this precaution is taken, there will be a good *roar* to the fire, and the china will be successfully fired.

If any cracks begin to show in the kiln they should be very carefully plastered up with kiln clay, otherwise the fumes from the fuel will discolor and spoil the china.

THE PROCESS OF FIRING

52. Placing and Stacking China in a Kiln.—Before lighting the fire to heat the kiln, the first thing to do is to put in place the shelves upon which the china is to stand. Each piece of china, particularly if it is glazed, should be so placed that it does not touch any other piece, otherwise they will stick together. Further, a current of air should be allowed to play under and all around each piece, to prevent any danger of cracking or breaking. The china is stacked with the aid of asbestos pads, plattens, stilts, asbestos cord, etc. The beginner will probably start with firing only a few pieces at a time, but as he comes to fire more pieces these precautions in stacking must be followed.

The part of the kiln in which is the door is called the front of the kiln, and the part directly opposite the door is the back of the kiln. The front and top of the kiln give the lightest fire, or least intense heat, and the back and bottom of the kiln the strongest fire or greatest heat. This should be carefully borne in mind when desiring to give some articles a light fire and others a strong fire.

53. Length of Time for Firing, and Other Details. No specified length of time, in exact number of minutes, can be given for firing any particular piece of china; for instance, a greater length of time is required in warm or stormy weather than in weather that is the reverse. Certain colors, also, require a stronger firing than others; for instance, pinks, blues, grays, etc., require quite a strong fire, while greens, yellows, browns, etc., need only a medium fire, and purples a still lighter fire. The flesh tones and reds require only the lightest fire. Golds, and also luster colors, need only a light fire; they should not be overfired.

When starting the kiln the oil should be allowed to saturate the asbestos fibers for about 5 or 10 minutes before the match is touched. Then the oil should flow drop by drop for a while, and afterwards a little faster.

Generally from 2 to 3 hours will be found to be the proper length of time for firing. There are various methods of telling when articles have had sufficient fire. One is in the form of melting tests, or cones, placed in the kiln with the china to be fired. These are of varying hardnesses; and when they start to melt and turn over to one side it is then time to stop the firing. Many workers can tell whether a proper firing has been given by observing, through the peephole provided in the front and the top of the kiln, certain conditions. For instance, when the bottom of the kiln has gotten so red hot that it has become a very white red, approaching what is known as white heat, the operator stops the fire. There are other visual tests employed, such as the apparent even gloss over the china, etc.

Care must be observed—after the fire has been turned out— to allow the kiln and its contents of china to cool gradually; otherwise the china will become cracked and broken. After the fire has been turned out, the door of the kiln should be opened little by little, and several hours allowed, say three or four, for the china to cool off.

The intention here is not to give minutely detailed directions for firing china, but simply a general outline of the process. When a china kiln is purchased from a manufacturer or dealer there is also supplied with it a book giving full and explicit directions for setting up the kiln, its operation, lengths of firing, firing tests, etc.

DESIGNING DECORATION FOR CHINA

PLANNING THE DESIGN

54. Consideration of Shape of Article to Be Decorated.—Inasmuch as the foundation principle of china decoration is that one must start with a certain definite article, of definite shape, and decorate that, it is extremely important that the selected shape be good in line and form, whether it be for a plate, a cup, a vase, a jar, or perhaps some more elaborate article.

No standard rule can be laid down, nor can pictures be shown, to illustrate just exactly what is good and what is bad in the shapes of china. As a general proposition, however, the china decorator is safe in avoiding elaborate, top-heavy shapes, with useless curves and applied scrolls, or with weak and insecure-looking feet and handles. Much of the so-called decorated chinaware or bric-à-brac one sees in department stores and 10-cent stores is of this *bad* class. The decorator can always feel safe in chosing shapes of china that are simple and graceful in line and form, and that give the effect of firmness and solidity; for instance, a vase, or a sugar bowl, that is of a general cylindrical shape but somewhat wider at the bottom than at the top. A safe plan to be followed by the beginner, who is not sure of his own judgment as to what is good and what is not good in china, is to look over the high-grade articles of fine china displayed in the best china or jewelry stores, or examine the illustrations in the catalogs or trade-magazine advertisements of the makers of the best china. The shapes of china handled by such dealers, and made and sold by such manufacturers, can always be depended on as being good.

55. Consideration of Suitability of Design to Shape Selected.—There are some articles, such as circular plates, etc., the shapes of which are unchanging; but in the case of bowls, vases, cups, etc., the possible varieties are unlimited. To the china decorator who has carefully studied historic and modern styles of design motifs and has prepared designs in those motifs, as have those who have studied the work of the previous Sections, the shape of each new piece of china will suggest which particular historic or modern period style will be most appropriate for that particular shape. A tall, full-necked vase with practically straight sides would probably demand a decorative treatment suggestive of the Gothic. A vase with a full, rather spherical body and a thin neck might demand delicate Greek or Roman motifs, or perhaps a Renaissance treatment. A short, squatty bowl or vase, if decorated at all, would be most appropriately treated with so-called modern ornament, the characteristics of which have been treated in a previous Section.

The important point, therefore, is to have the decoration suit the shape; and not to spoil an artistic shape with a lot of meaningless scrolls, nor to waste one's time in decorating a shape that is bad, no matter how tasteful and artistic the decoration.

The matter of having the main lines of the decoration suit the structural lines of the article of china is also one that must be considered, but this will be referred to in proper detail later.

56. Consideration of Suitability of Design to Use of Article.—Just as simplicity and dignity of form are very necessary in the case of the shapes of the articles, so similar simplicity is advised for the decoration. The sensibleness of this will appear when it is considered that a great many articles of decorated china are intended for actual use. When the use, therefore, is considered, the china decorator will not paint the interiors of cups, cream pitchers, etc., but will confine the decoration to the outside. Similarly, a plate for frequent use will have most of the decoration consist of a band or border around the rim of the plate.

However, some articles of decorated china are for exhibition purposes only; plates, therefore, to be displayed on plate rails, or china closet shelves, may be painted over the entire upper surface; cups, bowls, vases, etc. for display can likewise be more freely decorated than those intended for actual use. However, even in the case of articles intended for display only, it would not be good taste to violate the proprieties from the standpoint of use of the article.   There would be little sense, for example, in decorating profusely the insides of cups, vases, bowls, etc.

Then, too, the thoughtful designer and decorator will want to consider the specific purpose of a certain article of china. For example, a short cylindrical bowl of a certain sort, with a flat cover with a handle, intended as a currant or marmalade . jar, could most appropriately be decorated with currants, or berries, and leaves, either conventional or naturalistic, but it would be decidedly out of place to decorate a cracker jar with a similar motif.

57. Consideration of Principles of Good Design and Coloring.—Previous Sections have treated on the principles of composing design motifs, the evolving of designs and patterns, the proper filling of specified areas or spaces, and originating and proper coloring of designs for certain purposes. These points must of course be borne in mind by the designer for china decoration. However, there are certain applications and modifications of these principles in the case of china decoration that need mention.

For example, when planning a decoration, whether naturalistic or conventionalized, for a cylindrical, or approximately cylindrical, object such as a vase or jar, or even a hemispherical object like a bowl, it must be remembered that the details will not appear as when spread out flat, but will be seen foreshortened. This means that some parts of the decoration will be nearer to the eye than other parts, and that these distant parts will appear to become narrower and smaller as they recede from the eye; that is, as they go around the sides of the vase or bowl. Therefore, if an equally repeating decoration is placed on the curving surface it should not be too bold, but should have at least five repeats as it goes around the curving surface. Two repeats would appear to divide the vase in half vertically, three would make it unbalanced, and four would tend to spoil the circular or cylindrical effect.

The decoration on a plate (which usually takes the band or border form) should contain motifs, or spots, so arranged and connected that there is the effect of forward movement and action. This can generally be suggested by connecting the equally spaced spots in the border by slanting or curving lines.

In the case of very tall articles like vases, jars, jugs, pitchers, etc., if well designed, the greatest weight or mass is at the bottom, and similarly the greatest share of the decoration, such as borders, bands, etc., should be at the bottom of the article. In this way there is expressed the upward or growth movement, so characteristic of nature and of the laws of gravity, and therefore so essential to good design.

Tall objects, like tall vases, jars, etc., should have long vertical lines, expressive of growth or upward movement, while curved flat objects like bowls, saucers, etc., should have curving lines leading to spots, thus expressing forward movement.

From the standpoint of tone and color, also, great care in planning the composition is required. However, the matter of color in designing for china painting will be discussed in a definite way later, under the treatment of color schemes and coloring of china, showing how theory of color in design should be applied practically to china-decoration work.

58. Consideration of the Medium and the Method of Working.—While there is nothing very hard and exacting about china colors or the china itself that would be especially restricting to the china decorator, yet he must not attempt to paint with the naturalness of a water-color study on rough paper. It must be remembered that the very facts that his colors are opaque, that the china is hard and glossy, and that the colors must be fired into the china, suggest certain restrictions that will cause him to work in a broad and bold, while at the same time artistic, manner. These things can better be learned by the decorator while working with the actual pigments than they can be explained verbally.

The purpose should be, on account of the character of the medium and method, to paint decoratively rather than naturalistically.

59. Consideration of Conventional versus Naturalistic Treatment.—In some forms of handicrafts and commercial designing for definite purposes, as in the case of stencil work, or carpet designing, there are certain definite physical limitations of material or processes, or of use to which the article or fabric is to be put, that almost compel the designer to use conventionalized motifs and designs. Preceding Sections have made plain the distinction between naturalistic, or pictorial, designs and conventional designs, so that no repetition of their respective characteristics is here necessary.

However, in the case of china-decoration designing these physical limitations of material do not exist, and therefore it is difficult to explain to the beginner just why he should use a conventional treatment rather than a naturalistic, or pictorial, treatment. The task is made still more difficult by the fact that there seems to be almost a tradition that china decoration should look as "natural" as possible. All who have in their possession, or who have access to, old china that has been in the family some time will see the profusion of large sprays of roses, and other flowers, flung across plates and pitchers so as to appear "as natural as life." Nevertheless, however treasured these pieces may be, or however well painted, they are not good in design; for the reason that as long as nature and natural forms are merely imitated and slavishly copied there is no creative art; that is, no design.

Perhaps the strongest argument for the use of conventional motifs and conventional designs for china decoration is that it is now the fashion to use them. By this is meant that the best work turned out by professional decorators of prominence, and by the most prominent schools and classes of china decorators, is of the conventional order.

From what has just been said it must not be imagined that purely pictorial and naturalistic floral and other studies are never to be used in china decoration. These, of course, have their place for exhibition or decorative articles; but they do not fall strictly into the classification of designed work, because no literal copy of a natural form is a design.

SOURCES OF IDEAS FOR DESIGNS

60. Importance of Original Ideas for China Decoration.—It is a simple matter for any one desiring to paint on china to secure patterns and pictures furnished by china-decorators' supply houses, and to copy these literally on a plate, cup, pitcher, or whatever article of china is being painted. It is even possible to secure transfer pictures that, placed in reverse position on the surface of the china, may be transferred to this china and thus painted, or rather touched up, with every degree of fidelity. But, for the conscientious designer, such copying or direct use of the designs of others is not honest work. In fact, it is no more honest than would be the deliberate cribbing and public use, by one commercial artist, of the published advertisement design or picture made by another artist; and in the latter case the plagiarist or cribber would be prosecuted for infringement of the copyright laws. The fact that the cribber of china-decoration patterns employs them simply for personal use does not alter the objectionable features at all.

Further, there is no true craftsmanship in turning out a design, or a completely decorated article, that is not entirely one's own. There is a source of great satisfaction and legitimate pride in making for oneself, or to give or sell to some one else, an artistic production that is entirely original, and of which no duplicate exists. It is very humiliating to exhibit to one's friends an article of painted china that has been decorated by oneself, or that has been bought as specially designed, that turns out to be readily recognized by every one as a stock pattern from the catalog of a china-decorators' supply house.

It is hoped that these points will impress upon the young china decorator the importance of getting up original designs for any work turned out.

61. Designs From Arbitrary Motifs.—The devising of design motifs from arbitrary forms, as well as the theory of such design practice and the practical application of such designs to various specific uses, have been treated in previous Sections.

In applying these arbitrary motifs to the circular, hemispherical, cylindrical, and other geometric surfaces typical of articles of china, it is simply necessary to use the motifs as designed, with as much elaboration of form and color as arbitrary motifs will allow, but to arrange them in a well planned out repeating system. The method of arranging these division and repeating

Fig. 18

lines on the surface of the china has already been discussed; and later, under Drawing and Painting the Design, will be shown the method of plotting the repeats and construction lines in the design itself.

In Fig. 18 is shown a simple design for china decoration, suitable for a plate, and based on the use of arbitrary motifs.

It will be observed that the border of the plate has been divided into eleven sections, or segments, each one of these then being filled by arrangements of curved lines and forms.   It is true

Design by Mrs. K. E. Hodgdon
FIG. 19

that the close student of historic styles will see in portions of this border decoration, and especially in the central spot, or rosette, suggestions of the severely conventionalized lotus; but nevertheless these forms as here used are arbitrary motifs. This design represents the use of arbitrary motifs of the more graceful and refined variety, and illustrates the possibilities of arbitrary units adapted to curving or circular forms.

The design as painted on the china was in pearl gray, gray-green, and shading green, the color scheme, as well as the drawing of the design forms, thus being conventional.

62. Designs From Severely Conventionalized Plant-Form Motifs.—A preceding Section has treated upon the study of plant forms, their analysis, and the use of parts thereof for the evolving òf conventionalized plant-form motifs; and the distinction between severely conventionalized, purely conventionalized, and partly conventionalized motifs and designs has been made plain. There remains, therefore, simply the application of these conventionalized plant-form motifs to the surfaces of decorated articles of china in the systematic repeats already referred to.

A typical example of the application to china of a severely conventionalized design is shown in Fig. 19, which is a design for the trays, of a decorated-china dresser set. The conventionalized full-faced flowers and leaves are used at the sides and ends of the borders in the form of interesting spots, these being connected by bands consisting of rows of full-faced blossoms. The color scheme that was used—pearl gray, apple green, yellow-green, and green-gold, with a touch of coral enamel in the small spots of the flowers—assisted in carrying out the conventional treatment.

63. Design From Purely Conventionalized Plant-Form Motifs.—In purely conventionalized designs it is always observable that every part of the design has been taken from some plant or floral form, and adapted to suit a certain space, material, or requirement. Such a design, as applied to china, is shown in Fig. 20, which is a small square piece of pottery for holding ferns or other plants. The gracefulness and interesting character of the flowers occupying the upper one-fourth and the symmetrically arranged stem and leaf forms in the lower three-fourths are apparent, and need no

detailed description. The entire color scheme is carried out in
Roman gold for the roses, matt gold for the stems and leaves, and
a yellow luster over the entire design and background, with
touches of coral enamel in the centers of the flowers.

**64. Design From Partly Conventionalized Plant-
Form Motifs.**—In Fig. 21 is shown the application to china
(in this case a cup and saucer), of a partly conventionalized
design, based on wisteria. The solid band, with the occasion-

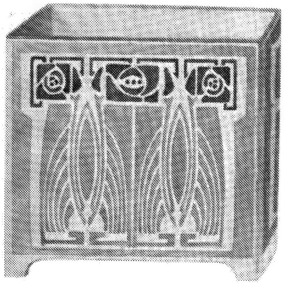

FIG. 20

ally repeating simple leaf form is, conventional, but the hanging,
or pendant, leaf and blossom forms on the cup are only partly
conventionalized, yet symmetrically arranged. This design
was carried out in moss green, pearl gray, and violet, the effect
being very delicate, in keeping with the character of the design
and also with the delicacy of the substance of the china itself.

65. Naturalistic Floral Designs.—It has already been
stated that the use of naturalistic floral subjects in a pictorial

manner for the decoration of a plate, a vase, etc. is really not designing and therefore, strictly, does not come under the head of any line of handicrafts designing.   However, there are certain classes of patrons who demand flower subjects, such as roses, violets, etc., spread across the decorated china, just as if they were loosely thrown or dropped there; and these patrons

Copyrighted by The Keramic Studio Publishing Company
Design by Mrs. L. R. Lightner
FIG. 21

must be accommodated and satisfied.   Therefore, the china decorator will at times be called on to portray such naturalistic floral subjects.

It is possible to secure excellent full-color reproductions of studies of flowers of all kinds made by some of the greatest water colorists of the present time, and then to simply copy them on the china.   As has already been pointed out, however, the more satisfactory method to the conscientious china decorator is to secure natural specimens of the desired flowers— from field, garden, conservatory, etc.—and to make his or her

own studies in water color from these flowers, and then afterwards paint them in china colors on the article to be decorated.
The proper use of color for various kinds of floral subjects will
be taken up later.

In Fig. 22 is shown a typical example of the use of flowers
in a naturalistic or pictorial manner for the decoration of a
plate for exhibition on a plate rail. Here roses have been

FIG. 22

used, and it will be observed that they have been drawn and
painted with the greatest fidelity to the natural specimens.
As a matter of fact, there is no design here, in the strict meaning
of the word; there have simply been used just as many roses
and leaves as could be accommodated by the limiting circle
of the plate. This specimen is introduced here merely as a
typical example of this class of work for those who like it—but
not as a design.

66. Figure-Subject Designs.—Much of what has already been said regarding the inappropriateness of using floral subjects pictorially in the decoration of china will also apply to the use of figure subjects on china. This applies not only to the use of the human figure, draped or undraped, but also to the use of animals, birds, etc. for the same purpose. Subjects of this kind find their most appropriate use in pictorial illustra-

FIG. 23

tions for books, magazines, and newspapers, and for advertisement work; and likewise for mural decorations; but they seem decidedly out of place for the decoration of china. However, certain patrons demand pictorial figure subjects just as they demand pictorial floral subjects, and they must be satisfied.

The young designer for crafts work, in which china decoration may be included, may not have had occasion to train and perfect himself in drawing direct from the human figure so as to be able to make his figure studies direct from the posed model, although practice in doing such figure drawing acceptably is not especially difficult to obtain. The optional Sections in this Course which treat of figure drawing and animal drawing will be found of great assistance in such work. If, however, the china decorator has not had sufficient experience to do such original drawing satisfactorily, figure and animal studies, and pictorial composition subjects of a decorative character,

FIG. 24

suitable for application for china decoration, can be obtained in the form of reproductions in color from supply houses dealing in materials for china decorators. The matter of the proper use of color in these figure subjects will be taken up later.

In Fig. 23 is shown a typical example of the use of a figure subject for china decoration, in this case a somewhat elaborate exhibition plate for a plate rail, china closet, or bric-a-brac stand. The rather idyllic figure, with pink draperies, reclining on sunny verdure and attended by the conventional cupid, makes a suitable decoration for those who have a liking for this class of decorated china. It is introduced here, not as a design (for it is not a design in the real sense of the word), but simply as a specimen of this class of work. In Fig. 24 is reproduced the figure subject shown in the central panel of Fig. 23, the purpose of the illustration being to show almost full size how the painting of the figures and the landscape accessories, etc., was done.

COLOR SCHEMES AND COLORING FOR CHINA

67. Color Theory Applied to China Painting.—The practical application of a knowledge of harmonious coloring and of good color schemes is, of course, made by the china decorator as he actually paints on the china; but as a preliminary design is almost always prepared for any decorative work to be done, it is in the coloring of this preliminary design that the knowledge of harmonious coloring should first be applied.

It is not the purpose here to discuss the theory of color, color harmony, color matching, the classes of color harmonies, etc. All this has already been fully treated in a preceding Section, which treats on the use of color in design work in general. This Section should be referred to again in order to keep the knowledge of color theory fresh in the mind. The purpose here will be to give some helpful hints on color combinations, and coloring in general, as specifically applied to china decoration.

The laws of complementary colors apply literally. For instance, color theory has shown that red and green are complementaries; so are yellow and violet; and so also are blue and orange. Now, in china-painters' pigments the nearest to a standard red is the pigment known as ruby purple; the nearest to a standard yellow is mixing yellow; and the nearest to a standard blue is Sevres blue. Thus, in planning for color combinations one is safe in using red contrasted with green, yellow contrasted with violet, and blue contrasted with orange. But if the red is a yellow-red then the contrasting blue would have to be a reddish, or violet, blue; or if the yellow is a greenish yellow the violet would have to be a reddish violet, and so on

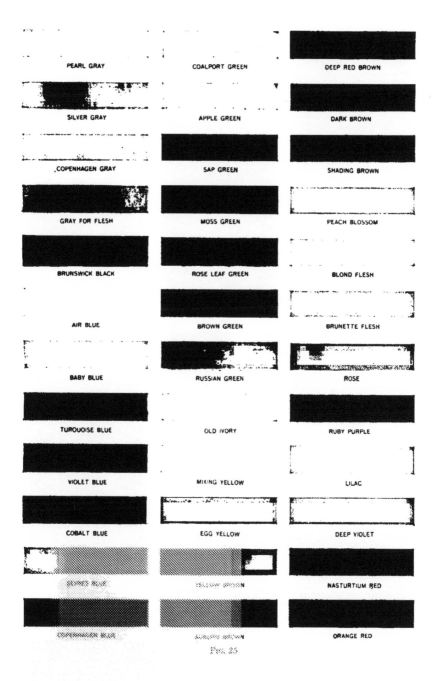

PEARL GRAY	COALPORT GREEN	DEEP RED BROWN
SILVER GRAY	APPLE GREEN	DARK BROWN
COPENHAGEN GRAY	SAP GREEN	SHADING BROWN
GRAY FOR FLESH	MOSS GREEN	PEACH BLOSSOM
BRUNSWICK BLACK	ROSE LEAF GREEN	BLOND FLESH
AIR BLUE	BROWN GREEN	BRUNETTE FLESH
BABY BLUE	RUSSIAN GREEN	ROSE
TURQUOISE BLUE	OLD IVORY	RUBY PURPLE
VIOLET BLUE	MIXING YELLOW	LILAC
COBALT BLUE	EGG YELLOW	DEEP VIOLET
ROYAL BLUE	YELLOW BROWN	NASTURTIUM RED
COPENHAGEN BLUE	AURORA BROWN	ORANGE RED

FIG. 25

with the other primary and secondary colors. If one color is modified, its contrasting color must be modified with the complementary color of the hue used to modify the first color.

In this way all the classes of color harmony—contrasted, dominant, complementary, analogous, and perfected—can be used and applied practically in china painting. For instance, the application of dominant harmony, in the color scheme for a tall cylindrical vase, would be to paint the greater portion of the lower part in deep, dark, rich yellow-browns, and the upper part in light yellow-browns, running thin lines or small spots of the dark yellow-browns occasionally up into the light yellow-browns, and small portions of the light yellow-browns down into the dark yellow-browns.

It is well to go over the possibilities of the various classes of theoretical color harmony and to test out for oneself the various successful color schemes and pleasing color combinations that can be devised.

68. Examples of Typical China Colors.—There are reproduced in Fig. 25 examples of some of the principal china colors, with the name of each placed under it. It must be remembered that only a few of the many colors of pigments available for china decorators can be reproduced here, and that their hues and values can be reproduced only approximately. The limitations of colored inks used for printing in colors prevent anything except an approximation, in each case, to these china-painters' colors. However, the hues in the reproductions shown in Fig. 25 are sufficiently close to the originals to give a good idea of the colors named, and to assist one in recognizing various colors as used by the china decorator, so that he can know how to order from the dealer what he wants, and also know what colors to use in the painting of various floral and figure subjects.

69. Some Specimen Harmonious Color Combinations.—It is, of course, impossible to give in tabulated form an absolutely authentic list of combinations of china-painters' pigments that, if combined, are sure to be harmonious. The trade names of colors differ greatly among various dealers, and, also, the decorator may use one of the colors too dark and its contrasting color too light. However, the following suggested list of color combinations that are good when used in the proper proportions, which proportions must be found by trials and experiments, should prove helpful to the designer.

SUGGESTED LIST OF HARMONIOUS COLOR CONTRASTS

Black and white.
Black and gold.
White and gold.
Black and any color.
White and any color.
Ruby purple and Coalport green.
Light nasturtium red and light blue.
Best pink and apple green.
Egg yellow and violet.
Lemon yellow and lilac.
Banding blue and yellow-red.
Blue and orange.
Green and red.
Orange and dark blue.
Violet and yellow or green.

SUGGESTED LIST OF HARMONIOUS COLOR COMBINATIONS

Red with yellow, white, brown, etc.
Light yellow with dark green, blue, or violet.
Light yellow with light brown, red, etc.
Blue with black, deeper (or lighter) blue etc.
Green with blue and yellow.
Orange with light brown, red, or yellow.
Violet with red and blue.
Pearl gray with Copenhagen blue.

SUGGESTED LIST OF STRIKING COLOR COMBINATIONS

Sultan green with peacock blue.
Dark green with silver.
Olive green with red.
Ivory yellow, or light green, with dark green.
Maroon with gold.
Yellow-brown with violet.
Ruby purple, or crimson-purple, with dark green.

70. General Hints for Coloring.—The color scheme to be employed must of necessity be influenced by so many considerations other than mere color theory. For example, the first consideration is: What is the article being decorated, and for what is it to be used? Thus, if one were making a design for the decoration of some china table service—cups, saucers, sugar bowl, cream pitcher, etc. to be used constantly, the question of color contrasts, color harmonies, or striking color schemes would not enter to any great degree. All that would be needed would be well-arranged bands or spots of gold, or perhaps of some simple delicate colors in light tints, arranged in a simple and consistent style on the various articles decorated. In a case like this, where the table service is actually to be used, certainly no striking color schemes would be employed. However, if articles of china were to be painted for gift or exhibition purposes, as plates for plate-rail decoration, vases, etc., for ornamentation, and other articles of similar purpose, then the matter of good color contrasts and color harmonies would have to be carefully considered.

The china decorator cannot expect to evolve beautiful and original color schemes out of his head, as it were, or even from printed lists in tabulated form. He must go out and observe colorings in nature and in places where they are used artificially. A visit to a flower garden or a conservatory, a noting of the multitudes of hues and tints there displayed, their contrasts and their harmonies, will offer many helpful suggestions. Visits to, and observations in, department stores and millinery shops, interior-decorating establishments, etc., will be of even greater practical assistance in suggesting good color schemes to the china decorator.

In painting the preliminary design in water colors, as well as when doing the painting on the china, the best color effects are often obtained by first of all using a wash of gray; that is, a monochrome wash, as an undertone, then painting the colors over it. This undertone wash of gray is not a flat wash, but it is practically a painting in of the high lights, semitones, and dark shaded values in monochrome (gray) before any color is applied, this monochrome study being like a photograph, but without sharp detail. Then the local colors, the reflected colors, and the touching up of lights and shadows with proper colors may be attended to. Snappy effects are secured by washing one color partly over another color that is lighter or darker, but when painting with the china-painters' pigments on the china this can be done only after the first color wash has been fired.

The china decorator must remember and apply all that has been taught in previous Sections about light, shade, shadow, local color, reflected color, simultaneous color contrast shown in shadows, etc. For instance, in a study where there are red apples shown against green leaves, the mistake should not be made of painting the red apples in one solid red throughout, and the green leaves in one solid green throughout. In the first place, the modeling of the apple; that is, the light, shade, and shadow values, must be expressed by various undertone planes of light, shade, and shadow properly blended. Then, as to color, this will not be a uniform red hue throughout, but the red of certain parts of it, adjacent to the leaves, will have a greenish hue due to the reflected green hue from the leaves. If the apple were resting on a sheet of white paper, the parts of it adjacent to the paper would appear pink, because of the reflected white light from the paper combining with the red of the apple. Careful observation of the exact colors, hues, and values of all details of a study should be made, and then everything should be painted as it really appears, not as one thinks its color is. This applies of course to naturalistic, or pictorial, studies.

71. Coloring for Conventional Designs.— When arbitrary motifs and conventionalized plant-form motifs are used in the preparation of conventional designs for china decoration, the coloring may also be conventional. By this is meant that, when the designer uses an arbitrary geometrical form in a design, or conventionalizes some detail from a plant form so that it no longer resembles nature, he is also allowed to take certain liberties with the colors of nature. If, for example, he were using a conventionalized grape design, with symmetrically

Design by Miss E. Mason

288   ⸸ 15   FIG. 26

288 $ 15   FIG. 27

Fig. 29

Painted by Charles C. Curran

288 § 15   FIG. 30

FIG. 31

Fɪɢ. 32

288　§ 15　FIG. 33

FIG. 35

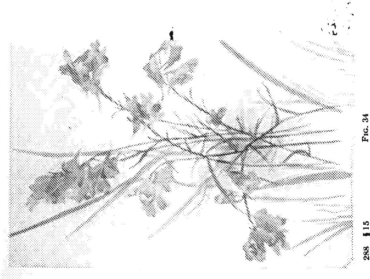

FIG. 34

288 § 15   Fig. 36

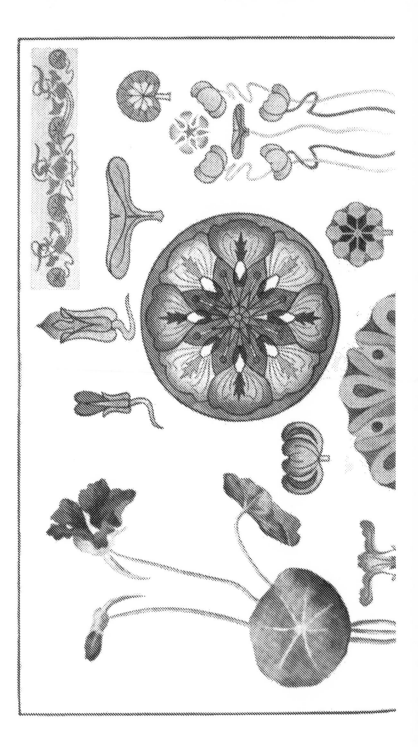

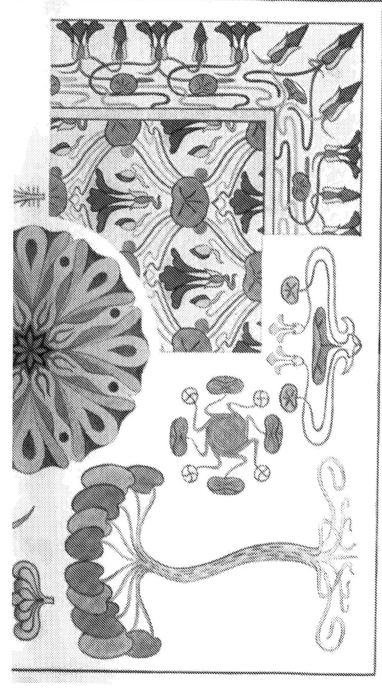

FIG. 37

Fig. 38

Fig. 39

arranged and equally repeating bunches of grapes, he need not feel bound to use blue or purple for the grapes, red-brown for the stems, and green for the tendrils. He is at liberty to use a single color, or even gold, for all the parts, if he so desires. In conventional designs, one is not required to use the colors of nature.

For this reason, in planning a color scheme for such conventional work, the considerations should simply be those of the most harmonious color contrasts and color combinations, which considerations have already been presented. Therefore, just as the beginner in china decoration should start with the use of simple conventionalized motifs and designs, so he should start with simple color arrangements. At first, only one color, in very conventional arrangement, should be attempted, and then two simple contrasting colors. As a matter of fact, for conventional designs the color schemes should always be kept simple, nothing elaborate being attempted.

72. In Fig. 26 is reproduced a typical example of a proper conventional color scheme for the conventional decoration of the coffee pot, sugar bowl, and cream pitcher of a coffee set, the scheme being very simple, only gold and two colors of luster being used. First, the entire design was painted in black color outline, and after that was dry a coat of matt gold was applied to all the portions indicated. Then the first firing was done. For the second firing, the gold portions were gone over again and the lusters were applied, black luster being used for the background and orange luster for the leaves, stems, and flowers. For the third firing, the black luster and the orange luster were applied again, for it is only by repeated applications of lusters that the required depth and evenness are gained. For this third firing, the black outline was put over the gold on the handle, the border, and the base.

73. Coloring for Flowers, Etc.—When flower and fruit subjects are painted in a very naturalistic manner, the colors must also be those of nature, and the light and shade values, and proper hues for all details, must be carefully studied from the actual specimens.

Either one of two general methods of painting the flowers may be employed. By the first method, the modeling of the flowers, leaves, and stems may all be done in tones of gray, the high lights, semitones, and deep shades, as well as shadows, being indicated only in gray values, so that the effect is that of a photograph, no colors at all being shown. This monochrome painting is then fired, and, after firing, the local and reflected colors of the various flowers, leaves, etc. are put on at their proper places. The gray, or monochrome, painting will then show through the color sufficiently to give the modeling effects.

74. By the second method, the local colors of the various details are first placed and the painting is then fired. After firing, the modeling of high lights, shades, shadows, etc. is accomplished by means of white, gray, and black worked over the previously fired applications of local color. By this method, it is sometimes necessary to use more local color, in conjunction with the modeling grays, on the second painting.

75. The system of painting various types of flowers naturally divides itself into a classification of colors; that is, flowers of different colors.

For example, the principal red flowers, for china decoration work, may be considered as being roses, poppies, holly berries, currants of various kinds, etc.; and these are usually painted with the pigments known as carnation red, nasturtium red, and blood red, depending upon whether it is the high lights, the body tones, or the deeper portions that are being painted.

In the case of yellow flowers, some of the chief specimens are daffodils, buttercups, dandelions, chrysanthemums, roses, sunflowers, primroses, etc., and egg yellow and mixing yellow will be found best for painting their local color, yellow-brown being used for the shades and shadows.

For blue flowers, such as corn-flowers, bluebells, forget-me-nots, and similar flowers, various china-painter's blues are suitable, such as corn-flower blue, turquoise blue, blue-green, etc.

In the case of flowers that are variegated yellow and red, such as nasturtiums, honeysuckles, tulips, autumn leaves, etc., the use of nasturtium red, ivory yellow, yellow-pink, etc., depending on the particular flower being painted, gives the best results. For purple flowers, like morning glories, sweet peas, lilacs, violets, clover, etc., the pigments known as pansy purple, violet, violet of gold, etc. are used.

It must be understood that suggestions cannot be given here for the painting of every floral subject that may come up for painting. Very frequently dealers in china-painters' colors can provide little manuals at small cost giving information as to the use of various pigments and the most suitable ones for various kinds of flowers, leaves, backgrounds, etc. The present purpose is simply to give a general idea of the colors used in the actual painting of floral studies, so that the designer of china decoration will be able to make his or her preliminary colored sketch, in water colors, of such a character that it can be carried out in china-decorators' pigments.

76. Reproductions of color schemes for conventional, semiconventional, and naturalistic floral designs are shown in Figs. 27, 28, and 29, respectively.

In Fig. 27 are shown conventional designs for plates, borders, panels, corners, etc., based on the columbine. An inspection of the illustration itself will show the character of the colors employed, and how the effects are secured. Suggested color schemes in connection with this series of treatments are as follows:

1. Background, cream; panels, yellow-brown; stems and leaves, pale green or brown; flower, yellow; outline, green, brown, or gold; band, gold with design in black.

2. Background, white; leaves and stems, pale green; flowers, dull blue, or a pinkish, bluish, or gray violet; outline, dull blue, green, or brown; small band, design of the color of the flowers on a green ground.

3. Design, in two shades of gold on cream, white, or tinted ground; outline, black; small border, flat enamels on a gold ground with black outlines.

4. Background, white; panels, pearl gray; flowers, pink; leaves and stems, gray-green; outline, gray-green for leaves, brown for flowers; small border, gold on a pink ground.

5. The simple cup and saucer design made of leaf and stem repeated can be carried out in any monochrome with outline.

77. The yellow-azalea design in Fig. 28 is an example of a suitable color scheme for a semiconventional treatment of floral forms in china decoration. If applied to the decoration of a tray, plaque, plate, vase, or other large article of chinaware, a suitable color scheme (in the preliminary water-color design, and expressed in terms of water-color pigments) would be as follows: Flowers, Naples yellow and white, warmed with touches of chrome orange and burnt sienna; stamens, Chinese white tipped with emerald green; stems, burnt sienna, mixed with new blue to produce darker effects in the shadows; leaves, gray-green with touches of Antwerp blue, Hooker's green and burnt sienna; broken outline, burnt sienna.

78. The panel of roses reproduced in Fig. 29 is typical of the kind of naturalistic or pictorial floral decoration popular among a certain class of decorators and their patrons. Directions for painting such a rose panel, first in water colors as a preliminary sketch, and then in china paints for the actual painting, are given below.

For the water-color study the color scheme is: Background, gray made of yellow, cobalt blue, and a touch of red; dark leaves, Payne's gray, Hooker's green, and a little carmine; roses, carmine, with bright touches of vermilion; light leaves, Hooker's green and gamboge, with darker shades made by lemon yellow, Hooker's green, and gray.

For the actual painting on the china, for the first fire, paint shadow leaves with violet and blood red; the light leaves, with moss green and yellow; the roses, with ruby and blood red. For the second fire, paint the background with violet and yellow, and a little brown-green; touch up the roses with ruby and washes of blood red, with a little carnation in the reflected lights. Touch up leaves with brown-green and moss green, and stems with blood red and moss green.

79. Coloring for Flesh, Figure Subjects, Etc.—The craftsman-designer, trained in decorative design work, does not commonly have occasion to use figure subjects in china decorating. However, any china decorator will probably have occasion at some time or other to use figure subjects, in the portrayal of which it is necessary to know how to treat the flesh of the face, hands, feet, or even of the entire figure, if in the nude. A few hints as to such treatment may be useful.

There are two general methods of portraying and coloring figures for such work. First, the figure may be painted in boldly with one or two colors used flat, as is observable in the case of the figures painted on old Greek vases. Figures so painted resemble those produced by the method of treatment used in certain classes of decorative pen-and-ink illustrations, consisting of bold heavy lines and masses. This is a good method for the beginner to use for figure subjects.

80. The naturalistic, or pictorial, method of painting the figure is more difficult, because it requires not only a very carefully detailed and modeled preliminary painting, but requires great care and skill in the blending of values and hues. After the tracing and transferring of the design onto the china have been very carefully done, the features of the face (ears, eyes, chin, hair, etc.) and the details of hands and feet should be carefully outlined with a very fine brush known as a liner. The pigment used should be what is known as flesh shadow. The shadows on the face, hands, etc., should then be very carefully painted with this same pigment, flesh shadow; and, between the high lights on the flesh and the shadows, there should be painted some flesh gray, which should be purely and softly blended into both the high light and the shadow, and kept light in value, thus forming a neutral value between the shadows and the lights. Thus, the face is simply painted in planes of color, flesh shadow and flesh gray, the high lights being the white of the china, and is then ready for the first firing.

After the first firing, a thin coat of soft flesh tint is placed over the entire face, hands, feet, etc., and while still moist another painting with flesh shadow is done on the shadow portions, but no repainting with the gray is done, because the gray values from the first painting show through with sufficient distinctness to show the modeling. Then the eyes should be painted, and the hair, lips, etc. repainted, and the subject given a second firing. After the second firing, all details of the flesh or figure study should be again touched up, using mostly soft flesh tint. The subject is then given the third firing.

When painting hair, eyes, etc., which is done after the first firing, the color to be used of course depends on the kind of hair or eyes of the subject. The overwash (for second firing) for light hair should be yellow-brown; for dark hair, hair black with a little banding blue; and, for chestnut-colored hair, hair brown. For blue eyes, any desired shade of blue is used; for dark eyes, finishing brown; and for gray eyes, flesh gray.

There is reproduced entire in Fig. 30 and in part in Fig. 31, an example of figure and flesh painting for ceramic work; and a careful inspection of these reproductions will reveal the colors employed for such a study. However, since the instruction that has been given in this and previous Sections does not include the painting of flesh and figure studies in full color, such a color study, and its application to china, would probably be a more ambitious attempt than the student would want to make at present. Therefore, no detailed discussion of the method and pigments employed, in making either the water-color study or the actual china painting itself, will be advisable. The portion of this study reproduced in Fig. 31 is full size of the original, and careful study should be given it, for the blending of the colors and the character of the pigments employed are clearly shown.

DRAWING AND PAINTING THE DESIGN

81. Making the Sketch Design in Colors.—In all lines of crafts work, where the success of the finished article depends on the careful and skilful carrying out of an accurate plan, the best results are secured by making a preliminary sketch design. The case of china decoration is no exception. The china decorator who would attempt to paint direct onto the china without drawing and painting a preliminary sketch design would have to be very expert indeed; certainly the novice could not expect to do it successfully.

The advantage of having a preliminary color sketch is that it shows the form and color of the design and how the general scheme of decoration is to be carried out in each article, so that the appearance of the completely decorated article can be seen at a glance, and if the first plan is not satisfactory it can be altered in the sketch until it appears as desired.

The sketch must, of course, be made in water colors on smooth cold-pressed paper (water-color paper) or on Bristol board. The more pictorial it is made the better it will carry out the idea of the proposed decoration on the china. Before using the water colors for such a preliminary sketch, the designer must have a comprehensive idea of the appearance of the main china-painters' pigments and how to recognize them by name; and then what water colors should be used to get, in the sketch, approximately the effects that it is desired to secure on the completely painted article, with china colors. This will not be particularly difficult, for dealers in china-painters' materials will upon request furnish charts showing the appearance of all the main china-decorators' pigments, before and after firing. It is then a simple matter to match these colors with water-color pigments on paper, and thus determine the water-color pigments to be used to match certain china colors.

In painting the water-color sketch for a conventional decoration, a few simple colors used flat, just as they are to be used on the china, will give the effect. In painting the sketches for naturalistic floral decoration and figure subjects, considerable care must be exercised, and it will require some skill to do this well.

82.   Hints on Making Flower Studies in Water Colors.
In the case of painting flowers with water colors, very often a single touch of the brush will suffice to indicate a petal, while a bold stroke will represent a stem or a leaf. Further, the freehand brush stroke is much more expressive than the pencil outline carefully filled in with flat wash. In Fig. 32 are shown brush drawings of a number of simple sprays of different flowers and other natural forms, which indicate the kind of work suitable for first practice work. The next step in the practice work

is to copy good facsimiles of flower painting; not pictures of masses of flowers, but decorative sprays in which a few individuals play an important part and a good deal of the character of the flower is shown. Flowers and other plant forms are almost always at hand in the field, garden, or conservatory. Cut flowers change rapidly, but most of them keep long enough to make a sketch. Choose at first simple, single flowers that have color which may be represented on white paper without a background; do not attempt elaborate flowers like the garden rose and the chrysanthemum.

Place a single flower, like the wild rose or cosmos, against a white ground so that the relation of its hues and values to the white paper may be studied; block in the forms, very lightly, with the pencil, indicating the center of the flower and the radiating lines separating the petals. Let the pencil lines be merely a guide to the proportions and the placing of the parts, and depend on the brush to fill in and correct the form. Paint the center first and then each petal. The first painting should show the saucer shape of the flower. A dark petal may be kept separated from a light one by a tiny line of dry paper. Cast shadows and dark accents may be strengthened afterwards. Fig. 33 shows a cosmos blossom rendered in two stages in the manner above described.

Leaves should be painted before the stems. The beginner is apt to paint the stems first and sometimes gets more than he wants, forgetting that stems are covered in many places by leaves. A single brush stroke often suffices for a simple leaf, or, when one side is in light and one in shade, two strokes separated by a thin line of paper; it is sometimes more expedient to carry the lighter color over all, and make the separation with another wash, as in Fig. 32. Only very conspicuous veining should be indicated and then never by means of hard lines; one will observe that in nearly all leaves the veins are made evident by little planes of dark and light coming together; sometimes the dark plane is quite thin but it never forms a wiry line.

Do not draw flowers too small, rather make them larger than life size unless they are very large; very small flowers do not make good subjects for decorative painting. Give stems their proper width, making them neither thick and clumsy nor shriveled; green stems should look sappy—woody stems are full of character and require close study. Special note should be taken of the manner of branching of stems and the changes of direction that they take at the joints. Although botanical correctness is not essential in flower painting, any knowledge of botany is helpful in that it assists the observation and tends to prevent glaring mistakes in structure. The local color of the blossom may always be carried throughout the stems and the leaves. When painting a red flower, look for red in the whole plant—you will surely find it; this helps to hold the color together and prevents glaring contrast. Beginners paint leaves too green; they fail to note the effect of light and shade on the local color. The lights on shiny leaves are bluish, and sometimes almost white. Light shining through a leaf makes it appear yellowish green. Leaves in half light are a rich green, and in shadow a dull, grayish green. Bright greens and strong contrasts in leaves should be subdued in order that they may not claim attention before the flowers. The management of leaves and stems is usually more difficult than that of flowers, because there are apt to be so many more of them that they require some degree of elimination and arbitrary arrangement.

83. Figs. 34 and 35 show two reproductions of water color studies of two simple floral groups, the work being done largely in brush strokes. The colors employed for the two studies are so simple as to be readily understood by any one familiar with the pigments in the average water-color box. The reproduction in Fig. 36 is that of a broadly rendered study of the iris flowers and leaves. For the background, a light wash of new blue should be used. The blossoms should be rendered with a slightly grayed purple, made by combining crimson and blue with a small amount of gamboge. The pollen on the lower petals should be expressed with gamboge modified with a little purple. The leaves, stems, and buds should be rendered in Hooker's green, No. 2, modified with a touch of purple and an occasional touch of gamboge where they have a yellowish tinge. The darker accents in these green parts are made with more purple added to the green.

In Fig. 37 are shown some reproductions of naturalistic, or pictorial, water-color studies made from the nasturtium, then conventionalized partly and as a whole, and designs made therefrom to suit definite geometrical shapes (circles, triangles, etc.) and for all-over repeating patterns and borders. It is advisable to study these carefully and to practice not only the making of copies of them but also the preparation of similar studies and conventionalizations of other flowers. They will thus be useful in showing not only how to render the preliminary water-color studies for conventionalized floral decoration, but also the method of painting them on the china.

84. Hints on Painting Figure Subjects in Water Color.—Underlying every water-color rendering of a figure subject—such as face, bust, full figure, figure composition, animal subjects, etc.—must be a very accurate and artistic drawing. The edges of the planes of light and shade, as well as color values, should first be outlined in pencil and the details of the features drawn in, for errors in drawing must be corrected before the color is applied. The next step is to wash in the masses of the shadows. Burnt sienna, modified with a touch of cobalt, makes a good foundation value. The edges of the shadows in a figure study in colors should be softened in places, and variation secured by touching on other colors. However, only simple masses and simple color should be used at first. When the shadow washes are dry, the whole figure or face, as the case may be, should be washed in with a tint composed of orange, crimson, and a little new blue. This same tint may also be produced with diluted cadmium deep, and a touch of vermilion and cobalt. Indian red, diluted, is useful in rendering flesh tints of older subjects. Touches of blue should be applied to indicate the cool lights. Vermilion is used for the warm color of the lips and crimson with cadmium (orange) for the deeper color of the cheeks. The lights in the hair are cool, whether it is golden or dark, and the shadows are warm. The local color appears in the half tones.

In making studies of figure and animal subjects, one should not get into the habit of using only one set of colors in their portrayal, even for the basis. Neither should the water-colorist adhere to any particular formula when working in full color; rather he should faithfully portray the values and colors in nature just as they appear to him. The models should be posed at first in a strong light that comes from one direction, with a dark background, so that the broad contrasts in values may be seen. It is well to remember that, when painting indoors, in general the lights are cool and the shadows are warm, which means that various values of blue are evident in the lights, and various values of red and brown prevail in the shadows. However, even this rule should not be followed too closely. Individual taste and judgment, so necessary in all art work, must be brought into play with particular care and effectiveness in making figure studies in color.

In painting figure studies in water colors, it is remarkable how much form can be suggested by simply using solid masses of dark color contrasted with the lighter tone of the paper. Such a figure study in colors is reproduced in Fig. 38. The general effect in such a study is secured with black and one other color over a tinted paper. A little vermilion was used on the cheeks and lips; but this could be omitted, if necessary. Heavy charcoal paper was used, on which was washed a tint of ivory black and raw sienna water color. Then the outlines of the picture, which had previously been drawn direct from life on a separate sheet of paper, were transferred to the charcoal paper. Ivory black was used for the deepest tones, and a red-violet, composed of crimson and a little Prussian blue, for the other dark tone.

In Fig. 39 is a typical water-color study of a figure subject, rendered in full color. Although it has the appearance of being a quick sketch it was in reality most carefully executed. A warm gray charcoal paper was used. The figure was first accurately drawn in black Conté crayon, and considerable modeling was suggested. Then color and white were added to the high lights. In some cases color was added to the background to give variety. A few thin washes were added to some shaded portions to suggest color, as in the case of the burnt sienna tones on the shadow of the hair and the blue wash in the shadows of the dress. A wash of diluted orange or vermilion over the crayon tone gives the color of the shadow in the face.

85.´ Making the Full-Size Drawing or Design. Usually, the preliminary water-color sketches may be made small, especially if the decoration of the china is to consist of fairly simple conventionalized motifs. But the drawing from which the tracing is ´to be made must be the full size as it is to appear on the china, though it need be in pencil outline only. In the case of elaborate floral or figure studies, in addition to

FIG. 40

the small and rather rough color sketch to show the general treatment, there should also be a full-size water-color sketch from which to paint, so as to secure accuracy.

From the full-size drawing, in each case, there is to be made the tracing to be transferred to the surface of the china.

The details on the small-scale sketch may be plotted in roughly in perspective; that is, foreshortened, but when the full-size outline drawing of conventionalized decoration is being made it must be plotted accurately so as to repeat a specified number of times upon the allotted space or surface. First of all the size and shape of the article to be decorated must be known.

86. Full-Size Drawing for Decoration of a Plate. Suppose that a number of articles of chinaware for a dinner service are to be decorated with a conventional repeating design, and that the prevailing shape of the articles throughout the set is uniform, as illustrated in Fig. 40.

It is evident that the simplest shape for which to lay out the decorative pattern or design is the plate, because it is practically flat; so it may be advisable to make the drawing for the plate first.

The number of repeats will depend on the nature of the design and the size of the plate; therefore, this number must first be decided upon and then the surface of the plate divided into the required number of equal divisions, which in this case may be taken as sixteen.

Plates and other articles may have their surfaces plotted out into equal divisions for the repeats, direct on the china, by means of various mechanical devices. One of these is the ring divider, previously described, which is shown in use in Fig. 41,

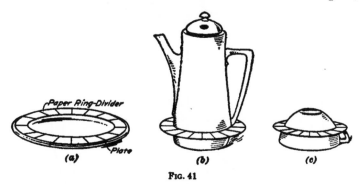

(a)   (b)   (c)

Fig. 41

where in (a) it is laid on top of the plate, in (b) it is slipped up over the bottom of the chocolate pot, and in (c) it is laid over the cup in a reversed position. In each case the ring is held steadily in position with the left hand, while with the right the selected divisions are marked on the china surface with a wax crayon. The vertical lines to divide the surfaces of the china into sections, or segments, may then be drawn freehand or with the aid of a flexible ruler or tape.

To make the full-size drawing for the plate, the exact size of the outside circumference of the plate should be laid off on the paper from the plate itself, and it will then appear as the circle a d b c in Fig. 42. The sixteen equal divisions of the circumference to correspond to those on the plate, can then be marked off by use of the ring dividers; or if the home-made divider is used it must be folded four times, then when it is unfolded the creases will form sixteen radial lines, some of which, as *o a*, *o h*, *o f*, etc., are shown in the illustration, and the circle will be divided into sixteenths. In one or two of the sixteen divisions, or segments, the design can then be drawn, as shown at *a h*, *h f*, Fig. 42, and from this drawing transferred direct to the surface of the china plate.

87. Full-Size Drawing for Decoration of a Cylindrical Cup, Etc.—A different problem is encountered when

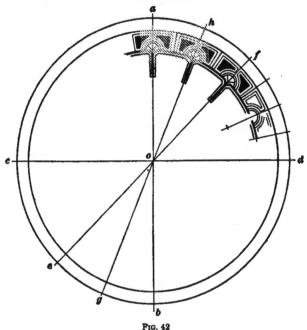

Fig. 42

it comes to laying out the full-size outline design to be traced and transferred onto a cylindrical cup, such as shown in Fig. 40, or onto other cylindrical articles, such as the cream pitcher, sugar bowl, or chocolate pot. In the first place, the perspective sketch in colors, whether small scale or full size, must show the repeating details of the conventionalized decoration getting apparently smaller and closer together as they get farther and farther around the sides of the cup and thus farther away from the eye. Unless so shown the sketch gives no effect of roundness to the cup. The failure to show this perspective, or foreshortening, of the decoration, is a very common fault in the preliminary sketches of most china decorators. In Fig. 43 (a) is shown an example of this faulty method. The surface of the cup is supposed to be divided into sixteen vertical members or sections by black lines, and on the upper part of each alternate line a heavy black stroke is added. Eight of these sections and four heavy strokes (three full and two half ones), show on each half of the cup. The mistake in the treatment in view (a) is that each one of the eight visible sections

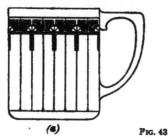 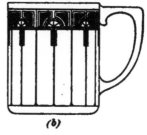

(a)   FIG. 43   (b)

is shown of equal width, and the heavy strokes exactly the same distance apart, thus destroying the effect of foreshortening, or perspective. The proper effect of roundness is secured as shown in Fig. 43 (b) by making the sections appear to decrease in width as they go around the sides of the cup.

The method of plotting out these sections accurately for the perspective sketch is illustrated in Fig. 44. The same design motif is used as was used on the cup in Fig. 43.

The circumference, or cylindrical surface, may be marked off into sixteen equal sections by means of the ring divider or the home-made divider, as previously explained. The top of the cup may then be placed on the surface of the paper and a line very carefully drawn around it with a lead pencil, thus making a circle of the same size as the circumference of the cup, and on this circle should be marked the division points taken from those marked on the cup. Let it be assumed that the semicircle *9–8–7–6*, etc. in Fig. **44** (*b*) is the lower half of the circle made by the cup; then, as the circumference has been divided into sixteen parts, the semicircle will contain eight of these parts, denoted by the division points *1, 2, 3, 4, 5, 6, 7, 8, 9* marked on it.   Now vertical parallel lines projected upwards, by means of a straightedge, from these points will locate in view (*a*) not only the exact width of the cup as represented by the diameter *1–9* of the semicircle, but the proper positions of the dividing lines separating the eight sections in the foreshortened design; the sketch can then be made as tall as the

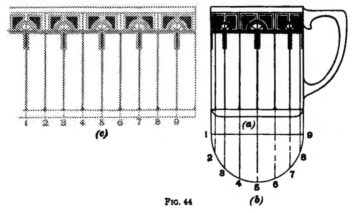

Fig. 44

cup itself, and the details of the decoration can be drawn in freehand.

88.   It is next necessary for the designer to lay out the entire *development* of the cylindrical surface of the cup; that is, a strip or rectangle as high as the cup and as long as the entire circumference of the cup and divided into sixteen parts.   This length of circumference may be measured by wrapping a strip of paper, or a tape measure, around the cup.   It may also be determined by taking ordinary pencil compasses or dividers (which may be bought at a stationery or notion store for 5 or 10 cents) and setting them so that the points are a distance apart corresponding to *1–2*, *2–3*, etc., in Fig. 44 (*b*), and then walking, or stepping, them along a base line as in Fig. 44 (*c*), marking the points *1, 2, 3, 4, 5, 6, 7, 8, 9,* etc., until seventeen points have been located; the distance from point *1* to point *17* will equal the length of the sixteen divisions of the circumference.   When the cup is truly cylindrical, the length of the development, or the circumference, will be found always to be 3.1416 times the diameter; thus, a cup having a diameter of 3 inches has a circumference of 3×3.1416, or about $9\frac{7}{16}$ inches. After these points have been laid off on the base line, parallel vertical lines should then be drawn through them, as in view (*c*), forming the exact size of the full-size sections on the surface of the cup.   The details of the design or pattern can then be drawn in freehand as shown.

89. Full-Size Drawing for Decoration of Hemispherical Cup.—The china decorator will often be called on to decorate surfaces such as that of the cup shown in Fig. 45 (*a*). This shape is not exactly hemispherical, only approximately so; its contour is rather that of the *ogee* curve, having portions of it approximately flat.

The method of making the foreshortened view, as in (*a*), with the pattern properly drawn thereon, is similar in some respects to that used for the cylindrical cup in Fig. 44, but requires some additional work.

Begin by drawing a horizontal line to represent the top edge of the cup, as in Fig. 45 (*a*), and on and above this draw a semicircle equal in diameter to the diameter of the cup.   This semicircle *1-2-3-4-5-6-7-8-9* is then divided into eight equal parts, as before, and lines are projected down from the division points to intersect the top line of the cup at points *2, 3, 4, 5, 6, 7, 8,* as shown.

Below the top line of the cup, in Fig. 45 (*a*), at a distance equal to the height of the cup, draw a line parallel to the top line to represent the bottom of the cup, and on and beneath this line draw a semicircle, as *1-2-3,* etc., having its center on the projection of the line *5-5*.   This small semicircle is then divided into eight equal parts as marked by the points *1, 2, 3, 4, 5, 6, 7, 8, 9.*   From these points, vertical lines are projected upwards to the line representing the bottom of the cup, and from the points where they intersect this line, connecting lines are drawn to the points *1, 2, 3, 4, 5, 6, 7, 8, 9* at the top of the cup. It will be noticed that the line *5–5* is straight and the others are curved, and all may be drawn in freehand. When these connecting lines are all drawn, the surface of the cup as

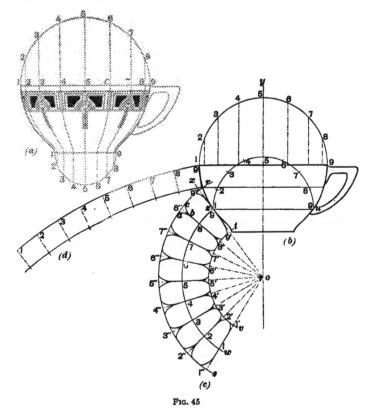

FIG. 45

it appears in the foreshortened view will be properly laid out, and the design or pattern can be drawn in freehand upon these construction lines as guides.

90. To lay out the development of the surface of a cup whose contours are of the general ogee shape is a somewhat more complicated process than the development of the surface

of a cylindrical cup.   The method of making such developments
is shown in Fig. 45 (*b*), (*c*), and (*d*).

First, on the vertical center line *y o* draw the outline of the
elevation of the cup, as in Fig. 45 (*b*).   On account of the shape
of the cup, it will be advisable to make the development in
two parts, one showing the development of the surface of the
cup from the bottom line at *t* up to the circumference at *r*,
the other from the circumference at *r* to the top *9*.   Next, in
view (*b*), place a straightedge or ruler so that it touches points *r*
and *t*, and at the point where the ruler intersects the center
line mark the point *o*.   From *o* as a center, draw a line, as *o x*,
tangent to the cup, and at the point where it touches the cup
locate the point *z*.   With *o z* as a radius, draw an arc *z w*.
Then, with *o* as a center, draw arcs *r s* and *t v*.   At the point *z*,
draw a horizontal line *z u*, whose length is the diameter of the
cup at that point, and on and above this line draw the small
semicircle *1–2–3–4–5–6–7–8–9* equal to half the circumference
of the cup at *z u*.   Divide this semicircle into eight equal parts,
as shown, and with the dividers space off like distances on
arc *z w*, marking the division points *1, 2, 3*, etc., then from point *o*
through these points *1, 2, 3*, etc., on arc *z w*, draw lines intersecting arcs *t v* and *r s*, thus marking the points *1′, 2′, 3′*, etc.,
and *1″, 2″, 3″*, etc., and also determining the sections of the
lower surface of the cup from the bottom *t* up to the height *r*.

Since the lower part of the cup is not exactly a part of a
cone, but is curved vertically as well as horizontally, little
three-cornered nicks, as *a b c* in view (*c*), should be taken out
of each segment at top and bottom to make it approximately
fit the irregularity of the cup.   The size of these nicks must be
found by trial.

To make the development of the upper part of the cup from
the circumference at *r* to the top *9*, first extend the center line
downwards an indefinite distance.   Then place a straightedge
or ruler tangent to the widest part of the cup, as at *9*, and intersecting the center line *y o* extended.   Mark the point of inter-
section, and, using that point as a center, draw the arc *9–1* shown
in view (*d*).   With the same center, also draw another arc
beginning at *r* and paralleling *9–1*.   Then draw the semicircle

1–2–3–4–5–6–7–8–9 equal to half the circumference of the top of the cup, as in view (*b*). Divide this into eight equal parts and mark like distances off on the arc *9–1* in view (*d*). Then, using the same center as was used in drawing the arc *9–1*, draw radial lines across the parallel arcs at the points of division, as *9–8–7*, etc. These lines are divisions between the sections of the upper part of the cup, and will be extensions of the division lines on the lower part of the cup, as *9′–9″*, *8′–8″*, etc.

When both sets of developments are made, the design may be drawn in freehand upon these construction lines.

91. Importance of Accurate Developments.—While the importance of such accurate developments as just described may not be at once apparent in the case of the simple conventionalized repeating patterns illustrated, yet when the pattern is more elaborate, and the sections or segments of the decoration require accurate joining, the necessity for such accurate layouts will be seen. Any repeating pattern to be painted on a curved surface will appear more finished and artistic if first laid out accurately on a carefully developed preliminary sketch.

92. Tracing and Transferring the Design.—When the design or pattern has been carefully drawn full size in outline, it is only necessary to make a careful tracing of it and transfer it to the surface of the china in the manner previously described.

The design having been properly transferred to the surface of the china, the painting and firing are then done as already described.

EXAMPLES OF DECORATED CHINA

93. Purpose in Showing Typical Examples.—In Figs. 46, 47, 48, and 49 are reproduced some photographs of collections of china decorated by some of the best china painters working at this line of handicraft. The reproductions of these specimens are shown, not that the designs may be copied, but for the purpose of showing what is best in china-decoration designing. Through past experiences or associations, some may have been unknowingly led to believe that the best china decoration consists of naturalistic flowers and leaves spread indiscriminately across a plate, vase, or the like. One purpose of this present Section is to demonstrate that the most appropriate decoration for china is the conventionalized motif, whether arbitrary or plant-form. The reproductions of photographs in Figs. 46, 47, 48, and 49 are introduced to emphasize this fact, and to give an idea as to how expert china decorators apply conventionalized motifs and designs in their work. It

Copyrighted by The Keramic Studio Publishing Company

Fig. 46

is hoped that these examples will be closely studied, and that they will influence the student to prepare only the highest type of designs for his work in connection with this Section.

94. Specimens of Decorated Plates, Cups, Vases, Etc.—In Fig. 46 the chocolate pot is beautifully decorated with a conventionalized rose motif, the stems coming down to divide the surface into sections, as before explained. The small jar has a similar decoration, but the motifs at the top are purely arbitrary, and very skilfully arranged. The decoration on the bread plate is of a more dainty floral style than the other two articles.

In Fig. 47 the decoration on the pitcher is of the boldly con·
ventionalized floral type; and the symmetrically repeating spots
in the borders of the plate, cups, and saucers are very cleverly
arranged.

The collections of articles of china in Figs. 48 and 49, both as
to shape of the articles and as to decoration, are so varied as to
furnish very interesting material for, and a means of securing
acquaintance with, the best there is in this class of work.   The

FIG. 47

specimens shown range from severely conventionalized patterns of arbitrary motifs to the more delicate floral conventionalizations, although the severe arbitrary motifs are the most
prominent.

The collections reproduced in these illustrations are worthy
of being studied with the greatest care and thought, and if this
is done it should result in the cultivation of a high standard of
taste in the student.

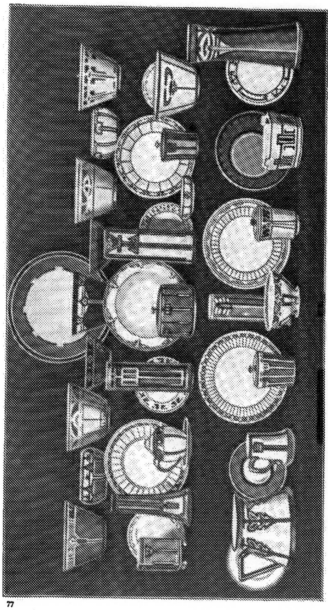

Fig. 48

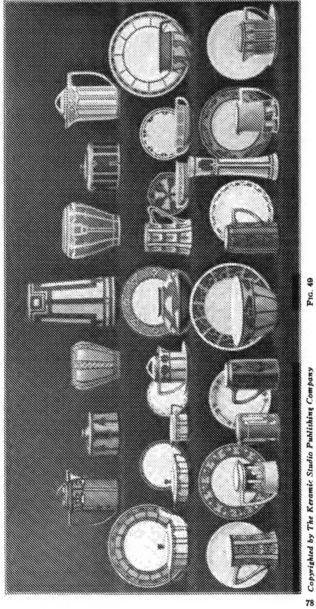

FIG. 49

CHINA-DECORATION DESIGNING EXERCISES

GENERAL INFORMATION

95. Required Work in China-Decoration Designing. It is advisable to make plain again that this course of instruction is purely a course in *designing for* handicrafts work, and that the purpose of this present Section is to give instruction in *designing for* china decoration. Although considerable space is devoted to painting and firing china, it is introduced simply to show the technical requirements with which the student of china-decoration designing must be familiar in order to make practical designs. He must not get the idea that he is studying with a school of china painting, to whom he can write for information regarding troubles he is having in handling the pigments and doing the firing. The purpose is simply to give training in the making of good designs for china decoration.

Therefore, the required work in this Section will consist of original drawings or designs for the proposed decoration of china, these original designs to be in the form of drawing plates.

96. Character of the Drawing Plates.—The drawing plates are to be four in number. The most suitable paper to use will be a good water-color paper, such as Whatman's, coming in sheets about 15¼ in. × 19¾ in., which should be cut in half, thus making therefrom two sheets each about 15¼ in. × 9⅞ in. These must be mounted or stretched on the drawing board, and thus about ⅜ to ½ inch of the edge will be needed for the paste, so that the sheet, when cut off from the board after the rendering is completed, cannot be over 9 in. × 14 in. in size and have unspoiled edges. Therefore, after every sheet has been mounted on the board, and has dried, the first thing will be to lay out a 9″×14″ space, which represents the final size

of the plate when trimmed.   The plate will therefore be spoken
of as being 9 inches wide by 14 inches high.

Each plate is to be worked upon vertically, it being divided
by a horizontal center line into two rectangles 9 inches wide by
7 inches high.

———

PLATE 1

97. Exercise A, Plate 1.—In the upper 9″×7″ rectangle
of the plate arranged vertically, lay out the contours of a china
plate 6 inches in diameter, or of a china tray about 5 inches by
7 inches, if desired.   Design an original decorative treatment
for this plate or tray, and draw it full size therein, using a
purely naturalistic or pictorial treatment—sprays of roses,
violets, buttercups, etc.—spread across the surface without any
effect of repeat, but arranged in a pleasing manner.

Paint this design very carefully in water colors, using the
natural colors of the flowers, and working direct from the actual
flowers themselves or from studies made direct from the flowers.
This is to be a completely finished product, *not* a rough sketch,
every detail being painted with exactness and care so that it
will appear like the finished plate or tray.

98. Exercise B, Plate 1.—In the lower 9″×7″ rectangle
of the plate arranged vertically, lay out the contours of the same
china plate, or tray, as the case may be, and at the same size,
as used for Exercise A.   Instead of using for this exercise a
naturalistic, or pictorial, arrangement of floral forms, design a
very carefully arranged and symmetrically repeating pattern
of conventionalized motifs, either arbitrary or plant form.   The
design, which, of course, must be absolutely original, should
consist mainly of a border, and some filling if desired, but
should be entirely conventionalized.

This design also should be painted with the greatest degree
of care and finish, and should look like the finished decorated
plate or tray.

99. Purpose of Exercise A and B.—The purpose of
making two kinds of designs for the same shape of plate or

tray, one purely naturalistic and the other severely conventional, is to enable the student to demonstrate for himself which character of design is the more artistic, which requires the greater degree of inventive skill, and which is the more suitable for china decoration. The student, after completing Exercises A and B, is expected to compare the two and decide for himself.

100. Final Work on Plate 1.—Letter or write the title, Plate 1: China-Decoration Designing, at the top of the sheet, and place on the back class letters and number, name, address, and date of completing the plate. Roll the plate, place in the mailing tube, and send to the Schools for examination. Then proceed with Plate 2.

PLATE 2

101. Exercise A, Plate 2.—In the upper 9″×7″ rectangle of the plate arranged vertically, lay out the contours, full size, of a saucer standing on edge (so that it shows as a circular shape), and of a hemispherical cup seen in profile, standing in front of the saucer in a position similar to that in Fig. 21.' Using the same conventional arbitrary motifs for each, design decorative patterns for the cup and saucer of a purely conventionalized character, repeating at regular intervals and foreshortened on the cup. This design may be similar to, but not a copy of, the designs in Figs. 42 and 45.

After all details are accurately drawn, the designs should be carefully colored with water colors so that they will appear in every respect like the completely decorated cup and saucer after being painted and fired.

102. Exercise B, Plate 2.—In the lower 9″×7″ rectangle of the plate arranged vertically, lay out accurately the developments of the surface of the hemispherical cup used in Exercise A, after the method shown in Fig. 45, and as described in the accompanying text directions. It is to be understood, of course, that neither the shape of the cup in Fig. 45 nor its decoration is to be copied. After the surface developments, and the accurately spaced and divided sections, or segments, have been laid out, several of them should be filled in freehand, *in outline only*, with the decorative pattern used for the cup in Exercise A. To give the best effects one of the segments full of decoration should then be colored, although one or two others should be allowed to show in outline only in a manner suitable to be used for making the tracing to transfer to the china surface.

If in making the developments for Exercise B it is found that the arcs or other construction lines and points will extend beyond the limits of the lower 9"×7" rectangle, another sheet of paper should be fastened to the drawing sheet where needed to accommodate any such construction lines, this extra sheet being detached before Plate 2 is sent to the Schools.

103. Final Work on Plate 2.—Letter or write the title, Plate 2: China-Decoration Designing, at the top of the sheet, and place on the back class letters and number, name, address, and date of completing the plate. Roll the plate, place in the mailing tube, and send to the Schools for examination. Then proceed with Plate 3. ────────

PLATE 3

104. Exercise A, Plate 3.—In the upper 9"×7" rectangle of the plate arranged vertically, lay out the contours, full size, of a cream pitcher, similar in shape to the one shown on the extreme left in Fig. 40, and design a suitable decorative pattern for its surface. Use a design that, while composed of conventionalized motifs, is not so severely conventional as the design of arbitrary motifs used for the cup on Plate 2, and yet is not a naturalistic floral study. Make the design of conventional floral motifs, semiconventionalized; and consider the decoration of the lower, or heavier, part of the pitcher as well as the border design for the upper part.

After all details are accurately drawn, the design should be carefully colored with water colors, so that it will appear in every respect like the completely decorated cream pitcher after being painted and fired. Care should be taken to follow the proper principles of coloring as applied to china decoration, and as discussed in the portion of the text devoted to color schemes and coloring for china decoration.

105. Exercise B, Plate 3.—In the lower 9"×7" rectangle of the plate arranged vertically, lay out accurately the development of the surface of the cream pitcher used in Exercise A. The method of doing this is similar to the method illustrated in Fig. 44 and described in the accompanying text.

After the surface development, and the accurately spaced and divided sections, or segments, have been laid out, a number of them should be filled in freehand in outline only with the decorative pattern used for the pitcher in Exercise A, and one or two of the segments full of decoration should be painted in colors, as before explained.

In the course of making the development of the surface of the pitcher the center point for the arcs may extend into an adjoining rectangle and perhaps even beyond the limits of the sheet. This difficulty can be taken care of, as explained for Exercise B of Plate 2, by fastening an additional sheet of paper to the drawing sheet where needed to accommodate any extended construction lines, this extra sheet being detached before Plate 3 is sent to the Schools.

106. Final Work on Plate 3.—Letter or write the title, Plate 3: China-Decoration Designing, at the top of the sheet, and place on the back class letters and number, name, address, and date of completing the plate. Roll the plate, place in the mailing tube, and send to the Schools for examination. If all required redrawn work on previous plates has been finished, the work of Plate 4 should be taken up at once.

PLATE 4

107. Exercise A, Plate 4.—In the upper 9"×7" rectangle of the plate arranged vertically, lay out the contours, full size, of a 4-inch plate, suitable for plate rail, or bric-à-brac decoration, and a cylindrical vase about 6 inches high and 3 inches in diameter, and design suitable decorative patterns for each, not necessarily using the same motifs. The design should be of the semiconventional floral type, very free in treatment, but *not* of the naturalistic floral-spray type. Consider the decoration of the base of the vase as well as that of the top.

After all details on both plate and vase are accurately drawn, the design should be carefully colored with water colors, so that they will appear in every respect like the completely decorated articles after being painted and fired. Care should be taken to follow the proper principles of coloring as applied to china decoration, and as discussed in the portion of the text devoted to color schemes and coloring for china.

108. Exercise B, Plate 4.—In the lower 9"×7" rectangle of the plate arranged vertically, lay out accurately the development of the surface of the cylindrical vase used in Exercise A. This development is very simple to make, being simply a rectangular strip spread out horizontally, after the method shown for developing the surface of the cylindrical cup in Fig. 44.

After the surface development, and the accurately spaced and divided sections, or segments, have been laid out, several of them should be filled in freehand, in outline only, with the decorative pattern used for the vase in Exercise A. One or two of the sections should be colored, as before explained.

If any of the construction lines of the development extend beyond the edges of the sheet, this difficulty can be taken care of, as previously explained, by fastening an additional sheet of paper to the drawing sheet where needed to accommodate any extended construction lines, this extra sheet being detached before Plate 4 is sent to the Schools.

109. Final Work on Plate 4.—Letter or write the title, Plate 4: China-Decoration Designing, at the top of the sheet, and place on the back class letters and number, name, address, and date of completing the plate. Roll the plate, place in the mailing tube, and send to the Schools for examination.

If any redrawn or rerendered work on any of the plates of this Section has been called for and has not yet been completed, it should be satisfactorily finished at this time. After all required work on the plates of this Section has been completed, the student taking up the Handicrafts Designing Course as his specialty may consider the technical training given by his Course as finished. It simply remains now for him to read and profit by the material in the concluding Section of his Course devoted to the methods of selling designs and obtaining a position.

If the student has chosen to study the work of the Industrial Designing Course, he should proceed with the next Section of his Course at once.

TILE AND PARQUETRY DESIGNING

PURPOSE

1. Requirements for Practical Design Work.—Preceding Sections have given instruction in drawing, rendering, and the principles of design and color. These separate lines, while in themselves valuable accomplishments, are not sufficient to enable any one to make practical workmanlike designs for any definite line of industrial art work. For instance, although the training so far given will enable one to prepare all-over patterns based on geometric repeats and to color them, he should not yet expect to be able to prepare practical designs for tiles, parquetry, linoleum, carpets, wallpaper, etc., that will be so artistically attractive, and so correctly executed technically, that he can sell them to manufacturers of these products. The very necessary feature that his designs would lack would be technical accuracy and suitability for the purpose intended; and to be able to prepare designs that fulfil these requirements the student-designer must become acquainted with the processes by which such products are manufactured or otherwise prepared and the consequent technicalities that must be followed in making the designs.

The mistake is frequently made by students of design of thinking that, because their designs are nicely drawn and attractively colored, they are perfectly suitable for tiles, wallpaper, fabrics, etc., though prepared without any knowledge of how such products are manufactured. For this reason, when their designs are returned to them by the manufacturers as

§ 16

unavailable (because unsuitable), they feel a personal resentment against the manufacturer, believing that he is not honest in his reasons for rejecting their designs.   The sooner the young designer comes to appreciate the absolute necessity for knowing the technical processes of manufacture of the products for which he designs, the better able will he be to understand why technical knowledge must supplement artistic training.

2.   Scope of Training in This Section.—That the student of designing may pass with the least difficulty from the purely theoretical stage of his art training to its application to practical industrial work, the simplest forms of commercial designing are taken up first.   By "simplest forms" is meant those lines of commercial designing in which the artistic designs required are, through necessity, along comparatively simple lines, and the processes by which the objects or fabrics are produced are comparatively simple.

Perhaps no lines of commercial or industrial art work could be simpler, from the standpoints mentioned, than tile work for floors, walls, or ceilings, and parquetry work for hardwood floors.   In both cases the effects are secured on the very simple lines of laying bricks in a pavement or floor boards on a floor. However, before the art student can make designs for such work he must know just what kinds of tiles are used, how they are made, how they are laid in position, etc., and similar points about the various kinds of woods and the sizes and shapes of the pieces for hardwood parquetry flooring.

Therefore, there will first be presented the technical requirements of tile and parquetry work from the viewpoint of manufacturer and workman, and then will be explained the process of preparing artistic designs for such work.

TILES

CLASSIFICATION OF TILES

3. Meaning of the Term "Tiles."—When the term *tiles* is used, it is generally understood to refer to the flat slabs or pieces of burnt clay, similar in composition to burned-clay bricks, used for floors, roofs, gutters, etc. However, for purposes of convenience, the term tiles, in this connection, will be used to designate the small pieces (slabs, cubes, mosaics, etc.) of material used for floors, walls, hearths, etc., which pieces, on account of their symmetrical shapes, lend themselves to the formation of decorative spot or repeating patterns or designs. The materials of which these tiles are composed— whether of baked clay, marble, or glass, and whether unglazed or glazed—is not of so great concern to the designer as are the shapes and colors of the individual slabs or pieces, and the different ways in which they may be combined with best decorative effect.

In the present consideration of tiles for decorative purposes the classification will be as follows: *encaustic floor tiles, mosaic tiles, wall and hearth tiles,* and *faience tiles.*

4. Encaustic Floor Tiles.—The term **encaustic tiles** is applied to those unglazed geometric-shaped baked-clay tiles, either plain or decorated, that are colored in the clay or painted and then fired; such tiles, placed in decorative geometrical patterns, are used for pavements or floors.

5. Mosaic Tiles.—Tiles are known as **mosaic tiles,** whether composed of baked clay, marble, or glass, when made in small squares, circles, hexagons, strips, etc., and fitted together in more or less intricate geometric patterns or even for the delineation of floral designs and pictorial work.

6. Wall and Hearth Tiles.—The designation of **wall and hearth tiles** may be given to that class of tile work composed of large squares, hexagons, strips, etc., of glazed clay tiling or marble used for lavatory, hospital, and restaurant walls, and for hearths, fireplaces, etc. Such tiles may be plain, or they may have patterns or pictures on them. If of the latter class, the design or picture is complete on the single tile, thus distinguishing these tiles from *faience tiles*, described below.

7. Faience Tiles.—Tile work is spoken of as being composed of **faience tiles** when the square or rectangular tiles are all highly glazed or enameled by a special process, and the decorative work or the pictorial work extends across the joints of the tiles and requires a number of adjoining tiles to express the decorative or pictorial composition.

ENCAUSTIC FLOOR TILES

MANUFACTURE AND USE

8. Kinds and Sizes of Encaustic Floor Tiles.—Encaustic tiles may be either plain or decorated; but it is only the decorated tiles, or those that may be laid in decorative patterns, that will be considered at present. Plain geometrical floor tiles, made for laying in decorative patterns, are obtained usually in the following sizes and thicknesses: 6 in.$\times$6 in.; $4\frac{1}{2}$ in. $\times 4\frac{1}{2}$ in.; 3 in.$\times$3 in.; $2\frac{1}{4}$ in.$\times 2\frac{1}{4}$ in.; $1\frac{1}{2}$ in.$\times 1\frac{1}{2}$ in.; $1\frac{1}{16}$ in. $\times 1\frac{1}{16}$ in. The tiles are made in these sizes so that, when larger ones are twice cut through diagonally, the four smaller (triangular) ones formed have their longest side the same dimension as the large square originally cut. In this way smaller square tiles (say $4\frac{1}{4}$ in.$\times 4\frac{1}{4}$ in.) may be halved diagonally into two triangles each, so that when four such triangles are put together point to point they will form one large square about 6 in. $\times$6 in. In this way multitudes of patterns can be formed. There are also used straight halves, thirds, quarters, etc., of the 6-inch sizes, thus making strips for borders, etc., these strip sizes being 6 in.×3 in.; 6 in.×2 in.; 6 in.×1½ in.; 6 in. ×1 in.; etc. There are also made octagonal sizes, 6 in.×6 in.; 4¼ in.×4¼ in.; and 3 in.×3 in. These octagonal pieces will combine readily with each other, as well as with the squares and strips. The thickness of all the foregoing is usually ½ inch.

9. Manufacture and Colors of Encaustic Floor Tiles. The plain encaustic tiles, to be laid in decorative geometric patterns, are of one color all the way through, and are baked until they are rendered sufficiently impervious to resist permanent discoloration in ordinary use.

The decorative encaustic floor tiles are those in which a pattern of clay of one color is inlaid in the surface of a tile body of a different color, while both clays are in a soft condition, and is burned in as a part of the tile itself. The surface of the tile is perfectly level, and the pattern or design is generally complete on a single tile, but may sometimes extend over a series (as of four, for instance), a large number of varied designs being thus produced.

Encaustic tiles are made either by the plastic process or the dust process. In the plastic process, a die or plaster relief of the desired pattern is modeled and placed at the bottom of a box mold, due allowance being made for shrinkage. Tiles are then made by compressing clay into the mold, the relief pattern previously placed in the mold producing a sunken pattern on the clay, which clay is then dried and removed from the mold. Colored clay of another hue in a semi-liquid state is then poured into the hollows formed by the die, and the tile is again dried and leveled, and then baked or fired until one hard component mass results.

In the dust process of making encaustic tiles, the clay is worked into a liquid condition in a huge mixing vat. This liquid clay is then passed through a series of sieves of extreme fineness, and is afterwards brought back to solid form by being passed through a filter press or by a similar mechanical process. The solid matter is then thoroughly dried, reground to a state of fine meal-like dust, and sifted, after which it is slightly moistened and compressed into shape in hollow steel molds between two dies by means of a powerful screw press. When the tile is taken out it is quite solid and can be easily handled. It is then dressed or trimmed as required, and dried very carefully for some days, after which it is baked or burned to a state called *bisque*. If a glazed surface is desired, the tile is then dipped in glaze and allowed to dry.

A third class of tiling, which has features resembling the foregoing, may be called *incised* tiling; these tiles are made with sunken lines or patterns which, in common with the joints between the tiles, are filled with cement when the tiling is laid. The prices of paving or flooring with such encaustic tiles, plain or decorative, vary with the colors used in forming the design, the cheapest being those in which buff, salmon, red, chocolate, gray, and black predominate. White, blue, and green are from two to three times as expensive, and are seldom made larger than 3 inches square. _____

DESIGNING

10. Geometrical Basis of Arrangement.—In Fig. 1 is shown a typical floor or pavement made of plain encaustic tiles combined with decorative encaustic tiles bearing floral or conventional patterns, mostly of rosette form. The process of designing conventional rosette patterns for the decorative tiles is a simple one. To one who has been trained to conventionalize floral forms and fill therewith definite shapes, such as squares, octagons, etc., the task of designing single tiles will not be a difficult one. A reference to preceding Sections devoted to design composition, and space filling, historic styles, etc., will not only refresh the student's mind as to methods of designing such spot ornament, but will offer suggestions and specimens that can be used bodily for such tiles. Once the individual tiles are designed, it simply remains to combine the plain and the decorative ones on a geometrical basis.

Since the stock sizes are already known, and the relative costs of various colors are known, the process of making a floor design really consists of simply arranging tiles of known sizes, shapes, and colors in geometric patterns. Such designs are usually drawn out first very carefully in lead pencil on white

paper of any kind, preferably water-color paper, at a scale of
1 inch = 1 foot; that is, 1 inch on the drawing will represent
1 foot on the actual floor. However, this scale is not arbitrary,
and if the size of the floor or the fineness of the pattern demand
it, the scale may be
½ inch = 1 foot, ¾ inch
= 1 foot, or even 1½
inches = 1 foot.

**11. Coloring the
Design.**—After the
design is drawn
sharply in pencil, it
should be colored in
opaque water color or
distemper, either com-
posed of ordinary
water-color pigments
mixed with Chinese
white and a few drops
of clear mucilage to

Fig. 1

serve as size, or consisting of specially prepared designers' moist
(opaque) colors ready for use on the design. After the coloring
is done, the main lines of the geometric design should be again
lined up with a hard pencil, or with opaque color (light or
dark), or India ink used in a ruling pen.

The field of the design should indicate the entire floor to be
covered, and show the whole scheme of treatment, but it is
necessary to finish up in detail and color only enough of the
design to show what the arrangement and coloring are to be,
say a corner and two short sections of border, as well as some
of the most important repeats of the field.

MOSAIC FLOOR TILES

MANUFACTURE AND USE

12. Kinds and Sizes of Mosaic Floor Tiles.—The term mosaic is applied to that class of tiling in which the entire pattern is made up of small pieces, regular or irregular in shape, set in cement and leveled off to form a smooth surface. The art of laying mosaic floors was well known to the Romans, by whom the component parts were termed **tesseræ**, from the word meaning checkered.

Mosaic tiling in which the small elements, or tesseræ, composing the design are made of clay, is known as ceramic mosaic, and is distinguished from marble mosaic, in which the tesseræ are of marble, and also distinguished from vitreous mosaic, in which the material is glass. The modern mosaic tiled floor is composed of pieces cut by dies into uniform sizes. The usual sizes of these pieces, or tesseræ, are $\frac{3}{4}$ in. $\times \frac{3}{4}$ in. and $\frac{1}{2}$ in. $\times \frac{1}{2}$ in. Smaller pieces may be necessary when working out a special pattern. These tesseræ may be square, round, or hexagonal, as will be pointed out later when the designing of mosaic tiled floors is discussed.

13. Colors of Mosaic Floor Tiles.—All colors of tiles may be obtained, but—as stated in regard to the large encaustic tiles—the darker colors, such as gray, chocolate, black, etc., are the cheaper, while white, blue, etc. are comparatively expensive.

For the designs for mosaic floors that are laid out on the simple geometric basis, a limited range of harmonizing colors well placed will give the best results. However, when floral or pictorial devices in mosaic are attempted, a great range of hues and tone values can be used.

14. Laying Mosaic Floor Tiling.—It being assumed that the design for the floor is made (the method of doing which will be discussed later), and that the tesseræ of the proper colors are all selected and at hand, there are two methods that may be used in laying the tiling. The first consists in placing the tesseræ one by one in position on a prepared bed of cement and subsequently leveling the surface before the cement has set.

The more usual method, however, is to affix the tesseræ at the manufacturer's works, face downward, with glue on a full-size drawing of the proposed floor design.

15. Making the Full-Scale (Reversed) Drawing. The small-scale design, already mentioned, having been prepared to a scale of ¼ inch = 1 foot, or even larger, the next step is to make a full-size setting-out plan of the mosaic, showing the complete design. This drawing is made in pencil on cartridge paper, or manilla detail paper, which may be bought in rolls 5 feet wide and containing 50 yards. In case the space to be covered by the design is very large, it will be necessary to paste together, edge to edge, large sheets of this cartridge paper so as to obtain a surface of sufficient area for the design. To serve as a check on the accuracy of the small-scale drawing, the actual area available for the mosaic is measured in the building where the work is to be done and the full-size drawing must agree with these measurements. This is a simple way of insuring that the mosaic will fit properly when laid in place.

This full-size drawing is made reversed; that is, it is so drawn that if the drawing were turned face downwards it would exactly fit the space to be occupied by the mosaic. The reason for making the drawing thus is that the tesseræ are subsequently gummed on the face of the cartridge-paper drawing and then turned over and laid in place on the floor. On this large reversed drawing the border must be drawn in first. If the floor is rectangular, as is most commonly the case, or if it is bounded by straight lines of tesseræ only, the border may be indicated by straight lines, since square tesseræ will then be used without the necessity of cutting or reshaping any of them.

Fig. 2 (a) represents one corner of a rectangular lobby floored with a mosaic having an outer border like that shown. The method of drawing the full-size reversed plan of this mosaic, is shown in (b); the outermost band of white is indicated by two parallel lines 1⅛ inches apart, and the black band by two

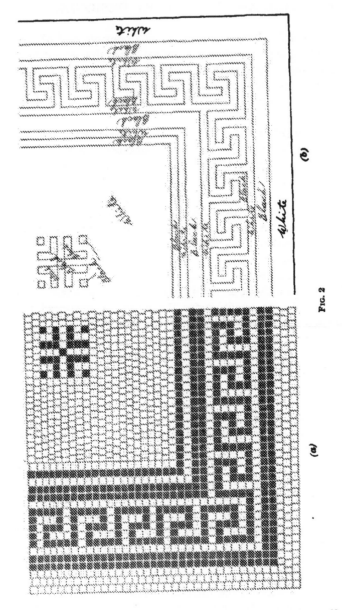

FIG. 2

lines 1¼ inches apart, followed by a band ⅜ inch wide, next
inside which the interlocking black-and-white outline is drawn.
The color of the tesseræ to be used for each band is plainly
written along it, as shown in the illustration.

In case the border is composed of figures or designs containing
curved lines, it will be necessary to show on the full-size drawing
more than the mere outline, for the mosaic cannot then be
made of square tesseræ. Many, and perhaps all, of the blocks
will need to be cut and shaped to conform to the curves of the
figure; and in order that this may be done easily and rapidly
by the workmen, it is necessary to divide the design by lines
into small areas, each of which represents a tessera. Of course,
none of these small areas should be of such size or shape that
it cannot be covered by a single tessera cut to the correct outline. If the curve of the outline is very gradual, it will be
possible to use square tesseræ, without shaping or cutting, allowing the cement to fill the wedge-shaped spaces thus formed
between adjacent tesseræ.

16. Dividing Reversed Plan Into Sections.—After
the full-size reversed plan has been drawn, and the colors to be
used in the various portions have been marked, the drawing is
cut into pieces or sections of convenient shapes containing
about 4 or 5 square feet each. By thus dividing the entire
plan into Sections the work is greatly facilitated, since it would
be very inconvenient to handle the entire mosaic in a single
piece, after the tesseræ have been affixed to the paper, because
of the weight. Moreover, there would be considerable likeli-
hood of tearing the cartridge paper in handling large and heavy
sections. The plan is cut along straight or curved lines,
according to the nature of the design, and, wherever possible,
the cuts should be parallel to the joints between the rows of
tesseræ.

An example of the way in which a full-sized plan is cut is
shown in Fig. 3 (a), the dotted lines showing the positions of
the cuts. The pieces are numbered consecutively, the numbers
being put on the *backs* of the sections and not on the faces to
which the tesseræ are affixed and on which the border lines

are drawn. However, owing to the impossibility of showing these numbers on the back of the plan in (a), they have been placed on the front. A small-scale plan, like that shown in (b), is made to show the relative positions in which the sections are to be placed when laying them upon the floor. This is known as the **key plan,** and the figures indicate the appearance and positions of the numbers that are marked on the back of drawing (a).

17. Affixing Tesseræ to Plan Drawing.—After the full-sized plan drawing has been divided and numbered, the

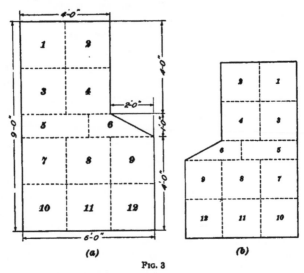

FIG. 3

sections are taken to the work bench, where the tesseræ are to be affixed. A section is laid out flat on top of the bench, with the lines of the border or design facing upwards. Within easy reach are the loose tesseræ of the necessary colors as called for on the plan. There is also a bowl containing a fairly thick solution of gum arabic and water, with a brush for applying it. The workman dips the brush into the gum solution, and paints over with the gum a portion of the surface of the paper, and upon this he places row after row of tesseræ, pressing each slightly so that it adheres firmly to the paper.

The tesseræ are placed closely, edge to edge, and the workman should take care that the faces of the tesseræ in contact with the gum or glue are perfect; for, if any corners are missing, there will be flaws in the mosaic, since the faces next to the paper form the surface of the mosaic. The method of affixing tesseræ composing a straight border is shown in Fig. 4. It will invariably be found, after all the tesseræ have been gummed to the paper, that the surface exposed to view is very rough and uneven, due to variation in the thickness of the tesseræ. However, this need cause no concern, as this surface is bedded in a floating of cement, which will fill all irregularities.

18. Cutting Tesseræ to Shape. When the shapes of individual features of a design are not geometric, but are curved or irregular, the tesseræ of the regular cubical or other shapes cannot be employed.

Fig. 4

The shaping of tesseræ to suit various intricacies of the design is carried out by the use of a metal block and a sharp-edged hammer, as shown in Fig. 5. The block *a* is a piece about 9 inches long cut from an iron bar 3 inches square in section, while the hammer *b* has a sharp edge like an adz. An enlarged view of the hammer, known in the trade as a **martello**, is given in Fig. 6 (*a*) and (*b*). The cutting part is sharpened to a small angle, the inner face *a* being straight and the bevel *b* being put on the outside. To cut or shape a tessera, it is laid on the iron block and struck with the sharp edge of the hammer, the latter being held so that the beveled face *b* is at right angles to the surface of the tessera at the moment of impact. In this way a few sharp strokes will bring the block roughly to shape. If it is desired to have the block very accurately shaped, one corner of the cutting edge may be rested on the iron block,

with the right hand gripping the body of the hammer, the handle of which should point toward the right. Then, manipulating the tessera with the left hand and rolling the cutting edge forwards with the supported corner as a fulcrum, the tessera may be shaped by a sort of chiseling action. In Fig. 5 the workman is shown cutting a tessera to fit the curved design indicated on the drawing. This design is usually divided by pencil lines into a number of parts, each of about the same size as a tessera. The workman then cuts a block to fit each shape, resulting in a finished design made of tesscræ.

Fig. 5

19. Laying the Mosaic.—Each section of the divided full-size plan having been covered with tesseræ of colors according to the design, it should be laid aside long enough to allow the gum to dry. When all the sections are finished and dry, it is necessary to lay them in their proper relative positions, according to the key plan, to make certain that they fit together properly and form a continuous surface showing the desired design. For example, in case a border consists of repetitions of some geometrical or other figure, it is very important that the sections shall, when fitted together, show the figures correctly spaced at regular intervals and properly in line as well. After the various sections have been found to fit together properly, they should be taken to the place where the work is to be laid, or else packed in cases ready for shipment.

The surface on which the mosaic is to be laid consists of an approximately smooth bed of concrete. On this the sections of mosaic are laid, with the cartridge paper uppermost, their relative positions being determined by the key plan made when the full-size reversed draw-ing was cut into sections. After being laid, the mosaic is then stamped or rammed down tight with the proper implements and rolled perfectly flat and level.

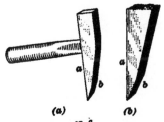

20. Removing the Paper, Rubbing Down, and Polish-

(a)

(b)

IG. 6

ing.—The mosaic should be allowed to stand for several days, depending on the season and the condition of the weather, to permit the cement to set and thus hold the tesseræ firmly in place, after which the cartridge-paper facing may be removed by wetting and simply peeling off the tough sheets of paper, exposing the even surface of the mosaic. If any of the blocks are chipped or imperfect, they should be replaced by perfect ones.

The roughness of the faces of the tesseræ must now be removed by grinding with grit stone and the proper implements, after which the surface of the mosaic is polished with cement and water rubbed on with the proper implements. The polishing here indicated does not mean the production of a glossy surface, but rather the removal of all roughness not smoothed out by the initial rubbing with grit stone.

DESIGNING

21. Use of Special Design Paper.—The fact that each individual tessera, or small tile, is of a regular geometric shape, and all are of the same size, of necessity impels a geometric basis for the design of a mosaic tile floor. This is clearly illustrated in Figs. 9, 10, 11, and 12, which are reproductions made direct from the designs, but on a smaller scale.

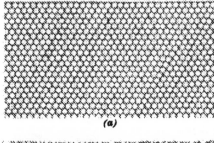

(a)

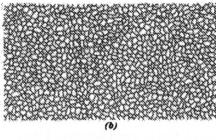

(b)

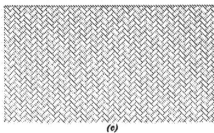

(c)

Fig. 7

On account of this accurate geometric basis, special papers are used by mosaic tile designers, the geometric patterns being printed thereon. These papers not only insure accuracy in the design, but save the designer a great deal of trouble, which he would otherwise have, in being obliged to draw this geometric network of lines himself.

Some of the most common forms of patterns for these design papers, all of which are printed in a pale gray or pale salmon ink, are shown in Figs. 7 and 8. The printed portions on the sheets of design paper are of course considerably larger than the small sections shown. The scale of the patterns is about the same as those on the design paper.

In Fig. 7 (a) is shown the pattern of circles, fitted together in a honeycomb-like network, a pattern that is used a great deal, because these circular tesseræ lend themselves readily to the securing of a diversity of effects, both for fillings and for borders. It is on design paper of this circular pattern that the fields, or fillings, of the designs in Figs. 9 and 10 were designed.

In Fig. 7 (b) is shown an irregular all-over pattern of pieces of various sizes and shapes without any geometric regularity. Design paper such as this is employed in designing backgrounds or fields such as shown in Figs. 13, 14, and 15. The pattern in Fig. 7 (c) is the herringbone brick pattern used for rectangular tiles of that shape. It is evident that interesting patterns can be devised upon such a basis.

In Fig. 8 (a) the pattern of the background shows a narrow brick effect, the tiles being narrow and rectangular.

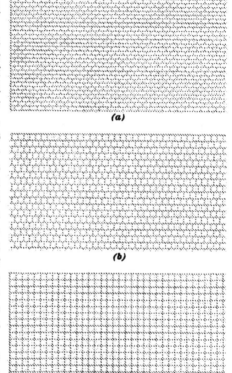

(a)

(b)

(c)

FIG. 8

Design paper of this pattern would be used for a background such as that shown in Fig. 16. The decorative work, being of a pattern that is of specially designed shape, is not worked out on such paper but is laid out freehand, the special available shapes of the tesseræ, however, being kept well in mind.

The pattern shown in Fig. 8 (*b*) is similar to the one in (*a*) except that the tiles are square, the bricklike arrangement remaining the same. The field, or filling, in Fig. 11 was designed upon such paper.

In the pattern of Fig. 8 (*c*) the tiles are also square, but are not bricklike in their arrangement, but are arranged geometrically one below the other. Such design paper was employed when designing the borders for Figs. 9 and 10.

22. Basis of the Designs.—The process of designing the kind of geometrical repeating patterns and borders that are suitable for mosaic tile work is not at all difficult for one who understands the evolution of designs, design composition, color, etc., which have been explained in previous Sections. The general design of the border and of the filling should first be blocked out roughly within the scaled shape of the proposed floor surface. When this basic work has been clearly blocked in, the printed design paper, which is very transparent, may be laid over the roughly blocked-in design and fastened securely with thumbtacks. The shapes of the individual parts of the design will then be plainly visible through the thin design paper, and the process of coloring the design may be taken up at once.

23. Coloring the Design.—When once the design has been blocked out on the design paper, whether it consists of squares or of hexagons, or a combination of both, the first step in coloring is to know just what colors to use. The colors shown in Figs. 9, 10, 11, and 12 are very accurate and may be relied upon; but it would be well for the young designer to secure from tile makers, or from dealers in tiles, mantels, etc., samples of tesseræ of various colors and shapes.

Any opaque water-color pigment, such as the designers' moist colors previously referred to, will be suitable for this work. A medium-size water-color brush, such as a red sable, No. 3 or No. 6, should be used, the very pointed tip being cut off or burned off by touching lightly to a hot iron. This leaves a stubby, blunt, but not ragged, tip, with which the color can be applied in dabs or spots to the individual checks, squares, or hexagons on the design paper. The brush is held exactly perpendicular to the paper when doing the coloring. The results of applying color in this way are shown clearly in Figs. 9 to 13.

24. Examples of Mosaic Floor Designs.—Previous Sections have treated of the artistic principles of design and color; and it is therefore assumed that, from the study of these, the student now knows how to get up repeating designs that are interesting, and to color them attractively. The present work, therefore, is to consist of applying this artistic training to the definite field of mosaic tiling. However, it will assist the young designer to show him examples of practical designs actually prepared by commercial designers, so that he may have some idea as to how to start in getting up original designs.

In Figs. 9, 10, 11, and 12 are shown reproductions of portions of designs made of simple circular, hexagonal, rectangular, or square tiles, upon geometric bases such as have been described. In Fig. 9 the border is extremely simple, being suggestive of prehistoric or savage ornament. It is composed of large and small squares alternating, and set up diamond shape. The repeating spots in the field, or filling, based on circular tesseræ, are equally simple in form, the distances separating the spots being equally spaced. In Fig. 10 the border is somewhat more elaborate and quite interesting, being an elaborate form of the Greek fret, or key, pattern. The Greek fret is used a great deal for tile borders because it is so easily adapted to mosaic tile work, its form having in fact originated from the manner in which the bricks or tiles in old Greek and Roman pavements were laid. The spots in the field of Fig. 10 are simply the corner positions of diamond repeats.

The designs in Figs. 11 and 12 are somewhat more elaborate than those of Figs. 9 and 10, but the simplicity of their spacing is readily seen. The field of Fig. 12 is particularly rich in design.

25. Elaborate Floral Subjects in Mosaic.—The designs heretofore considered have been comparatively simple, being based on geometric repeats and underlying meshwork on the design paper. However, the designer is not confined to the use of geometrically ruled design paper and tiles of uniform shapes. By cutting or breaking the tiles in irregular pieces, and not attempting to conform to a geometric basis, decorative or pictorial work of considerable elaborateness may be produced, as shown in the designs illustrated in Figs. 13, 14, 15, and 16.

Obviously, squared or meshed paper cannot be employed for the making of color sketches for such designs. The general setting of the design must be sketched or painted in on ordinary white paper, such as water-color paper, and then gone over with a sharp pencil and the general forms and placing of the individual irregular tiles then put in. This, in conjunction with the full-size working drawing, will indicate to the workmen how the irregular pieces of the required colors are to be combined to secure the desired result. Such sketches are made in opaque water color, as before.

In setting, or laying, work of the kind illustrated in Figs. 13, 14, 15, and 16, the tesseræ are placed piece by piece in the cement bed by the workman, aided by a full-size drawing of the entire design, or may be made up in sections at the factory, as is the case with the geometric mosaic tile work.

In Figs. 13 and 14 are shown two quiet and dignified designs that were used on the floor of a church vestibule. It will be observed that the torches and ribbons, the book, and the swags are all composed of pieces of mosaic tiling of the proper colors. The tesseræ are not of regular shape, but are cut and split to fit the proper places.

In Fig. 15 is shown a series of specially designed shapes that, while not for mosaic floor work, could easily be used for that purpose. These mosaic shapes show the possibilities of mosaic tile work in connection with a fireplace. Again it will be noted that the backgrounds and decorative parts are composed of tesseræ of irregular shapes, while the pieces in the border are rectangular in shape. The large rectangle shown in (a) represents a panel over the mantel shelf; the odd-shaped piece in (b) shows the panels about the fireplace opening; and the long rectangle in (c) shows the mosaic tiling of the hearth. A careful study of these designs will show clearly the sizes and colors of the pieces needed to produce the decoration, the backgrounds, and the borders.

The design shown in Fig. 16 is very elaborate and shows the possibilities of decorative mosaic tile work. The original color

Fig. 17

sketch to scale, and the full size drawing, would be prepared as before described.   In this design tesseræ of irregular shapes are necessary in order to carry out portions of the design, as, for example, the peacocks, the flowers, the leaves, etc.   Such a design would be suitable for a vestibule floor at the base of a flight of stairs, where a good view of the design would be obtained by persons descending the stairway.

26. Figure Work in Mosaic.—Pictorial subjects can be portrayed with great fidelity by means of mosaic work, as is clearly shown in Figs. 17 and 18. The available colors are practically unlimited, and the little individual pieces may be split and cut to any desired shape.

In Fig. 17 is shown a very fine piece of modern mosaic work, which serves as a panel in a London church. The subject, entitled, "Time, Death, and Judgment," is copied from a well-known picture of that title by the late G. F. Watts. The mosaic has very faithfully reproduced the picture itself, and gives evidence of a great deal of time having been spent upon it, as will be seen by the fact that it is not composed of a number of cubes but that each piece is specially cut to fill the place for which it is intended, so as to give the best results in the building up of the pictorial mosaic.

In Fig. 18 is shown in colors another example of pictorial figure work in mosaic. In such work the cartoon is very often finished in color, so that no mistake will be made by the workman in carrying out the work. It will be noticed how carefully the tesseræ are cut to shape to form the delicate curves of the face and of the folds of the drapery.

WALL AND HEARTH TILES

MANUFACTURE AND USE

27. Glazed and Enameled Tiles.—Tiles used on walls of bathrooms, restaurants, and other public buildings usually differ from the various types of floor tiles heretofore considered in that wall tiles are usually glazed or enameled, while floor tiles are not. A great variety of decorative methods is possible in wall tiles which would be unsuitable in floor tiles. The glazes or enamels that are used, and the tile bodies themselves, must harmonize in their physical properties, fusibility, and dilatation (power of expanding in all directions) or the glazes will chip or peel. Tiles of coarse body are frequently covered with a layer of fine china clay in a liquid state as a basis for the white or colored glaze. Glazes of different character are formed by the several methods of application, such as spraying, dipping, or immersing, irrigation or pouring on, and volatilization. Volatilization is the familiar *salt glazing*, which is performed by throwing saline substances into an active kiln at the close of the baking or burning operation. The salt is converted into vapor by the intense heat, and attaches itself to all exposed surfaces and forms there a thin layer of transparent glass. The brilliant decoration called *luster* is produced by painting the design over the glaze or enamel with pigment composed of metallic salts mixed with a strong reducing agent and refiring in a special kiln, which subjects the tile or other object to the action of heated gases and smoke.

28. Embossed and Intaglio Tiles.—Embossed tiles are those in which a pattern or design is executed in relief on the surface, which is generally glazed in addition. Intaglio tiles are those in which the pattern is sunk or depressed. In both classes the soft lead glazes, during the baking or burning process, will flow from the higher portions of the pattern to the hollows, producing a beautifully soft effect. Tiles which are a peculiar combination of slight relief and glazing or enameling are variously described as having *raised outline, slip outline,* or *tube-line* decoration, the outline of the pattern being raised slightly above the general surface of the tile as a guide for the glaze or enamel painting.

29. Painted and Printed Tiles.—Painted tiles are usually considered as being of two kinds: those in which the color decoration is applied to the once-fired (or *bisque*) tile before glazing, which method is called *under-glaze painting;* and those in which the painting is carried out in prepared vitrifiable colors on the glaze, the tile being then refired, which method is called *over-glaze painting.* However, there is no difference in the actual methods of designing for these two kinds.

In some cases tiles for wall decoration are put together in panels before or after being glazed, and a picture is painted on the panel and, of course, extending across the joints of individual tiles. The tiles composing the panel picture are then taken down, separated, and fired.

In case a tile of a certain pattern or design is to be reduplicated in large quantities, methods of line and chromolithographic and other color printing have been devised, the design being laid on the tile by means of transfers. The Dutch tiles, used around hearths and elsewhere, showing the familiar quaint and spirited designs of ships, horsemen, etc., are examples of this type of decorative tiles.

Further descriptions of glazed tiling will be taken up later when faience tiles are discussed.

30. Sizes and Colors of Wall and Hearth Tiles. The white wall tiles, of the larger sizes, known as earthenware glazed tiles, commonly used in bathrooms, restaurants, dairies, etc., are usually 6 in. × 6 in. Sometimes octagons and hexagons of smaller sizes are used. Then there are smaller rectangular tiles of many varying sizes, used chiefly for the *field* of the side wall; that is, the part above the dado at the lower part of wall. The usual colors are white and cream, but olive, blue, buff, ivory, etc. are available; and these tiles of various sizes of plain colors, combined with printed or painted tiles used for friezes and borders, produce very interesting arrangements.

Hearth tiles are usually 6 in. × 6 in.; 4¼ in. × 4¼ in.; and 3 in. × 3 in. The available colors are as described for wall tiles. There are also used for this purpose floral patterns and conventional designs in the form of printed tiles; and also decorated and embossed tiles.

As in the case of the encaustic tiles and mosaic tiles previously discussed, the young designer should secure samples of wall and hearth tiles of all sizes and colors, which can be done with little trouble by visiting the dealer or the manufacturer. Every effort should be put forth to visit the tile manufacturing plant, if possible, to see the processes by which the tiles are made and glazed.

31. Basis of Pattern Arrangement.—In Fig. 19 is shown a typical wall tile arrangement for a bathroom wall, and in Fig. 20 an arrangement of tiles for a hearth. While the fact that the square and rectangular forms of the tiles themselves necessitate to a certain extent a geometrical arrangement, yet more freedom of treatment is allowed here than in the case of mosaic floor tiles. This applies to the designs of individual tiles as well as to the broad treatment of the entire wall.

In this class of work there is required, not only a sketch made to a scale of, say, $\frac{1}{2}$ inch = 1 foot, or 1 inch = 1 foot, showing the appearance of the entire wall when the proposed tile treatment has been completed, but also a scaled sketch of the patterns of the individual decorative tiles, such as those used in borders, etc. Such color sketches are laid out on water-color bristol board, or on regular water-color paper mounted or stretched. All parts of the drawing should be carefully drawn in pencil before the coloring is started.

32. Character of Designs for Wall and Hearth Tiling. Wall designs for glazed tiling for bathrooms usually show a large expanse of white tiling in both dado and field, the individual tiles being somewhat larger in the former than in the latter. This expanse of white is usually relieved by a frieze of decorative tiles in delicate colors and a band or strip of decorative work at the top of the dado separating it from the field. Sometimes the Greek fret, or key, design is used for this latter purpose, the frieze being composed of the anthemion, or honeysuckle, ornament. The preparing of other suitable designs should present little difficulty to one well trained in the artistic principles of designing for all-over patterns, borders, strips, fields, etc., as explained in previous Sections. He simply needs to apply his artistic design training to the work in hand. Several specimens of practical designs, however, such as are actually used in the tile trade, are shown in Figs. 19 and 20, so that the young designer may have a basis upon which to produce original designs.

Fig. 19 is an example of a bathroom or lavatory wall faced with white tiling. A dado, or wainscoting, is emphasized half way up the wall by the insertion of a course of colored decorative tiling, done in gold and capped with a band mold. At the floor, a special plinth, or base, course is inserted. A decorative frieze is put in near the ceiling line immediately under the angle cove, and makes a suitable and effective framing for this apartment. Specially designed tiles form the door frame, and can be selected from manufacturers' catalogs. It will be noticed that special curved tiles are used at the junction of the floor with the wall and also between the wall and the ceiling. The purpose of these curved tiles is to do away with angles where dust and dirt may accumulate and which are hard to keep clean.

The designer in laying out such work must remember that it is always cheaper to select stock tiles than to have them made special. He will also find that he will be able to get tiles kept in stock at much shorter notice than those that have to be made especially for one job.

This design possesses the charm of cleanliness, and makes the room bright and attractive. While the general constructive features shown in Fig. 19 should be observed in all rooms of this character, sufficient distinction can be obtained by the selection of appropriate decorative designs.

Fig. 20 shows a typical arrangement of hearth tiles, in the so-called Dutch style, showing windmills, sailboats, etc. The wooden mantel is painted a mouse gray, the tiles being blue and white and surrounding the fireplace opening, which is trimmed with a brass angle and set off with andirons to match. The hearth is made of red tiles. In designing for tile arrangements of this character it is necessary to make not only a complete sketch of the entire scheme in a pictorial way, as in Fig. 20, but also scaled or full-size designs for the individual tiles. Although pictorial work has not been taken up in the preceding Sections, yet these simple pictorial devices can easily be managed by the design student in view of the thorough training he has had in drawing and in certain forms of rendering.

33. Coloring the Design.—When the design has been carefully laid out, it may be colored with ordinary transparent water-color pigments. The color sketch may be made in any pleasing colors, well combined, and the tile manufacturer or tile setter can then adapt it to the available colors he has in stock. It would be better, however, for the young designer to become acquainted with the principal colors used in such glazed wall and hearth tiling by looking over the stock of the merchant or manufacturer, and employing only such colors as those for which stock tiles are available.

FAIENCE TILES

MANUFACTURE AND USE

34. Meaning of Term "Faience."—In the strictest meaning of the word one cannot speak of tiles as being faience, but on account of the association and use of faience with glazed tiling it may be considered as coming under the heading of tile work.

The word **faience**, pronounced *fay-yans'* (the last syllable being accented and th. *a* in it being pronounced like the *a* in father) was originally applied to the glazed and richly colored or enameled pottery manufactured at Faenza, one of the chief seats of the ceramic industry in Italy in the 16th century. It is now, however, applied indifferently to all the various kinds of structural and decorative glazed or enameled earthenware or stoneware used in building, with the exceptions of glazed or enameled bricks and sanitary pottery. Beautiful effects can be obtained with a judicious use of faience, owing to the large range of colors available and to the soft and rich effects of the covering glaze. The color is always bright and permanent, and the surface capable of being easily cleaned when necessary.

35. Glaze and Enamel.—Both glaze and enamel are practically glass and both may be colored; but the term **glaze** is applied to transparent glass coating, and the term **enamel**

to an opaque coating.   Glazes are prepared by fusing sand or other silicious material with potash or soda to form glass. The addition of oxide of tin to the lead glaze produces an opaque white enamel; and both glaze and enamel are variously colored by the addition of metallic oxides.

36.   Applied Faience.—The term **applied faience** refers to faience that is made in thin slabs or tiles, which are then used for the various classes of tile work, particularly for walls, as previously discussed.   These faience tiles may be prepared by either of two principal processes, the *plastic process* or the *dust process*, both of which were described when unglazed encaustic floor tiles were discussed.   In the plastic process the pieces are usually made from 9 in. × 12 in. up to 20 in. × 40 in., with remarkable accuracy.

From the above description there will be apparent the distinction between ordinary glazed wall tiles of specified square patterns, and faience work where specially designed panels are produced on a large scale with beautiful design and coloring.

DESIGNING

37.   Basis of the Design.—The basis, structurally, upon which the tiles are arranged is, of course, geometric, being composed of large panels, squares, and rectangular strips.   However, since the decoration or picture runs over the joints of adjoining tiles, and since quite a number of adjoining tiles are required to produce the decoration, this geometric basis is not so apparent as in the case of mosaic tiling.

The available shapes, colors, and patterns of faience tiles should be known to the designer, although, of course, special designs are always being made up.   It is then not a difficult matter for the designer to apply to this class of work the training in artistic designing that he has already received.   The problem in the case of faience tile decoration is not so much the construction of all-over repeating patterns surrounded by borders, as has been the case in the designing of the classes of tiles previously discussed, but the problem is to cover a wall surface, a panel, a lunette, etc. with appropriate decoration.

38. Making and Coloring the Design.—There should first be made a small-scale design (say ½ inch to the foot, or 1 inch to the foot) of the proposed wall surface to be covered with faience tiles.   This surface may be merely the dado, but frequently is the entire side wall, in which case it should be broken up into dado, side wall, or field, and frieze.   Moldings in relief can also be employed.   The design may be made on smooth white or tinted bristol board with opaque color in which Chinese white plays a large part.

The designer here has ample opportunity to apply what he has learned regarding design composition, space filling, decorative motifs, coloring, etc.   However, in making such application he must first become familiar with actual examples of faience tile work that have been prepared and set up.   This can best be done by visiting buildings where such work is erected and examining it carefully, but particularly by visiting factories where such tiles are designed and made.   An excellent plan is to call on the manufacturer or the merchant and ask to look over old books of patterns that they may have on hand. These will serve to give the designer a clear idea of what is being done, and will serve as suggestions to him for the preparation of original designs for this class of work.

39. Examples of Designs in Faience Tiles.—As suggestions of the class of work done in high-grade faience, the decorative wall surfaces shown in Figs. 21 and 22 are presented. Fig. 21 illustrates the use of faience in the decoration of an interior wall surface by means of tiles forming a molding, dado, molded dado capping, and panel molding enclosing a panel of plain tiles.   The whole is surmounted by a cornice.   This scheme could be carried out in many different ways, so far as color is concerned, to harmonize with the design of the remainder of the building in which the finishing is placed.

In Fig. 22 is shown, in colors, an example of faience more elaborate than that in Fig. 21.   There is the plinth molding, as in the case of the design in Fig. 21, but it is made in two heights, while the dado is decorated with panels of embossed tiles, giving relief to the plain tile border and furnishing filling for it.   The

Fig. 21

dado capping consists of two molded members filled in between with decorated tiles, which could be either embossed or plain, at the pleasure of the designer.   The general wall face above the dado is filled in, as shown, with plain and embossed tiles, giving a very pleasing effect; and the whole wall face is finished with the capping, frieze, and molded cornice.   The frieze, as will be seen,

Design by The Rockwood Pottery Company.
Used by permission.

FIG. 23

is somewhat elaborate in treatment, but yet does not look heavy when considered in conjunction with the plain wall face beneath.

40. Dull-Glaze Tile, or Della Robbia.—Tiles in color with a dull, or matt, glaze are frequently used very effectively as wall decorations, for both interiors and exteriors. Very interesting pictorial effects, in flat masses of harmonizing colors, are thus obtained on walls of public buildings. For example, one large railroad station has a frieze of pictures, in Della Robbia tile work, running around the side and end walls of the large waiting room, portraying scenes at the various termini of that particular railway system and at various scenic points along its route. This is not only decorative, but is a far more attractive method of calling attention to the scenic and other attractions of that particular railroad than the rather antiquated system of framed photographs and lithographs hung about the waiting room.

This dull-glaze tile is also used on exteriors, for it will very well withstand the action of the elements.

In Fig. 23 is reproduced in black and white a large seal, set in a circular leaf border, the original of which was executed in dull, or matt, glazed tile in colors. As can readily be seen, the device is made in sections, the circular, or seal, portion including the band of lettering, being made in four segments, and the leaf border being composed of sixteen sections. The design overruns the dividing lines of the various sections, as shown. In pictorial dull-glaze work, as in purely decorative work, the entire composition must be laid out, and the cutting lines dividing the individual tiles must be carefully considered.

PARQUETRY

CLASSIFICATION OF HARDWOOD FLOORS

41. Hardwood Floors in Patterns.—While not in any sense related to tiled floors so far as material is concerned, the matter of designing for parquetry is closely associated with designing for tiles on account of the fact that both forms of work are for structural construction of floors and both are based upon geometric repeating motifs.

Leaving out of consideration for the present ordinary hardwood floors, which consist simply of straight strips and need no special design, hardwood floors in patterns are usually considered as coming under two general classes, **parquet flooring** and **parquetry flooring.**

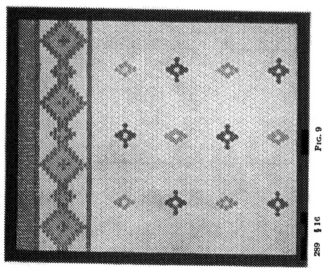

Fig. 9

Fig. 10

Fig. 12

Fig. 11

FIG. 13

FIG. 14

(a)

(b)

§ 16

FIG. 18

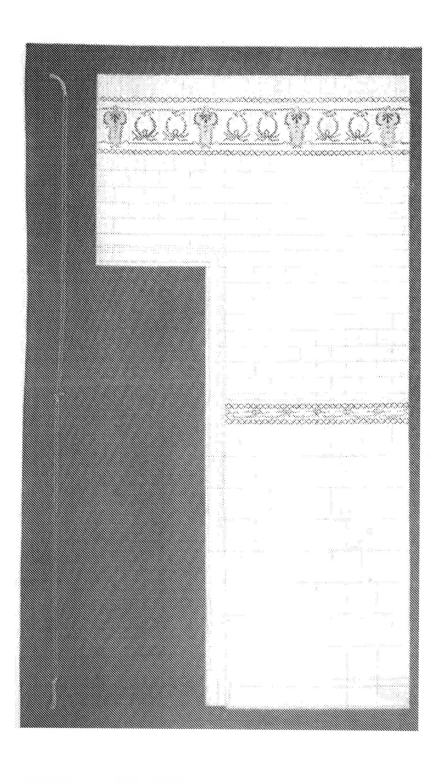

Fig. 20

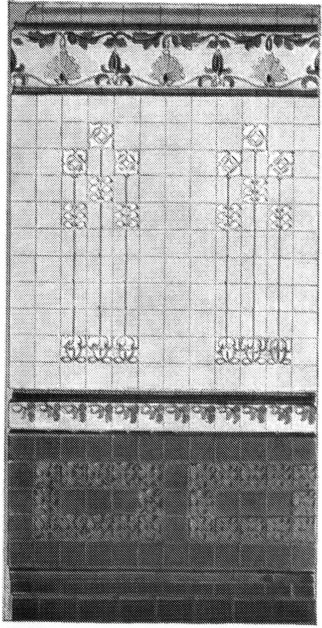

Fig. 22

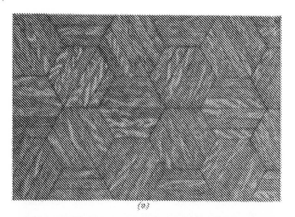

(a)

(b)

(c)

Courtesy of Wood-Mosaic Company, Inc.

(a)

(b)

(c)

(d)

(e)

(f)

(g)

(h)

(i)

(j)

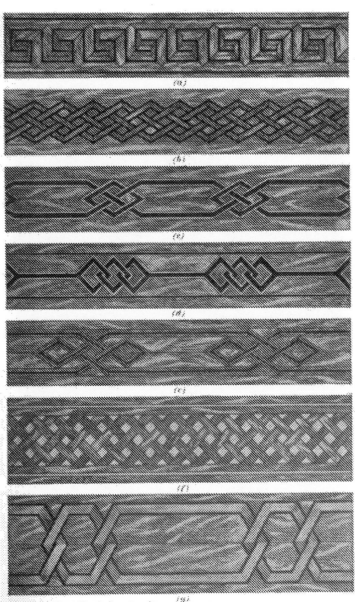

(a)

(b)

(c)

(d)

(e)

(f)

(g)

FIG. 57

(a)

(b)

(c)

(d)

Fig. 38

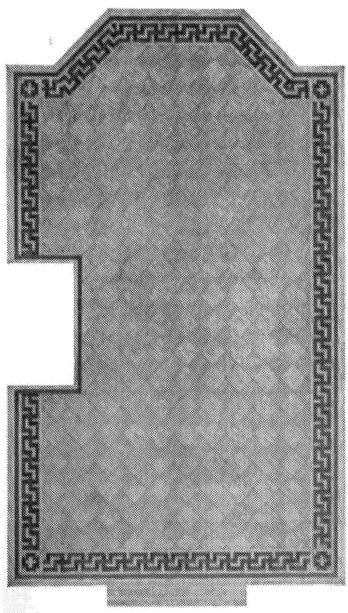

Fig. 20

42. Definition of Parquet Flooring.—The term **par-quet flooring** is applied to flooring composed of boards or strips tongued and grooved and laid and otherwise worked into strip patterns by the carpenter, in the same manner as a cabinet-maker would work.

43. Definition of Parquetry Flooring.—When **par-quetry flooring,** or, briefly, **parquetry,** is spoken of, the reference is to flooring that is composed of flooring strips, or so-called wood carpet. The general term **wood mosaic** may be applied to parquetry because the manner in which the strips, squares, etc. of wood are put together, so far as arrangement is concerned, is precisely the same as the putting together of tiles in tile-mosaic work.

The present treatise will discuss this work under the head of parquetry flooring.

_____

PARQUETRY FLOORING

_____

MANUFACTURE AND USE

44. Kinds and Sizes of Wood Strips.—The woods ordinarily used for parquet and parquetry flooring are plain white oak, quartered white oak, selected white maple, dark cherry, walnut, dark oak, red mahogany, and white mahogany. In certain special cases the so-called rare and fancy woods are used.

In the parquet flooring the strips are so made at the mill that the tongue and groove come in the middle of the edge of the strips or boards, a feature differing somewhat from that of ordinary flooring. This insures a tight, even contact of both top and bottom edges. In parquetry flooring, in addition to long strips, there are also pattern pieces of geometric formation and standard sizes, such as squares, rhombs (equilateral parallelograms having oblique angles), and herringbone patterns. Sometimes the effect is secured by veneering on a backing of pine or chestnut. In Fig. 24 are shown several common patterns that can be made up of parquet strips.

The parquetry strips used for parquetry flooring are of different widths, such as $1\frac{1}{2}$ inches, $1\frac{1}{2}$ inches, and 2 inches;

and $\frac{5}{16}$ inch thick. The lengths of the strips run from 4 feet upwards.

45. Wood Carpet.—When short pieces of parquetry strips are pressed tightly together, side by side and end to end, and

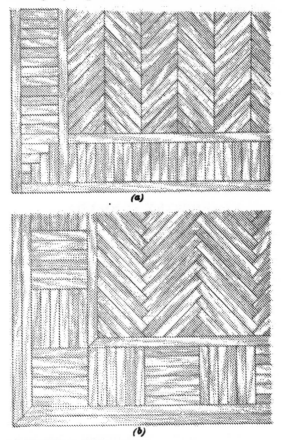

(a)

(b)

Courtesy of the Wood-Mosaic Company, Inc.

FIG. 24

mounted or glued onto cloth, in more or less intricate patterns, the product is called in the trade wood carpet, or wood-mosaic carpet. Various arrangements of the parquetry strips are used to secure interesting patterns. Sometimes the pattern is simply of parallel strips run across the width of the carpet; in other cases the strips are combined to form 8-inch squares, the directions of the grain of the strips in adjoining squares being at right angles to each other. In other cases the strips are combined to form hexagons, diamonds, rectangular sections, etc.

In Fig. 25 (a) and (b) are shown two patterns for wood carpet that are widely used. In (a) the pattern consists of 8-inch hexagons, diversity being secured by causing the strips to run in different directions. Each hexagon consists of six parallel strips all running in the same direction; in one hexagon they run horizontally, in the one above it they run in a left-oblique direction, and in the one below in a right-oblique direction. In (b) the pattern consists of 8″×16″ sections, the six strips in the vertical rectangles running vertically, and the six strips in the horizontal rectangles running horizontally.

Wood carpet, after the strips are glued in the proper patterns, is trimmed on the ends, and may be transported to the place where it is to be laid in 2-foot slabs or in rolls.

46. Parquetry Patterns.—Special patterns in parquetry work are used both for fields and borders, their interest and elaborateness consisting of the different directions of the grain and the different colors of woods used. These fancy parquetry patterns are made of strips, blocks, and sections of hardwoods of various colors, $\frac{5}{16}$ inch thick, glued edge to edge and backed by cloth or canvas. Many interesting patterns, for both fields and borders, can be gotten up by the judicious use and matching of such woods as oak, walnut, mahogany, maple, etc. Specimens of interesting patterns will be shown later, when the designing of parquetry is discussed. For the present it will be sufficient to show simply one specimen of field parquetry, as illustrated in Fig. 25 (c). This is composed of straight strips of light oak, mitered at 45° at both ends, and triangular-shaped pieces of dark oak or mahogany.

Fancy parquetry of this kind is usually made up in sections 4 feet long and 12 inches wide, unless they are for narrow borders, and thus are taken to the building where the parquetry is to be laid.

47. Laying Parquetry.—The proper kind of a subfloor must first be laid or the parquetry placed over it will be uneven. This subfloor should be of well-dried pine, in narrow, matched, boards. The boards should run diagonally across the floor, and be so arranged that sections of the parquetry will not be parallel to the subfloor boards. If parquetry is to be laid in a house where there are old floors, care must be taken to meet the above conditions.

The parquetry is secured to the subfloor by wire brads (nails). If the subfloor is of hardwood, 1-inch brads are used, but if of softer wood 1¼-inch brads are used, these being driven through the tops of the parquetry strips, and the heads sunk below the surface and the holes filled with putty.

DESIGNING

48. Basis of Design.—From what has been said as to the composition of parquetry, or wood mosaic, it must be evident that designs for this class of work must be on a geometric basis. Not only are the available pieces of certain standard sizes, but the colors also are limited to a certain few; for this reason the scope of the designs must necessarily be somewhat restricted, even more so than in the case of mosaic tile work.

However, the young designer has considerable opportunity, even in this class of work, to apply what he has learned about design composition, repeats, space filling, coloring, etc. and the exercise of good taste in making the patterns.

49. Making and Coloring the Design.—First of all, the shape and size of the proposed floor space to be covered by parquetry must be determined by measurements. Then a scaled drawing—½ inch to the foot or 1 inch to the foot, depending on the intricacy of the pattern to be used—should be laid out on white water-color paper or artists' bristol board.

The designer, of course, must be familiar with the kinds and colors of woods used, and the sizes and thicknesses of strips, squares, hexagons, etc. available. Further, all of the various manufacturers of parquetry throughout the country have on hand design books of patterns used, photographs of floors they have laid, instruction books on laying floors, etc., to all of which the serious young designer can have access if he goes about it in the proper way. The use of all these preliminary helps is necessary before the designer starts to draw and color his designs.

Having laid out the scaled drawing of the floor to be covered, he then plans the patterns of the borders and fillings. The amount of money that is available for the floor will, of course, influence the degree of elaborateness of the parquetry design. Taking an average case, however, the designer would usually plan out the border first, and then the filling, keeping both appropriate to the general style of the building in which the floor is laid. Examples of design patterns used for borders and for fillings will be given later, when examples of parquetry designs are discussed.

In coloring the design, either water colors or opaque colors may be used. As previously stated, the available colors are limited to those characteristic of the various hardwoods, light oak, dark oak, maple, walnut, mahogany, etc. To be sure that the coloring is correct, the young designer should secure, from firms that manufacture hardwoods, samples of the principal kinds of hardwoods, and keep these before him as he does the coloring. Experiments with the various pigments in the color box will readily show him what pigment or combination of pigments should be used to portray the different kinds of woods.

50. Things to Be Considered When Designing Parquetry Floors.—In making designs for parquetry floors the main effort should be to secure the effect of a flat level surface. One should feel that, when walking over a floor, he is on a secure surface, and that he will not stumble over anything or fall through anywhere; and patterns such as glaringly contrasted interlacings, or the effect of strips or blocks being piled one on top of the other, should therefore be avoided. Simple interlacings when on a small scale do not give such an effect of unevenness or instability, especially if the tones of the adjoining colored woods are not too widely contrasted.

Further, the pattern for the field, or filling, of the floor should be designed so that it will look well when viewed obliquely and very much foreshortened. An all-over repeating pattern that would be suitable for a side wall of a room, because frequently looked at squarely from in front, would not necessarily be suitable for a floor, even if the limitations of the wood strips and slabs would allow the pattern to be constructed of parquetry. Experience has shown that strips, squares, diamonds (rhombs), hexagons, etc., form the most satisfactory patterns, although every opportunity is given the young designer to experiment with other forms.

51. Examples of Border and Field Parquetry Designs.—In the parquetry industry there are certain standard designs for borders and fields that, by experience, have been found to be workmanlike and thoroughly practical from both the artistic viewpoint and the workman's side of the trade. The designer of parquetry must be familiar with these standard patterns and arrangements, so that he may be able to combine them skilfully when getting up a scheme for a floor treatment; but this does not mean that he will be prohibited from using originality in getting up still other designs.

In Fig. 26 (a) to (j) and Fig. 27 (a) to (g) are reproduced designs for borders of various widths, for parquetry fields, and for a complete installation.

In Fig. 26 (a) is shown a 3-inch border of two strips of oak enclosing a very narrow strip of mahogany; that in (b) is a 3-inch border of two strips of oak enclosing a narrow strip of walnut; in (c) is a 3-inch border of two strips of mahogany surrounding a narrow strip of maple; in (d) is a 4-inch border consisting of a strip of oak flanked by narrow strips of maple and mahogany; in (e) is an 8-inch border with interlacing strips of cherry, outlined with maple, over an oak background; in (f) is an 8-inch border having interlacing strips of cherry on an oak background; in (g) is an 8-inch border consisting of a Greek fret, or key, pattern made of cherry over an oak background; in (h) is an 8-inch border with oak background and a double-hexagon interlace, the narrow lines and S-shaped forms being of walnut; in (i) is a 10-inch border of oak and walnut, the narrow strips in the diamond interlace and the edging being of walnut; and in (*j*) is a 12-inch border of oak and walnut with a hexagonal interlace, the narrow strips being of walnut.

In Fig. 27 are shown some examples of borders running up to 18 inches in width. Borders are made even wider than those shown in Fig. 27, some being as wide as 24 inches. In Fig. 27 (*a*) is shown a 12-inch border having a Greek fret, or key, pattern of oak and walnut on an oak background; in (*b*) is a 12-inch border having a Moorish or Celtic interlace of oak, outlined with mahajua (a dark wood from tropical America) on an oak background; in (*c*) is a 12-inch border with interlacing strips of mahogany, outlined with maple, on an oak background; in (*d*) is a 12-inch border with an interlace of dark English oak, outlined with maple, on an oak background; in (*e*) is a 12-inch border with an interlace of rosewood and oak on an oak background; in (*f*) is a 16-inch border with a straight-line interlace of oak with background blocks and narrow edging lines of maple; and in (*g*) is an 18-inch border with a bold interlace of primavera, outlined with rosewood, on an oak background.

In Fig. 28 are shown four of the more elaborate parquetry designs used for fillings, more intricate and of higher grade than the ordinary so-called wood carpet. In using such parquetry fillings care must be taken, when making the design, that the border is bold and strong enough to hold the field pattern down to its proper scale. Further, the border should harmonize, in its general design, with the design used in the parquetry field. In Fig. 28 (*a*) is shown a design consisting of squares with diagonal crosses in each, giving a Greek effect, the dark wood being walnut, and the lighter wood oak; in (*b*) is a parquetry pattern consisting of a very clever interlace composed of mahogany and maple strips over an oak background; in (*c*) is an eight-pointed-star effect of mahogany on an oak background, the mahogany strips forming the stars being laid so as to suggest an interlace; and in (*d*) is another design consisting of squares containing diagonal crosses made of oak over a mahogany background. The effect of a level, even floor is maintained in all of these examples.

It will be seen that the combinations that can be devised for such parquetry fields are practically unlimited; and, even if it is not necessary to get up new and original patterns, considerable·ingenuity may be employed by the designer in combining borders with fields and adapting them to rooms of different shapes and sizes.

In Fig. 29 is illustrated a combination of Greek fret, or key, border and wood-carpet or parquetry field that is very popular and makes a very harmonious floor pattern. The clever manner in which the corner for the Greek fret border is arranged should be particularly noted.

The student must understand that when he is making a design for a parquetry floor his finished sketch must exhibit the degree of completeness shown in Fig. 29 in order to be acceptable and to make the proper impression on a client or customer.

TILE AND PARQUETRY DESIGNING EXERCISES

GENERAL INFORMATION

52. Required Work in This Section.—As in the case of previous Sections dealing with practical design work, the required work in this Section will consist of original designs for tile and parquetry work, drawn and rendered as a practical commercial designer would prepare them. Directions for doing this work technically have already been given in the text.

These drawings and original designs are to take the form of drawing plates, which the student will prepare and submit in the usual manner.

53. Character of the Drawing Plates.—There are to be four drawing plates in this Section—the first two to contain original designs for tiles for specific purposes, and the last two to contain original designs for parquetry work. For these plates it will be best to use Whatman's cold pressed drawing paper (known as water-color paper), although any good grade of white drawing paper that will take wash and color well will be suitable. The paper may be purchased in sheets approximately 15 in.×20 in., and each one then divided into two 10″×15″ sheets. It is not required that the student shall use the regular printed pattern paper, such as used by professional designers, for this design paper is rather difficult to secure except by those connected with the business. The student, when such background patterns are required for this plate work, can rule them with pencil. In connection with the description of each plate detailed directions are given as to what kinds of drawings or designs are required.

_____

PLATE 1

54. Exercise A, Plate 1.—In the upper half of the 10″×15″ plate—that is, within the 10″×7½″ space—lay out a 7″×5″ rectangle; and over the entire rectangle rule in pencil a background of squares, or squares in which circles may be drawn freehand, similar to patterns in Fig. 7 (*a*) or Fig. 8 (*c*). These little squares or circles may each be $\frac{1}{16}$ in.×$\frac{1}{16}$ in., each one representing a separate $\frac{1}{2}″×\frac{1}{2}″$ tessera; therefore, on the drawing, there will be sixteen of these squares to each inch, and as each square represents one $\frac{1}{2}″×\frac{1}{2}″$ tessera, each inch on the drawing will represent $\frac{1}{2}×16=8$ inches on the floor   The 7″×5″ space on the drawing, therefore, will represent a floor space of 56 in.×40 in., or 4 ft. 8 in.×3 ft. 4 in. This space may be considered as one corner, or one-fourth the area, of a 9′ 4″×6′ 8″ bathroom floor.

Within this 7″×5″ rectangle, therefore, make a design for one-quarter of a mosaic-tiled bathroom floor, using any selected design and color scheme. Show one-fourth of the entire border, and the filling, or field, that goes with it. Every latitude is allowed the designer, but a plain field, with perhaps a few small, well-placed spots, and a Greek fret border, and a color scheme in delicate blues, greens, and white, is suggested.

55. Exercise B, Plate 1.—In the lower half of the 10″×15″ plate—that is, within the 10″×7½″ space—lay out a 7″×5″ rectangle. Within this rectangle lay out a background of squares or circles (depending on what background pattern was used for design in Exercise A) showing the *full-size tesseræ*, each one ½ in.×½ in.   This 7″×5″ rectangle will then contain 140 such ½″×½″ squares; that is, it will be 14 squares wide by 10 squares high

On this background lay out, full size, and in colors, as much of the corner of the design made in Exercise A as the 7″×5″ rectangle of Exercise B will accommodate.   Mostly border will show, but if the border of the design has not been made too wide, some of the filling, or field, should also be visible on this full-size drawing.

56. Final Work on Plate 1.—Letter or write the title, Plate 1: Tile and Parquetry Designing, at the top of the sheet, and on the back place class letters and number, name, address, and date of completion of the plate.   Roll the plate, protected by a sheet of tissue paper, place in the mailing tube, and send to the Schools for examination.   Then proceed with Plate 2.

PLATE 2

57. Exercise A, Plate 2.—In the upper half of the 10″×15″ plate—that is, within the 10″×7½″ space—lay out a 7″×5″ rectangle.   Within this rectangle make a sketch in colors—on a scale of ½ in.=1 ft.—for the side wall of a bathroom 10 feet high, showing glazed white tile with frieze and dado-top in colored decorative work.   Or, if preferred, make a design for mantelpiece and hearth with square tiles.

58. Exercise B, Plate 2.—In the lower half of the 10″×15″ plate—that is, within the 10″×7½″ space—lay out a 7″×5″ rectangle, and within this rectangle draw, in colors, and *full size*, such section of the decorative portion of the sketch design in Exercise A as can be accommodated within the available space.   If the design in Exercise A is composed of the smaller rectangular tiles such as are commonly used for bathroom walls, a number of such tiles can be shown.   If the large 6″×6″ hearth and fireplace tiles are employed in the design, it will, of course, be necessary to make the available rectangle 6 inches high.

59. Final Work on Plate 2.—Letter or write the title, Plate 2: Tile and Parquetry Designing, at the top of the sheet, and on the back place class letters and number, name, address, and date of completion of the plate. Roll the plate, protected by a sheet of tissue paper, place in the mailing tube, and send it to the Schools for examination. Then proceed with Plate 3.

PLATE 3

60. Exercise A, Plate 3.—Divide the upper $10'' \times 7\frac{1}{2}''$ rectangle of the $10'' \times 15''$ sheet into two equal parts vertically, making two rectangles 5 in. $\times 7\frac{1}{2}$ in.

In the left-hand $5'' \times 7\frac{1}{2}''$ space lay out a design 4 in. $\times 6$ in. for a simple parquetry or hardwood-floor pattern for a field or filling of hardwood strips, using only one kind of wood. Color the design appropriately to show the matchings of strips, and the kind of wood used, also showing markings or grain of wood. Note in pencil at margin of the sketch the name of the wood used for this field pattern.

In the right-hand $5'' \times 7\frac{1}{2}''$ space lay out a design 4 in. $\times 6$ in. for a somewhat more elaborate parquetry or hardwood-floor field pattern than that shown in the left-hand space, using two or three kinds of wood. Color the design appropriately to show the matchings of the strips and the various kinds of wood used, also showing markings or grain of wood. Note in pencil at margin of the sketch the names of the different kinds of wood used for this field pattern.

61. Exercise B, Plate 3.—In the lower half of the $10'' \times 15''$ plate—that is, within the $10'' \times 7\frac{1}{2}''$ space—lay out five or six strips for borders of parquetry or hardwood. These strips may be 8 or 9 inches long and from $\frac{1}{2}$ in. to 2 inches in width, with the proper spaces of white-paper background left showing between them. The patterns for the strips or borders should be original designs, ranging from simple work on the narrow strips to more elaborate treatment on the wider ones. The extent to which the complication of a design may be carried, and still be possible of execution in wood, is indicated by the text illustrations. These strips, or border designs, are to be carefully colored and the grainings indicated to show properly the kinds of wood used; and notations in pencil are to be made on the margin to indicate the names of the different woods employed in the making of the borders.

62. Final Work on Plate 3.—Letter or write the title, Plate 3: Tile and Parquetry Designing, at the top of the sheet, and on the back place class letters and number, name, address, and date of completion of the plate. Roll the plate, protected by a sheet of tissue paper, place in the mailing tube, and send to the Schools for examination. Then proceed with Plate 4.

PLATE 4

63. Exercise for Plate 4.—On the 10"×15" sheet to constitute Plate 4 lay out a rectangle 6 in.×11 in., or 7 in. ×12 in. if desired. Let this space represent, on a scale of ½ in. =1 ft., a floor 12 ft.×22 ft. (or 14 ft.×24 ft.), to be covered with parquetry or hardwood flooring.

Make a design therefor, for a filling, or field, with an appropriate border, for this parquetry flooring, coloring it appropriately to indicate the various kinds of woods used, and their markings. As before, indicate in pencil on the margin the names of the various woods. This design is to be in every respect a finished drawing and rendering, and is to show exactly the appearance of the completed hardwood floor.

64. Final Work on Plate 4.—Letter or write the title, Plate 4: Tile and Parquetry Designing, at the top of the sheet, and on the back place class letters and number, name, address, apd date of completion of the plate. Roll the plate, protected by a sheet of tissue paper, place in the mailing tube, and send to the Schools for examination.

If any redrawn work on any of the plates of this Section has been called for and has not yet been completed, it should be satisfactorily finished at this time. After all the required work on the plates of this Section has been completed, the work of the next Section should be taken up at once.

LINOLEUM AND OILCLOTH DESIGNING

PURPOSE

1. Necessity for Specialized Training.—To prepare satisfactory and salable designs for any line of industrial design work, it is necessary to know something of the methods of manufacture and use of the articles or fabrics. This is particularly true in the making of designs for linoleum, interlocking cork tiling, and oilcloth of various kinds. It must not be imagined that, because the patterns used for these products are so apparently simple, the designs can therefore be made for them without knowing how they are to be carried out in the finished material.

2. Scope of Training in This Section.—There have heretofore been considered those classes of decorative work for floors and walls in which the materials, such as tiles or hardwoods, are applied to, and become a component structural part of, the floors and walls. It is therefore appropriate that there should next be considered those lines of industrial design work that are equally simple in their patterns, but are in the form of separate and distinct fabrics applied to the floors or walls.

In this Section, therefore, will be taken up the designing of linoleum, both plain and inlaid, including interlocking cork and rubber tiling—fabrics that are closely associated with linoleum—and oilcloth for floor, table, and wall use. Preceding the directions for designing for these lines of work there will be presented descriptions of the manufacture and use of these fabrics in so far as these considerations influence the designing.

§ 17

LINOLEUM

CLASSIFICATION OF LINOLEUM

3. Definition of Linoleum.—The term linoleum is used to designate that separately and superficially applied floor covering consisting of a cork, (or rubber) and canvas composition, in most forms of which the patterns and colors extend entirely through the fabric.   It may be made in small blocks, or in large sheets or rolls, but, unlike tile or parquetry, it is a separately applied fabric and does not become a component part of the floor on which it is laid.   There are several classes of linoleum; namely, *cork tiling, inlaid linoleum*, and *printed linoleum.*

4. Cork tiling, as its name indicates, has the form of tiles and is made from a cork composition.   These tiles may be square or rectangular, or of such grooved contours, or dovetail-shaped outlines, as to. interlock at the edges, thus forming, when laid, an even floor surface.   By the judicious use of several harmonizing and serviceable colors the decorative possibilities of such flooring are many.

5. Inlaid linoleum does not differ materially, from the designer's standpoint, from cork tiling, although its decorative possibilities are greater.   In cork tiling the tiles are of uniform shape and size, are individual, and are laid separately, but in the case of inlaid linoleum the pieces or sections of linoleum, the composition of which will be described later, are all mounted on jute or burlap, and thus form one continuous sheet or roll, the linoleum extending all the way through the thickness of the fabric.

6. Printed linoleum is made in sheets of one solid color and the pattern is printed thereon in heavy oil colors.   It is evident that printed linoleum, while not so durable as inlaid linoleum, because the pattern can actually be worn off by continued use, offers greater possibilities for the decorative designer, because the patterns may be more intricate and diversified.

CORK TILING

MANUFACTURE AND USE

7. Composition of Cork Tiling.—In making cork tiling, bulk cork is finely granulated, and then, in closed molds and by intense hydraulic pressure, is compressed to a small portion of its original bulk. No cementing materials are needed in this process because the high temperature to which the cork is heated during the compressing process liquefies the natural gum of the cork, which serves as a binder and forms the compressed cork particles into a homogeneous mass, which is practically block of natural cork.

8. Shapes, Sizes, and Colors of the Tiles.—One class of cork tiling is made up of square or rectangular pieces accurately fitted together. These square tiles are made in a great variety of sizes, as 3-inch, 4-inch, 4½-inch, 6-inch, 8-inch, 9-inch, 10-inch, and 12-inch. Rectangular tiles are usually made 6 in. × 12 in. and 8 in. × 16 in.

Another class of tiling is composed of interlocking sections, fitting together with edges constructed on the general principle of the dovetailed joint in carpentry. There are various styles of interlocking shapes put out and patented by different manufacturers, but the principle of interlocking edges is the same in all cases. These tiles are usually about 3 inches square, or slightly more. In Fig. 1 is shown, on a small scale, a group of four such interlocking tiles, two light and two dark, and the manner in which they fit together. The dimension figures placed on the lower left-hand one will show the size of each one. These tiles are about 3 inches square and $\frac{5}{16}$ inch in thickness.

These interlocking shapes themselves offer great possibilities to the designer, and the fact that cork tiling can be made in any desired color gives him additional opportunities. The colors usually carried in stock by manufacturers are white, black, light green, dark green, light blue, dark blue, red, slate, light brown, and dark brown.

9. Laying Cork Tiling.—Cork tiling may be laid on any kind of subfloor, as wood, concrete, or metal. The cork tiles are laid individually, with tight joints cemented under pressure with liquid cement, thus hermetically sealing the entire

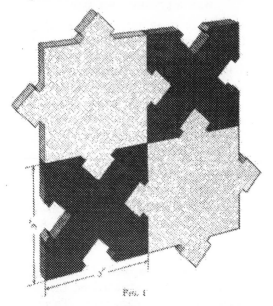

Fig. 1

surface and making it non-absorbent and impervious to liquids. Such a floor requires no especial care other than ordinary cleaning and occasional washing with soap and water.

DESIGNING CORK TILING

10. Principles Governing Cork-Tile Designs.—To one who has had some knowledge of mosaic tile work, and designing therefor, the making of designs for cork-tile floors will not introduce any new principles. However, in the case of cork tiling, the designer is considerably restricted on account of the shapes of the individual tiles being limited strictly to geometric forms. For this reason, he must make his designs on ruled section paper, or paper having the outlines of the tiles printed in pale ink, a small section of which is shown, full size, in Fig. 2. Such design sheets are made 13 3/16 inches by 14 1/16 inches in size. The design is made by coloring the sections desired to make the decorative pattern and filling in the others with the ground color.

11. Colors Available.—While cork tiling can be made up in any desired colors, it is well for the designer to become accus-

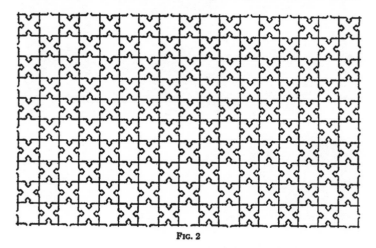

FIG. 2

tomed to getting his effects with the colors that the manufacturers usually carry in stock, such as white, black, light green, dark green, light blue, dark blue, red, slate, light brown, and dark brown.

12. Keeping in Touch with the Commercial Product. The manufacturer and his designers usually determine the patterns to be used for cork tiling, the public seldom having opportunity to express preference of taste one way or the other. Therefore, the designer should keep in touch with the cork-tile floors that are being laid, or should look over the patterns in the manufacturers' catalogs. The designer who has had training in the evolution of designs, space filling, etc., will have found numerous suggestions for getting up such geometric patterns presented in connection with his work in those subjects.

TYPICAL DESIGNS FOR CORK TILING

13. Specimens of Commercial Cork-Tile Patterns. In Figs. 3, 4, 5, 6, and 7 are shown typical examples of cork-tile patterns for fields and borders. Fig. 3 shows the square

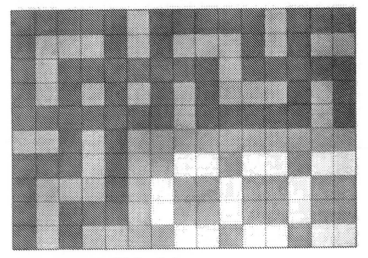

Used by permission of David E. Kennedy, Inc.

FIG. 3

tiles; and Figs. 4, 5, 6, and 7 the interlocking tiles, which style of shape, it must be remembered, is simply one manufacturer's patented style; there are other styles of interlocking edges on the market.

In Fig. 3 is shown parts of the filling, the border, and the corner of a floor laid in square tiles. By the skilful use of tiles of different tone values and color hues an interesting effect of a checkered field with a Greek fret, or key, border is secured. In the illustration, the three colors are represented by different values of gray. The very dark squares represent rich maroon red, as in the border fret design; the medium-gray squares indicate the warm gray brown background; and the lightest gray squares stand for light steel blue.

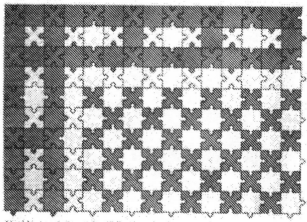

FIG. 4

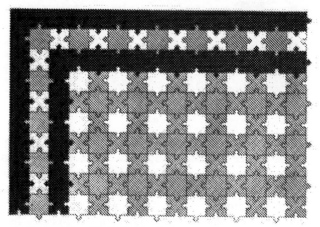

FIG. 5

With very little ingenuity the designer can readily form other interesting designs based upon the square tiles.

14. In Figs. 4 and 5 are shown two examples of floor patterns composed of interlocking tiles laid on lines running horizontally and vertically. The color schemes that were employed
may be followed by studying the contrasts of dark gray and
light gray. In Fig. 4 the dark gray represents dark brick-red
tiles, while the light gray represents white tiles, the strong bold
border according well with and holding in the red-and-white
checker effect of the field. In Fig. 5, the black represents black

Used by permission of David E. Kennedy, Inc.

Fɪɢ. 6

tiles, the dark gray indicates dark yellow-brown tiles, the light
gray in the border indicates white tiles there, while the light
gray in the field represents light steel-blue tiles at these places.
In this case the border of black bands and white spots on the
dark-brown background is very strong, and serves as an excellent finish for the blue-spotted field with dark-brown background.

15. In Fig. 6 the interlocking tiles are arranged on a
series of diagonal lines crossing each other at right angles.

FIG. 7

Considerable variety in pattern arrangements may be secured by this method. The very dark gray portions in Fig. 6 represent deep rich blue tiles in the actual floor; the medium value of gray represents rich sap-green tiles; while the light gray indicates a background of light warm-gray tiles. The border of the green and blue cross-line interlace is a rather unusual one because of its pattern, but it harmonizes well with the green and blue-spot pattern of the field. If the border had been made on the principle of a simple Moorish interlace it would have been even more interesting.

16. In Fig. 7 is reproduced in dark gray and light gray an interesting field, or rug, pattern, the dark gray representing blue tiles, and the light gray representing light warm-gray tiles of the background. A design such as this, where the field fuses into and becomes a part of the border, is an interesting treatment, both in design and in coloring, and lacks the hard mechanical characteristics of a field with separate border.

The examples in Figs. 3, 4, 5, 6, and 7 were reproduced direct from the designer's sketches, and at the same size, thus showing the scale to which designers work and how sketches for this class of work are made.

INLAID LINOLEUM

MANUFACTURE AND USE

17. Composition and Sizes of Linoleum.—The composition of linoleum is not unlike that of cork tile, although linoleum is made in large sheets or rolls, whereas the tile is in individual blocks.

Linoleum is a mixture of ground cork and oxidized linseed oil spread in a uniform layer upon canvas or burlap. The linseed oil is oxidized by exposing it in thin films to the influence of air, thus making a substance that possesses a certain amount of elasticity. After adding rosin, kauri gum (gum from the New Zealand kauri-pine tree), and the pigments of the desired colors, the oxidized oil is then mixed with the ground cork, and firmly pressed upon the canvas or burlap backing, to which it then adheres.   Afterwards it is coated with oil paint and thus made waterproof.

The distinctive feature of inlaid linoleum is that the design extends all the way through the fabric, which will therefore preserve continuity of design until the prepared surface is worn clear through.   Inlaid linoleum, or mosaic linoleum, as it is sometimes called, is prepared by first cutting pieces of colored linoleum pulp by means of dies, and then arranging them side by side on the burlap or canvas, thus forming a sort of tile pattern in different colors.   The burlap and pulp are passed under a heavy heated plate, which is brought down on them with a tremendous pressure, literally welding the parts into one homogeneous mass and uniting them perfectly with the burlap backing.

A process producing similar results is one wherein the dry pulp in granular form is sprinkled on the burlap backing through a series of stenciled plates or patterns, after which it is submitted to heavy pressure and heat as before, and thus becomes a solid fabric.

Inlaid linoleum is much more expensive than printed linoleum, on account of the intricacies of its manufacture, but it has many advantages; it is not so attractive, however, to the designer, for the limitations of the present method of manufacture impose such decided restrictions that one can work out nothing but very simple patterns.

Linoleum is made up in rolls of varying widths, from 5 to 9 feet, or over that for special orders.   The number of yards to the roll also varies to suit special cases.

18.   Laying Linoleum.—Linoleum is of such a composition that, when unrolled from the large rolls and spread out, its very weight will cause it to lie flat on the floor without any special fastening being required.   In some cases, however, where the floor is rough, or it is required to place sections of linoleum edge to edge, small brads, called **linoleum nails,** are used to fasten the edges to the floor.   In other cases brass binding strips are used.

DESIGNING INLAID LINOLEUM

19. Principles Governing Designs for Inlaid Linoleum.—The principles that govern the designing of patterns for inlaid linoleum are not unlike those that apply to designs for mosaic tiling, cork tiling, etc. Inasmuch as the fabric is composed of pieces of different colored linoleum stamped or cut out by dies, and then fitted together by pressure so as to make a complete fabric, these pieces must not be too complicated in shape, or the fitting together will be difficult and expensive. For this reason the designer must use mostly the simpler geometric shapes, as squares, octagons, crosses, etc., although symmetrically curved shapes can also be used.

20. Making the Design.—Designs for linoleum are made on cold-pressed white drawing paper, illustrators' board, or even heavy manila paper, and usually painted with opaque pigments of the desired hue to represent the actual linoleum colors. These colored designs are made in 9-inch repeats and the full scale of the finished fabric. For one who has made designs for mosaic and other tiling, for hardwood floors and parquetry, and for cork tiling, no further details as to actually drawing and rendering the design need be given.

21. Keeping in Touch with the Commercial Product.—There is a greater variety of patterns put out by manufacturers of inlaid linoleum than is the case with patterns for cork tiling. While the designer is expected to use originality in getting up designs, he will be assisted thereto by carefully studying patterns that are now on the market. This can be done by observing those actually in use, or those being displayed and sold in stores. The best way is to look over the sample books put out by manufacturers; these can readily be seen at carpet, furniture, or department stores.

TYPICAL DESIGNS FOR INLAID LINOLEUM

22. Specimens of Commercial Inlaid Linoleum Patterns.—Even though there are many limitations that restrict the designer in the use of other than simple geometric lines and forms, yet the pattern books of manufacturers of inlaid linoleums show evidences of the ingenuity of designers for this product. The four designs grouped in Fig. 8 give a general idea of the straight and curved forms that are most practicable for linoleums.   Squares, pentagons, hexagons, octagons (regular or irregular), rectangles, etc., of varying sizes and colors can be so

Fig. 8

skilfully combined as to give beautiful effects.   Fig. 8 is shown simply to give an introduction to the general line forms, straight and curved, that can be used most appropriately for this purpose, while Figs. 9, 10, and 11 are reproductions of standard linoleum patterns a little less than one fourth full size, 2 inches in the illustration representing 9 inches in the original.

23. Fig. 9 (*a*) shows a small scale reproduction of a simple but dignified, pattern, consisting of dark-brown rectangles, represented by dark gray in the figure, combined with light-brown squares of two sizes, represented by light gray. In the full-size pattern on the actual linoleum, the rectangles are $2\frac{1}{8}$ in.$\times 4\frac{1}{4}$ in., the small squares $2\frac{1}{8}$ in.$\times 2\frac{1}{8}$ in., and the large squares $4\frac{1}{4}$ in.$\times 4\frac{1}{4}$ in., thus showing that linoleum patterns are designed on a repeat basis of 9 inches square, as will be found by actually laying out such a pattern.

Fig. 9 (*b*) shows, in gray values and on a little less than one-fourth scale, another straight-line geometric pattern, consisting of dark-blue rectangles, represented by the dark gray, and dark-brown beveled-end oblongs represented by the medium gray, combined with cream-colored squares and octagons, represented by the light gray, making a harmonious color scheme. The dark-blue rectangles are $2\frac{1}{4}$ in.$\times \frac{11}{16}$ in., the dark-brown oblongs are $1\frac{3}{4}$ inches wide by $2\frac{5}{8}$ inches long, the small light squares are $1\frac{1}{4}$ in.$\times 1\frac{1}{4}$ in., and the large light octagons $3\frac{1}{8}$ in. $\times 3\frac{1}{8}$ in. Again, if this pattern is laid out full size, it will be shown that the pattern is designed upon a repeat basis of a 9-inch square.

24. The pattern for inlaid linoleum reproduced, on a small scale, in grays in Fig. 10 (*a*), is an artistic and serviceable one, based entirely on straight-line forms. It is so popular that it is made in various color schemes. One form of it shows the main background, the part outside the crosses, of a general light mottled olive-green, with the dark inside portions of the crosses in deep mottled blue-green surrounded by wide white outlines; the tilted squares, or diamond shapes, are a deep rich mottled red-brown. Another color scheme for this same pattern shows the general background in light mottled olive-green as before, with the dark inside portions of the crosses in deep rich mottled red-brown surrounded by wide light-cream outlines, the tilted squares being a rich mottled sap green. A third color scheme shows the background in a light mottled olive-green as before, with the dark inside portions of the crosses in a rich mottled blue surrounded by wide light-cream

(a)

(b)

Fig. 9

(a)

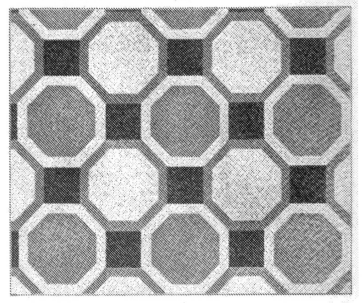

(b)

Fig. 19

(a)

(b)

Fig. 11

outlines, the tilted squares being a rich mottled green. It is this latter color scheme that was photographed and reproduced in grays in Fig. 10 (*a*).

The pattern reproduced on a small scale and in grays in Fig. 10 (*b*) shows, in the original, a very effective color scheme of two values of green on a light mottled écru background. The very dark mottled grays indicate a deep rich dark green, almost black, in the original; the medium values of mottled gray represent the rich mottled sap green in the original, and the light mottled grays represent the light mottled écru background.

25.   The pattern shown on a small scale in Fig. 11 (*a*) is another popular design issued in a variety of color schemes. One scheme shows a general background of pale green and pale cream checks alternating, the large interlaced figures being dark blue with a hollow square of black in the center, the small interlaced figures being in black. Another color scheme for this same pattern shows the background of pale green and pale cream checks alternating, as before, the large interlaced figures being sap green with a dark blue-black hollow square in the center, the small interlaced figures being in blue-black. A third color scheme for this same pattern shows the background of light-brown and pale-cream checks alternating, the large interlacing figures being a dark rich maroon-red with a dark hollow square in the center, the small interlaced figures being a rich black. It is this latter color scheme that was photographed and reproduced in grays in Fig. 11 (*a*).

The rather more free and graceful design reproduced on a small scale in grays in Fig. 11 (*b*) is unusually rich and attractive. The general background, shown by a very light mottled gray in the illustration, was a light mottled brown in the original. The outer and darker bands of the large tilted squares, and the horizontal and vertical members of the rosettes and their centers, shown in medium-dark gray in the figure, were a cool mottled dark green. The inside bands of the large tilted squares, as well as the left-oblique and right-oblique members of the rosettes, represented by a medium-light mottled gray

Fig 12

in the figure, were a warm dark mottled brown. The small dark solid squares, and the dark hollow rings at the center of each rosette, were a deep rich mottled red.

In Fig. 12 is reproduced full size, in grays, a portion of the original linoleum pattern shown on a small scale in Fig. 11 (b), and it demonstrates clearly the scale on which it is necessary to work when designing for this class of linoleums. The details should not be allowed to get smaller than the rosette in Fig. 12.

26. Application of Design Composition to Linoleum Designing.—One who has faithfully studied the Section of his Course devoted to design composition, and has prepared the various evolutions of design patterns based on squares, triangles, etc., using arbitrary motifs of lines, dots, masses, etc., will see how such practice work can be applied directly to linoleum designing. Without such preliminary training in design motifs and design composition, however, he would not be able to prepare attractive original designs for such a line of work.

PRINTED LINOLEUM

MANUFACTURE, USE, AND DESIGNING

27. Methods of Manufacture.—Printed linoleums are of the same physical composition as inlaid linoleums, but instead of the design patterns being produced by the methods that have been described for inlaid linoleum, the desired lines, tones, and masses are printed onto the surface of sheets of one-color linoleum. The process by which this printing is done is exactly the same as that by which printed oilcloth is produced, namely, from blocks or rollers. Therefore, a full description of this printing process will be deferred until the manufacture and designing of oilcloth is taken up.

28. Designs for Printed Linoleum.—In making designs for printed linoleum the same materials and methods of working are used as were previously described, but the scope of the designer's art is considerably enlarged and his ingenuity is given wider sway. The reason for this is that there no longer exists the mechanical restriction of the tile inlay process, but all the freedom of the printing process for producing patterns may be employed.

In color effects for printed linoleum design, the golden brown of the linoleum pulp is made use of very frequently as the fundamental tone of the design. This color can be imitated on the palette by a mixture of burnt sienna and Vandyke brown. Considerable variety of effect in color and in texture may be obtained by working over this ground color by hatchings or by representing on it geometrical forms or spots.

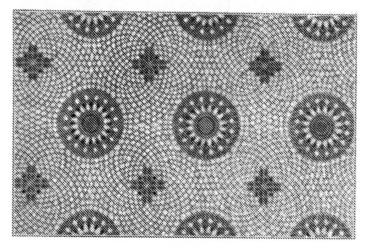

FIG. 13

In Fig. 13 is shown a popular pattern of printed linoleum that is composed entirely of lines and spots printed in five colors on a ground of linoleum color, which is, in reality, the color of the prepared and painted burlap. This background of linoleum color forms the principal color scheme in the circular spots and also shows around the smaller spots, which only partly cover the spaces formed by the intersections of the crossing lines.

Notwithstanding the fact that this pattern has been a good seller and therefore a profitable one to the manufacturer, it is best, as a general rule, to avoid preparing designs that introduce large circular forms. Such patterns are seldom popular with the public, and the fact that this pattern was popular is an exception to the general rule, and goes to show the uncertainty of popularity in designs.

OILCLOTH

CLASSIFICATION OF OILCLOTH

29. Definition of Term Oilcloth.—The term **oilcloth,** as used in this connection, refers to the oil-treated cloth, with patterns printed on it, that is used for a cheaper grade of floor coverings, as well as for wall coverings, table covers, etc. The term oilcloth will always refer only to the printed fabrics, and never to those in which the patterns are produced by the inlay method. There are three principal kinds of oilcloths: *floor oilcloth, table oilcloth,* and *wall oilcloth.*

30. Floor Oilcloth.—The oilcloths manufactured for floor coverings are the thickest and heaviest made, because they must be able to stand the hard usage of being constantly walked upon, and having furniture and other heavy objects pushed about over their surfaces, without the oilcloth becoming buckled up or wearing through. The patterns are printed on the surface. Method of manufacture will be discussed in detail later.

31. Table Oilcloth.—The oilcloths manufactured for use as table covers are made on the same methods as floor oilcloths, but are thinner and more flexible, because they need not stand such rough usage and because they must be draped over the edges of tables, as are other table cloths. Such oilcloths also bear decorative patterns printed on their surfaces.

32. Wall Oilcloth.—The wall oilcloths are intended to take the place of wallpapers where there is occasion for special sanitary methods being employed, as in hallways, kitchens, laundries, bathrooms, etc. The dirt or dust that accumulates on such oilcloth-covered walls can be wiped off with a damp cloth and thus they are always kept clean. Wall oilcloths, which are known under various trade names, are designed in a great variety of artistic patterns, resembling in every way high-grade wallpapers.

FLOOR OILCLOTH

MANUFACTURE

33. Composition and Sizes of Floor Oilcloth.—Strong canvas of an open weave, composed of flax and hemp, is the backing used for floor oilcloth, the canvas being woven in 6- and 8-yard widths on special looms. The lengths woven sometimes run as high as 100 to 113 yards.

A long section, say 100 feet, of this canvas backing is stretched out in a frame, coated with a "size" (composed largely of glue), and then smoothed with pumice stone. A thick paint, made of linseed oil and ocher, is then mixed and then several thick coats of it are laid, with a trowel, on each side of the canvas, each coat being treated with pumice stone. When the paint is dry, the treated cloth is ready to be taken to the printing room to have the patterns printed on its surface, after which it is put up in rolls of varying widths—6 feet, 9 feet, and larger sizes.

PRINTING FLOOR OILCLOTH

34. Preparing Printing Blocks.—The decorative patterns on floor oilcloth are printed from wooden or metal blocks, whose surfaces are coated with oil paint and then pressed down on the surface of the cloth by hand or by machinery, thus making the pattern.

In Fig. 14 are shown four blocks of an eight-color pattern. All the forms that are to be represented in one color in the finished design are traced on one block. The superfluous wood is then cut away, leaving the desired form in relief. This operation is then repeated on another block for another color, and so on throughout the pattern until each detail of the design is provided for.

Where the colors come together, the edges are apt to be blurred and ragged; therefore, **outline blocks** are prepared, usually in metal. These are printed last and even up the rough edges, as they contain only the outlines of the figures. They give a finish to all the forms and make them stand out sharply and clearly. It does not necessarily follow that these outline blocks are to print a different color from the colors printed on the design. Sometimes they make a black outline around certain details, and at other times they are the same color as one of the two adjacent forms that they even up. It is necessary, however, for the designer to bear in mind that an

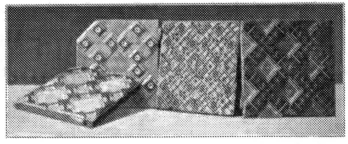

FIG. 14

outline block must be cut for every design of oilcloth, whether it is executed in two colors or ten. A two-color design requires three blocks, the third block being an outline block. Fig. 15 shows several examples of outline blocks.

The matrix, or mold, for these metal blocks is made by burning the lines, or forms, into a wooden block to a depth of about $\frac{3}{16}$ inch, by means of tools heated by electricity. Probably, in time, metal blocks will entirely supersede wooden ones. The matrix having been made, any number of castings can be taken from it, affording duplicate blocks for the different printing machines, and permitting the same pattern to be printed on different machines at the same time, while old or worn-out blocks can easily be replaced.

FIG. 15

35. Hand Printing.—When oilcloth is printed by hand, the design is usually manipulated by two men. The prepared jute burlap, which forms the backing, is rolled about a rod at one end of a long, low table beside which the two men stand. Immediately behind them is a rack to hold the different blocks required to print the pattern and slabs or pads containing the different colors. The color, which consists of oil paint, is spread evenly over the pad and the blocks are lifted from the rack and pressed on the color pad, and then transferred to the surface of the cloth and pressed firmly into place. In this manner, each successive color is applied to the design until all but the outline blocks have been used.

At this stage of the work, a plain **mash block,** as it is called, is laid over the surface of the oilcloth and heavy pressure exerted, which forces the design and color firmly against the fabric. The use of the mash block also tends to spread the color somewhat and destroy the evenness of the edges, but the application of the outline block trues up these edges and makes the forms clear-cut. On the sides of each block are fastened small wooden projections and a screw head to act as a guide in printing the pattern, so that each form will fall in its proper place.

When one set of impressions is complete, the fabric is moved forwards on the table a proper distance and the next section is printed; and so the operation is repeated over each section of cloth, until the end of the roll is reached. The printed cloth as it proceeds from the end of the table is carried over long, low drying racks, where it remains for several days until the surface is perfectly hard and dry.

36. Machine Printing.—Oilcloth printed by machinery is similar in process of manufacture to that made by hand, and there is so little difference in the quality of the finished fabric that it is likely that machine work will supersede hand work entirely in the near future.

In the oilcloth-printing machine, the material is, as before, passed over a long, low table with a metal top. Above this, the different printing blocks are set at regular intervals, each with a roller carrying color immediately beneath it. The rollers revolve constantly in a trough containing the paint, and as the blocks are raised from the cloth after impressing their design, these color rollers pass under them and distribute the color across their surfaces. While this is being done the fabric moves forwards the proper distance on the table, so that in each case the impression made by one block falls into position to receive the proper impression from the next block beyond. Thus, the blank fabric fed into one end of the machine from a large roll emerges from the other end entirely printed, the outline block being the last of the entire series, as in hand printing.

The blocks for machine printing are much larger than the blocks for hand printing, as they extend the full width of the material, and in this way very large quantities may be turned out in a very short time. Hand work, however, is still used where samples are being made up or new goods are being prepared for the market.

DESIGNING FLOOR OILCLOTH

37. Principles Governing Floor-Oilcloth Designs. The artistic principles governing designs for floor coverings apply to oilcloth quite as much as to mosaic tile work, parquetry, and linoleums. Oilcloth designing affords a most excellent opportunity for the application of these principles, as the limitations of its manufacture and the space usually alloted for the repeat, being simply 9 inches, tend to prevent the designer from producing coarse and sprawling patterns. This should be particularly considered, as the tendency among some carpet designers is far too strong in this direction.

The rules governing a design for floor covering are few. First of all, the design should be such that the floor appears flat. Any tendency to show an undulating or coarsely interwoven element is not only out of place, but annoying. Any attempt to show a modeled or rounded surface or lumpiness, or arrangement of colors that produces the effect that some parts are lower than others, is bad in design and will surely condemn the goods. In a floor covering, the feeling of stability is paramount, as one does not wish to feel that there are even imaginary obstacles in the way or unknown depths into which one might fall through jagged holes.

This principle is constantly violated by designers; therefore, there are frequently seen patterns of floor coverings representing large bunches of elaborately modeled flowers and leaves, or occasionally animals and landscapes, so realistically treated that one would almost suppose the designer was trying to impress the user and observer that they were intended to be hung on the wall as decorative elements rather than spread on the floor as utilitarian details. The effect that a pattern impresses on one in a dimly lighted room when he views it with partly closed eyes is almost identical with the constant impression that is unconsciously produced on us at all times when the object is in our full field of vision, even though we do not really look at the object at the time. If one walks across a dimly lighted room where one of these distracting patterns covers the floor and if in so doing he partly closes his eyes, a feeling of uneasiness and uncertainty immediately takes possession of him. The effect is not restful, and the pattern is therefore not a good one to have around. If this test be tried on such ideal floor coverings as the best oriental rugs or good mosaic and tile effects, there is not the slightest uneasiness; and, even though the pattern possesses decided contrasts in light and shade or color, there will be a feeling of restfulness as one melts into the other and produces a delightful unity of effect. Floor coverings that stand such a test as this also fill another and important office, namely, that of being a proper background for objects in the room, such as furniture, etc. Although these principles of good designs for floor coverings are most frequently violated by carpet designers, yet the designer of floor oilcloth needs also to observe care in applying them.

38. Color in Oilcloth Designs.—A most important part in the general effect is produced by **color**, although in the manufacture of oilcloths this detail is practically taken out of the designer's hands, as the manufacturer is likely to accept a design executed in one set of colors and print it in entirely different ones. There should, however, be a definite intention on the part of the designer in the color scheme of his design, and he must determine whether he wants to produce the general effect of a neutralized bloom or blending of all the colors, or to contrast some strongly with others; and the fact that the designer cannot control perfectly the colors that his design is to be printed in should make him all the more careful of making the design interesting in point of form and arrangement.

39. Classes of Designs.—The designer must be able to produce three classes of designs: (1) designs that are good floor covering, pleasing in form, and harmonious in the theory of design, to suit the public that is educated and knows what a design should be; (2) those where elaborate floral devices, in bunches or strewn in garlands, form the principal theme in loud and contrasting colors, that a certain number of unedu cated people can best get their money's worth in noise and brilliancy; and (3) a class of design for the great middle class that knows these florid and ostentatious designs are in bad taste, but that does not feel itself equal to the appreciation of the first lot and therefore must be content with simple, inoffensive patterns, whose main virtue lies in the fact that even though one cannot say they are good, he cannot say they are very bad.

The majority of oilcloth patterns are made by public design-ers or designers for the trade, a large number of whom are women. Some manufacturers employ special designers, but even in such cases they buy of outside designers when the designs suit their purpose. The price of an oilcloth design is standard—$10. If the manufacturer wants a design at all, he pays $10 for it, no matter whether the designer be a beginner or one well known. If the manufacturer does not want the design, he, of course, has his reasons for such choice, and will not take it at any price.

40. Sources of Ideas for Designs.—In historic styles of decorative art, much profit can be derived from a careful study of diaper patterns, particularly those characteristic of the Oriental and Gothic styles, as these styles are based on geometrical principles and therefore well suited, with slight modifications, to print in the geometrical manner required for oilcloth and linoleum.   It should be borne in mind, however, that in borrowing forms and ideas from historic styles one must be careful in his selection, as symbols and elements may be taken that are highly unsuited to the design of floor coverings. We find much in the history of decorative art associated with religious ideas, and throughout all time the greatest perfection in ornament has been in some way associated with some intellectual conception of a religious idea.   For instance, it is a well-known fact that the cross emblematic of Christianity enters largely into historic wall decorations in the Gothic style.   This should be most carefully used in oilcloth design, and must surely be of such a form as not to suggest the slightest symbolism, for one large class of buyers would reject it as a symbol of Christianity, while another large class would reject it as too sacred to walk on.

It is always possible to create new designs based on well-known arrangements of geometrical lines, and the combination of geometrical forms and severely conventionalized floral forms may produce an endless variety of design combined with a large degree of originality.

Fig. 16 is a design, by a student, based on simple tangent circles cleverly broken by severely conventionalized leaf forms. It requires but little study to observe that this design is strongly Gothic in feeling and but a variation of many Gothic all-over patterns exhibited in the mural paintings of that period.

Close adherence to geometrical all-over patterns will prevent the student from getting far astray in oilcloth design. Sprawling scrolls and attempts at naturalism should always be avoided, for even though one of these designs is occasionally put out by a manufacturer, they are all bad for a student to strive for as they are inappropriate and inartistic; and, despite the vulgarity of public taste, the proper and artistic forms are the ones that survive.   Naturalistic renderings of floral and vegetable forms suggest a delicacy of handling entirely out of harmony with printing in heavy oil paints.   The principal aim of the purchaser is to secure a design that is interesting and will wear well; the finer the lines the more the design will be affected by wear, and the longer the design wears the more popular will be its sale; therefore, the more successful will be the designer.

Adaptations of the forms so popular in L'Art Nouveau have found their way into oilcloth design, but have not attained any great popularity in this field.   It is probable that this is

FIG. 16

due to the fact that the character of this style is not thoroughly understood by the public, and that the oilcloth designer has not been able to reconcile it properly with the limitations of oilcloth manufacture.

41.   Originality an Essential.—All designers should avoid the error of presenting to the manufacturer a design that is partly copied or suggested from the design of some other manufacturer, or from sample books. The experienced manufacturer will detect the fraud at once. He is experienced in buying designs and has devoted considerable time to the study of designs shown in the sample books of his rivals. He has watched the market to know what designs are good sellers and what are poor ones, and if he decides to deliberately copy a popular design of some other manufacturer, he will do it, with a perfectly clear conscience, by buying a sample of the goods themselves and handing it to his block cutter to vary sufficiently to make the design his own property. The manufacturer, therefore, will not buy designs that suggest in the slightest degree some other popular pattern. It is necessary to point this fact out very strongly, because young designers very frequently present for sale to manufacturers designs that have already been on the market or are but a slight variation from an existing pattern.

42. Importance of Satisfying Public Taste.—Widely different patterns frequently attain remarkable successes and sell in larger quantities than other designs that are on the market at the same time, thus necessitating the manufacture of millions of yards of one pattern throughout a period of several years. It is naturally the desire of manufacturers to become possessors of patterns that please the public in this manner, as it simplifies matters for them materially. It is the aim of every designer to prepare patterns that will be good sellers, and to avoid submission of patterns that are not likely to sell well. The successful oilcloth designers whose goods are most sought after are those whose patterns most frequently attract the public and cause a sufficient run of one kind of goods to make it worth while to buy the designs and prepare them for printing.

Designers, manufacturers, and salesmen all admit that they have never been able to analyze the public taste sufficiently to determine just what the qualities are that cause a pattern to be popular. Fortunately, however, for the designer, one thing is certain, and that is that the public is very fastidious and demands a large number of designs from which to select, and consequently the manufacturer is making up new designs and getting out additional sample books every season. The poor sellers are withdrawn from the market and the good sellers are pushed, and the spaces in the sample books left by the removed examples are filled with new designs that the manufacturer hopes will bring better returns. Occasionally, the same pattern is printed in many different colors, in order that the public may not be limited in their choice to one scheme of coloring.

43.   Preparing Designs.—Designs should be made on a good quality of white drawing paper, and should exactly repeat within a 9-inch square. There may be more than one repeat in this square, but no matter how many there are the above conditions must be fulfilled, or the design cannot be reproduced. The drawing paper must be carefully stretched, and when the design is entirely completed, the paper should be cut from the board, leaving a 1-inch margin or blank on the lower and right-hand sides, but should be trimmed close to the pattern on the other two sides. This is done in order that the prospective purchaser may view the pattern in his double mirror, which shows a complete set of four repeats surrounded by a white border.

Every designer should have a similar mirror for testing his patterns. It consists of two pieces of looking glass arranged at right angles, so that when the design is placed in the angle it may be seen repeated in each direction. The mirror is also useful for the construction of certain geometrical units used in reproduction, as a number of remarkable forms can be obtained by arranging a few abstract forms in the angle between the two glasses.

The colors used in designs may be checked off on the margin at the upper right-hand side, but the little blocks containing these color checks should be free from the edges of the design. A ¼-inch to ½-inch block for each color is sufficient, and black and white count as colors and must appear in the scale.

Usually, one color is employed for the outline, but any color or black or white may be used.   If two colors are used in the outline, let it be for some good reason and explain the reason, or the block cutter will probably reduce the design to one color in order to save the cost of the extra block.   The outline is

FIG. 17

necessary to clean up the printing, and it frequently helps the appearance of the design on paper.   Therefore, in finishing up a design, care should be taken as to the color and placing of the outlines, in order to get the best effects possible.

44.   Observing Care in Outlining.—In Fig. 17 is shown a design, drawn by a student, that is not properly outlined.

The large circles are outlined but the cross form is not, and in Fig. 18 the simple rosette in the center is outlined, but the interlacing circles are not. Where it is desirable to avoid the effect of an outline, it can be applied in the same color as the form around which it is placed, thereby fulfilling the printer's requirements of a clean edge but not appearing in the finished goods.

FIG. 18

In Fig. 19, however, it will be observed that all the outlining is properly considered and that each color in juxtaposition with another color is separated therefrom by a black outline.

The outline should be firm and well considered. It must be neither thin and wiry nor thick and clumsy so as to be misconstrued into a detail of design. Oilcloth designs do not admit of minute details. Every element introduced must be

large enough to admit of a strong outline, or it cannot be properly printed.   However, where designs are made for inlaid
linoleum, outlines are useless and out of place.

45. Economy in Use of Colors.—In all printed fabrics,
whether wallpapers, oilcloths, or linoleums, the manufacturer
desires to get a maximum effect with a minimum cost of pro-

FIG. 19

duction, and as each additional block means additional cost
it is certainly important that as few colors as possible be made
to serve the given purpose.   All other things being equal, the
designer that can handle his designs in four colors and produce
the appearance of six by skilful repetition or juxtaposition in
dots and lines stands the best chance of disposing of his work.
On the other hand, if a manufacturer takes strongly to a design

he is likely to spare no pains or expense to reproduce it satisfactorily, even making two blocks at times for the printing of one color if, by so doing, a better effect can be obtained.

46. Some Amateur Designs Analyzed.—Figs. 17, 18, and 19 were made by students working on practically the same problem; that is, an oilcloth design based on circles in combination with other geometrical forms. These three designs illustrate how three different designers can draw three separate ideas from the same material, and it is not unreasonable to say that the relative value of these designs is exactly proportional to the amount of study and brain work the designer has put into his drawing.

In Fig. 17 the designer has attacked the problem by swinging together a number of circles to cover his space and filling in the space that they failed to cover with a simple geometrical form. He did not consider that the average manufacturer is opposed to designs based on coarse circles, and therefore the circular element in his design is the most prominent.

In Fig. 18 the designer has evidently considered the fact that the manufacturer is opposed to circular forms and has endeavored to disguise his circular forms by breaking them with simple interlacings where they intersect. He has failed, however, to disguise them satisfactorily, because the circular forms on this design are red and the background against which they appear is green. By this strong contrast the conspicuousness of the form is increased, and although the design is better and shows more care and thought than Fig. 17, it is still too evident that the circle is the fundamental principle of its construction.

In Fig. 19 the considerations are entirely different; the designer has evidently carefully thought over his problem. According to the problem, he must use circles and he may use other geometrical forms. He knows that the manufacturer is opposed to circular forms, and attempts to disguise them. Large circles tangent to the small circles are used, with intervening spaces filled with rectangular forms, the outlines of the rectangular forms being composed of arcs of broken circles.

Everywhere throughout the design is the evidence of variety and contrast of curve, so that the attention is distracted from the circular forms in the general effect of the whole. Having accomplished this, the designer has evidently given considerable thought to his color combinations and has been careful that while the adjacent colors harmonize satisfactorily they do not contrast so strongly as to give undue evidence to the predominance of the circle; and where the circular form is conspicuous, it is not too large nor so prominent as to dominate the design.

It is interesting also to note in connection with these three designs the fact that Figs. 17 and 18 are not properly outlined, while Fig. 19 is. The designer that best understood the conditions of the problem was the one that was most careful to execute his design not only in accordance with the limitations of the problem, but in full accordance with the limitations of the printing machinery and the demands of the manufacturer.

47. Requirements for Producing Salable Designs. A design, in order to be salable, must be thoroughly practical and must contain some good points of its own aside from its practicality, or the manufacturer will not go to the expense of having the blocks cut. An infinite amount of variation can be played on certain geometrical forms that have been made use of throughout all history for surface decoration; but it should be borne in mind that many of these have been used so often, with slight variations, that they have become thoroughly exhausted, and the designer should not be despondent if some of his first patterns submitted to the manufacturer were rejected on the ground that the same pattern had been manufactured before.

A design that may be entirely original with the designer may be based on certain geometrical lines that make its general form so familiar to the manufacturer that the effect on him, whether right or wrong, is precisely the same as though he actually had seen it before.

The successful oilcloth designer must be wide awake. He must be able to turn over every kind of decorative form in his mind and decide if they can be applied successfully to oilcloth, and if so, how. He must understand well the principles of his craft, keep constantly in touch with the best things that are being done, follow carefully the public taste and keep in advance of it. He also must not be led into the following of the style or manner of other designers because they are successful, for the details of all their designs that cause them to be successful are the only details of those designs that cannot be copied; that is, the individuality of the man that made them. It is the individuality of the designer that characterizes his work, in the same manner as it is the individuality of a person that characterizes his handwriting. The same idea can be conveyed by several people in several styles of writing or methods of expression, but one of these persons will express it better, write it better, or state it more clearly than the others, and it is the individuality of this person that impresses itself in his writings.

In the same manner, several designers may take the same idea and work it into a design and get several different results, one of which will be better than the others. It is the individuality of this one designer that has brought his design into prominence compared with the others, and one cannot copy that design, and vary it somewhat in order to disguise the theft, without destroying the originality of the original designer and substituting the personality of the copyist, thereby probably destroying the popular value of the design itself. A person that is weak enough to copy the design of another, rather than invent work of his own, will impress his weakness on his copy of the design to such an extent as to neutralize entirely the strength of the original. Therefore, it should ever be borne in mind, to create all designs from original motives and to carry them out without thought of other existing patterns.

TYPICAL FLOOR-OILCLOTH DESIGNS

48. Specimens of Commercial Floor-Oilcloth Patterns.—Sample books of floor oilcloths, as put out by various factories and to be seen at any dealer's shop, show a great variety

(a) (b)

(c) (d)

Fig. 20 40

Fig. 21

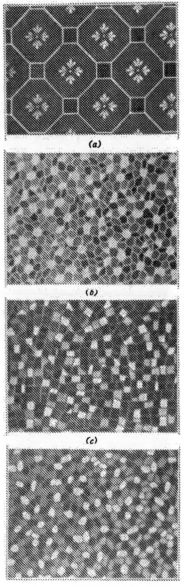

(a)

(b)

(c)

Fig. 22

of styles, from the simplest diaper pattern in two or three colors to elaborate floral scrolls in imitation of wallpaper and carpet designs, printed in six or eight colors, as clumsy and ungraceful as they are inappropriate.

In Fig. 20 four of these elaborate patterns are shown, but it should be borne in mind that their appearance is greatly improved by photographic reproduction, as the varying contrasts of color and shiny surface of the paint are thereby lost. There is no doubt that the simple diaper patterns shown in Fig. 21 are far more suitable for this class of work than the elaborations shown in Fig. 20.

The simple mosaic work represented in Fig. 22 (b), (c), and (d) is a very popular style of design; this illustration shows what a great variety in so simple a pattern can be obtained by the judicious use of proper colors. Of these designs (a) and (c) were executed by Philadelphia manufacturers, but (b) is the work of a British firm.

Almost every manufacturer runs a pattern similar to these, for the reason that it is one of the best "sellers" ever produced, and for a similar reason the simple tile pattern illustrated in Fig. 22 (c) can be found among the products of nearly all manufacturers. It is a well-known fact in the trade that whenever a given pattern attains an unusual sale, all the enterprising manufacturers will copy it, making but slight modifications, in order to each get his share of the trade.

The oilcloth designer never knows when his pattern is going to make a hit. He may be well pleased with his design and feel that it is bound to meet the public approval, but his opinion must not only be ratified by the public but also by the majority of the buyers in the manufacturing establishment where he proposes to sell his design, as every person connected with the manufacture of the goods, from the superintendent to the order clerk, will have a personal opinion as to the value of the design and prophesy its success or failure according to his own ideas.

TABLE OILCLOTH

MANUFACTURER

49. Composition and Sizes of Table Oilcloth.—The general principle upon which table oilcloth is made is the same as that for the manufacture of floor oilcloth. The basis, or backing, is a well-woven cloth, and the pattern is printed in oil colors on the upper surface. However, table oilcloth is much thinner, lighter, and more flexible than floor oilcloth because no thick coats of linseed oil and ocher are applied to the cloth, the weave itself is finer and closer meshed, and the oil coating is given only to the upper side, the surface on which the pattern is to be printed.

The chief characteristic of table oilcloth is that the surface is glazed with a waterproof oil preparation, completely covering the meshes of the woven cloth. This gives an excellent surface on which to print the pattern in oil pigments, and makes the cloth waterproof on one side, having a surface that can be washed without injuring the cloth or the surface decoration.

Table oilcloth is usually made up into rolls of convenient widths. A width of 5 feet is considered a good size because it can be most advantageously adapted for table sizes.

PRINTING TABLE OILCLOTH

50. The Printing Rollers.—Table oilcloth consisting of individual repeating designs that are on a comparatively small scale is usually printed from rollers after the same process as machine-printed floor oilcloth that is printed from rollers. The process of transferring the design from the designer's colored drawing to the rollers may be the zinc etching process, as in line illustrating work, or it may be by lithography, the patterns being transferred to aluminum sheets that are curved into cylindrical form to fit the rollers. There is no need to discuss in detail the processes used for transferring the patterns to the rollers; it is sufficient for the designer to know that the printing process is such that he may go into as much detail as he wants to in making his designs. As will be shown by the specimens of table oilcloth reproduced in following pages, patterns, and even pictorial work, including details on a very small scale, may be used in design. Of course the details must not be too small, or composed of lines that are too fine, for they would then not stand the wear and tear of ordinary usage.

DESIGNING TABLE OILCLOTH

51. Principles Governing the Designs.—Much of that which has already been said regarding designing for floor oilcloth will apply to the designing of table oilcloth. The design must be so made that its details make the surface look flat, and not undulating. The feeling of stability and evenness must be preserved on a table-oilcloth surface so that objects will not appear to roll or fall off the table. Further, the rules of good color harmonization should be observed, for, by doing so, beautifully rich effects can be produced.

In this class of work there exists for the designer the same necessity for keeping in touch with what the public likes, and therefore buys, as in the case of floor oilcloths. A simple way to do this is to make the rounds of shops and stores where table oilcloth is shown, look over the patterns the dealer keeps in stock, and inquire from the salesman what are the ones that sell the best. Another method is to borrow from the salesmen in these shops or stores any copies of the manufacturer's sample books of table oilcloth he may be willing to lend, or perhaps give, and to find out from the salesman, the dealer, or perhaps from the manufacturer himself, which designs are popular and which are poor sellers.

52. Preparing the Designs.—In preparing designs for table oilcloth the same considerations apply as when making designs for floor oilcloth. First of all, the demand must be studied and consideration given to the classes of designs that have been used and are being used; those that are pleasing artistically and suit people of good taste; those that are designed to suit the taste of the uncultured mass who like bright, gaudy effects, with large floral groups; and those that will suit the vast number of middle-class people who know that crude and gaudy designs are out of place as table coverings, but who do not care for nor appreciate the more appropriately designed patterns.

Sources of ideas for table oilcloth designs may be the diaper repeats of the Gothic or other historic styles, or from any geometric repeating pattern. However, in table oilcloth the stiff and formal geometric repeating pattern is frequently varied and its monotony reduced by having a border composed of leaves, flowers, etc., sometimes conventionalized and sometimes naturalistic. Actual pictorial scenes are also sometimes used, although the taste of such usage is questionable. Specimens of table oilcloth designs of these various kinds are shown in Figs. 23 to 27, inclusive.

The actual preparation of the design, making the drawing, coloring it, etc., is along the same lines as described for floor oilcloth, white water-color paper, properly mounted or stretched, and water color pigments being used. The adherence to the 9-inch square when designing repeats need not be absolutely strict and rigid, as was the case in designing floor oilcloths, but if the designer becomes accustomed to making his designs about

9 in. ×9 in. he will find that such a size is a good one to show the effect of the pattern when completed.

The matter of outlining need not be so seriously considered when designing table oilcloths because the process by which the drawing is transferred to the printing rolls is different from that of producing floor oilcloth, and greater latitude in patterns is therefore allowed, as can be seen by looking at the specimens reproduced in Figs. 23 to 27. However, since the general tendency of the patterns is to become smaller in scale on table oilcloth than on floor oilcloth, great accuracy in drawing and rendering must be employed. Further, there exists here, also, the same necessity for economy in the use of colors. Most frequently the effects in table oilcloth are secured by printing the design in a dark color on a light-colored ground; as blue on white, dark brown on light brown, dark red on light red, and these limitations should be taken into consideration when making the designs.

TYPICAL DESIGNS FOR TABLE OILCLOTH

53. Specimens of Commercial Table-Oilcloth Patterns.—The makers of table oilcloth put out sample books every year or season, that show hundreds of varieties of patterns. Reproductions of some of these patterns are shown in Figs. 23, 25, and 26, and in Figs. 24 and 27 the pattern in each case is reproduced almost full size to show the scale upon which such designs are made.

54. Large Floral Patterns.—Floral patterns, particularly if the arrangement be naturalistic, do not seem to be the most appropriate kind of decoration for a table surface, because one instinctively hesitates to set heavy objects, or objects that may be tipped over, upon floral forms. However, a large class of people are attracted by such patterns and want them, and since the demand is for such patterns the manufacturers make them up for table oilcloth.

Four such designs, on a somewhat reduced scale, that is, slightly less than one-fourth the size of original, are shown in grays in Fig. 23. Whether or not one concedes the appropriateness of such patterns for table-oilcloth use, he must admit

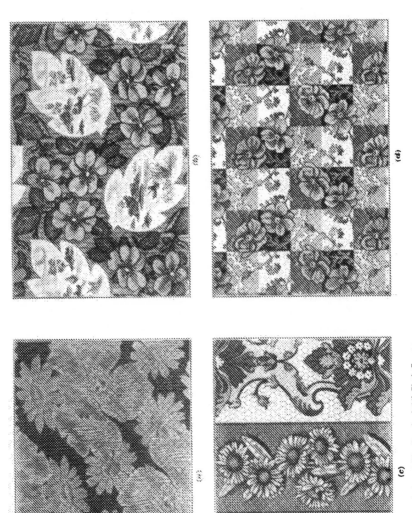

47

(a)

(b)

(c)

(d)

"*Meritas." Used by permission of The Standard Oil Cloth Company.*

that they are artistic; that is, well drawn and designed, and (in the originals) attractive in color. The large floral forms in view (a), were, in the original, red-yellow and pink, on a deep rich red background, giving a very pleasing effect. In view (b) is shown in grays a design where, in the original, little land-scapes in varying shades of yellow and brown on large leaf forms alternate with pink and red floral forms on a background of brown leaves and bands. This design, while not what the ultra-artistic person might select, is nevertheless very popular; and the designer should be familiar with just such designs if he wants to keep in touch with the public taste and public demand. In view (c) is shown in gray an attractive, although somewhat gaudy, design introducing, in the original, floral forms in yel-lows and browns, some naturalistic and some conventionalized, on wide brown and écru stripes in the background, these stripes themselves being decorated. In view (d) the design repro-duced in grays shows the wild rose floral pattern somewhat naturalistically placed over the rectangles of different tone values, and which in the original were écru, light brown, medium brown, and very deep brown. These rectangles tend to draw the floral pattern together and give it more stability, thus making it the most appropriate of the four in Fig. 23 for table-oilcloth use.

In Fig. 24 is shown, at almost full size, a full-page illustra-tion of the pattern shown reduced in Fig. 23 (d) so that there may be seen not only the scale at which such designs are usually drawn, but also the method of rendering the lines, dots, and masses composing such a design.

55. Small Geometric Repeating Patterns.—Without question the most appropriate patterns for table oilcloth are those consisting of small geometric repeats. These repeats form an even surface all over the table, there is no feeling of unrest and instability, and the general effect is one of dignity. It might be said that a table oilcloth would be just as useful without any pattern on its surface. To some extent this is true, and there are made table oilcloths in pure white, cream, and other solid colors. There are also table oilcloths made with a marbled pattern; that is, a white ground with irregular

"Meritas." *Used by permission of The Standard Oil Cloth Company.*

FIG. 24

lines running over it, in imitation of the black, gray, blue, etc. veinings of a marble slab. But, the purpose of the small geometric repeating pattern is not only to be decorative but to prevent occasional slight soiling of the cloth from being too noticeable.

Specimens of small geometric repeating patterns for table oilcloth are shown in Fig. 25 (a), (b), (c), and (d). These four patterns are shown with the details full size, and the designs are therefore shown exactly as they are in the oilcloths themselves, except that they are in grays instead of colors. In view (a) is shown a design which, in the original, was in blue lines and checks on a white ground. The lines, etc. are all very simple, but the spacing is so well thought out that the effect is light and delicate. In view (b) is shown another simple design based on small squares formed by double-ruled horizontal lines crossed by double-ruled vertical ones. In the original the center of each spot was formed by four solid blue squares, an effect of vignetting being given to the spot by using dots and outlines of decreasing weight and size in the squares that surround the four heavy blue ones. In (c) is a beautiful example of a simple geometric pattern consisting of horizontal lines crossed by vertical lines, resulting in squares and rectangles, which, in the original, were filled in with dark-blue and light-blue values. The small geometric repeating pattern shown in (d) is somewhat more elaborate than those in (a), (b), and (c), but the effect is rich and the pattern very serviceable. The original showed rich dark-green spots on a light-green background.

It must always be remembered that the same pattern is used by manufacturers in various color schemes. For instance, the pattern shown in (d) is made not only in dark green and light green, but also in black, dark red, and white; and in dark brown, light green, and cream. Considerable skill may be employed by the designer in devising different sets of color schemes for the same pattern.

56. Patterns With Fields and Borders.—Inasmuch as the pattern of a table cloth receives a certain degree of finish

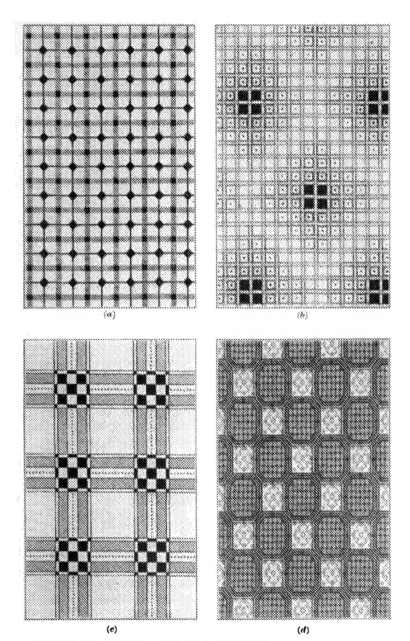

(a)

(b)

(c)

(d)

"Meritas." *Used by permission of The Standard Oil Cloth Company.*

FIG. 25

if it possesses a border, like a woven table cloth, a rug, etc., manufacturers use designs for table oilcloth showing fields and borders. Four such designs, on a scale about one-fourth the size of the original, are shown in Fig. 26. In view (a) is shown an exceedingly artistic design for a field and border, very suggestive of a damask table cloth. A design of this kind requires the exercise of the very best artistic talent. In view (b) is shown another artistic design, in which the field repeating pattern is particularly clever in design. In view (c) is a design in which the field is perfectly plain, and the border is in very close imitation of a lace curtain border. In view (d) is a clever design showing a field designed on a geometric repeat, the border being strong and bold.

In Fig. 27 is a full-size reproduction of the pattern in (d) of Fig. 26, showing exactly the scale on which such a pattern is designed, and just how the effects are secured by tones, dots, lines, etc. It should be studied carefully, noting the skill and accuracy displayed in the drawing, the beautiful gradations of tone values, and the general artistic character of the design. Thus there is illustrated the necessity for the designer of oilcloth to observe care in planning his design composition and to use the greatest skill and accuracy in drawing and rendering the details of the design.

The examples shown should thoroughly convince any one that oilcloth designing, far from being simple child's-play in lines and squares, offers opportunities for the use of the highest degree of artistic talent and creative ability.

WALL OILCLOTH

MANUFACTURE

57. Composition and Sizes of Wall Oilcloth.—The method of manufacturing wall oilcloth, by coating one side of durable linen or other fabric with an oil composition, is so like the process of making table oilcloth that no additional data need be given as to the method of its production. The weight

(a)　　　　(b)

(c)　　　　(d)

"Meritas."　*Used by permission of The Standard Oil Cloth Company.*

Fig. 26　　　　§ 17　289

FIG. 27

§ 17   289

and flexibility of wall oilcloth are practically the same as those of table oilcloth.

A great deal of wall oilcloth is highly glazed on the one side, and is, of course, washable, being made in patterns suggestive of tiles and used for bathrooms, halls, restaurants, etc. But not all wall oilcloth is glazed; much of it is finished in a dull, cloth-like surface, its patterns being as highly artistic as the highest grades of wallpaper, but with a surface that can be cleaned just as readily as a glazed surface, because the coating is an oil preparation. Either the glazed or the dull surface makes an excellent surface to receive the printed patterns, produced as previously described.

Wall oilcloth is usually made up in rolls 12 yards long and 48 inches wide. The designer should bear these dimensions in mind, particularly the width, when making his designs.

PRINTING WALL OILCLOTH

58. Fine Details Possible.—Wall oilcloth is printed from rollers by methods similar to those used for table oilcloth, and there are no technical difficulties to prevent the designer from using small and finely detailed ornament if occasion requires. The possibilities in this direction can be seen from the typical examples of wall oilcloth shown in Fig. 28.

DESIGNING WALL OILCLOTH

59. Principles Governing the Designs.—The principles to be borne in mind when preparing designs for wall oilcloth differ in marked degree from those governing the designing of floor or table oilcloth. There no longer exists the necessity, nor the desire, for severely geometric repeating patterns such as are used on floors, the chief consideration being to prepare patterns for wall surface decoration; that is, patterns that are seen vertically.

In making designs for patterns for wall oilcloth, the simplest are those tile-like patterns used for walls of bathrooms, kitchens, etc. These patterns are used for such purposes because they imitate real tiling. Rectangles, squares, etc., in brown or blue on white, sometimes relieved by leaf or rosette forms, are standard patterns for this class of wall oilcloth.

Aside from the simple patterns just described, the designer may indulge to the fullest extent his artistic tendencies and training, in both drawing and coloring, in the preparation of all-over repeating patterns. This will be seen from the specimens illustrated in Figs. 28, 29, 30, and 31.

60. Preparing the Designs.—First of all, it is necessary to know the nature of the designs demanded by the public. The best way to learn this, is to see what the stores and shops are selling, particularly to look over the sample books of designs put out by the manufacturers, which any dealer will be quite willing to show. The purpose in such investigation is not to copy existing designs, but to find out which designs are popular, and which are not and therefore are not wanted by manufacturers. The designer then comes to realize that there are designs on the market made to suit people of no particular taste or culture, but who buy freely; designs of a higher grade for people of culture; and designs for the persons of average culture; that is, designs that are not extremely high in artistic worth, nor yet very bad.

Sources from which ideas for designs may be secured have already been discussed in previous Sections, when design motifs, design composition, space filling, and historic styles, etc. were treated. The methods of designing repeating patterns based on conventionalized floral or other designs have been thoroughly explained; it is, therefore, only necessary to apply them to all-over patterns for wall surfaces, having due regard to the differing requirements of public taste.

The actual making and coloring of the designs for wall oilcloth offers no new feature. Water colors on stretched white water-color paper are employed. No particular restrictions are offered as to the length and the width of the repeat, except that it must be remembered that the wall oilcloth is usually made up in a 48-inch-width roll or strip, and the lateral repeats must conform thereto.

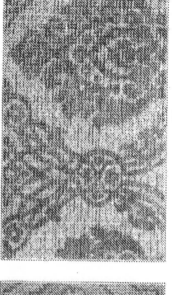

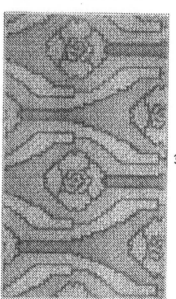

(d)

(e)

"Sanitas." Used by permission of The Standard Oil Cloth Company.

FIG. 28

55

The colors for wall oilcloth designs must be used with economy. Usually, one dark color is printed over a lighter ground to get the effect. Thus, if the design is limited to the two colors it will be more likely of sale than if rendered in more than two colors, in which case the manufacturer would probably have to transpose the design to a two-color scheme.

TYPICAL DESIGNS FOR WALL OILCLOTH

61. Specimens of Commercial Wall-Oilcloth Patterns.—While access may usually be had to manufacturers' or dealers' sample books, in which are shown scores of patterns for wall oilcloth, it will be helpful to have some specimens of patterns reproduced in these pages for immediate reference. Such patterns are shown in Figs. 28 and 30; and to show the scale and method of rendering, one design from each figure is shown full size in Figs. 29 and 31, respectively.

62. Decorative Patterns for Dull-Surface Fabric. Beautiful effects in decorative all-over patterns are secured on the dull-surface wall oilcloth, opportunity being given to show all softness of line and mass that is usually shown on decorative wallpapers and fabrics.

Four patterns for such decorative wall oilcloth, printed in grays and considerably reduced in scale, are shown in Fig. 28. A close inspection of them will show the degree of elaborateness possible. In the originals, the effects are produced by two colors, a dark one on top of a light one. In the original of the design in view (*a*) was shown a pattern in dark brown on light brown that is distinctly modern, based on Austrian secession motifs, interest being added by making the down strokes connecting the spots somewhat slanting, instead of perfectly vertical. The original of the design in view (*b*) is a delicate pattern of dark brown and salmon on a buff background, the *Art Nouveau* influence being clearly shown in the growth of the stems and the shape of the spots containing the leaves and the flowers. In the original of the design in view (*c*) was shown a severely conventionalized arrangement in dark rich tones,

"*Sanitas.*"   *Used by permission of The Standard Oil Cloth Company.*

Fig. 29

over which was printed, in black, a network of lines, thus giving a tapestry effect. Design (d) was a beautifully rich design, based on a Gothic diaper repeat, that is suggestive of a woven fabric or wallpaper pattern. A pattern such as this may be made in dark red on light red, dark green on light green, dark brown on light brown, brown on light buff, etc., thus giving a variety of rich effects with the same pattern.

In Fig. 29 is shown a reproduction, full size, of a portion of the pattern shown in Fig. 28 (d), thus giving an idea as to the scale upon which such details may be designed, and it should be studied with great care. The system on which the large details of such a pattern repeat can be readily understood by any one who has studied the theory of repeating patterns.

63. Patterns for Glazed Tile-Effect Fabric.—The purpose of glazed wall oilcloth is to imitate, and to a degree take the place of, real glazed tiling, for use in bathrooms, halls, kitchens, etc. Many of the designs for this purpose are therefore made in imitation of tiles—square, rectangular, etc. However, liberties are taken with the actual tile sizes, the shapes on the wall-oilcloth patterns sometimes being made smaller and being relieved by floral spot designs introduced symmetrically.

In Fig. 30 (a) is shown a plain rectangular tile pattern in blue and white, with little vertical spot ornaments introduced as shown, which would be very suitable for a bathroom. In view (b) is shown a checker effect in blue and white of large squares, alternating decorative and plain, that would be suitable for a kitchen wall. Note that, although the general plan of repeat of the squares is geometric, the rosette decoration in the darker square consists of a cleverly designed conventionalized floral motif based upon the acanthus, in the center, surrounded at the four corners by smaller floral forms. In (c) the tile arrangement is cleverly devised vertically and horizontally so as to form or surround a small square, which is then filled with conventionalized leaf and berry ornament, thus making a dark spot of accent. In (d) is shown another tile effect based on the geometric repeat, every alternate square

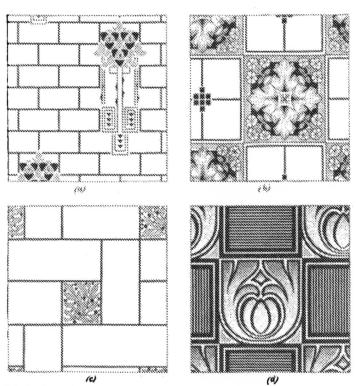

(a)   *(b)*

(c)   *(d)*

"*Sanitas.*"   *Used by permission of The Standard Oil Cloth Company.*

FIG. 30

FIG. 31

(in checker effect) being decorated by a curved line motif showing the *Art Nouveau* influence. In the original of this pattern only the dark blue parts are glazed, the lighter parts being of dull surface. This alternating of glazed and unglazed surfaces produces a satiny effect that is very pleasing.

In Fig. 31 a portion of the pattern shown on a small scale in Fig. 30 (*d*) is reproduced full size, so that the scale upon which such designs are drawn may readily be seen, as well as the method of drawing the lines dots, and tones to get the effects.

Besides the illustrations of full-size sections of linoleums and oilcloths reproduced in these pages, it is well, as has been explained before, to look over the sample books of linoleum, cork tiling, floor oilcloth, table oilcloth, and wall oilcloth in department stores, furniture stores, carpet and rug stores, etc. These books are accessible to any one who courteously requests permission to look them over, and a knowledge of their contents will materially assist the designer to prepare practical and salable designs for these purposes.

LINOLEUM AND OILCLOTH DESIGNING EXERCISES

GENERAL INFORMATION

64. Required Work in Linoleum and Oilcloth Designing.—The student will now be asked to prepare original designs for linoleums, cork tiling, and oilcloths, to serve as a test of his understanding of the requirements of this line of work, and by practice to prepare him for doing commercial designing in this field. Such original designs he will have no difficulty in making, if he follows out the directions for methods of working as given in this Section, and observes the requirements as explained.

These original designs are, as before, to be arranged in the form of drawing plates to be submitted to the Schools for examination and help.

65. Character of the Drawing Plates.—These drawing plates will be six in number, the first one requiring original designs for cork tiling; the second, a design for inlaid linoleum; the third, for printed linoleum; the fourth, for floor oilcloth; the fifth, for tile oilcloth; and the sixth for wall oilcloth. Each plate is to be about 10 inches wide and 15 inches high. With the exception of Plate 1, on which there are to be two designs, each plate is to contain one design full size; that is, a 9-inch square, which is the repeat size for linoleum and oilcloth designs. This will leave a narrow side margin of ½ inch, but rather wide top and bottom margins of 3 inches. However, to make these top and bottom margins appear less awkward the design may, if desired, be extended upwards and downwards over the edges of the 9-inch square, thus showing more of the repeat.

The original designs on the plates are to be made in colors and with great exactness; therefore, a rather smooth watercolor paper should be used. Water colors should be used for the rendering.

The plates, as before, are to be prepared and submitted to the Schools one by one for examination, the student working on the subsequent plate while the submitted plate is being examined and returned to him.

PLATE 1

66. Exercise A, Plate 1.—In the upper half of the 10-inch by 15-inch sheet arranged vertically, lay out a rectangle about 8 inches wide by 6 inches high, and fill it with an outline pattern, or groundwork, like that used for the design for square cork tiling in Fig. 3. This may be done by ruling horizontal lines at distances of ¼ inch, crossed by vertical lines at distances of ¼ inch, thus making quarter-inch squares over the entire 8-inch by 6-inch rectangle.

Upon these squares as a groundwork make an original design for a floor arrangement of square cork tiling showing corner, parts of top and left-side border, and the filling. Use three of the colors allowable for cork tiling, as explained in the text, and render carefully.

67. Exercise B, Plate 1.—In the lower half of the 10-inch by 15-inch sheet arranged vertically, lay out a rectangle about 8 inches wide by 6 inches high and fill it with an outline pattern or groundwork, like the design paper used for designing interlocking cork tiling.   This may be done by making a tracing of Fig. 2 of the text and then transferring it a number of times to the 8-inch by 6-inch rectangle on the plate, and then strengthening in the lines with a sharp pencil, until the entire rectangle has been covered by this outline pattern.

Upon this design paper as a groundwork make an original design for a floor arrangement of interlocking cork tiling showing corner, parts of top and left-side border, and the filling, similar to, but not in any respect a copy of, the designs in Figs. 4, 5, and 7 of the text.   Use two or three of the colors allowable for cork-tile work, as explained in the text, and render with great care, so that the color washes do not overrun the lines of the groundwork where they should not overrun, and all color washes are smooth and even.

68. Final Work on Plate 1.—Letter or write the title, Plate 1: Linoleum and Oilcloth Designing, at the top of the sheet, and on the back place class letters and number, name, address, and date of completing the plate. Roll the plate, place in the mailing tube, and send to the Schools for examination. Then proceed with Plate 2.

_____

PLATE 2

69. Original Design for Plate 2.—On a 10-inch by 15-inch sheet arranged vertically, lay out a 9-inch square, and within this square design one repeat of an original pattern for inlaid linoleum similar to, but not in any respect a copy of, Figs. 8 to 12 of the text, and designed in accordance with the principles there described. The scale at which the smallest details may be drawn can be understood from the full-size illustrations given in the text.

The design should be colored with washes of water color, carefully applied to show exactly what the finished inlaid linoleum will look like.

70. Final Work on Plate 2.—Letter or write the title, Plate 2: Linoleum and Oilcloth Designing, at the top of the sheet, and on the back place class letters and number, name, address, and date of completing the plate. Roll the plate, place in the mailing tube, and send to the Schools for examination. Then proceed with Plate 3.

PLATE 3

71. Original Design for Plate 3.—On a 10-inch by 15-inch sheet arranged vertically, lay out a 9-inch square, and within this square design one repeat of an original pattern for printed linoleum, similar to, but not in any respect a copy of, Fig. 13. Before starting the design a clear understanding must be had of the difference between printed linoleum and inlaid linoleum, as explained in the text, and how much greater freedom is allowed the designer of printed linoleums than is allowed for inlaid linoleums.

The design should be drawn with the greatest accuracy, and carefully rendered in water colors, so as to show exactly what the finished printed linoleum will look like.

72. Final Work on Plate 3.—Letter or write the title, Plate 3: Linoleum and Oilcloth Designing, at the top of the sheet, and on the back place class letters and number, name, address, and date of completing the plate. Roll the plate, place in the mailing tube, and send to the Schools for examination. Then proceed with Plate 4.

PLATE 4

73. Original Design for Plate 4.—On a 10-inch by 15-inch sheet arranged vertically, lay out a 9-inch square, and within this square design one repeat of an original pattern for floor oilcloth, similar to, but not in any respect a copy of, Figs. 17 to 22, inclusive, of the text, and designed in accordance with the principles there described. It must be remembered that the examples of floor oilcloth illustrated are only about one-fourth full size, and the proper enlargement of scale must be observed when making the original design required on this plate.

As before, the drawing and rendering must be done with the greatest accuracy.

74. Final Work on Plate 4.—Letter or write the title, Plate 4: Linoleum and Oilcloth Designing, at the top of the sheet, and on the back place class letters and number, name, address, and date of completing the plate. Roll the plate, place in the mailing tube, and send to the Schools for examination. Then proceed with Plate 5.

PLATE 5

75. Original Design for Plate 5.—On a 10-inch by 15-inch sheet arranged vertically, lay out a 9-inch square, and within this square design an original pattern for table oilcloth, similar to, but not in any respect a copy of, Figs. 23 to 27, inclusive, of the text, and designed in accordance with the principles there described. The text illustrations showing full-size sections will give a correct idea of the scale upon which the decorative motifs in the design may be planned.

As before, the drawing and rendering must be done with such care and accuracy that the design will show exactly how the finished table oilcloth is to look.

76. Final Work on Plate 5.—Letter or write the title, Plate 5: Linoleum and Oilcloth Designing, at the top of the sheet, and on the back place class letters and number, name, address, and date of completing the plate. Roll the plate, place in the mailing tube, and send to the Schools for examination. Then proceed with Plate 6.

PLATE 6

77. Original Design for Plate 6.—On a 10-inch by 15-inch sheet arranged vertically, lay out a 9-inch square, and within this square design an original pattern for wall oilcloth, similar to, but not in any respect a copy of, Figs. 28 to 31, inclusive, of the text, and designed in accordance with the principles there described.   The text illustrations showing full-size sections will give a correct idea of the scale upon which the decorative motifs in the design may be planned.

The drawing and rendering of the design, as before, must be executed with great care and accuracy.

78.   Final Work on Plate 6.—Letter or write the title, Plate 6: Linoleum and Oilcloth Designing, at the top of the sheet, and on the back place class letters and number, name, address, and date of completing the plate.   Roll the plate, place in the mailing tube, and send to the Schools for examination.

If any redrawn work on any of the plates of this Section has been called for, and has not yet been completed, it should be satisfactorily finished at this time.   After all the required work on the plates of this Section has been completed, the work of the next Section should be taken up at once.

CARPET AND RUG DESIGNING

PURPOSE

1. Necessity for Specialized Training.—It has already been shown that the designer who desires to specialize on some individual line of industrial design work must know more than the artistic side of designing.

When one has acquired the theoretical idea of the application of natural forms to design, it is necessary that he should understand the mechanical limitations of certain forms of machinery or methods of production in order to fit himself to design for some specific purpose. The preparation of a design for a carpet or other woven fabric differs in no way from the preparation of a design for any other fabric or object, except so far as the mechanical limitations of the methods of reproduction are concerned. Both may be based on the same natural type severely conventionalized to suit the material and the machinery that are to produce the result, and the more intimate the designer is with the limitations of these methods of production, the better and more economically can he design for some specific purpose.

Many of the most practical carpet designers learn their craft while helpers in the designing room of a factory, and although this is an admirable way of acquiring the practical experience necessary to prepare a good design, it has the disadvantage of being a tedious process, for manufacturers are usually slow in recognizing the artistic ability of employes occupying subordinate positions. A man with original ideas and ability as a draftsman and designer can train himself, in a short time, to occupy the position of a first-class carpet designer by studying mechanical limitations of a certain kind of manufacture. The helper in the design room learns only the technical features of carpet production and is kept copying the ideas of others, so that his own individuality is never expressed. He soon becomes a mere machine, and therefore is in the worst possible condition to become a successful designer.

The head of such a designing department usually is a graduate of a technical art school, and he is apt to keep to himself much of the theory of design and at the same time make little effort to absorb the practical side from his helper.

The public, or free-lance, designer, however, must understand both the theoretical and the practical side. He must have a thorough knowledge of his craft, possess inventive genius, and thoroughly understand the practical and economical sides of manufacture in the production of his fabrics.

2. Scope of the Training in This Section.—Foregoing Sections have dealt with the designing of decorative work for floors themselves, as tile and parquetry, as well as designs for linoleum, oilcloth, etc., which are fabrics applied to the surface of the floor. Now will be taken up the designing of superficially applied floor coverings that are woven, thus giving greater scope for the use of patterns that are intricate and interesting, both in design and in coloring.

It must be definitely understood that the training given here is in designing carpets, not in weaving them. It is true that the carpet designer must have a clear idea of the particular kind of carpet for which he is making his design, and a general knowledge of the process of weaving that particular class of carpet; and such information will be given as a preliminary to the designing methods and practices discussed in the case of each class of carpet. But only such mechanical details of manufacture will be taken up as are required as a foundation knowledge upon which the designer may base his artistic designs.

CARPETS

CLASSIFICATION OF CARPETS

3. History of Carpets.—The original meaning of the word **carpet,** called in old French *carpite*, referred to wrapping cloth, of a very coarse weave, in which packages or loads were wrapped or packed for carrying upon backs of men or animals. Later these wrapping cloths were used by men carriers to protect themselves from cold or inclemency, to wrap up their feet and limbs. The next development in its use was to spread the *carpite* over the cold stone floors as a protection to the feet. As its use for this purpose progressed, and the civilization of man developed, he attempted decoration in the weaving of these cloths, introducing designs and colors into the threads or strands in the fabric.

The cold mountain districts of western Asia—Persia, Turkey, and Syria—where the art of weaving these cloths, which will now be called **carpets,** started, produced carpets of wool, camel's hair and goat's hair, combined with flax; and carpets and floor coverings made there were practically indestructible. Some carpets have been in use in certain Persian palaces ever since the 16th century.

It is likely that carpets were used as early as 3000 B. C. in Egypt. Cyrus the Great possessed magnificent carpets and rugs in the days of his and Persia's greatness; and Alexander found many of them as he progressed in his conquests through Asia and India. But carpet making in its finer sense, that is, hand-made fabrics, has always been at its best in the Orient.

It was in the time of Louis XIV, in France, that the weaving of carpets by machine looms was first carried on upon a large scale. The weavers and the weaving of carpets then spread to England, and then to the United States, where the carpet industry is carried on principally in the states of Pennsylvania, New York, Massachusetts, and New Jersey.

4. General Types of Carpets.—In this treatise there will be discussed only machine-made carpets, which are the carpets for the artistic designing of which the services of the commercial designer are needed. There are three main classes of carpets, depending upon their method of manufacture, as follows:

1. Carpets that need to be woven of colored yarns with the aid of the Jacquard machine (to be described later) attached to the loom. Under this head come *Brussels carpets*, *Wilton carpets*, and *ingrain*, or *Kidderminster*, *carpets*.

2. Carpets for the weaving of which no Jacquard machine is needed. Under this head are *Axminster*, or *moquette*, *carpets*, and *Axminster chenille carpets*.

3. Carpets upon which the design or pattern is printed on the pile yarn with blocks or cylinders, either before or after the carpet is woven. The general class of carpets known as **tapestry carpets** come under this head, and they are variously called *tapestry Brussels*, *tapestry Axminster*, *Smyrna*, etc.

5. Brussels Carpet.—The carpet bearing the name *Brussels* is a machine-made worsted carpet, of linen, or of cotton-and-linen, web, the pattern being produced by the Jacquard mechanism (which automatically picks out certain colored yarns and brings them to the top of the fabric to form the pattern). The surface is thus raised in ridges of loops of **uncut pile**, and each yarn is of different color and shows frequently in the back of the fabric, thus distinguishing the carpet from tapestry Brussels, which shows no such marking.

6. Wilton Carpet.—The carpet called *Wilton* is woven in the same manner as Brussels carpet, and on the same kind of loom, but it differs from Brussels carpet in that the pile is not in ridges, but the loops of yarn that come up and form the pile are cut after they come to the surface, thus forming tufted ends; and the surface is known as **cut pile**, or **velvet**, surface.

7. Ingrain, or Kidderminster, Carpet.—The chief characteristic of the class of carpets called *ingrain* in the United States and *Kidderminster* in England is that they are two-ply carpets; that is, the same figured pattern shows on each side of the fabric, although in different colors. These carpets differ from Brussels and Wilton carpets in that they belong to the non-pile class of woven fabrics; that is, no loops come up to form the pile, but the yarns are braided tightly over the upper web of cross threads, then go through the fabric and are braided over the lower web of cross threads.

8. Axminster Carpet.—As previously indicated, *Axminster* carpets are woven in the loom without the aid of the Jacquard mechanism. All the yarns that are evident on the surface are in the form of tufts, thus being what is known as **tufted pile,** this long soft pile being all displayed on the surface and none being stowed away in the body of the fabric. Originally such carpets were hand-woven.

In England, but not in the United States, Axminsters are chenille-woven and are known as **chenille carpet.** In this process, a soft tufted or fluffy cord of cotton, wool, silk, or worsted is made into a woven "fur" cloth by a separate weaving process, and this cloth is afterwards cut into strips and woven onto the web backing.

9. Tapestry Carpet.—The carpet to which the general term *tapestry* is applied is a woven fabric with a pile surface, but the design in colors is produced not by bringing a multitude of colored yarns to the surface, but by printing or dyeing (with blocks or rollers) the yarn, either before or after weaving. This printing operation is so devised that the color goes through the entire fabric to the backing, and thus renders it a very durable and wearable fabric.

BRUSSELS CARPET

MANUFACTURE

10. The Principle of Woven Fabrics.—Heretofore there have been considered types of decorative floor coverings in which the patterns were produced by mosaic work or by various printing processes. There will now be considered a fabric floor covering in which the pattern is produced by weaving colored yarns together in various ways to form designs or patterns in color.

The simple principle upon which a carpet is woven is to interweave strands of yarn running crosswise of the fabric

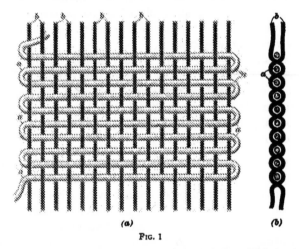

(a)   *(b)*

Fig. 1

through those running lengthwise of the fabric. This is clearly illustrated in Fig. 1, where the black threads *b* representing the strands of yarn that run lengthwise of the fabric are crossed at right angles and interwoven by the white strands *a* that run crosswise of the fabric. It will be noted that each white crosswise thread goes first under, then over, then under, then over, etc., the black lengthwise threads. In this manner a compact fabric is formed.

11. Warp Threads and Weft Threads.—In Fig. 1 (*a*) the threads or yarns *b* running *lengthwise* of the fabric are shown in black; these are called **warp threads;** the white threads *a* running *crosswise*, of the fabric are called **weft threads.** This terminology for the two kinds of threads in weaving must be clearly understood and carefully remembered, for hereafter all lengthwise strands will be referred to as the warp threads, and all crosswise strands as the weft threads.

12. Heavy Fabrics Such as Carpets.—It is evident that while such a fabric as is shown in Fig. 1 (*a*) will hang together because properly woven, it would not be thick enough, nor sufficiently staunch and durable, to serve as a floor covering. Therefore, more layers of yarns, both warp and weft, must be incorporated into the body of the fabric.

In Fig. 1 (*a*) is shown the front, or face, view of the fabric, and in (*b*) is a section taken lengthwise of the fabric along the warp threads; therefore, the ends of the weft, or crosswise, threads *a* show as little dots or circles, and the warp, or lengthwise, threads appear as snake-like black lines winding over, and under, and between the dots, in guilloche-like formation.

13. Yarns and the Method of Weaving Them in Brussels Carpet.—Fig. 2 is a longitudinal section of a foundation weave of a carpet, and the method is similar to that shown in Fig. 1 (*b*), except that two sets of weft threads *a* are used. While a weave such as that shown in Fig. 2 would form a fabric, it would not be sufficiently heavy to be designated as a carpet,

FIG. 2

nor would it be decorated with a pattern or design. Other warp threads, or yarns, are therefore inserted, so that the section lengthwise of Brussels carpet will be as shown in Fig. 3, in which can be seen all the threads, or yarns, in their proper places. The black dots, or sections, marked *a* are the ends, or sections, of the flax weft threads, called the *filling;* threads *b* are the cotton *chain warp* threads winding over and under the weft threads. Threads *c* are of heavy jute, and are used as a warp; they are called *stuffer chain* because they stuff the fabric and make it thick and springy. The heavy worsted threads, or yarns, *d* are used as warp, and called the *figuring warp*, because it is these yarns that come up and form the figure or design pattern on the surface of the carpet. There may be two, three, four, five, or six colors of this figuring warp, depending on the intricacy of the pattern and the color scheme to be employed.

Note carefully that the *right-hand* side of Fig. 3, where the heavy loops appear, represents the surface of the carpet.

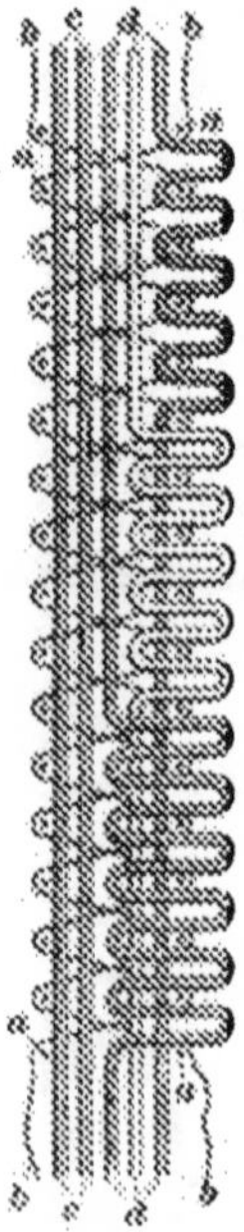

14. Characteristic Weave of Brussels Carpet.—As will be seen by reference to Fig. 3, the characteristics of Brussels carpet are that its surface consists of loops of the figuring-warp threads or yarns coming up through the surface and forming what is known as the **pile.** Being in the form of loops that are uncut, it is called uncut pile. These figuring-warp threads are interwoven with the basic foundation of the fabric, any one selected color extending the entire length of it, and coming up to the surface only when needed to form part of the pattern, and being hid in the body of the fabric when not so needed. Thus the figuring threads are not expensive to dye, but are expensive in the weaving, because so much of their length lies hidden in the fabric. However, this is compensated for by the fact that the carpet is thereby made more firm and durable.

FIG. 3

15. Frames.—The figuring-warp threads or yarns that form the colored design are of various colors, and various numbers of sets of colors. In the cheaper classes of Brussels carpet, only two or three sets of colors are used; but in the better grades, four, five, or even six colors are employed to get the best effects in bringing out the pattern.

Each one of these sets of colored yarns is called a **frame;** therefore, if a certain carpet is to be woven to show a color scheme of three sets of colors, that is, three sets of colored yarns, it would be known as a *three-frame* carpet.   If four sets of colored yarns are used, it is a *four-frame* carpet, and so on, up to a *six-frame* carpet.   The manner in which these sets of colored yarns, or frames, are used in the weaving is as follows:

Suppose a three-frame Brussels carpet is being woven, such as is shown in cross-section in Fig. 3, the yarns of the frame being the three marked *d*.   First it must be evident that, in the weaving, these figuring-warp threads or colored yarns must be wound on separate spools or bobbins somewhere above the loom, from which they gradually unwind as needed.   Each set, or frame, of colored-warp yarns is wound on a separate bobbin; they could not all be wound on one cylinder, or beam, as is the chain warp, because they (the pile-warp colored threads or yarns) form loops at irregular intervals, as threads *d* of Fig. 3, and are used in varying proportions.   The colored warp yarns, used to make the pattern, therefore unwind from the spools or bobbins above the loom, come down through the guiding wires and thence go into the surface of the fabric as it is being woven.

16. Forming the Pile and the Pattern in Colors. The colored warp yarns, running lengthwise in the loom, are looped over wires that run crosswise of the fabric, the loops thus forming the pile.   This process is accomplished by the action of the Jacquard machine attached to the loom, wires and hooks coming down and automatically lifting up to the surface and looping such colored yarns as are needed to form the pattern.   The action of the Jacquard machine is such as to raise certain desired warp threads and permit wire rules, or weft threads, to pass under the raised threads and over those that lie below.   These raised threads are usually called the *shed*.

17.   The Jacquard machine is caused to operate by a series of perforated cards like that shown in Fig. 4, in which the black dots represent holes in the card.   These cards are prepared as follows: After the design for the carpet is made, in the manner to be described later, it is turned over to the draftsman, or copyist, who transcribes it to squared design paper of the proper kind.   This squared design paper with its design

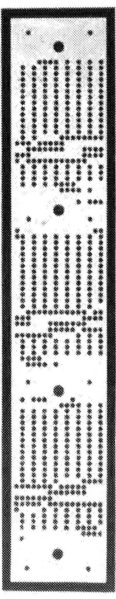

FIG. 4

painted, or checked off, thereon is then turned over to the operator of what is known as the piano machine, which has a keyboard resembling that of a typewriter; and the operator, following the design, square by square, by punching certain keys on the machine translates this design onto cards such as shown in Fig. 4, each hole of which represents one of the squares on the design paper. These cards are then strung together edgewise by means of cords and are fed into the Jacquard machine in such a way that they press against a series of pins and cause the long wire hooks to which the colored warp yarns are attached to be released. Where the holes exist in the cards the pins pass through and the hooks are not released; therefore, the colored warp yarns represented by the holes in the cards are lifted, and appear as loops of the desired color on the surface of the carpet. The Jacquard cards are all of the same size and are linked together to form a chain, several thousand of them being required to weave a carpet of a certain pattern.

18. Planting.—As already mentioned, the colored threads of the figuring warp are carried in frames, and in the simplest color arrangements each frame is composed entirely of one color; that is, all the colored yarn, to be used as figuring warp, wound upon any particular spool or bobbin is of one color. If this system were unalterable there could then never be more than six colors in any carpet, six frames being the limit of what it is practicable to incorporate in the body of the carpet. However, by the method known as **planting,** quite a number of additional colors may be incorporated in the carpet pattern. Thus the designer is not necessarily restricted to the employment of the same number of colors in his pattern as the number of frames in his loom, and on this variation of the color scheme depends the important details of the design. The designer's ingenuity is taxed to produce the best arrangement of comparatively few colors to produce the best results. The designer may use six or seven colors in a five-frame fabric, but to do this must make use of the planting system, which, as already stated, means the introduction of two or more colors in one frame so that each will contribute its share to the fabric without interfering one with another; that is, each one of the four frames may be a solid color, but in the case of the fifth frame, the spool or bobbin may be filled with two, three, or more, colors and thus woven into the fabric.

Each of the five frames could be a planted frame if desired, but as a rule three or four of the frames are run full in solid color and the remainder are planted.

Planted designs possess mechanical limitations that must be understood by the designer. One cannot bring out a planted color throughout the design at any or every place he chooses, as he can with the color from a full frame. Planted colors exist only in those warp threads or yarns in front of which they are placed, and they cannot be brought up in the design where these threads or yarns do not pass. For it can be seen that the planted warp threads exist in the fabric as a series of longitudinal stripes, and the order of these stripes cannot be disarranged to bring the colors to the surface elsewhere. The designer must, therefore, keep this limitation in mind and exercise care and ingenuity not to produce a distinctly striped effect. An ingenious designer will so arrange his figures and distribute his colors that the finished design will give no indication of the fact that the colors have been planted. To do this will require considerable practice and experience on the part of the novice. Planting in Brussels carpet is sometimes referred to as *chintzing*.

The considerations that must be borne in mind by the designer, when making carpet designs in which intricate color effects are to be secured by planting, will be discussed when the matter of designing for Brussels carpet is taken up.

It is not necessary to describe further in detail, nor to illustrate by photographs or diagrams, the processes of weaving or the Jacquard mechanism. Enough has been said regarding the composition of the fabric of Brussels carpet, and the weaving of the fabric, to give the designer a sufficient knowledge of it to start to make designs.

19. Sizes of Brussels Carpets.—All carpet is woven in strips, the length depending upon the amount desired for a certain purpose, the size and weight of the roll when made up, etc.

The standard width of Brussels carpet to be used for the filling or general field, that is, when a carpet is laid to form a repeating pattern, is 27 inches, or three-quarters of a yard. Borders for such carpet, for making them up into large rug size, may be 13 inches, 18 inches, or $22\frac{1}{2}$ inches wide, although the 18-inch width is the one most commonly used.

Brussels stair and hall carpet is sometimes woven the full 36 inches, 1 yard, wide. Stair carpets are occasionally woven with two side borders and a filling, while the same border is sometimes woven separately to be attached to the regular hall carpet designed to match the filling of the stairs. Stair carpets are also made in widths of $\frac{1}{2}$ and $\frac{5}{8}$ yard, with borders to match, and the fillings are woven in various widths, such as $\frac{3}{8}$, $\frac{1}{2}$, and $\frac{5}{8}$ yard.

Repeats can be woven in various lengths up to $1\frac{1}{2}$ yards, under which conditions very broad and bold effects may be obtained. If a repeat must be long, it is usually arranged on a drop pattern, so that there may not be too much waste in getting the goods to match properly when a carpet is fitted.

A small pattern that is so designed that it cannot be matched in less than a yard is an unprofitable design for the retail dealer to carry, and a thoughtful designer must take this into consideration, as it is likely to prevent the disposal of his design.

Such designs have been made by thoughtless designers and manufactured by unobserving manufacturers, and often have been sold to retail dealers, the defect remaining unknown until the cutter would endeavor to fit a room, when he would find that a yard or more in each length would have to be wasted in order to secure a satisfactory repeat.

— ——

DESIGNING

20. Application of Design Principles to Carpet Designing.—The theory and principles of artistic designing and coloring have been treated in previous Sections, and the time has come to apply them to carpet designing by combining the artistic knowledge already secured with technical knowledge of the processes of carpet manufacture.

There are definite technical limitations imposed upon the artistic designer when he comes to make designs for carpets that are not imposed in any other line of design work, and these limitations must be given special consideration.

21. A Design Must Be for a Definite Kind of Carpet. The first thing to be borne in mind by the carpet designer is that he is to make a design for a *definite kind of carpet*. One does not make simply *a carpet design;* but he makes a design for Brussels carpet, or a design for Wilton carpet, or a design for some other definite class of carpet. In the present consideration, the designer is about to make a design for Brussels carpet. His first duty is to learn how Brussels carpet is woven, how many colors of yarns are used, how they are arranged as frames in the fabric, how certain ones are lifted up by the Jacquard mechanism and formed into loops, how additional colors may be planted, etc., and to what widths and sizes, and with how many loops or points to the inch, Brussels carpets are woven.

The purpose of this treatise so far has been to give such information; but if at any time opportunity is offered to supplement this information by a visit to and trip through a carpet manufacturing establishment, it would be well to do so. There can be seen the entire process of designing and weaving a Brussels carpet, which operations will reveal, with still additional clearness and force, the peculiar technical restrictions imposed upon the designer of Brussels carpet. Further, should any student desire to secure an authoritative textbook on the weaving of Brussels and other classes of carpets such a textbook will be recommended on request.

22. Classes of Patterns Suitable for Brussels Carpet. From the very character of the fabric and the method of weaving, it is evident that designs for carpet must be of the **repeating pattern** type, because woven by mechanical means. While a certain amount of monotony must necessarily result from such repeating patterns, yet the thoughtful and clever designer can avoid or disguise such monotony by carefully balancing the forms and colors in the design. The principles under which successful repeating patterns are made have been treated in previous Sections, and if necessary they should be referred to again to refresh the memory. It will then be found that side-to-side repeats, drop repeats, diamond, or lozenge, repeats, ogee repeats, etc., may all be applied to carpet patterns. The design may be constructed so that the lines of the repeat are emphasized, or so that they are hidden, as the case may require.

In laying out such repeats it must be borne in mind, first of all, that carpet, being laid on the floor as it is when in use, is viewed differently from any other kind of fabric; namely, in diminishing perspective, and at an angle. In preparing repeating patterns, therefore, the designer must bear this feature in mind, and must design repeating patterns that will always be satisfactory when viewed at an angle and very much foreshortened.

23. A Repeating Pattern of Isolated Motifs.—A satisfactory arrangement of a repeating pattern for carpet is to take some simple and graceful form or design motif and distribute it over the desired surface in a series of spots. The advantage of this method is that the individual motif or form may be turned in different directions at different parts of the design and thus fulfil the ideal requirements of a floor decoration;

namely, that the pattern will appear very much the same, no matter from what direction it is viewed. An added advantage of such an arrangement is that, in Brussels carpet, this separate-spot, or separate-motif, idea enables *planting* of colors to be done with good effect, the units or motifs, as they appear in different places on the fabric, being colored with different hues and values and an interesting pattern in colors thus secured.

Fig. 5

This principle is illustrated in a simple way in Figs. 5 and 6. In Fig. 5 the motifs or units are exactly alike except that they run at different angles, one set inclined toward the upper left-hand corner and the other set toward the upper right-hand corner. Fig. 6 also shows units laid, or placed, in different positions by the turn-over method of repeat. If the pattern is used for a carpet, it would appear satisfactory at any angle.

24. The Drop Repeating Pattern.—The drop repeat, the method of designing of which has already been fully discussed in another Section, is very suitable for carpet manufacture, because the width of the section of carpet that is woven usually contains only one repeat. As has been learned, Brussels carpet is usually 27 inches in width; but, by using a

Fig. 6

drop-repeat pattern when making the design, it is possible to make the apparent width of the repeat twice this, or 54 inches.

The method of thus increasing the apparent width of the repeat by the use of the drop pattern is shown in Fig. 7. The distance *a b* represents the complete width of the woven carpet strip, 27 inches. The rectangle *a b c d* represents the amount

necessary to be worked out in the design in order that the
Jacquard cards may be properly punched to weave the pattern,
and includes one complete repeat. Along the vertical line *b c*,
and at its center, is found the same repeat dropped, this being
the top of the rectangle *e f g h*, which rectangle represents
another width of carpet that fits side to side with the first

Fig. 7

strip so as to make a perfectly connected design. Thus it will
be seen that the same details or motifs do not repeat in this
design in less than twice the width of one roll or strip of carpet,
as is shown at *d* and *k*, where the flower at *d* is completed in
the section at *k*, directly opposite it on the right, and 54 inches
away from it. If this same general pattern were to be laid out
as a direct side-to-side repeat, these motifs would repeat every

27 inches horizontally; but by means of the drop pattern there can be produced, without additional labor or expense, a carpet design of apparently twice the width, which in many cases is a decided advantage.

Another advantage of the drop repeat is that it considerably reduces the chance of waste in cutting and fitting the widths together to suit the size of a room. This saving is clearly shown in Fig. 8, where in (a) the drop pattern is shown as its repeats would recur in a room; and in (b) the side-to-side repeating pattern appears as laid out upon the same floor space. This floor space is assumed to be 13 feet 6 inches wide by 15 feet

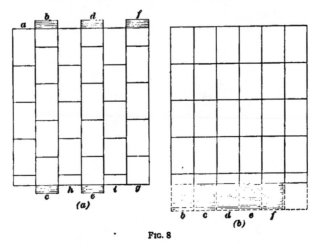

Fig. 8

long, the width requiring just six widths of 27-inch carpet to cover it. If, as in Fig. 8 (a), the one who lays the carpet begins at the upper left-hand corner and cuts off from the roll what is required for the length of the room, there will be four complete vertical repeats and a little over in each strip; then, when the next strip toward the right is laid, it will be necessary, in order properly to match the pattern, to waste a little at each end as indicated by the shaded portions b and c. In the same manner the same amount of waste occurs at d and e in the fourth strip, and at f in the last strip, while the third and fifth strips show no waste because they are cut to cover the length of the room.

In Fig. 8 (*b*), however, where the side-to-side repeat is used, and the drop repeat is not taken advantage of, the waste is much greater, as shown by the shaded sections at the lower end of each strip, this amount of waste being nearly 4 yards. For this reason it is well to keep the length of the repeat short,

(b)

Fig. 9

whether or not it is a drop repeat, for with a long repeat there is often more waste in cutting than where the repeat is moderate in length. In Fig. 7, for instance, the repeat is entirely too long for economy. Had the lozenge form been turned to a horizontal position it would have been much more advantageous.

25. The Multi-Symmetrical Repeating Pattern.
Perhaps the most suitable of all repeating patterns for carpets
is the multi-symmetrical repeating pattern. The process of
evolving such a pattern is shown in Fig. 9. Suppose the width
of the carpet strip to be 27 inches, as it is in Brussels carpet.
This would be represented by line $a\,c$ in view (b). An isosceles
right-angle triangle would then be laid out, as $a\,b\,c$ in (b). If
corner a is considered the point from which all lines will grow,
then any kind of a pattern may be drawn within this right-
angled triangle.

With such a simple pattern as the leaf and scroll growth
shown in (b), an interesting multi-symmetrical pattern can be
formed as follows: Considering a as the central point of a
large design to be formed, place triangle $a\,b\,c$ of view (b) in
the position shown by $a\,b\,c$ in view (a). Then the triangle
with its decorative motifs is folded over on the line $a\,c$ as an
axis, until it takes the position $a\,c\,b_1$. In practical work, the
process would be to make a tracing of $a\,b\,c$ and then reverse
it on line $a\,c$ and transfer it reversed so as to become triangle
$a\,c\,b_1$. A new decorative form, perfectly symmetrical, is then
formed at $a\,b\,c\,b_1$. The resulting ornament may then be
folded over again, this time on line $a\,b_1$ as an axis, to form a
repeated section at $a\,b_1\,c_1\,b_2$. Again the resulting decoration
may be folded over, on line $b\,b_2$, and reduplicated at b_2, c_2, b_3,
c_3, b, thus filling the entire square $c\,c_1\,c_2\,c_3$ with symmetrical
decoration, all of which seems to radiate from center a. But
the process described above does not conclude the repeating, or
multi-symmetrical, possibilities of the simple decorative details
shown in triangle $a\,b\,c$. Triangle $a\,c_3\,c$ may be repeated by
folding the triangle over on line $c_3\,c$, thus making triangle $c_3\,a_1\,c$.
Similarly, triangles $c\,c_1\,a_2$, $c_1\,c_2\,a_3$, and $c_2\,c_3\,a_4$ may be formed.
This completes the entire square $a_1\,a_2\,a_3\,a_4$ which in turn may
be repeated indefinitely on all four sides by folding over, in
turn, on axes $a_1\,a_2$, $a_2\,a_3$, $a_3\,a_4$, and $a_4\,a_1$.

A strong advantage of this multi-symmetrical repeating
pattern is that it is an ideal one for a floor covering pattern.
No matter from what direction it is viewed, or from what
angle, the carpet pattern in such a scheme will appear to be

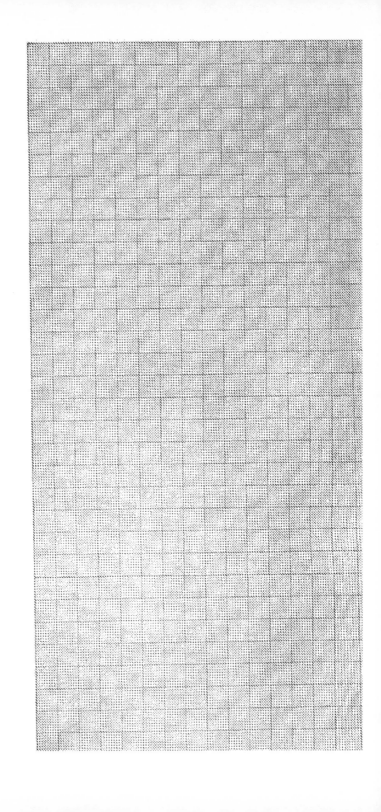

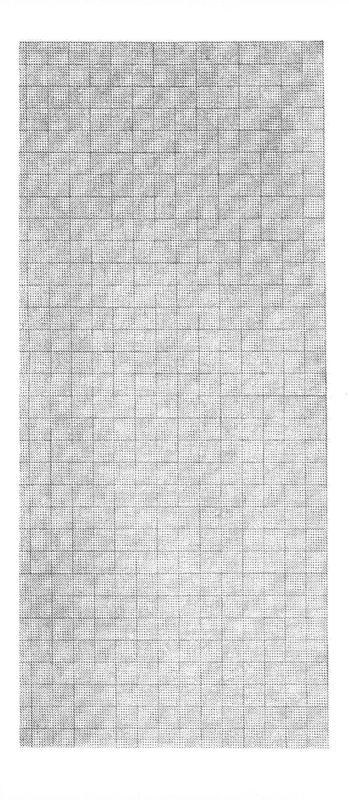

viewed in the proper position, and in correct foreshortening of details. A still more important advantage is that the design can be made to extend across two widths of carpet, as before described, a 27-inch layout giving the effect of a 54-inch repeat. In this way, when cutting or punching the cards for the Jacquard machine, cards need be made to cover only section $c_3\ a_1\ c\ a$ of the pattern shown in Fig. 9 (a), and when these have been run through their motion in the Jacquard machine may be reversed and the section $a\ c\ a_2\ c_1$ be woven. This process is convenient when carpets in short lengths are being woven; but ordinarily in long carpet lengths Jacquard cards would be cut for the whole repeat, as $a_1\ a_2\ a_3\ a_4$.

26. Obtaining Suggestions for Designs.—Students who know nothing about carpets, and also practical carpet designers, should embrace every opportunity to go over the stocks of retail dealers and learn, in connection with these, the character of designs that are most popular, and study at the same time the designs of wallpapers, furniture, and other elements of interior decoration that are presenting themselves in the market. From the character of furniture exhibited in the windows one can determine the styles of carpets and wall-papers that will soon be in demand. The reason for this is easily understood. The intelligent purchaser endeavors to furnish his house with various articles that are harmonious in style, and one usually selects his floor coverings and wall coverings to match his furniture rather than his furniture to match the coverings.

With the delicately carved and simply modeled furniture that was characteristic of the earliest Renaissance there were wall decorations of delicate arabesques adapted from carvings; and as the later Renaissance introduced the absurdity of rococo ornament in furniture, accompanied by elaborate carving and much gilding, there were likewise reproduced, in meaningless wall decoration and elaborate pilaster ornament, an excess of meaningless forms everywhere. With the period of the Empire that followed these absurdities, and the return of classic models and simple, severe furniture, with occasional ornaments and festoons carved and gilded, came wall decorations of the same severe character corresponding with it in style. Likewise, later when there came the introduction of the severe "Mission" furniture, and the later reproductions of furniture on the Gothic model, wall decorations tended to tapestry effects based on Gothic ideas, and floor coverings occasionally became simple and severe in design so as to be in harmony with their surroundings. Similarly, in the more modern period there came the influence of the furniture and wall covering styles of certain European countries, the two lines always being kept in harmony.

27. Blocking Out the Design on Squared Paper. Designs for all classes of carpets are laid out and rendered on a special design paper, ruled in vertical and horizontal lines to form squares or rectangles.

In Fig. 10 is shown a reproduction, on a small scale, of a full sheet of design paper such as is used when making designs for Brussels carpet. This figure is introduced simply to show the number of squares on a full-size sheet of design paper, but must not be confused with the actual width, in inches, of a strip of Brussels carpet. In Fig. 11 (a) is shown a small section of this 8×8 to the inch Brussels design paper in which the squares are the actual size of those on the paper upon which the carpet designer lays out his designs. In (b) is shown a full-scale paper of 8×9 to the inch, such as is sometimes employed in designing Brussels carpet.

The rows of squares running lengthwise of the design paper represent the warp threads or yarns in the fabric, and those running crosswise represent the weft threads. Designs for carpets are made full size; that is, the same size as the pattern on the carpet itself. Therefore, the full size of the printed portion of the design paper is at least 27 inches wide, the width of one strip of Brussels carpet, and sometimes it is as wide as 32 inches, so as to allow portions of the surrounding repeats to show. This is why, in Fig. 10, there are thirty-two large squares, although Brussels carpet is only 27 inches wide. The kind of design paper illustrated in Fig. 11 (a) shows each square

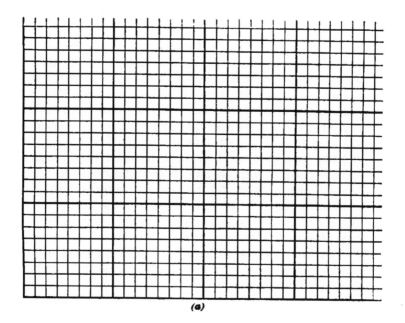

(a)

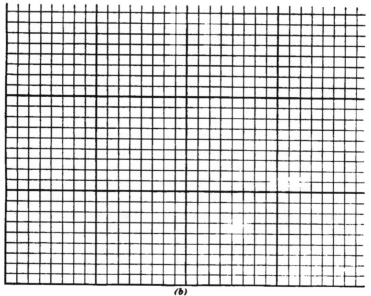

(b)

FIG. 11

inch ruled in heavy lines, and each square inch is divided into eight squares in width and eight squares in length; that is, eight warp threads and eight weft threads to the inch. In a 27-inch-width carpet there would therefore be 8 times 27, or 216, warp threads in the width; that is, in *one frame;* but if the carpet were a five-frame carpet for instance; that is, five layers of 216 warp threads in each layer, there would be 5 times 216, or 1,080, warp threads. In some of the higher grade and more expensive carpets there are nine or ten rectangles to each inch in width; that is, 243 or 270 warp threads, to the entire 27-inch width of the carpet. The design paper to be used in any particular case must always be determined by the grade of Brussels carpet being made by the particular mill or factory for which the designer is working, and design paper of that particular *pitch* must be secured. No designer should ever start to make a design for Brussels or any other kind of carpet until he has a full understanding of the kind of squared design paper he must use.

There is no specified rule for the length of the repeat in any carpet design, but 27 to 36 inches is a suitable length for small designs, and 45 to 54 inches for larger ones. The designer's judgment must be used in this matter, and a length should be selected that prevents certain features in the design from being repeated too frequently.

Taking such design paper as that of Fig. 10 and Fig. 11 (a) as an average, it will be observed that every inch, vertically and horizontally, is ruled in heavier lines, so that the small squares may be conveniently counted by the designer. These small squares are the ones that are of most practical use to the designer and the weaver. Each square in the design paper, therefore, corresponds to one loop of thread in the warp that comes to the surface of the loom and forms the pile of the carpet. The fineness or coarseness of the weave depends on the number of lengthwise divisions to the inch, ordinary Brussels carpet being made with 8 or 9 to the inch, while exceedingly fine carpet has as many as 13. As a horizontal row of loops appears, the various colored yarns brought to the surface unite to form the pattern or design, and it is therefore evident that each square on the design paper must be accounted for by the designer to the weaver, so that the loom may be arranged to bring to the surface at the proper point the proper color of yarn.

28. The experienced designer usually roughs out his sketch directly on the design paper, using for this purpose charcoal or crayon and, at the beginning, giving no heed to cross-sections or squares. Some designers pin up before them on a drawing board (arranged vertically, horizontally, or inclined, to suit the designer's preference) a sheet of squared design paper, and, over this, then pin a sheet of tough transparent tracing paper on which the preliminary design is freely sketched in with charcoal.

Long sinuous curves with free open drawing indicate the general trend of the main features of the design, and finely drawn details are worked up afterwards. In doing this, the designer never loses sight of the fact that in his completed work the lines and figures must be represented by a series of checks, and he instinctively avoids such geometrical forms as are too minute to be boldly expressed in this manner. Long delicate curves extending in a horizontal direction are impossible, as they must necessarily be made up by a series of long straight lines separated from each other just 1 square; bold decided curves, however, may be drawn in almost any direction. In Fig. 12 are shown examples of renderings of curves, which serve well to illustrate this point. On one side are shown the outlines of the forms that are to be represented, while on the other side are the results of these curves worked out on the squares. A careful study of the extent to which the sinuous and graceful curves of these petal and leaf forms must be altered so as to portray them by means of the squares, and the supplementing of this study by actually working them out on squared paper, will show just what forms may be allowed in carpet designing, and what forms are too fine and delicate to be properly portrayed by weaving.

29. Arranging Colors for a Solid-Frame Design. There is perhaps no form of artistic design work in which a thorough knowledge of color and its application to design is more required than in that of designing for carpets. In a successful carpet design, good colors properly harmonized outweigh every other consideration. Form must always be secondary to color. No matter how skilfully and cleverly the design is drawn from the standpoint of line and form, these cannot fulfil in greatest measure their purpose unless these

FIG. 12

forms are colored in such harmonious hues and values as to present to the eye a neutralized bloom. It is well known that a design, even though badly drawn and with poor arrangement of form, if colored in a pleasing manner, will be more popular and better in every way than a skilfully drawn design that is poorly colored.

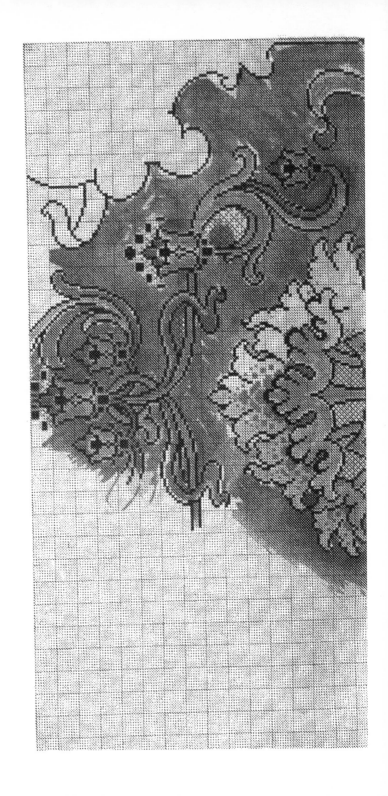

Fig. 13

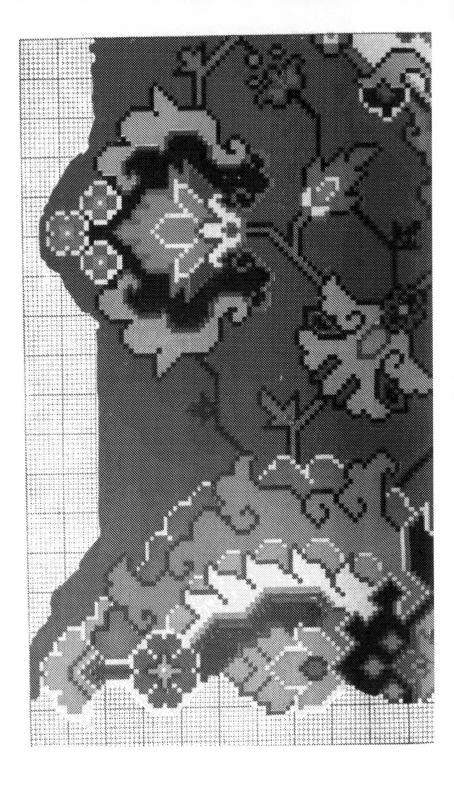

128 Ends

FIG. 14

It is not the purpose here to again discuss the theory of color, or to describe how harmonious color schemes can be devised, for these subjects have been fully treated in a previous Section. It now simply remains to apply the instruction there given to the preparation of harmoniously colored carpet patterns. The colors that may be used in a design will, of course, depend on the colored yarns that are available and the number of colors the manufacturer wants to use in the proposed carpet; that is, whether it is to be a two-, three-, four-, five-, or six-frame carpet; and the designer must conform to these limitations.

30. Arranging Colors for a Planted Design.—If the carpet is a solid-frame carpet; that is, if each one of the two, three, four, five, or six spools is filled with yarn of only one color, the designer may color his design in any way that suits his fancy, so long as he uses no more colors than there are frames in the carpet, because he knows that at any and every place all over the surface of the carpet he could dig down and find any or all of the colors he is allowed to use.

However, if he wants to use in his design any more than the six colors, he must resort to *planting*, which has been previously described, so far as the weaving operation is concerned. The considerations that must be borne in mind by the designer when planting colors in a design will now be taken up.

To understand best the procedure, an actual example of such a planted design must be referred to. First, of course, the design and color scheme are blocked out, as shown in Fig. 13. In Fig. 14, however, is shown how the designer arranges for the planting of the frames of color. The designer of this carpet first made his outline design to show the drawing and arrangement of the spots of ornament and other details. Let it be assumed that the carpet is to be woven as a six-frame carpet. The designer may decide that in the case of two of his colors he will use them all over the surface of the fabric. As shown by a reference to Fig. 14, these two colors are black and red. These two are solid frames, and are full frames, because they extend entirely across the width of the carpet. By his trial color sketches, on tracing paper, or otherwise, he may determine that dark gold and écru are two other colors that he will want to use freely in the spots of ornament; and so these two colors are considered solid frames, although not full frames, because there will be portions across the fabric where they will not be needed. The designer now finds that, out of the six frames allowed, four have already been used as solid frames; namely, black, red, dark gold, and écru; which leaves him only two frames for coloring the rather intricate ornament within the spots. Since two colors could not possibly enable him to produce good results, he must use more colors, which means that in these two remaining frames he must plant his colors.

The designer therefore paints strips of colors across the bottom of his design to show just where in the width of the design certain colors are to appear. As will be seen at the bottom of Fig. 14, strips of black, red, dark gold, and écru run entirely across the fabric, although the dark gold and écru are interrupted at the places where they are not needed. The fourth and fifth strips from the bottom represent the planted frames. The fourth strip from the bottom represents the frame planted with green and blue-green, in sections as shown, representing how the yarns are wound on the spool or bobbin for this frame. The fifth strip from the bottom represents the frame planted with pink and light gold, in sections as shown, again indicating how the yarns are wrapped on the bobbins for this frame.

The placing of these strips and portions of strips of color can be done after the preliminary trial color sketch has been made. Once they are placed in this way, they indicate just how many vertical rows of squares on the design paper, representing a corresponding number of warp threads, the designer may use for any one color. In this way he has eight colors at his disposal, and the chart or guide of color strips at the bottom of the design paper will show him just where he may use these colors throughout the width of the design.

Some designers paint the colors right on the design paper, as shown at the bottom of Fig. 14, and then, aided by the vertical cross-section lines in the paper, simply run imaginary vertical lines, or bands, up through their painted design to show where the different colors may be used. Other designers paint these colors on horizontal strips of paper and then shift these strips up and down over the design as a guide to determine the placing, or planting, of the colors. Either method will serve the purpose.

31. Ticking-In, and Coloring the Design.—As previously indicated, the design for the carpet is first laid out simply in pencil on the design paper, and the color schemes accurately determined after various trials. The design in this preliminary state is carried about as far as is shown in Fig. 13.

Different designers use different methods of starting the work, and each must determine for himself, after some practice, which method will best attain the proper results. Some designers carefully draw out the figures, in pencil, before filling in with color; others start in with the color and "feel" for a pattern and the color scheme at the same time. In Fig. 13 is shown a design commenced in this manner; the main figures have been "roughed out" in charcoal and afterwards ticked-in with dark blue; then the different areas are filled in roughly with the local color. These trial color areas should be washed in with thin color so that the ruled lines are not obliterated, and the colors can then be altered without the application of two coats of the heavier opaque color, which would be likely to chip off if the design were much handled.

The figures drawn in outline on the design paper are likely to appear much more perfect than when filled in with color; therefore, it is advisable to "rough in" the general design in color, as it brings to light at once any bad drafting and gives the designer an opportunity to remedy this defect before it is too late.

In the factory, where the busy designer has a number of helpers, he would not carry his design quite so far as is shown in Fig. 13, but after roughing it out would hand it over to the helper, trusting to him to carry out the effect and color scheme that he has indicated by ticking-in. The designer himself, however, needs to be familiar with the helper's work as well as his own.

For *ticking-in* and *putting on*, it is well to use old or worn red sable brushes, or new ones whose points have been purposely cut off, or burnt off by touching them to a red-hot iron, to make them fit the size of the checks.

The use of the large squares on the design paper can be observed in the bold treatment of the pattern shown in Fig. 13, as the designer may here tick-in only one-half of each of the figures and a helper can reproduce the other side by counting the squares. The beginner, however, must learn to carry out his entire pattern from start to finish in general scheme.

The color scheme of the design must be decided on beforehand and the figures carefully outlined, and the color of each indicated by a touch of the proper tint. The experienced designer will make use of the checker effect to get the best possible drawing.

32. Fig. 14 shows the method of rendering in opaque color, the broad washes of opaque color indicating the solid colors, and the outlines and little details of decorative motifs are ticked-in as just described. Every carpet design to be submitted to a manufacturer should always be rendered with the degree of accuracy and finish shown in Fig. 14, although it is not always best to make the color washes so opaque as to cover the ruled squares. A careful inspection of the background of the design in Fig. 15, especially the red background for the decorative spots, will reveal the ruled cross lines. In the original painting, which was, of course, larger, they were even more distinct, and therefore useful to the weaver.

33. The carpet whose design is shown in Fig. 14 is a good example of a five-frame Brussels carpet. Any one of the colors, red, gold, sage, dark blue, and écru, that appear in the design, can be traced so that it will be found somewhere in the repeat to occupy each and all of the 256 little squares that extend across the entire width of the fabric. If this carpet were woven in only one color, it would require 256 warp threads of this color to be wound at the back of the loom; this would make one full frame, as each frame contains 256 bobbins, holding 256 pile warp threads. As these warp threads are consumed in the weaving with unequal rapidity, according to the frequency with which the different threads are drawn to the surface to form the pattern, it is impracticable to wind them all on one big bobbin or beam. Where a pattern calls for five colors, there must be a frame with 256 bobbins on it for each individual color. A five-frame Brussels carpet, therefore, has $5 \times 256 = 1,280$ colored warp threads fed into the fabric constantly at the back of the loom. At each pick of the Jacquard mechanism, 256 ends of warp thread are raised and a wire thrust under; then the weft thread binds them into place and 1 vertical *pick* of the pattern is formed. The remaining 1,024 colored warp yarns are hidden and lie idly in the body of the pattern.

This is the principle of the five-frame weave; the four-frame weave requires $4 \times 256 = 1,024$ ends, and the three-frame, 768 ends, etc. Thus we see that the five-frame carpet has 256 more ends of warp in its body than a four-frame and 512 more ends than a three-frame carpet. It is evident, then, that the five-frame carpet is much heavier and contains much more material than the latter, and is therefore more costly, regardless of the character of the pattern.

34. A Fully Rendered Design for Brussels Carpet. Fig. 15 shows, on a small scale, how a fully rendered design on design paper will appear. This illustration shows not only the accuracy of the ticking-in, but the harmony of colors that must be produced in the rendered design.

It will be observed that the colors are rich and pure, even though they have been used almost opaque at places. This should be an object lesson to the beginner in coloring his designs on design paper. When Chinese white is used with water-color pigment to make the pigment opaque, there is at times a tendency for the Chinese white to give a bluish tinge to the resulting color, making it cold and dull. This is generally due to the use of too much Chinese white. In such a color mixture, the pure rich color should predominate, and only enough Chinese white should be used to give the pigment a slight body. If too great difficulty is experienced in making the opaque color sufficiently rich and pure, the designer should purchase some jars of designers' moist colors (opaque) already mixed and ready for use. Or, if necessary, he may render his designs in heavy water-color pigments, placed thick (not in thin washes) without attempting to mix therewith Chinese white.

The carpet for which Fig. 15 is a design is another example of planting.

TYPICAL EXAMPLE

35. Specimen of Body Brussels Carpet.—The student of carpet designing is expected to visit carpet stores, and,

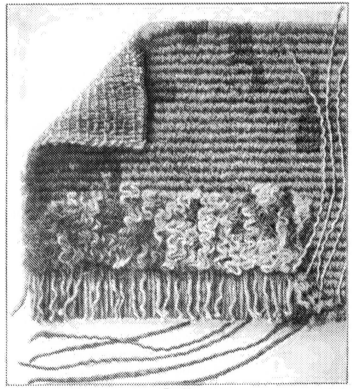

FIG. 16

if possible, carpet mills where the fabric is woven, and examine the actual specimens of body Brussels, pulling out some of the

Fig. 15

weft threads slowly and noting how they weave in with and around the warp yarns, and the amount of crinkle or waviness of the warp yarns as the loops are made.

However, as a step toward such investigation, there is shown in Fig. 16 a photograph of a small section, full size, of a specimen of body Brussels carpet. This was photographed direct from the actual fabric, and is therefore practically as valuable for purposes of research as would be the actual carpet itself. To show how the fabric is backed, one corner of it has been turned over. Some of the linen weft threads at the bottom have been purposely pulled out so as to show how the soft fluffy colored warp yarns that form the pattern are looped over and under these weft threads, these loops running in horizontal ridges and being uncut. A close inspection will reveal how one set of colored warp yarns lies above a set of another color, coming to the surface when needed for the pattern. The stuffer-chain warp, of smaller and more compact warp yarns, is also shown running through the body of the fabric next to the backing.

This photograph of a specimen of actual carpet full size is a graphic illustration of the processes of weaving and designing body Brussels described in the foregoing pages.

A specimen of *tapestry Brussels*, produced by a different process, to be described later, will be illustrated and commented on in the proper connection.

WILTON CARPET

MANUFACTURE

36. Characteristic Weave of Wilton Carpet.—Wilton carpet is woven in the same manner, and on the same kind of a loom, as Brussels carpet, except that in Wilton carpet the loops of colored figuring yarn that come to the surface to form the pattern are *cut*, which makes Wilton carpet belong to what is known as the **cut-pile**, or **velvet**, class. In fact Wilton carpet is usually called velvet carpet by the dealer. Therefore, one who knows how Brussels carpet is woven, including the action of the Jacquard mechanism and the loom, knows also how Wilton carpet is woven.

The characteristic feature of the manufacture of Wilton carpet is that the wire which passes transversely across the fabric and under the loops of warp yarns has on one end a sharpened knife edge which, as the wire is drawn out, cuts the upper surface of the loops, thus making of each loop two fuzzy tufts. From the nature of this feature, it is necessary that a rather

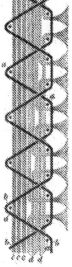

better class of warp yarns be used for Wilton carpets than for Brussels, and that these warp yarns be carefully placed in the fabric so that they will not be easily pulled out when the loops are cut, or when the carpet is in use.

37. Section of Wilton Weave Compared With Brussels Weave.—In Fig. 17 is shown a section, taken lengthwise of the fabric, of the weave of Wilton carpet, showing how the warp and the weft threads are placed. Note carefully that the *right-hand* side of the figure represents the surface of the carpet. The little black dots marked *a* are the ends, or sections, of the flax weft threads; threads *b* are the cotton chain warp winding under and over the weft threads; those marked *c* are the heavy stuffer-chain threads or yarns that give body to the carpet; and threads *d* are the worsted warp yarns (figuring warp) that come up in loops and form the pattern. By com- .

FIG. 17

paring Fig. 17, the longitudinal section of Wilton carpet, with Fig. 3, which is the longitudinal section of Brussels carpet, the first difference in weave noticeable is that the chain warp weaves over *two* weft threads at a time on the surface and then down through the fabric and under one weft thread at the bottom of the fabric. In this way the tufts, or cut loops, of warp yarns on the surface are held more compactly and have less danger of being pulled out. The most noticeable feature of the section of Wilton, Fig. 17, as compared with the section of Brussels, Fig. 3, is the manner in which the figuring warp yarns are placed; each yarn running along for some distance hidden in the surface of the fabric, and then coming to the surface as a loop, which is then cut, by the wire, into tufts.

Aside from the few distinguishing features referred to above, the weaves of Wilton and of Brussels are similar.

38. Frames, Planting, and Sizes of Wilton Carpet. Since the method of weaving Wilton carpets is practically the same as weaving Brussels carpets, the principle of introducing the colored warp yarns in layers, or frames, in the body of the fabric, and of planting colors in any frame when necessary, is the same.

Wilton carpets are 27 inches, or ¾ yard, in width, just as are Brussels carpets. In length, the pattern, or repeat, is usually about 36 inches. Ordinarily in Wilton carpet there are more crosswise wires to the inch used than in Brussels, which would require more squares to the inch in length on Wilton design paper than on that for Brussels. Therefore, if a carpet is designed on Brussels design paper and then is afterwards woven as a Wilton carpet, the longitudinal repeat will be somewhat shorter than was originally intended.

DESIGNING

39. Classes of Patterns Suitable for Wilton Carpets. Inasmuch as Wilton carpets are woven on the same kind of loom, and in the same way, as Brussels carpets, there is no mechanical requirement or other necessity that compels the designer to learn anything additional regarding styles of repeating patterns that are most suitably employed for Wilton carpets. In fact, he may design for Wiltons, so far as artistic designing and coloring are concerned, just as he did for Brussels.

40. Blocking Out and Rendering on Squared Paper. The kind of squared paper suitable for designs for Brussels carpet is shown in Figs. 10 and 11. Designs for Wilton carpet may be made on this kind of paper, but, if so, may come *short* in the length of repeat because there are more crosswise wires to the inch used in Wilton than in Brussels carpet. The number of divisions to the inch depends, of course, on the fineness of the weave of the loops of yarn. Thus, the design paper may consist of 8×8 divisions to the inch, or perhaps 8×9 to the inch, as shown in Figs. 10 and 11, or even 9×9 or 10×10. The designer's duty is first of all to find out from the manufacturer the fineness or the weave, and thus learn what kind of ruled paper is to be used, and then make his designs upon this kind of paper.

The process of first blocking in with charcoal, then testing for color schemes, and planting if necessary, then ticking-in and coloring with opaque color, may be followed in the case of Wilton designs just as was done in making designs for Brussels carpet.

41. A Fully Rendered Design for Wilton.—The reproduction of a carpet design in Fig. 18 gives the general appearance of a full-size design on regular design paper, for a Wilton border.

As in the case of Fig. 15, the design in colors for Brussels carpet, it should be noted that the design in Fig. 18 for the Wilton border, although rendered in semi-opaque colors, is pure, rich, and fresh in color, and there is no dull or cold effect observable.

The carpet for which this design is made also shows evidence of the planting of colors, where the red, blue, sage, and écru, and the three tones of dark brown, have been introduced in the pattern, making the total number of colors seven. In studying the planting system here, Fig. 18 must be viewed from one side, for borders are woven in long strips. It will be observed, too, that neither the red nor the écru extends over the full width of the border. All the middle tone of the brown is planted with red, but by carefully observing one can see that nowhere in the pattern do these colors come in the same vertical line.

TYPICAL EXAMPLE

42. Specimen of Wilton Carpet.—As in the case of the designer of Brussels carpet, the student preparing to make designs for Wilton carpet should not only become familiar with

FIG. 18 § 18 289

the process by which such carpet is woven, as presented in the foregoing pages, but should examine carefully specimens of Wilton carpet as displayed in carpet stores (where it will frequently be called **velvet** carpet by the salesman, because the cut pile forms a sort of velvety surface).

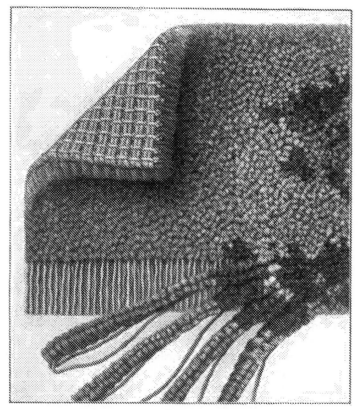

FIG. 19

The specimen of carpet selected for an example, a photograph of which is shown in Fig. 19, is therefore one that shows a typical **velvet** carpet, although its weave (as can readily be seen) does not in every particular agree with the diagram of the Wilton weave shown in Fig. 17. In Fig. 17 the figuring yarns

289—24

come to the surface in loops that are cut and thus become tufts, but a great part of each yarn strand lies in the body of the fabric. In Fig. 19, however, the cut pile is in the form of individual cut loops or tufts attached to the weft threads, but the principle of cut-pile surface is that of the Wilton weave, which is the particular characteristic that is always noticeable in a Wilton weave; namely, that the loops of warp yarns are cut to form the pile. In Fig. 16, the full-size specimen of body Brussels, the rows of loops running transversely across the fabric were very evident. In this specimen of Wilton, Fig. 19, the rows made by the loops are still there, but, as the loops are cut, the ends of the yarn are fluffed out, stand up, and spread out, and thus cover the pronounced effect of rows.

It can be clearly seen here that the backing is of strong linen thread, and that there are additional warp threads running through on the backing to give greater body to the fabric.

This specimen of Wilton is typical; but one who would make designs for such carpets should continue his investigations and research, visiting carpet stores and mills, as previously advised.

INGRAIN, OR KIDDERMINSTER, CARPET

MANUFACTURE

43. Characteristic Weave of Ingrain Carpet.—The method of weaving ingrain carpets (called Kidderminster in England) is quite different from that of weaving Brussels and Wilton carpets, previously described. In both Brussels and Wilton, the warp yarns were brought to the surface of the fabric and looped; in Brussels the loops remained uncut and in Wilton they were cut, these fabrics being known as pile carpets. In weaving ingrain, or Kidderminster, carpets, however, the figuring yarns are tightly stretched over the intersecting linen threads, the surface of the fabric thus being fairly flat and no surface loops or pile being formed.

The chief characteristic, in the simplest form of two-ply ingrains, is that the two figuring yarns change places as they pass across the fabrics, one color being on the upper side and the other color on the under side of the fabric. This enables the pattern to be the same on both sides of the fabric, but in reversed colors. Thus, if one side of the fabric shows écru figures on a green background, the other side of the fabric will show green figures on an écru background.

The above simple two-ply arrangement, which allows the designer the use of only two colors in his design, can be elaborated upon, thus producing three-ply ingrain carpets. The three-ply refers not only to the three sets of colored figuring yarns, but also to an arrangement whereby not only the three regular sets are used, but where warps of various colors are used crossing the wefts of various colors. In this way the colored warps and the colored wefts may be combined to make some quite elaborate color schemes.

44. Cross-Section of Ingrain Carpet.—It must be clearly understood that, in ingrain carpet, the pattern is formed mainly by the *weft* yarns, which is just the reverse of the method used for Brussels and Wilton, where the *warp* yarns form the pattern. In ingrain carpets, while the heavy, closely woven *weft* yarns, which run crosswise of the fabric, form the greatest body of the color scheme, the *warp* threads, running lengthwise of the fabric, also assist in the color scheme by their diversified colors. Thus, in a two-ply ingrain carpet, there may be four colors—two weft and two warp.

FIG. 20

For the above reason, when looking at Fig. 20, the cross-section of ingrain carpet, it must be remembered that the section is taken *across* the fabric; that is, across the warp threads, and *not* along them as in the case of the sections of the Brussels and the Wilton shown in Figs. 3 and 17. Therefore, in Fig. 20 the little black dots and white dots lettered *d* indicate the *warp* threads running lengthwise of the fabric; the white interlacing yarns lettered *b*, and the black interlacing yarns lettered *c*, represent the figuring *weft* yarns which, in ingrain carpet, form the greater part of the colored pattern of the carpet.

The cross-section in Fig. 20 shows only the simplest kind of a two-ply ingrain. The cross-section of three-ply ingrains, of course, would show three sets of dots to represent warp threads, and three sets of intertwining yarns to represent weft figuring yarns.

45. Sizes of Ingrain Carpets.—Some ingrain carpets are woven in squares 9 feet by 9 feet and called *Kidder squares*, or *art squares*. In designing for such seamless squares, or for the carpet woven in strips, as is other carpet, the repeats should be from 18 to 27 inches wide and not more than 2 feet long.

DESIGNING

46. Classes of Patterns Suitable for Ingrain Carpets. The designer of ingrain, or Kidderminster, carpet must consider first of all whether his design is to be for an ingrain carpet woven in the regular 18-inch or 27-inch strips, or for a Kidder square, or art square. If the design is to be for ingrain strips, the classes of patterns described for Brussels and Wilton may easily be adapted, if the comparative coarseness of the ingrain weave is carefully considered. It is well to avoid the drop repeat in any kind of ingrain designing, for if the pattern is to be adapted to the art square the repeat must of necessity be plain side-to-side repeat; otherwise it would not balance well on both sides of the square.

If an ingrain design is being prepared for an art square of seamless carpet, about 9 feet by 9 feet in size, the repeats of the pattern of the border must correspond to the dimensions of the repeat of the filling; that is, 9 inches, 18 inches, 27 inches, etc., so as to make the repeating patterns of both border and field symmetrical.

47. Blocking Out and Rendering on Squared Paper. The kind of design paper to use when making designs for ingrain carpet depends on the kind of weave employed—whether for a two-ply or for a three-ply carpet, and whether in two, or four or more colors. However, a standard cross-section paper suitable for ingrain designs is shown in Fig. 21, where each inch in width is divided into eight spaces, representing the thin warp threads—sometimes used only as binders and sometimes colored—and each inch in height is divided into sixteen spaces, representing the weft figuring yarns that form the greater portion of the body colors of the carpet.

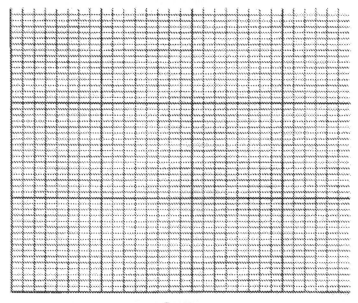

Fig. 21

The method of blocking out the design, testing for color schemes, then coloring on the design paper, as described for Brussels and Wilton carpets, should be followed here. Since the method of weaving ingrain carpet is such that the planting of frames of colored yarns cannot be resorted to, the designer of ingrain escapes this complication and his work is much simplified. For this reason, a two-ply ingrain carpet, with two colors, offers the simplest kind of a problem that the carpet designer can expect to meet.

48. A Fully Rendered Design for Ingrain.—While Fig. 22 was originally a design made for Wilton carpet, adopted from one of the designs of William Morris, the great designer and craftsman of England, it could be very well adapted to ingrain carpet. There are but four colors—two blues, two yellows, a red and a green. Since it is quite practicable to produce four colors in an ingrain carpet of the better class, by having the warp threads colored as well as the weft yarns, this pattern could be produced as an ingrain with little modification.

The flowers and leaves in the pattern are honestly conventionalized, in both drawing and coloring, to suit them to their purpose, a perfectly flat effect being thereby secured, one that is thoroughly suitable for a floor covering. It is not a pattern that would attract the public at first sight; but the public taste is improving, and the use of such frankly conventionalized floral patterns trains one to appreciate them and gives a feeling of satisfaction that can never be attained by such gaudy floral designs as are very commonly seen even on expensive carpets.

TYPICAL EXAMPLE

49. Specimen of Ingrain Carpet.—As in the case of Brussels and Wilton carpets previously discussed, the designer of ingrain carpets should first of all seize every opportunity to examine and handle specimens of ingrain carpets as seen in store and factory.

For assistance along this line, however, there is shown in Fig. 23 a photograph of a piece of ingrain carpet, full size. By turning over one corner, as shown, it is clearly seen that ingrain carpet has no backing; that is, it is reversible. The same pattern appears on both sides of the fabric, but the colors are reversed.

In the piece of carpet from which the photograph was made, the part shown at the top of the illustration had light green leaves on a white background and on the reverse side white leaves on a light green background; on the part shown at the bottom, red ornament appeared on a white background, while on the other side was white ornament on a red background.

FIG. 22

§18   289

When the weft yarns, which in ingrain carpet form the greater part of the body of the colored design, are pulled out or unraveled, the warp threads show clearly. In some of the cheaper classes of ingrains there are only two sets of warp threads and these are uncolored, in no way helping with the

FIG. 23

color scheme. In the specimen shown, however, there are four sets of warp threads—white, yellow, green, and red—all helping in the color scheme.

The illustration shows how ingrain carpet is woven, but should be supplemented by a study of specimens of the actual fabric.

AXMINSTER CARPET

MANUFACTURE

50. Classes of Axminster Carpets.—Axminster carpets, classified according to their methods of weaving, may be divided into two general kinds: *Royal Axminster*, or *Moquette*, and *Chenille Axminster*. The methods of weaving of these two carpets differ so radically that they must be described separately.

FIG. 24

51. Characteristic Weave of Moquette Axminster.—The term moquette is a French word used for Axminster, and is one commonly applied to that class of carpet in the United States. All Axminster carpets are of the tufted-pile class, or velvet carpets; that is, the pile loops are cut and tufted, but the tufting material is not woven in by the Jacquard machine, as in the case of Wiltons, but is tufted in. Originally, in the hand-made carpets of this type, there was first woven a square meshwork of interlacing warp and weft threads, and then the softer yarns of the desired colors were tied in by hand in tufts at the intersections of the warp and weft threads. Later a process of weaving both the groundwork and the pile tufting on a hand loom was devised.

In the modern machine-woven Royal Axminster, or moquette, there may be one or two sets of weft threads used for filling and binding, in addition to the tufting displayed on the surface; and for the groundwork and the stuffing there may be two or three sets of warp threads.

52. Section Through Moquette Axminster Carpet. While there are many different weaves of moquette carpets, depending on the weight, thickness, degree of length and richness of the tufting, etc., a typical section of moquette weave is that shown in Fig. 24, the *right-hand* side of the illustration representing the surface of the carpet. This section is taken along the length of the warp threads, and crossing the weft threads, just as are the sections of Brussels and Wilton carpets shown in Figs. 3 and 17, respectively. The little black dots marked *a* are the ends or sections of the jute weft yarns used as filling weft; thread *b* is the intertwining linen warp thread or yarn, called the chain warp, that passes over the top weft threads, then down through the body of the fabric and under the bottom weft threads; the long cotton warp yarns *c* are the stuffer warps, which help to give weight and body to the fabric; and at *d* can be seen the pile tufts of colored yarns and their method of tufting in under the top weft threads and over the stuffer warps.

The noticeable feature of the section of moquette Axminster shown in Fig. 24, as compared with the sections of carpets previously shown, is the arrangement and tying in of the tuft warps, to make the velvet pile.

53. Characteristic Weave of Chenille Axminster Carpet.—The process of weaving chenille Axminster carpet is so complicated that it is necessary to give here only the principle under which it is done.

There is first woven what is called the chenille *fur*, which is to form the velvety surface of the carpet fabric. The fur is woven by a special loom mechanism in one large *cloth piece*, but in strips of color, each strip corresponding with its appropriate horizontal row of colored squares on the design paper. This cloth piece of fur is then put in a cutting machine where it is pressed under heat and cut into strips, ready to be woven in on the body of the fabric.

The fabric, or backing, for the chenille is woven separately, like ordinary carpet, but of course to the same scale as the chenille fur. The problem then is to incorporate the strips of chenille fur with the body, or backing, so as to make a homogeneous and compact fabric. The chenille fur, in horizontal strips, is woven into or upon the specially woven carpet backing in such a way that the binding threads or loops are picked up, the fur strips forced under, and the binding threads then tightened. The detailed mechanism by which this is accomplished need not be discussed in this connection.

54. Sizes of Axminster Carpet.—The 27-inch width for regular strip carpets applies to Axminster as well as to other classes of carpets, on account of the convenience in repeat and in cutting. However, Axminster is also woven in 18-inch widths, especially for stair carpets, because the lateral repeats allowable in an 18-inch-width pattern are suitable singly for stair carpets and hall runners, and in multiples of this 18-inch repeat for strip carpets and rugs.

DESIGNING

55. Classes of Patterns Suitable for Axminster Carpet.—What has already been said about the kind of patterns suitable for Brussels, Wilton, and ingrain carpets will apply also to Axminster carpets, so far as actual repeat arrangements are concerned. However, when it comes to the amount of detail to be introduced, the fineness of the individual details of ornament, etc., the designer of Axminster carpets must simplify these features more than for any other class of carpet. The reason for this is that the size of the little squares on the design paper is larger, as required by the coarser weave, which subject will be discussed in connection with blocking out and rendering the design on squared paper.

The designer of Axminster, therefore, requires considerable preliminary practice in reducing decorative forms to the restrictions imposed on him by the coarseness of the weave, and therefore of the squared design paper.

56. Blocking Out and Rendering on Squared Paper. There are numerous *pitches* of Axminster design paper; that is, divisions or small rectangles to the square inch, depending on the quality of the weave. Standard sizes, or pitches, of design paper are 6×7 spaces or 7×7 spaces to the square inch, although papers having spaces ranging in number from 5×6 to 10×10 spaces to the square inch are used. Two specimens of Axminster design paper are reproduced in Fig. 25 (a) and (b).

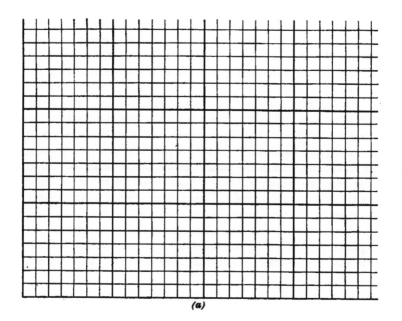

(a)

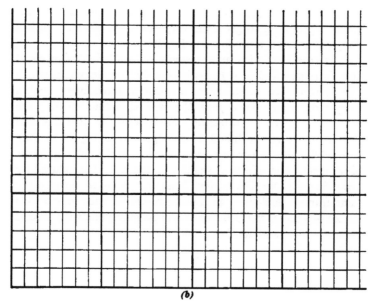

(b)

Fig. 25

The designer of Axminster carpets has the greatest opportunity of any of the carpet designers to use color. As a matter of fact, a well-trained color sense is absolutely essential for the designer of Axminster carpets. He is practically unlimited in his choice of colors. Each row of tufts per inch on the carpet may be of a different color; thus, if the design were 30 inches long and each inch contained seven rows of tufts, there would be allowable 30 times 7, or 210, separate colors in a pattern 30 inches long. But the pattern might be 40 inches long, thus allowing 280 separate colors. Each separate tufting colored yarn has a separate spool. Thus it is seen what a great choice of color is allowed the designer.

The method of first blocking out the design in charcoal on squared paper, then testing for color schemes, and then ticking-in with opaque color, has already been described and need not be repeated here.

57. A Fully Rendered Design for Axminster Carpet. Because of the characteristics of Axminster carpet, as just described, the designer can, if he desires, combine colors in the greatest profusion to get some very elaborate effects. Such a design in colors is reproduced in Fig. 26.

It is true that such an extremely naturalistic design could also be reproduced in a Brussels or a Wilton weave, in which case it would be necessary to arrange to have every bobbin carry a different-colored yarn, the method of thus securing the pattern being called *chintzing*. Such work, in Brussels and Wilton, involves the fullest knowledge and ability in making planted designs, as a great variety of colors in the different forms of ornament and effects of shading in the color is produced by arranging, side by side, various hues and values of yarns in the same frame. A flower can thus be produced with four or five values of yellow, where beside it will be found one with several values of blue, and another in red, etc.

FIG. 26 §18 283

58. Specimen of Axminster Carpet.—The process by which an Axminster carpet is produced, including the weaving of the backing fabric, the weaving of the "fur" to form the velvety pile, and then the weaving of the two so as to make

FIG. 27

one fabric, is so complicated as to make it almost necessary for the designer to inspect the actual fabric.

However, much can be learned from a study of a photograph, full size, direct from the carpet itself. Such a photograph of a piece of Axminster carpet is shown in Fig. 27. There is evident at once the furry surface of the pile; that is, there are seen no such regular rows of loops as in Brussels, but the pile spreads over the surface of the fabric in an irregular stipple effect very much like the short fur on certain animals. The carpet is very firmly backed—as can be seen at the turned-over portion in Fig. 27—by the linen warp and weft threads. Interwoven with the warp threads are the strong weft threads carrying the rows of fur. At the lower part of the illustration this fur is very clearly shown, as well as the fact that it is fastened to the weft threads that carry it, some of the strips of fur having been purposely unloosened and spread out separately to show just how this material is incorporated with the body of the fabric.

TAPESTRY CARPETS

MANUFACTURE

59. Characteristics of Tapestry Carpets.—In this consideration of tapestry carpets it will be of chief importance to discuss, not particularly the weaving, but the method by which the colored pattern or design on the surface is produced.   Heretofore, it has been shown that the colored patterns on Brussels, Wilton, ingrain, and Axminster carpets have been produced by weaving the colored yarns in such a way that the particular colors of yarns required to make the pattern were brought to the surface when needed.   In the case of tapestry carpets, however, the colored pattern is produced by printing, or dyeing, colors onto the fabric from large rollers or drums just as type is printed from in newspapers.

These carpets may be of the Brussels type of weave; that is, with the uncut loops; in which case the product is called **tapestry Brussels;** or they may be of the cut-pile, or velvet, class of fabrics, when they are commonly known as **tapestry Axminster.**

60. Section Through a Tapestry Carpet.—In Fig. 28 is shown a section, taken lengthwise of the warp, and crossing the weft, through a carpet of the tapestry-Brussels class, the *right-hand* side of the illustration representing the surface of the carpet. A comparison of this section of tapestry Brussels with the section of body Brussels shown in Fig. 3 will clearly show that there is not nearly the weight to tapestry Brussels that is possessed by body Brussels, because there are not nearly so many sets of warp figuring threads. As a matter of fact, there is only one set of warp threads or yarns coming to the surface in loops, and it is upon these threads that the pattern is printed.

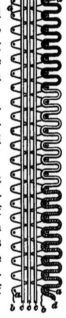

In Fig. 28 the regular weft threads are indicated as before by the little black dots *a*; the chain warp threads *b* binding the fabric together are shown going over and under the weft threads; threads *c* are the stuffer warp; and thread *d* is the warp yarn upon which the pattern is printed.

The printing of the pattern, which is the noticeable characteristic of this class of carpets, is represented in the illustration by the black, white, and gray shading of the surface warp.

61. Other Forms of Tapestry Carpet.—It is not only the Brussels, or looped-pile, type of carpet that can be made in tapestry form. Carpets of the cut-pile, or velvet, class may also be produced in printed form. The process is exactly the same as in the case of looped-pile carpets. Such cut-pile tapestries are usually called Axminster tapestry carpets, because their weave partakes of the nature of Axminster.

FIG. 28

62. Method of Printing for Tapestry Carpet.—To offset the comparative lightness in weight of the weave of tapestry carpet the weft is first dipped in glue, which adds considerable to its weight and also helps to stiffen the backing of the carpet.

The pattern on the surface of tapestry carpets may be printed in various ways. The most common method perhaps is to print, with color or dye, from rollers or blocks, the pattern colors on the pile-warp threads before they are actually woven into the fabric. It is evident that the *length* of any pattern color must be considerably greater on the straight, unwoven pile yarn than it is to appear when woven in the goods, because allowance must be made for the length of actual fabric space taken up in the formation of the loops. For instance, if the undulating line forming the loops at the top of Fig. 28 were to be stretched out straight vertically it would be considerably longer than $3\frac{1}{4}$ inches, as shown, and would probably be as long as 10 or 12 inches, depending on the depth of the loop. This will give an idea as to the allowance that must be made when printing the color on the warp yarns before weaving.

Another method, although not so commonly employed, is to have the carpet woven gray and then to have the pattern printed thereon direct from the rollers or blocks, just as a newspaper or a wallpaper is printed. It is evident, however, that, according to this method, the color cannot penetrate deeply into the warp pile.

The machinery used for the printing of colors in tapestry carpets is very elaborate and complicated and it would be of no practical value to the artistic designer to learn all the details of the processes. He can make just as successful designs for tapestry carpets without this detailed knowledge. However, the draftsman connected with the carpet mill, who translates the artists' design for carpet into a classified layout for arranging the colors on the color drum, must be fully acquainted with this printing process. However, such layouts are usually made by technical men who have been in the carpet business for years, and perhaps have devoted their lives to that specialty. The artistic designer need not thus specialize, unless he desires to do so.

63. Sizes of Tapestry Carpets.—As in the case of body Brussels carpet, or body Axminster carpet, tapestry Brussels and tapestry Axminster are made 27 inches in width, or three-quarters of a yard, for strip carpet, and the other sizes as previously specified for stair carpets, hall runners, etc.

64. Classes of Patterns Suitable for Tapestry Carpets.—From the standpoint of the anatomy of patterns or designs, that is, their outlines and masses, the same kind of repeating patterns are used on tapestry Brussels and tapestry Axminster as are used on body Brussels and body Axminster. However, there are certain features that must be understood by the designer of tapestry carpets that have not heretofore needed consideration, which apply in the blocking out and rendering of the design on squared paper.

65. Blocking Out and Rendering on Squared Paper. In the carpets previously discussed—Brussels, Wilton, ingrain, and Axminster—where the pattern was secured solely by weaving warp and weft threads or yarns, there were practically no limitations as to the *length* of the pattern. However, in the case of tapestry carpet the length of the repeat is limited by the circumference of the roller or drum that prints the colors onto the yarns. These rollers or drums vary greatly in size, and the designer's first duty is to find out just what size roller or drum is being used at the factory for which he is making the design. Thus, the pattern may be made 27 inches wide, the width of the carpet strip, or some divisor of 27, such as 9 inches, 18 inches, etc.; and the length of the pattern, in its elongated form, allowing for the reduction that comes from weaving, may be $3\frac{1}{2}$ or $4\frac{1}{2}$ yards. This consideration, however, applies to the draftsman in the carpet mill who lays out the *color board* for the printing drums.

66. The artistic designer of tapestry carpets blocks in and renders his design on the squared paper just as do designers of other classes of carpets, but he needs to exercise particular care and skill in doing the coloring, because allowance must be made for the running, or spreading, of certain colors on account of the great heat necessary in the steaming process. These features can receive the proper consideration only when the designer familiarizes himself with them by visiting carpet mills and watching the actual processes of weaving and printing tapestry carpets. Further, he must always work with a piece of tapestry carpet in front of him, preferably one in which the same colors have been used that he is about to use in his own design.

TYPICAL EXAMPLE

67. Specimen of Tapestry Carpet.—Of the various types of tapestry carpets, perhaps the best known is tapestry Brussels, and a photograph of a full-size section of such carpet is shown in Fig. 29.

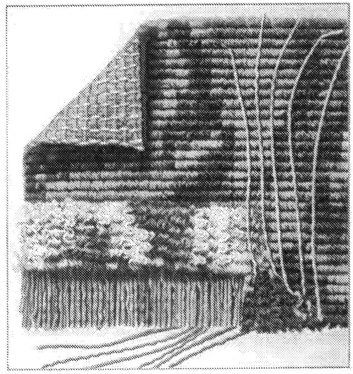

FIG. 29

As in the case of carpets previously discussed, the prospective designer of tapestry Brussels should become familiar with the processes of printing the yarns before or after weaving, as the case may be. Such complete knowledge can be obtained only by visiting the factory and watching the processes.

However, the full-size reproduction of the specimen shown in Fig. 29 will serve to show how certain effects are obtained by the tapestry printing process that can not be obtained by the ordinary weave. Soft gradations from dark red to light red, thence to light green gradually deepening to dark green, can be effected, because a certain amount of blending and gradation can be arranged for on the printing drums, and a certain additional amount occurs as the color spreads over, and down into, the loops of yarn.

As far as the backing and the weave are concerned, as will be shown by the turned-over and raveled portions in the illustration, there is very little difference between the tapestry Brussels and the body Brussels, except that the weave of tapestry Brussels is lighter, there being no warp yarns used except those that are printed upon. However, in some cases, as this one, additional warp threads of tough material are introduced to give firmness to the backing and weight to the fabric.

RUGS

CLASSIFICATION OF RUGS

68. General Meaning of Term "Rugs."—The distinction between carpets and rugs is that, while carpets are woven in long strips and laid on the floor by matching patterns and tacking the fabric to the floor, rugs are usually woven in one piece for a definite space or a definite size. There are some cases where rugs are made from strip carpet sewed together; but even in such cases these strips were originally designed to be sewed together in rug formation, particularly where a distinctly marked border surrounds the margin of the rug itself.

Rugs, broadly considered, may be considered as coming under two general classifications: (a) *oriental rugs*, and (b) *modern machine-made rugs*.

69. Oriental Rugs.—The term **oriental rugs** refers to those rugs that have been made, and are still being made, in the Orient; that is, in the eastern countries, Persia, India, Turkey, etc. Such rugs are all hand made; that is, woven by hand on hand looms, the result being individual and beautiful to a high degree.

70. Modern Machine-Made Rugs.—Modern conditions of house building, floor arrangement and construction, etc., are such that the householder does not desire his entire floor covered with carpet, but desires parts of it to show, particularly if the floor be of hardwood or parquetry. Hence rugs are employed; and this has created a demand for rugs that cannot be satisfied by the oriental product, even if the average householder could afford their cost. Machine-woven rugs of all kinds, therefore, are produced, and the carpet designer must be prepared to make designs for them.

ORIENTAL RUGS

71. Characteristics of Oriental Rugs.—It is not the purpose of this treatise on rugs to discuss their manufacture and designing, as was done in the case of carpets. The artistic designer who has been made familiar with the method of weaving and designing for carpets will also, therefore, have learned the weaving and designing of rugs, for the processes are the same, except, of course, that for one-piece rugs very wide looms are required for the weaving. The present purpose, therefore, is to present some descriptions of rugs of various kinds, together with illustrations of these rugs, that will serve as good examples of patterns and color schemes for the young designer.

The chief characteristic of the real oriental rug, as can be told by the average man as well as the expert, is the beautiful neutralized bloom of a vast assortment of rich color combinations all over the surface of the rug, in contrast to many of the sharp and precise color arrangements observable on machine-woven rugs. The reason for this distinctive feature is that oriental rugs were and are woven by hand. Men, women, and even children are engaged before the loom tying, by hand, the tufts of dyed yarn that are to form the pattern of the finished fabric. These yarns, in the best quality of rugs, are dyed with a vegetable dye that is permanent and unchanging throughout centuries, except so far as it acquires a softening effect that delightfully blends one color into another. These rug weavers receive a mere pittance of a few cents per week for their services, and in oriental countries a carpet that may have taken over a year to weave does not represent any large amount of money to the weaver; and sells for what would be considered an absurd price in this country.

Commercialism of late years has entered the far East, however, and rugs are now made there with aniline-dyed wools that fade and lose their freshness without acquiring the soft bloom so characteristic of the antique goods.

Every country in the old world had some particular guild of craftsmen that characterized the country, and the guild of most importance in oriental countries was that of the dyers. The dyers were divided into different classes according to the colors they could dye, and they lived in colonies regulated by the convenience of water facilities in applying their craft. The dyes were applied by dipping the skeins of yarn in successive solutions alternately, and not by mixing the dyes to form a color as in modern times. The exact method of doing this was one of the guild secrets, as was also the length of time it should hang in the sun to dry and soften. There are no books of recipes for these dyes, but each dyer has a mental list of various shades that he can compound at a moment's notice in order to satisfy the demand. The skill of these dyers can be judged when we understand that one of them, blindfolded, can run his hands over a rug and describe the pattern accurately from the feeling of the different colors in the wool, so familiar is he with the effect of the dyes on the fabric.

The imitation of the ancient dyes by the modern products of coal tar has degenerated the rug industry materially, as has also the demand in Europe and America for oriental fabrics, and the Wilton rug woven on the loom is in many respects preferable to what are apparently genuine oriental fabrics, but which are in reality cheaper imitations of the ancient goods woven expressly to sell in European and American markets. In many new fabrics that come from out-of-the-way parts of the Orient, the dyes and wool are found to be thoroughly up to the old standard, but the majority of importations are sadly inferior to what we are led to believe is the characteristic quality of an oriental rug. The reputation of Persia rested on its rugs, and there was at one time a law that forbade the introduction into that country of chemical agents to be used as dyestuffs, and any dyer convicted of using aniline in his craft was sentenced to have his right hand cut off. Whether the law was enforced or not, consignments of aniline-dyed rugs continued to pour out of the country. Some years ago, the Shah of Persia issued an edict, and had it printed in French as well as in Persian, in order that its circulation might be satisfactory, forbidding the use of aniline dyes in rugs and carpets; forbidding the introduction of aniline dyes into the kingdom either in dry or liquid form; forbidding the exportation of rugs dyed by any aniline process, and a number of other details all pertaining directly to the maintenance of the high quality of Persian carpets. Notwithstanding all this, the market is still flooded with spurious imitations of antique rugs that have undoubtedly been woven by hand in Persia.

72. Typical Examples of Oriental Rugs.—Rugs are classified under different names that usually indicate the city or community from which they come rather than any specific details regarding their manufacture. However, they are recognized usually by details of texture in the wool, the character of the knot employed to tie it, the material of the warp and weft, the length of the pile, etc.

A genuine oriental rug is usually a written page of history. The design is the development of a symbolism that has been handed from generation to generation, and that probably originated in Babylon or India many centuries ago. This inherited symbolism is the leading characteristic of all oriental designs, but the application of these designs to modern service requires their alteration to suit the mechanical limitations of the loom, and the designer can best serve his purpose by adapting the spirit that enters into these designs rather than the geometrical construction or outline itself.

While it is a simple matter for the design student, or other interested person, to get an excellent idea as to the various kinds of oriental rugs and their characteristics by visiting carpet and rug stores and asking to have these characteristics explained to him, yet he will be assisted toward such an investigation by studying several reproductions of oriental rugs as given in Figs. 30, 31, and 32. These colored reproductions were made direct from the rugs themselves, and reproduce with fidelity and exactness the colors of the original rugs.

73. In Fig. 30 is shown what is known to the trade and to collectors as a **Sehna,** which is one of the finest qualities of hand-made rugs known. The design in the body of this rug is what is known as the "Herati" pattern, or more commonly the "fish" pattern. It varies in size and method of treatment in different forms of rugs and is derived probably from ancient Chinese heraldic devices. The fish pattern is simple enough in itself and is admirable in its ground-covering qualities, as it works itself into an even bloom that conveys no definite idea of a fixed pattern but presents a satisfactory effect to the eye. The beauty of rugs of this character lies in the subdivisions of their color scheme, and in this manner the three sections of the ground are brought out by changing the color scheme of this pattern, which is uniform throughout the entire body. In the center medallion the colors are particularly soft, and when looking at it with partly closed eyes the divisions of the pattern can be clearly studied, while the colors melt into soft grays that are almost a monotone tint and yet are vibrating with color.

74. In Fig. 31 is shown a **Kirmanshah** rug. The designs of the Kirmanshah rugs run to floral patterns. The texture is looser than the average Persian rug, and the influence of Turkish ornament is very apparent. The colors are rich and in good taste, and the effect of pattern is much more prominent than in the Sehna rugs. The warp of Kirmanshah rugs is occasionally cotton, and the pile is tied with a Turkish

knot, showing the influence of the latter country. The pal-
mette and rosette forms that enter into the design are characteristic of oriental patterns and undoubtedly have been
derived from similar patterns that existed in antiquity.

75. In Fig. 32 is a **Feraghan** rug, which shows an open or
spread-out form of the fish pattern in the corners of the body.
This, on comparison with Fig. 30, will show the effects that can
be produced with this simple design by changing its color
scheme and the elements of its application. The Feraghan
rug in Fig. 32 is a modern rug. As in the ancient examples,
the fish pattern was worked out over the entire center field,
with the exception of small triangular corner pieces, as shown
in this example. The characteristics of the ancient pattern
have been carried out. The border is typical of the antique
Feraghan rug, but the solid red center and the medallion are
modern introductions due probably to an attempt to save labor
and produce in less time and with less skill sufficient rugs to
supply the market.

There are, of course, many other varieties of oriental rugs,
but the few examples illustrated will be sufficient to illustrate
to the design student the characteristics of the oriental product,
and to give him good suggestions for harmonious color schemes
when he comes to design carpets and rugs to be woven by
machinery.

MODERN MACHINE-MADE RUGS

76. Characteristics of Machine-Made Rugs.—The
superficial observer is not always able to tell the difference
between machine-woven rugs and oriental rugs merely from
the standpoint of the design and coloring. Many machine-
woven rugs are now made in such close imitation of the patterns
and coloring of oriental hand-made rugs that it requires a rug
expert to tell the difference.

The patterns characteristic of oriental rugs are seriously
imitated with more or less success. In the Wilton carpetings
produced by the modern loom, the carpet designer endeavors
to secure, with the means at his disposal, the effect of bloom

characteristic of the old oriental hand weaving. This can never be fully accomplished, owing to the limitations of the five frames and the planting. But inspirations can be drawn from the study of oriental patterns and worked up by the skilful designer into something that is suitable for modern weaving without being a direct imitation.

One characteristic of the machine-made rug is that it is usually made in uniform standard widths and lengths and the repeats, in both filling and border, tend to follow the 9-inch or 18-inch dimensions. There is less freedom, also, in the pattern of the field of machine-made rugs, there being a noticeable tendency toward repeating symmetrical patterns or motifs of a small scale all over the field. The border, too, has a geometrically accurate appearance. Then, too, a close inspection will reveal the color limitations of the machine-made rug as compared with the innumerable colors forming the neutralized bloom characteristic of the hand-made oriental rug.

77. Sizes of Machine-Made Rugs.—It has already been pointed out that carpets are frequently woven in patterns whose sizes are such that they can very easily be made up into rugs of uniform sizes. For instance, most Brussels carpet required by the average householder for covering entire floors is tapestry Brussels. Body Brussels is usually demanded not so much in strip carpet form as in the form of rugs. Manufacturers therefore want body Brussels designs that can be easily adapted for rugs.

78. The usual sizes for Brussels rugs are 6 feet by 9 feet, 8 feet 3 inches by 10 feet 6 inches, and 9 feet by 12 feet, the latter being a common size frequently called *room size* because suitable for the floor of the average room. If a larger rug than 9×12 is required, the enlargement will have to be on the 18-inch basis. Thus, if a wider rug were wanted it would be 9 feet +18 inches, or 10½ feet, wide by 12 feet long. If a longer rug than 9×12 were wanted it would be 9 feet wide by 12 feet +18 inches, or 13½ feet, long.

79. In the case of Wilton rugs, the sizes run the same as Brussels rugs, because the method of weaving is the same.

There are also Wilton rugs of smaller sizes, such as 3 feet by 5 feet 3 inches, 3 feet by 6 feet, etc. There is a style of Wilton rug called a *hall runner*, because it is made to fit more or less into narrow halls, which rugs usually are 3 feet by 9 feet, 3 feet by 12 feet, and 3 feet by 15 feet. Such hall runners of even narrower dimensions are also made in the Axminster weave.

80. Special Considerations When Designing Rugs. Special points must be observed in making a design for a rug, say Brussels or Wilton, that is to be composed of carpet strips sewed together. For instance, a 9′×12′ rug is made up of four strips of carpet each 27 inches, or 2¼ feet, wide by 12 feet long, which are sewed together. The two outer strips, the first and the fourth, contain the side border and its *return* on the corners to start the end borders. If the border is a full carpet strip wide (27 inches), of course no part of the field of the design will show on these first and fourth strips. However, if the border is 18 inches wide, then not only the 18-inch width of the border shows, but also 9 inches of the field. The two inner strips finish out the borders across the ends and also complete the major portion of the field of the design.

In designing a rug of this character, the designer must prepare his design for one-quarter of the entire space, which will require four sheets of design paper. The width of the design for a 9′×12′ rug will be 54 inches (4½ feet), while the length will include 72 inches (6 feet). Thus, one-half of the length and one-half of the width of the rug is expressed in the design, and the duplication of these details is effected through the mechanical devices in the loom. The designer need not concern himself about this detail, however, but must arrange his design in such a manner that the figures expressed in the rug will turn over and match properly. The design is usually executed at the lower left-hand corner of the rug, and the four pieces of paper are laid out as though they were one sheet, the proper number of warp and weft threads being accurately accounted for.

81. As it is desirable that rugs of this character should appear as if made of one piece, rather than of several pieces sewed together, the skilful designer schemes out his pattern so that the seams are hidden as much as possible. The first seam passes directly through the center of the drawing and can be used as a center line on which the figures duplicate or repeat to form the symmetrical devices on each side. If a 27-inch border is used, this seam can be hidden by the line of the border itself where it unites with the rug. A small wandering all-over pattern is most effectual for hiding the seam where it is desired that it should be suppressed, and a plain ground or filling is most likely to bring it into prominence. Where a plain ground is desired in the rug, as a whole or in a portion of the border, it is best that some of the design should extend beyond the seam at the end of the rug where the side borders and end borders unite, as the most objectionable place for the seam to show itself is at this point.

Designs for rugs smaller than 9 feet by 12 feet are adapted from the $9' \times 12'$ pattern. In rugs 8 feet 3 inches by 10 feet 6 inches, the two outside strips are $\frac{5}{8}$ yard instead of $\frac{3}{4}$ yard, making a reduction of $4\frac{1}{2}$ inches from the previous border from each side of the rug, or 9 inches in the entire width. If the pattern permits, this diminution in size is removed from the filling of the rug and the border is left as it was originally designed for the $9' \times 12'$ size.

Sometimes a border is composed of a number of subdivisions, so that when the smaller rug is prepared one of the subdivisions is omitted from the border, thus making it narrow. The two middle widths for the filling of the rug are left $\frac{3}{4}$ yard wide, and the length is reduced by dropping $\frac{1}{4}$ yard from the filling; though, if $4\frac{1}{2}$ inches has been dropped from the border, only $4\frac{1}{2}$ inches need be dropped from the filling.

In the next smaller size, 6 feet by 9 feet, the side strips are $\frac{5}{8}$ yard in width and the length is reduced an even yard. In making these corrections, care should be taken that no redesigning is necessary, as much trouble and expense can be saved by the observance of this rule.

82. Occasionally it becomes necessary that an entirely new pattern be drawn, but this rarely involves more trouble than the copying of the original design, with the omission of certain details and the alteration of others.

This practice of redrafting a design does not require the skill and experience of the head designer, but its easy accomplishment can be effectuated only through the forethought of the head designer in the planning of the original 9′×12′ rug. In this he has given due consideration to the separate sizes and has planned his border and filling so they can be cut down to the standard sizes without materially detracting from the general effect of the design.

In redesigning or redrawing the smaller sizes, it is nearly always necessary that there should be a reduction in the scale of the ornament, and as the beginner is likely to omit much of the detail in order to effect this reduction, the work requires the services of a more experienced man than does the reducing of the larger sizes. In this work the designer should be able to reproduce the original design on a smaller scale without losing the general effect and general appearance of the original.

The hall runners and other 1-yard-wide sizes are usually woven in one piece and are executed on the design paper accordingly. The 9′×12′ rugs have been woven in one piece also, but they are very expensive and have not as yet come into general use.

83. Typical Examples of Machine-Made Rugs.—The terms Brussels, Wilton, Axminster, etc., while terms covering rugs in general, do not represent all the names applied to rugs. A visit to any completely equipped carpet and rug store will reveal scores of trade names applied to rugs, such as Smyrna, Crex, Fiber, etc., but they all come under the general types of weaving and designing already discussed.

While the prospective carpet or rug designer should not attempt to prepare a design for any particular kind of rug without first examining carefully such a rug in a carpet store and if possible watching, in the mill, the process of weaving such a rug, it will assist him to that end to examine the reproductions of modern machine-made rugs shown in Figs. 33, 34, and 35, which reproductions were made direct from the rugs themselves.

These are all Wilton rugs 10½ feet by 12 feet, and are five-frame fabrics woven in conventional colors, red, blue, gold écru, and green. In each case the border is 27 inches wide, thus filling the entire width of a strip of carpet. This can be clearly seen, especially in the lower right-hand corner of Fig. 35, where the very distinct line running down vertically from the inner edge of the right-hand border and crossing the lower horizontal border indicates very clearly where the seam is. The other seam is also clearly shown at the lower left-hand corner, running down as an extension of the vertical center line of the medallion ornament in the center of the field.

These three examples undoubtedly owe their designs to inspirations derived from oriental patterns, but the coloring and general effect is far inferior to the softness of the Persian rugs, as may be seen by comparing any of them with Fig. 30. In general effect, they lack the softness of the hand-woven rug and express emphatically the hardness of a machine-produced carpet. The limited range of color, necessitated by the loom, prevents that soft bloom that is so characteristic of the oriental fabric. Compare the body of Fig. 30 with its imitation in Fig. 33, and observe how the Herati pattern assumes a machine-like and geometrical grouping in the Wilton rug that does not exist in its oriental prototype.

In the finer grade of Wilton rugs, many colors are introduced by planting, and the effect is thereby much improved, but this is a characteristic that is affected by style in carpets and varies with seasons. At the same time, designs that present the softness of bloom characteristic of oriental fabrics are not popular, owing probably to the fact that recent events in the world's history have filled the popular mind with a desire for brilliancy and loudness of color. In rug design, as in everything else, public taste is affected by entirely outside influences, and the relations of this country with some foreign power, be it oriental or occidental, are likely to bring some particular style into popularity and thereby affect all design.

84. In Figs. 34 and 35 will be found many forms similar to those in the oriental patterns, Figs. 31 and 32. The borders and medallions in the center appear to have been copied directly from some oriental example, although they may have been worked out from several sources of inspiration, but they lack entirely the spirit of the original fabric and fail to present that delicacy of tone that is the chief beauty of a Persian rug.

The designer of modern rugs and carpets must admit that with the means at his command the Oriental effects cannot be successfully imitated, and while a conscientious study of Oriental patterns is of the greatest value to the designer, he should not be led to the extreme of endeavoring to reproduce them, as the most successful efforts in this line must necessarily fall below the originals. But a proper adaptation of this system of space filling is far superior to the gaudy naturalistic floor coverings that are so frequently seen in the modern carpet and rug store.

CARPET AND RUG DESIGNING EXERCISES

GENERAL INFORMATION

85. Required Work in This Section.—There is but one sure test by which the student may demonstrate to himself and his instructors that he has properly absorbed the information presented in this Section, and by means of which he may prepare himself to do practical carpet and rug designing in that field. This test consists of actually preparing designs in colors, for the various classes of carpets designated, in accordance with the directions given, and submitting these designs for comment and helpful advice.

These required original designs will, as before, take the form of drawing plates, to be prepared and submitted in the usual manner.

86. Character of the Drawing Plates.—The drawing plates are to be six in number, five of which will contain two exercises each, the sixth consisting of a single exercise. The plates are to be 10 inches wide by 15 inches high, or, to be more exact, if water color paper is used, $9\frac{7}{8}$ inches wide by $15\frac{1}{4}$ inches

high. However, they will be spoken of as 10"×15" plates.
The rendering of each exercise on each plate is to be done in
water colors, and with the greatest care and exactness; just
as if the design were being made to be submitted to a carpet
manufacturer. The reproductions of actual carpet designs
shown in Figs. 15 and 18 will show the degree of care and
finish that should be apparent in all designs submitted.

In the cases of Plates 2, 3, 4, and 5, the upper 9"×9" space
(Exercise A in each case) is to contain a carefully executed
water-color sketch exactly *one-third* the size of the finished rug,
but *not* on a squared-paper basis, the sketch being 9 inches
wide, whereas the finished carpet would be 27 inches wide.
The lower 9"×4" space on each of these four plates is to be
covered with squares, drawn in pencil, and in each case they
are to be of the full size and arrangement of the respective type
of squared design paper employed in designing that particular
class of carpet. This lower 9"×4" rectangle of squared paper
is then to contain a section, *full size*, from the one-third-scale
color sketch above it, the rendering to be exactly as a working
design for a carpet is prepared when it is to be submitted to a
manufacturer.

PLATE 1

87. Exercise A, Plate 1.—In the upper half of the
10"×15" plate, that is, within the 10"×7½" space, lay out
an 8"×6" rectangle, within which draw, full size, a spot ornament, or series of them, that would be suitable for a carpet
design. Use as much freedom and artistic finish in the drawing as desired, and render in black-and-white or in colors, as
preferred.

88. Exercise B, Plate 1.—In the lower half of the
10"×15" plate lay out an 8"×6" rectangle. First divide this
smaller rectangle into 1-inch squares, and then, later, each
1-inch square into ⅛-inch squares, all of which may be done
by means of an ordinary foot rule or yardstick, using the ⅛-inch
divisions thereon. The result will be an 8"×6" piece of
squared design paper.

Now, make a tracing of the ornament designed in a free style for Exercise A, and transfer it (by rubbing or by transfer paper) symmetrically to the 8″×6″ rectangle of pencil-ruled squares. Next, tick in the decorative form; that is, with a brush go over the contours and masses of the design so that these are expressed entirely by series of little squares related to one another in the proper sequence and proportion, the process being similar to that shown in Figs. 12 and 13, which, however, are not to be copied as designs but are to serve to show the method of ticking-in. Render in black-and-white or in colors, as preferred.

89. Final Work on Plate 1.—Letter or write the title, Plate 1: Carpet and Rug Designing, at the top of the sheet; and on the back place class letters and number, name, address, and date of completion of the plate. Roll the plate, protected by a sheet of tissue paper, place in the mailing tube, and send to the Schools for examination. Then proceed with Plate 2.

PLATE 2

90. Exercise A, Plate 2.—In the upper part of the 10″×15″ plate, lay out a rectangle 9 inches wide by 9 inches high. Within this rectangle prepare a sketch design in colors for a 27-inch-width body Brussels carpet. The sketch will therefore be one-third the *scale* of the full-size carpet.

Every technical detail connected with the designing of a body Brussels carpet (as distinguished from any other kind cf carpet), as explained in the text of this Section, must be observed. Strips of color, after the manner shown in Fig. 14, must be placed beneath the colored design to indicate the number of the frames employed; and if any planting of frames is employed it must be indicated in the arrangement and extent of these color strips.

The design for this exercise must in every respect be a design for a **body Brussels** carpet, and for no other class of carpet.

91. Exercise B, Plate 2.—In the lower part of the 10″×15″ plate, lay out a rectangle 9 inches wide by 4 inches high, and fill it with ruled pencil squares such as appear on body Brussels carpet design paper, like those shown in Figs. 10 and 11.

Upon this squared design paper lay off, by ticking-in full size, a small section of the design in Exercise A, one-third of the width and about one-seventh of the height of the one-third-scale colored sketch in Exercise A. The details of the pattern on this design paper will then appear three times the size they appear in Exercise A, and will be the full scale at which body Brussels carpet designs are made; that is, the full size of the details in the carpet itself.

92. Final Work on Plate 2.—Letter or write the title, Plate 2: Carpet and Rug Designing, at the top of the sheet; and on the back place class letters and number, name, address, and date of completing the plate. Roll the plate, protected by a sheet of tissue paper, place in the mailing tube, and send to the Schools for examination. Then proceed with Plate 3.

PLATE 3

93. Exercise A, Plate 3.—In the upper part of the 10″×15″ plate, lay out a rectangle 9 inches wide by 9 inches high. Within this rectangle prepare a sketch design in colors for a 27-inch-width Wilton carpet. The sketch will therefore be one-third the *scale* of the full-width carpet.

Every technical detail connected with the designing of a Wilton carpet (as distinguished from any other kind of carpet), as explained in the text of this Section, must be observed. The design for this exercise must in every respect be a design for a Wilton carpet, and for no other class of carpet.

94. Exercise B, Plate 3.—In the lower part of the 10″×15″ plate, lay out a rectangle 9 inches wide by 4 inches high, and fill it with ruled pencil squares such as appear only on Brussels and Wilton carpet design paper, like those shown in Figs. 10 and 11.

Upon this squared design paper, lay off, full size, a small section of the design in Exercise A, one-third of the width and

about one-seventh of the height of the one-third-scale colored
sketch in Exercise A. The details of the pattern on this design
paper will then appear three times the size they appear in
Exercise A, and will be the full scale at which Wilton carpet
designs are made; that is, the full size of the details in the carpet
itself.

95. Final Work on Plate 3.—Letter or write the title,
Plate 3: Carpet and Rug Designing, at the top of the sheet;
and on the back place class letters and number, name, address,
and date of completing the plate. Roll the plate, protected
by a sheet of tissue paper, place in the mailing tube, and send
to the Schools for examination. Then proceed with Plate 4,
if all required uncompleted work on previous plates has been
finished.

PLATE 4

96. Exercise A, Plate 4.—In the upper part of the
10″×15″ plate, lay out a rectangle 9 inches wide by 9 inches
high. Within this rectangle prepare a sketch design in colors
for a 27-inch-width ingrain carpet. The sketch will therefore
be one-third the *scale* of the full-width carpet.

Every technical detail connected with the designing of an
ingrain carpet (as distinguished from any other kind of carpet),
as explained in the text of this Section, must be observed. The
design for this exercise must in every respect be a design for an
ingrain carpet, and for no other class of carpet.

97. Exercise B, Plate 4.—In the lower part of the
10″×15″ plate, lay out a rectangle 9 inches wide by 4 inches
high, and fill it with ruled pencil squares, such as appear only
in ingrain-carpet design paper, like those shown in Fig. 21.

Upon this squared design paper lay out, full size, a small
section of the design in Exercise A, using one-third of the width
and about one-seventh of the height of the one-third-scale
colored sketch in Exercise A. The details of the pattern on this
design paper will then appear three times the size they appear
in Exercise A, and will be the full scale at which ingrain carpet

designs are made; that is, the full size of the details in the carpet itself.

98. Final Work on Plate 4.—Letter or write the title, Plate 4: Carpet and Rug Designing, at the top of the sheet; and on the back place class letters and number, name, address, and date of completing the plate. Roll the plate, protected by a sheet of tissue paper, place in the mailing tube, and send to the Schools for examination. Then proceed with Plate 5, if all required uncompleted work on previous plates has been finished.

PLATE 5

99. Exercise A, Plate 5.—In the upper part of the 10″×15″ plate, lay out a rectangle 9 inches wide by 9 inches high. Within this rectangle prepare a sketch design in colors for a 27-inch-width Axminster carpet. The sketch will therefore be one-third the *scale* of the full width carpet.

Every technical detail connected with the designing of an Axminster carpet (as distinguished from any other kind of carpet), as explained in the text of this Section, must be observed. The design for this exercise must in every respect be a design for an Axminster carpet, and for no other class of carpet.

100. Exercise B, Plate 5.—In the lower part of the 10″×15″ plate, lay out a rectangle 9 inches wide by 4 inches high, and fill it with ruled pencil squares such as appear only in Axminster-carpet design paper, like those shown in Fig. 25 (*a*) and (*b*). Upon this squared design paper lay out, full size, a small section of the design in Exercise A, one-third of the width and about one-seventh of the height of the one-third-scale colored sketch in Exercise A.

The details of the pattern on this design paper will then appear three times the size they appear in Exercise A, and will be the full width at which Axminster-carpet designs are made; that is, the full size of the details in the carpet itself.

101. Final Work on Plate 5.—Letter or write the title, Plate 5: Carpet and Rug Designing, at the top of the sheet; and on the back place class letters and number, name, address, and date of completing the plate. Roll the plate, protected by a sheet of tissue paper, place in the mailing tube, and send to the Schools for examination. Then proceed with Plate 6, if all required uncompleted work on previous plates has been finished.

_____

PLATE 6

102. Exercise for Plate 6.—Within the entire space of the 10″×15″ plate arranged vertically, lay out a rectangle 9 inches wide by 12 inches high. Within this rectangle, make a sketch design in colors for a Brussels or Wilton rug to be 9 feet by 12 feet. The sketch design will then be on a scale of 1 inch = 1 foot; that is, the sketch will be one-twelfth the width and one-twelfth the height of the finished rug.

The designing of the rug—the proper proportions of border, filling, etc.—must be accompanied by the proper observance of the principles of space filling, border designs, etc., as taught in previous Sections, and must be done in accordance with technicalities of designing rugs, as discussed in the divisions on machine-made rugs, in this Section, which text should be reread by the student.

The sketch design should be drawn with the degree of finish noticeable in the text illustrations.

103. Final Work on Plate 6.—Letter or write the title, Plate 6: Carpet and Rug Designing, at the top of the sheet; and on the back place class letters and number, name, address, and date of completing the plate. Roll the plate, protected by a sheet of tissue paper, place in the mailing tube, and send to the Schools for examination.

If any redrawn work on any of the plates of this Section has been called for and has not yet been completed, it should be satisfactorily finished at this time. After all the required work on the plates of this Section has been completed the work of the next Section should be taken up at once.

WALLPAPER DESIGNING

PURPOSE

1. Necessity for Specialized Training.—Every specialized line of artistic designing, which is finally to result in the production of some special decorative product, requires on the part of the designer a preliminary knowledge of the particular process by which that product is manufactured.

The technical processes by which wallpapers are produced are not so complicated as those used in the manufacture of woven fabrics such as carpets, but they impose certain restrictions upon, and offer certain opportunities to, the wallpaper designer, and must therefore be well understood by him. Such technical knowledge is necessary, not only that the designer may make designs that are correctly drawn for reproduction and may be transferred to the printing rollers without alteration or adaptation, but because economy of printing can be planned by the designer so trained. For instance, a design for wallpaper that gives the effect of ten or twelve colors might be very effective and greatly desired by a manufacturer, but the cost of printing in that number of colors would be very great. However, a designer technically trained in the printing processes would know how to get this ten- or twelve-color effect by means of perhaps only six or eight colors properly arranged and superimposed. He would, also, perhaps be careful to use gold sparingly, except on the most expensive papers, knowing just why the use of gold is expensive. In this way his designs would be more practical, which means salable, than the designs made by an artist not so trained in the technical processes.

2. Scope of Training in This Section.—Wall coverings; that is, when the fabric is superficially applied, are not necessarily always wallpaper. The wall covering may be wood-paneling, or canvas, or burlap, or even silk, or leather in embossed patterns; but the use of these materials for such purpose is so comparatively rare, that the present discussion will be confined to **wallpaper,** because this product is the most commonly used form of wall covering, and the one for which the commercial designer's services are most needed.

It must be understood, however, that this treatise is not one on wallpaper manufacture or printing; and for this reason only such details of the wallpaper manufacturing and printing process will be presented as are necessary for the designer to know, so that he may prepare designs that are both artistic and practical.

WALLPAPERS

MANUFACTURE

3. The Principle of Printing Wallpaper.—The general principle upon which wallpapers are produced is to print from rollers, or blocks, the repeating patterns upon strips of paper 18 to 36 inches wide and 9 to 16 yards long. These strips are then pasted or glued onto the wall or ceiling so that the patterns or repeats match properly and form an all-over repeat or pattern entirely covering the wall or ceiling surface. The printing is done in black and white, colors, gold, or silver, upon a toned paper, so as to withstand rubbing and other wear, and thus be permanent.

4. Paper.—The kinds of paper upon which wallpaper patterns are printed differ in accordance with the quality of the wallpaper to be produced. Some of the cheaper grades of 18-inch width wallpaper that sell for 10 cents or 15 cents per roll are printed on paper of the cheapest kind, made from wood pulp—very much like the stock upon which newspapers are printed—and very easily torn. As the quality of the wallpaper design and pattern rises, the quality of the paper improves. In some of the higher grades the paper is very firm and tough, especially when made in imitation of embossed leather. There are also papers of a high grade made of fibers woven like grass cloth or burlap.

The sizes of these strips of paper vary with the pattern and the quality of the wallpaper. The cheaper papers—10 cents to 50 to 60 cents per roll—are usually about 18 inches in width and 16 yards long. However, some higher grade papers, especially those in solid tones and those in imitation of burlap or grass cloth, may run as wide as 30 or 36 inches, but their length is then only 8 or 12 yards. Such papers usually belong to the $1 to $5 per roll class.

5. Color Blocks and Rollers.—Wallpaper is printed by hand by the use of printing blocks, or by machinery with printing rollers. The design is applied to the block, or the roller, by processes of tracing, transferring, and carving, or machine engraving, the details of which transferring processes need not concern the designer.

Each color in the design pattern, or on the final wallpaper pattern, requires a separate roller or block for its printing. However, in estimating the number of colors in a wallpaper, a light background is never included, as this is printed on the natural-color paper by a special machine, called a grounding machine, before the regular printing of the decorative pattern is done. Thus, if it were desired to have a wallpaper showing a dark-brown pattern on a light-brown background, only one block or roller would be required. However, if the pattern were to be brown and green on a light-brown background, two rollers would be required, one for the dark brown and the other for the green.

The part of the pattern that is to print dark green, for instance, is traced from the design and transferred to the roller or block; and then the carving or cutting is done, either by hand alone, or assisted by mechanical processes, in such a way that the pattern is raised above the surface of the block or roller, the background being cut away, so that the raised portions will print just as does the raised surface of type when printing a newspaper or book. Similarly, that portion of the pattern that is to print dark brown is traced from the design, transferred to another block or roller, of the same size as the first one, and cut in raised relief. These two blocks, or rollers,

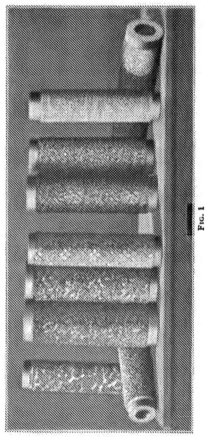

Fig. 1

then print, in two separate operations, over the same space on the paper, the result being the desired pattern in colors.

The necessity for extreme accuracy in making these rollers is evident. It is necessary that they imprint all the details of the pattern in the successive colors in exactly the proper positions in order to present a harmonious design and color scheme. This work is executed by skilled workmen and is often a slow and tedious process. The rollers are made from maple logs turned exactly to the required size, which is regulated by the length of the repeat. Where a design calls for a number of colors, each roller must be turned to exactly the same diameter, within the minutest fraction of an inch, before the design is executed on its surface. After being turned to the required size, the rollers are painted white, and, when dry, are given a traced impression of the entire pattern. Upon each roller is then marked its part of the pattern; and it is then given to the block cutter. The smallest details on these surfaces are made of solid pieces of brass, formed to the proper shape by being drawn through steel dies. These are then driven into the surface of the roller at the proper places. Circular dots, etc. are made of brass wire cut in pieces $\frac{1}{2}$ inch or less in length, and with the sharpened end driven, with a hammer, into the roller at the required point. Larger surfaces are outlined with thin strips of brass that are skilfully filed and bent to the required forms, and then sharpened on the lower edge so as to be driven into the wood after the outline has been cut in with a knife or a chisel. This outline of brass is driven firmly and solidly into the wood, somewhat less than $\frac{1}{4}$ inch of its length being left above the surface. When this work is complete, the spaces within these brass outlines are filled with heavy felt that has been soaked in hot glue. When the felt and glue dries, it forms a hard and perfectly solid printing surface within the brass outline. The rollers

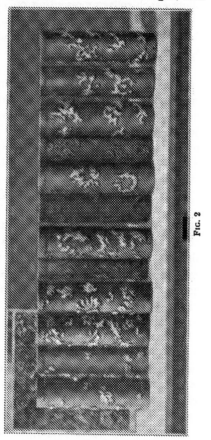

Fig. 2

are then placed on a lathe and turned up, or ground, to the finished diameter, which makes their circumference exactly equal to the length of the repeat on the paper. When all the rollers have passed through these processes and are finished to the exact circumference, they are ready for the printing machine.

Typical specimens of wallpaper rollers are shown in Figs. 1 and 2. Each one of the rollers shown in Fig. 1 represents a complete design, as can readily be seen by examining them. The rollers shown in Fig. 2, however, were all used for the same wallpaper—a twelve-color paper, therefore requiring twelve separate rollers—each roller representing only a fraction of the pattern.

The wallpaper itself that was printed from this combination of twelve rollers is shown at the left end of the illustration back of the first three rollers.

6. Colors.—The colors used in printing wallpaper are composed of a mixture of the required pigment ground in water and thickened with glue and dextrine. They must be of such consistency that they do not blur or blend one into another to any great extent, and at the same time they must be thin enough to flow readily from the surface of the felt belts and properly cover the rollers.

The colors are supplied to each roller by means of felt belts so adjusted that they pass through troughs containing the color and distribute it accurately to the printing rollers so that each receives just the proper amount. This amount is determined by experiment, as the belts are readily adjusted to change the amount of color being fed, and should it be found that as the paper passes through the machine too much or too little is being distributed, the belts can be adjusted in position so as to vary the amount.

It is evident, too, that since the amount of color can be varied as it is distributed on the rollers, and the amount of blurring and softness of effect can be regulated by the quantity of size or glue that is mixed with it, quite a variety of effects in design can be obtained if the designer understands the possibilities of these color mixtures and manufacturing details. In many machine-printed papers that possess a number of colors, this blurring is very conspicuous and frequently it is a means of rendering the paper more interesting than it would be were each detail in sharp outline.

Gold is not printed directly from a roller, as are the colors, but as the paper passes through the printing machine, the last roller with which it comes in contact impresses its design on the general surface in varnish that is much slower drying than the water colors with which the rest of the paper is printed. After all the water color has dried, this sizing of varnish is still sticky, and gold or bronze powder sifted over the paper will adhere to this sizing while it may be brushed off the rest of the paper. It is evident, therefore, that there must be distinctness of outline so that the surface covered by this varnish may be clearly determined and may not overlap any of the details of the design in colors.

7. Hand Printing.—The wallpapers of the highest grade, especially the imported ones, are printed by hand from flat blocks. The paper, which is in a continuous roll, is at the end of a long table, by which the printer stands, the paper being at his right. Behind him and also to his right are placed the tray of color and the color pad on which he places his block, the block being held by means of one or two handles on the back. He carefully transfers the block to the surface of the paper where it is printed by pressure effected by means of a long wooden elbow that the printer pulls straight, so as to brace the block against the paper with a thrust of the wooden elbow against the ceiling. The block, in printing, marks on the edge of the paper a guide so that the following block may be placed so as to impress the second color in its proper place. As the block is printed, the paper is moved along one repeat and carried over cross-bars, or sticks, in long loops or folds so as to dry thoroughly before it is rolled up to pass through the process again for the printing of the second color. Each color is thus applied successively until the entire surface of the paper is impressed with the design, and for each color applied the paper passes under the printer's hands and is impressed with a separate block.

Although the finest wallpapers are printed in this way, most of the hand-printed papers are imported from Europe. A few American manufacturers produce hand prints that compare very favorably with the imported article, but the price is so high and the demand for high-priced paper so limited, that most

FIG. 3

wallpaper designers in this country confine themselves to the preparation of designs for machinery production.

8. Machine Printing.—Most wallpapers, especially those of moderate and of low price, are printed by machinery, from rollers, such as have already been described.

In Fig. 3 is shown a machine on which a paper of eight colors is being printed. The paper is fed in at the bottom and on the opposite side of the machine, from whence it passes around a large drum, as shown, and comes in contact with the various color rollers, one by one successively, the second color being printed before the previous color has entirely dried. This causes machine-printed papers to blend their colors, and prevents the clean, sharp, distinction of outline that is characteristic of the hand-printed papers. After the printing is done from the successive rollers, the paper strip is then carried, in long loops, over a coil of steam pipes by means of which the colors are thoroughly dried before the paper reaches the opposite end of the long building, where it is rolled up by machinery and so cut that each roll contains exactly the same amount.

DESIGNING

PLANNING THE DESIGN

9. Principles of Wall-Surface Designing.—The designer of wallpaper must consider, above everything else, that he is attempting to beautify and make interesting the wall surfaces of a room in which some person or persons will spend a great deal of their time. The wallpaper designer's task, therefore, is not merely to fill a certain space with repeating patterns or designs, no matter how cleverly this pattern designing may be done. The best plan is for the designer to make only such designs as he himself would be content to have on the walls of his own room. If this standard is set, it is quite likely that he will refrain from designing such a crude scheme as large red flowers on a glaring green background, or some equally disturbing design and color scheme.

The requirements of decoration on wall surfaces differ in a marked degree, from those of decoration on floor surfaces. In the case of floor surfaces, perspective must be considered when laying out the repeats, as also the fact that the repeating details of the design are seen at an angle. In the case of wall decoration, however, the pattern is usually seen, not in perspective at an angle, but full face. Therefore, a pattern that might be suitable for carpet would not be suitable for wallpaper.

A further consideration when designing for any form of wall decoration is that the walls and their decoration must be considered in connection with the furniture, carpets, hangings, pictures, and other elements of the furnishings. Therefore, conspicuous floral patterns are always bad. Such designs can never hold one's interest long. One soon becomes weary of them, and after a while the presence of their self-asserting decorative elements becomes positively irritating and annoying.

Designs for wall decorations can be cheerful and even gay, but they should never be boisterous. The public's constant demand for novelty leads the designer to execute exaggerated floral effects with the idea of attracting the public eye and making the paper salable; but such designs are popular on the market but a short time, for when they are imposed on people of refined tastes their production is soon discontinued. The effect of novelty can be easily satisfied within the bounds of good taste, and it is the realization of this fact that enables the French and the English designers to create patterns that are more eagerly sought by American manufacturers than are the usual American patterns The foreign designers have become better acquainted with the principles of artistic design; and, while they are producing quite as many novelties as American designers, they confine these novelties within the bounds of good taste. These designers command suitable prices, and at the same time educate the people that use their designs to appreciate the value of good work, and thereby raise the artistic standard of the entire community. Decorative art has been systematically taught in this country for a comparatively few years, and American designers should soon compete with, if not excel, on equal grounds, their foreign competitors.

Hundreds of art students are being taught every year to design properly. The best manufacturers in the country are printing hundreds of designs every year that are educating the people to a higher standard of art The time, therefore, should not be far distant when none but good designs will be accepted by the mass of the people, no matter whether they are made by Americans or Europeans, or whether they are high-priced or low-priced; for a principle of good design can be applied to paper costing 25 cents per roll just as well as to paper costing $2.50 per roll.

It is the designer's duty, no matter what may be his branch of art, always to do the best he can and never give to the public or to his client a design of which he cannot approve. If the people to whom he is catering possess vulgar taste, it is his duty to educate them by giving them good designs, for as soon as their taste becomes refined they will accept none but the best, and if he has been in the habit of giving them inartistic designs, they will abandon him as soon as they know better.

10. Designing for Definite Rooms.—In the present perfected state of the art of wallpaper designing, one does not simply make a design for "a wallpaper," but he designs a wallpaper to go into some definite room of the house. The demand for designs suitable for special rooms is becoming more and more marked. People of wealth frequently order special wall coverings made exclusively for their own houses; and coverings having designs suited to similar purposes are produced by the manufacturers in large quantities, and therefore more cheaply, for that much larger class of people of less means, who nevertheless appreciate the artistic qualities of the special designs, and upon whom the manufacturers depend for the bulk of their sales. This tendency is the cause of the existence of such designs as the crown frieze, paneling in imitation of wood or leather, etc., which have been properly applied and appropriated to certain rooms, giving them much the appearance of having been designed to fit that especial room, and consequently are sought after by persons that desire these individual effects.

The designer and the interior decorator must have a definite idea as to the kind of pattern that is appropriate for an individual room. The former must be able to invent, and the latter to select, designs suitable to the different rooms of an ordinary house, from the parlor to the kitchen and the bathroom.

The manufacturer classes his various papers under headings that represent the rooms for which they are appropriate, and he endeavors to have as wide a variety as possible in the several designs included in each class. In the average city house, there should be sufficient contrast and harmony of tone and design from one room to another to prevent a feeling of monotony, as one goes through the house, without too great an impression of variety. The following styles are suggested as appropriate to the various rooms designated:

1. *The Hall.*—The hall should be rich and cheerful in color though not necessarily brilliant, unless the hall is very dark. The pattern should be bold but subdued in effect; it should be dignified and rather pretentious in drawing, severely conventional, suggestive of direct mural paintings in panels, or of cloth or tapestry effects.

2. *The Parlor or Drawing Room.*—The parlor or drawing room should be stately and pretentious in its pattern but in coloring more delicate than the hall; the tints should be lighter. Renaissance scrolls are frequently employed in rich embossed effects, as are also suggestions of materials such as silk, velvet, etc. However, many dainty naturalistic effects are used in parlor decoration, particularly in small houses. The parlor or drawing room is essentially an assembly room for state or dress occasions; it is used almost exclusively in the evenings, and its paper should be chosen to delicately harmonize with the suggestiveness of evening dress and dainty surroundings. It is usually the most pretentious room in the house and calls for an excellent quality of goods, showing skilful and chaste, rather than bold and aggressive, designs. The ceiling should usually be papered in plain tints or be hand-decorated in distemper.

3. *The Dining Room.*—The dining room should be cheerful in color and designed rather architecturally in subdivision, with a plain dado in wood or panel effect and fanciful frieze in tapestry effect with landscapes or figures. The side wall between the dado and frieze may be in plain colors or in panels,

but when panels are used in the side walls they should be avoided in the dado. The entire side wall may be omitted in the frieze treatment and its panels may be extended entirely to the ceiling, being filled completely with a tapestry effect repeated at intervals. The ceiling is often left plain or rendered in distemper to harmonize with the side-wall treatment, or it may be papered suggestive of wood paneling or embossed leather. Frequently a bronze effect is attempted, tufted at intervals with metallic buttons.

4. *The Library.*—The library should be rich but subdued in color, in tapestry or fabric effects if possible, and in any case suitable to the style of furnishings; of these the prevailing taste is Gothic, Italian Renaissance, Flemish, Elizabethan, Empire, etc. Other rooms on the first floor of the house are usually morning rooms, reception rooms, or, possibly, breakfast rooms, each of which should be rather more delicate in furnishing than the parlor and dining room, as they are essentially rooms that are used in daytime and their decorative elements should be so considered. Papers are seldom specially designed for the three last-named rooms, but the decorator is frequently called on to make selections for them and his judgment should be governed accordingly.

5. *The Kitchen.*—The essential point in a kitchen wall covering is utility, something that will reflect much light and keep clean. The ideal wall covering for a kitchen would be tiles or enamel brick; therefore, wallpaper patterns that are geometrical in design, suggestive of tile or brickwork, are entirely suitable, and designs of this character can be obtained in varnished papers, that are washable and can be kept nearly as smooth and clean as tile itself.

6. *Bedrooms.*—Bedrooms should contain delicate bright designs in cheerful decorative or naturalistic patterns of flowers. Stripe effects with floral details are exceedingly popular. The frieze treatment may be used, as the appearance of the stripes running from the ceiling to the floor gives an apparent height to the room.

An exceedingly popular treatment for bedrooms and sitting rooms consists of a subdivision of the wall into three parts, the lower two-thirds of which is covered with a plain tint or two-tone stripe, and the upper parts with a rather large and brilliantly designed floral pattern. A two-tone green stripe for the lower portion with a poppy frieze is very popular for bedrooms, as poppies are symbolic of sleep. But other combinations can be used, such as a two-tone yellow under a frieze of lilacs or Wisteria.

7. *Children's bedrooms* have received special attention from designers and decorators. Considerations of the lively imagination that children possess have been expressed in wallpaper design, as the child mind is likely to convert everything about it into a topic of conversation or wonder; therefore, to please these infant fancies, the English manufacturer has reproduced illustrations of Mother Goose rhymes in a wallpaper pattern, and also designs indicative of the different months of the year, suggested by drawings by Kate Greenaway. The propriety of these elements in wallpaper design, from an artistic standpoint, is hardly to be considered, since the decorative element in this case is subordinated to the educational and recreative element that must exist in the nursery.

11. Sources of Ideas for Decorative Motifs and Repeats.—Repeating floral or other patterns are by no means required on all wallpapers. As a matter of fact, many of the modern papers of the highest grade are quite plain, with effects either of fine vertical stripes or of tapestry or grass-cloth surface. A vast volume of wallpapers, however, is put out each year, designed for the medium-priced and the cheap trade, where repeating patterns of floral effects, either naturalistic or conventionalized, are very prominent. The designer, therefore, may always expect to be required to make designs for such papers.

As has been pointed out previously, the designer should go to nature for his suggestions when preparing floral designs for wallpaper patterns. This was fully discussed when the preparation of plant form motifs and their conventionalization was taken up, but it should be kept in mind and applied now that practical designing for wallpapers is to be done. The wallpaper designer does not make new designs for floral papers by adapting, twisting, and twining the floral forms seen on old papers. This is not designing, and the designer who expects to produce new and attractive floral designs must not pursue such a plan of copying and adapting, but must go direct to nature. The subject of the preparation of repeats of various kinds also has been treated fully, so that now it should only be necessary to apply the knowledge so gained to the specific field of wallpapers.

12. Designer Must Be Observant of Public Wants. In order that his wallpaper designs may be in harmony with other forms of interior decoration, and that he may be familiar with the current styles and public taste, it is necessary that the designer make frequent visits to the stores to keep in touch with what is being sold in the line of furniture, carpets, etc., as well as wallpaper. To be successful, he must keep in touch with the times, must be constantly on the alert for suggestions, must observe foreign patterns that use particular processes, and endeavor to prepare similar patterns suitable to American processes.

Inasmuch as current styles and public tastes differ from year to year, a statement as to what are now the styles would be useless. However, there are at all times only a few different possible styles, as, for instance, the general classification of plain papers, and elaborate floral papers. Some years, plain effects, in flat tones, fine vertical stripes, and burlap or grasscloth effects, may be used on the more expensive papers, and rich floral effects in brilliant colors on the cheaper papers. Another year the expensive papers may show floral effects. Thus there may be crown effects at the top of panels, landscape arrangements over the dado, decorative effects in imitation of mural paintings, etc.; but it is impossible to forecast, even from season to season, what the styles in wallpapers will be. For these reasons the designer should consult the local dealers, look over the newest stocks, and make every effort to learn what is being done in the designing world. Those living in large cities have an advantage, on account of the greater variety displayed, and the opportunity of observing the latest novelties and finest goods; but even those in small cities and towns can keep in touch with what is the latest through the medium of the trade papers.

13. Keeping in Touch With Manufacturers and Dealers.—Manufacturers have their designs prepared a year or more in advance of the market. In August of each year, the wallpaper men gather in New York to show their new goods to sell to jobbers all over the eastern part of the country. Sometimes, later in the year, they gather in other large cities for a similar purpose, and all experimental patterns must be out for execution at that time.

The experienced designer would do well, when convenient, to submit his designs to some local dealer, explaining his idea of the use of the design and asking advice as to a probable buyer among manufacturers. The designer must be particularly sure before submitting a design for sale that it is technically correct for reproduction. No matter how good a design is, it will not be accepted if it cannot be printed, as manufacturers have no time to redraw patterns. Certain advice from a manufacturer or an established designer would be most valuable, but it is not easily obtained even in communities where both manufacturers and designers abound. The former are usually too busy to enter into details, and the latter, jealous of their calling, are not anxious to explain the facts. But occasionally a wallpaper manufacturer will observe merit in a designer's work, although he is not anxious to purchase the design, and will suggest to the designer lines whereon he should work in order to arrive at more popular results.

DRAWING THE DESIGN

14. Laying Out Dimensions and Blocking-In the Pattern.—Before a wallpaper design is started, the size to which it is to be drawn must be definitely determined. This will depend on the character or grade of the paper to be produced, the size of the rollers ordinarily used by the factory for whom the design is to be made, etc. Thus the cheaper floral papers are usually 18 inches in width; while plain papers—vertical stripe and grass-cloth effects—and tapestry papers, are usually 30 inches or 36 inches in width.

Assuming that the width of a repeat of the wallpaper has been determined to be 18 inches, for instance, the designer first considers the lengths of repeats that are most convenient in ordinary reproduction; these are $11\frac{7}{8}$ inches, $12\frac{3}{4}$ inches, $14\frac{3}{4}$ inches, $17\frac{3}{4}$ inches, $18\frac{3}{4}$ inches, $21\frac{3}{4}$ inches, and $23\frac{3}{4}$ inches. He then lays off the required dimensions of the width of the paper and the repeat, in the center of a large sheet of Manila or brown detail paper, leaving an 8-inch or 10-inch margin all around the design. This margin permits sufficient freedom for the designer to draw in his general idea and indicate a portion of the repeat of all four sides. This large surface can be considered as a portion of the wall on which the designer is then arranging his paper. The leading lines should be sketched in with crayon or charcoal passing throughout the repeat to the very limits of the paper unless the design is to be composed of small geometrical figures, when the general effect of the design can be observed in smaller compass.

If charcoal is used and the lines are sketched very lightly at first, they can be easily erased, in order to make changes, by means of a small piece of chamois leather; if crayon is used the lines may be erased with a sponge-rubber, or with a kneaded eraser. Charcoal will give the best results for blocking in.

15. Trying Out Color Schemes.—After the dimensions and the general arrangement of the design have been blocked in, perhaps upon heavy tracing paper over the general construction lines, it is well to test out color schemes on a second piece of tracing paper pinned over the design. This tracing paper should be transparent and yet have a white, toothed (*not* glossy) surface that will take water-color washes.

In testing for color schemes the designer should bring into play all he has learned about color theory and color harmony; but must understand in addition thereto the peculiar requirements of color printing for wallpaper work.

He should always bear in mind that the design must be executed so that a distinct outline can be observed between each color and its neighbor. His mental conception of the finished paper may be one of softness and freedom from graduation from one part into another, but his execution of the design must not show any uncertainty as to where one color stops and another begins. If such uncertainty exists, the block cutters will never be able to get the repeats of their patterns cut accurately. All shading from one part into another is accomplished by means of planes of color, or gradual steps from one tone value into another, as shown in Fig. 4, which illustrates clearly how the natural floral or leaf form is portrayed by successive applications of flat colors so as to be suitable for wallpaper printing in colors. Exercises such as those shown in Fig. 4 should be practiced repeatedly by the wallpaper designer. Specimens of flowers and leaves should be secured, and careful drawings made thereof. Then must be determined the available number of colors that will be allowed for the printing of the wallpaper. All these separate colors should be laid out at the lower left-hand corner of the sheet in little squares, as shown in Fig. 4, for ready reference. Then, if a yellow flower, for instance, is to be shown in graded values, it should be painted all over first with a light value of yellow, then on the lower insides of the petals with a darker orange yellow, and then in the deepest shadow portions with a deep orange brown. Pink flowers, green leaves, etc., must be portrayed in a similar manner, as shown in Fig. 4.

It is absolutely necessary for the designer to be thoroughly familiar with this technique as well as with the details of manufacture, for on this depends the practical value of the wallpaper, and, outside of its merit as to design, its entire selling quality. The character of this technique can best be obtained by copying examples of any good designs. Hand-printed papers are admirable for this work when they can be obtained, and, when they cannot, it is best to use as copy some good quality of printed cotton goods, such as cretonne or sateen, as in most of these goods the printing is much more clearly defined than on machine-printed paper.

Fig. 4

16. In practicing all these exercises, as well as in making practical designs for wallpaper printing, it is best to proceed in the order of the relative depths of tone value, painting the lightest masses first and proceeding in the order of their depth to the darkest until the whole pattern is finished.

For instance, the tone value *a* in Fig. 5 would be the first one painted; it might extend over the entire form of the leaf and the darker tones be placed over it, but this is hardly necessary, as it can be carried a slight distance under the limits of the

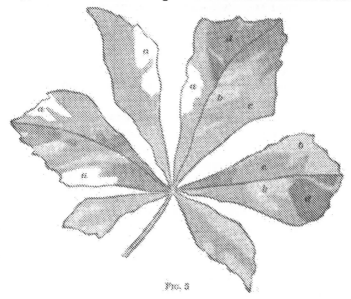

FIG. 5

tone value *b*, while *b*, when laid, can be carried a short distance under the tone value *c*, and *c* under *d*. When the design is executed on the printing machine, this is the order in which it will be printed to produce the most desirable effect, as it can be seen that, should there be a slight discrepancy in the register between these colors, the darker color will obliterate the lighter one, and thereby present a more even appearance than if a light color overlapped a dark one and caused a graying of the outlines. Therefore, if the designer observes this rule in preparing his design, he will find that much trouble will be saved in its reproduction and his ability will be much appreciated therefor by the manufacturer. Very small high lights are usually painted on top of other colors for convenience, but it is best to leave these in painting the dark colors, as it adds materially to the convenience of the color printers.

Where an outline is used to distinctly emphasize the edges of the form it is better that it should be dark. for light outlines do not clearly express themselves.

17. Final Drawing and Rendering.—When the stages of blocking-in the pattern, and testing for color schemes have been passed through, the final rendering of the design may be made.

Details of a design must not be elaborated or drawn with final accuracy before the arrangement of values and colors has been considered. The designer may picture in his mind a few leading lines and general effects of floral forms that he is desirous of using, and he may have a mental picture of whether the finished pattern is to present an all-over, a spotted, or a powdered effect, but his ideas may change as he works up the design, for as he pursues his way in his first preliminary sketches, new suggestions will come to him as the lines multiply and the general structure of the design is mapped out.

After thus beginning it is comparatively easy to alter and work out the structural lines until they are pleasing, and the details can still more easily be supplied. The designer should never attempt the slightest detail, however, until he is thoroughly satisfied with the general character of his composition.

As objectionable spotting or lining cannot be easily determined when the drawing is in outline only, the general forms should be darkened or spotted by means of charcoal or crayon.

By this method of procedure the design has been practically proved on the wall surface before any of its details are elaborated.

Assuming, however, that all these considerations have been attended to, the designer is now ready to draw and render the design. A third piece of tough tracing paper may be pinned over the preliminary blocking in and tests, and the design drawn thereon in soft pencil. From this tracing the design should be transferred for its final painting to a sheet of stretched drawing paper that has been coated with a background color. If the design is a large one, at least 3 or 4 inches should be shown beyond the repeat on all sides, while with smaller designs a number of complete repeats should be worked out. The stretched drawing paper on which the working drawing is executed should be large enough to permit a clear margin of at least 4 inches all around the finished design. Some designers make a margin of 6 or 8 inches on large patterns, and render this margin in a flat color that harmonizes or contrasts agreeably with the color scheme of the design itself. This border serves the simple purpose of framing the picture. The effect is still more striking when the design is separated from this border by a heavy line of contrasting tone or color that is lighter or darker than the border itself, as the case may require. The object of this should be obvious. It is the designer's desire and intention to show his work to the best advantage in submitting it for sale; and any detail that he can add to his finished design that will make it more presentable, is a perfectly legitimate way to commend his efforts to the attention of the prospective purchaser. Neat, accurate work is absolutely necessary. The color scheme should be definitely determined on before the final painting is commenced.

18. In rendering, it is advisable and often necessary to paint each individual color wherever it is to occur in the whole design at one painting, or at least in one day, and then apply the next darker color.

The necessity for so doing arises from the fact that many of the moist colors used by designers change color rapidly after exposure to light and air; therefore a color laid on a drawing one day may change sufficiently to be quite a different hue the next day, and consequently the inexperienced designer, whose rendering is likely to be slow, finds his work to be decidedly uneven in color when a number of days have been spent in the preparation of his design. This introduction of undesired values or hues may be avoided by first trying the entire color scheme on some portion of the design, and then putting on each color successively in the proper places all over the design, working with the one color continuously till all parts of that color are completed.

It is best to use as few colors as possible in the execution of any design, as the effect is more simple and the paper less expensive to produce. Printing machines for wallpapers are constructed to run a certain limited number of colors. The one shown in Fig. 3 carries only eight rollers and can print a pattern of only eight colors at one time, not counting the background, which is usually applied by a separate machine, called the *grounding machine*. The machine shown in Fig. 3, however, can print any number of colors less than eight, and it is therefore quite necessary that the designer should acquaint himself with the color capacities of the manufacturers to whom he proposes to submit his design. Six- and eight-color machines are common in the United States, though twelve- and sixteen-color machines exist in some places. The latter is about the highest limit for machine printing in this country. However, designs containing eight colors or less are the most acceptable ones to the average manufacturer, for it is expensive to cut the rolls for a multicolor paper, and every form of economy in printing a design is a point in favor of the designer.

TYPICAL EXAMPLES OF WALLPAPERS

SPECIMEN WALLPAPER PATTERNS

19. Diversity of Styles.—The prospective designer of wallpapers must, first of all, disabuse his mind of the idea, if he has it, that wallpaper patterns are always repeating floral patterns. Such is not the case; for not only does public taste demand a great diversity of effects, but the processes of printing wallpapers allow and encourage elaborate effects of all kinds. Thus, great freedom of choice is offered to the designer when he gets up his designs.

There is perhaps no branch of decorative design that permits the designer to use so unrestrainedly naturalistic effects and patterns as wallpaper designing. Such patterns are not difficult for the wallpaper manufacturer to produce. Among the diversified classes of wallpaper patterns that are prepared by designers and used from year to year, are plain-toned, grass-cloth, and burlap effects; conventional all-over repeating effects; naturalistic all-over repeating effects; vertical-striped effects; plain panel and crown effects; special decorative frieze effects; and geometrical pattern effects for glazed papers, etc. This list does not cover all the classes of papers that are in use or that can be seen in the sample books of wallpaper manufacturers and merchants; but the classification given is sufficiently broad to set the novice on the right track.

20. Plain-Toned, Grass-Cloth, and Burlap Effects. The simplest kind of wallpaper, from the standpoint of design, but not necessarily cost, is the plain, one-toned **ingrain,** or **cartridge,** paper. In a mottled effect it is sometimes referred to in the trade as **oatmeal** paper. Such plain papers are manufactured in rolls 30 inches wide, and in nearly all colors. Of course this class of wallpapers does not need the services of the designer as far as pattern is concerned, for there is no pattern; but the designer can always take advantage of the opportunities offered by these plain-toned papers when preparing wall decorations, or ornamental patterns for other work. Such plain papers can be used very appropriately in a room in which a figured or decorative paper would be out of place, and the plain surfaces of these papers can be stenciled or decorated in color to secure an unlimited variety of effects. This style of paper is sometimes used as the basis of a printed paper, thereby furnishing both the softness of the ingrain or oatmeal surface and the stenciled or stamped decoration.

A more interesting and refined plain paper is the paper made in imitation of grass cloth, or that made in imitation of burlap, in both cases the effects of woven surfaces are portrayed. In the case of grass-cloth papers the texture may actually consist of woven strips, or the surface be an imitation thereof.

21. In Fig. 6 is shown a small section, reproduced full size in black and white, of a typical grass-cloth paper that was printed in tan. This specimen will show just how the lines are drawn by the designer to give the effect of a woven surface. To do work of this kind requires great skill. A room whose walls are covered with paper of this kind possesses an air of quiet and dignified refinement not to be seen in rooms where figured papers are used. Sometimes flecks of gold are printed over the surface, giving a burnished or coppery effect. These grass-cloth papers, whether flecked with gold or not, are very

Fig. 6

costly, ranging in price from $1.50 to $5 per roll, depending upon whether they are imitation grass-cloth or the real weave.

An inspection of the dealers' sample books will reveal many other kinds of so-called *plain* papers; that is, papers not having a pattern, some in mottled effects, and some in imitation of other fabrics.

22. Conventional All-Over Repeating Effects.—The all-over floral patterns, conventional or naturalistic, represent by far the greatest volume of wallpaper patterns on the market. An infinite variety of such patterns is produced and sold.

In Fig. 7 is illustrated a design showing a conventionalized all-over floral repeat, showing an arrangement of poppies and their leaves decoratively treated and cleverly grouped in strong masses. The design is cleverly drawn, being based not only on a rectangular, or diamond, repeat as a basis, but also showing intersecting circles along which the diverging leaf growths are arranged. On the left side of the drawing, Fig. 7, is shown how the designer first blocks in masses, and on the right side is shown how the careful outline drawing is next made. In actual practice these stages would be two separate operations, on two separate sheets of tracing paper.

In Fig. 8 the interesting effect secured by the use of the conventionalized form of the closed gentian as the motif shows that the designer has gone a step farther than the mere geometrical

Fig. 7

repeat, and by the clever arrangement of the conventionalized stem growth and the leaves clothing the stems, has taken away any tendency toward stiffness of geometrical repeat, and yet has retained the artistic and practical convenience of an all-over repeat.

Fig. 9 shows another all-over pattern, similar in arrangement and treatment to the patterns in Figs. 7 and 8, the trumpet flower with accompanying leaf forms being used as the motif.

23. In Fig. 10 is an example of an all-over conventionalized floral pattern designed on a bolder and broader scheme than those so far discussed. This paper is an English hand-printed

FIG. 8

paper, bearing the name *Courtland*. This is an arrangement of decorative lilies and leaf scrolls, rendered in a color scheme composed of blue and green-gray with a touch of dull yellow in stems and stamens. This color scheme, therefore, is so skilfully arranged that, even though the details are very large, the flowers being 8 inches across, the colors are so delicate that

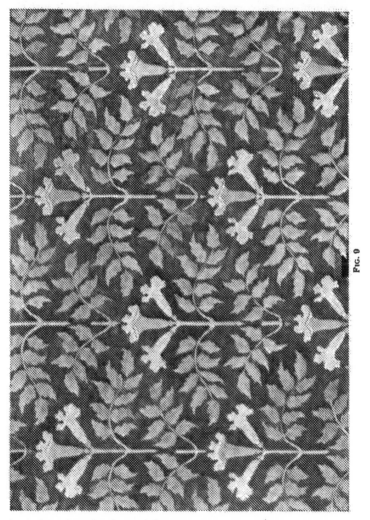

FIG. 9

it makes a perfectly satisfactory wall covering, and an excel-lent background for pictures, furniture, etc., there being not a harsh line or conspicuous tone or color in the entire design.

24. The paper reproduced in Fig. 11 is an English lithographed wallpaper in tones of red, green, yellow, and brown, in which effects of grading and blending are obtained just as if

Fɪɢ. 10

rendered by hand. In lithographed papers the blendings are accomplished by the use of stippling; that is, dots of various sizes and varying distances apart. However, in some of the highest grade papers the blending effect is accomplished by the use of stencil plates and the colors are applied with a brush, the harsh outlines being removed while the color is still wet, after the stencil plate has been lifted. It is evident that such

FIG. 11

papers must be very costly, for such effects can be obtained only after tedious manipulation and the expenditure of much time. However, it is with the ordinary roller-printed wallpaper that the student of this Course is concerned.

25. Fig. 12, a French design, shows a rather unusual arrangement of conventionalized small flowers and stems on

Fig. 12

very severely conventionalized leaf forms as backgrounds. This design made a very pleasing, though unusual, paper.

26. Figs. 13 and 14, while not strictly original designs, may be classed as conventional floral repeating patterns. Fig. 13 is a design based upon 16th century Italian arabesque work, and its skilful adaptation to wallpaper is very evident.

Fig. 14 is based upon the decorative embroidery pattern used on a priest's robe of the 16th century. Such special patterns,

FIG. 13

reproducing some historic form, are suitable for special purposes but not for general use.

27. Naturalistic All-Over Repeating Effects.—The matter as to whether or not naturalistic growths of flowers and leaves repeating in an all-over pattern are artistic, or are suitable for a wallpaper pattern is a debatable one. Some contend that naturalistic growths are inappropriate for such a purpose; others contend that, if the public enthusiastically welcomes such

FIG. 14

naturalistic floral patterns, then they are warranted. However, the demand for such patterns requires their treatment here.

Fig. 15

In Fig. 15 is shown a beautiful and elaborate floral pattern
of the naturalistic class. This is a French pattern that required
thirty-five impressions to reproduce. Such a pattern is mani-
festly very costly; for which reason American designers in
getting out such patterns use a process of adaptation, as follows: An elaborate pattern such as that shown in Fig. 15 is
copied and simplified in detail and in coloring so that a fair
reproduction of it may be printed in less than half the original
number of colors. Thus the hand-printed paper of France
becomes the machine-printed paper of America. Upon first
thought, this process of adaptation may seem to be an easy
one for the designer; but it requires much ingenuity, and is
usually the work of a certain class of designers who are clever
in such execution but who possess little inventive ability and
power to originate new designs.

28. In Fig. 16 is reproduced a characteristic American
machine-printed floral pattern of the naturalistic class. It was
printed in twelve colors on a plain white ribbed paper, in the
form of a spot repeating pattern, composed of bunches of pink
primroses and cream-colored narcissus. This is a side-to-side
repeat of two distinct groups of flowers forming alternate horizontal bands. Each repeat is arranged within a space 18 inches
wide by $21\frac{7}{8}$ inches high. This pattern is an example of the
style of naturalistic treatment that should be studiously avoided
by the beginner. The best critics characterize this style of
rendering as bunches of flowers thrown at the wall. They have
the appearance of cut flowers and their separate stems are
painfully evident. It should be borne in mind that the delicate
portrayal of a series of branches over the entire wall is likely
to become monotonous. The side walls of the room would be
inappropriate for such delicate details in reality; therefore, the
real appearance of the flowers should be avoided, and they should
be rendered with delicate conventional treatment that does not
pretend to be a counterfeit of nature.

29. Fig. 17 is an excellent illustration of the proper method
of arranging a naturalistic treatment of a floral pattern so as
to be more suitable for a wall decoration than is the crude

Fig. 16

arrangement in Fig. 16. The pattern in Fig. 17 is a French hand print, and the effect produced is that of a mass of green foliage entirely covering the wall, emphasized here and there by spots of sunlight and bunches of brilliant blossoms. The

Fig. 17

idea indicated in this pattern can be carried out to an almost unlimited extent with any other plant growth, without in any way violating any strict principles of design or of the nature of the growth.

30. Fig. 18 shows another French design of the naturalistic floral class, sometimes copied in American papers. To one who prefers, or who has designed, ingenious repeating patterns of a floral nature, the arrangement of details shown in Fig. 18 is almost a childish one. Combining tree foliage, huge sun-

FIG. 18

flowers, and a variety of small flowers and grasses in conventional perspective, as is done in this case, is very unique.

31. In Figs. 19 and 20 are shown several examples of naturalistic floral effects combined with rococo scrolls, bits of landscape, etc. These two reproductions of wallpapers also illustrate the difference between hand-printed and machine-printed wallpapers. It will be observed that in the hand-printed paper, Fig. 19, the details are perfectly sharp and distinct and probably determine accurately the appearance of the rendering on the designer's original painting. In Fig. 20,

FIG. 19

however, which shows a machine-printed paper, the tones are softened so that one blends into another very much as in ordinary water-color painting.

32.   Fig. 21 shows the floral styles of Figs. 19 and 20 applied to tapestry panel effects, to go over wainscoting, dados, etc.

The pattern in Fig. 21 shows how a strong effect is obtained by arranging the pattern of Louis XIV tapestry in a panel with a specially designed border surrounding it. This shows what can

Fig. 20

be done by using existing styles for severely conventionalized wall treatment rather than getting up specially designed styles to suit the conditions.

33. Vertical-Striped Effects.—A large class of wall-papers are made in patterns of vertical stripes of varying width, and require the ingenuity and skill of the artistic designer just as much as do papers of floral patterns. Such striped papers

Fig. 21

are generally used for bed rooms and similar apartments where restfulness and repose are required.

Some striped papers consist of very fine alternating stripes, from $\frac{1}{2}$ inch in width up to stripes of very much greater dimensions. These stripe effects may be secured by having a dark stripe, as green, alternate with a lighter stripe of the same color; or by having both stripes of the same hue and value, but one set printed in a dull finish and the other in a satin finish.

Striped effects are made more interesting by introducing at intervals along and between the stripes floral elements, either conventional or naturalistic. Such a vertically striped paper is shown in Fig. 22, and it will be observed that for striped

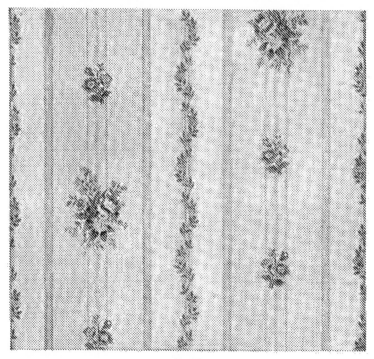

Fig. 22

papers there is just as much demand that the designer plan out proper repeats as for all-over repeats.

34. In Fig. 23 there is reproduced another striped effect. A rich effect is added by having the white dots, rectangles, and zigzag effects, placed over the darker background tone. The little baskets of flowers, delicately drawn and colored, give a dainty and refined effect to this striped paper. Both Figs. 20

and 21 represent papers that are most suitable for bed rooms or dressing rooms. No straight horizontal frieze is used at the top of such papers along the ceiling; such a frieze would be entirely too heavy. The paper is run right up to the top of the side wall and against the ceiling, and perhaps finished off with

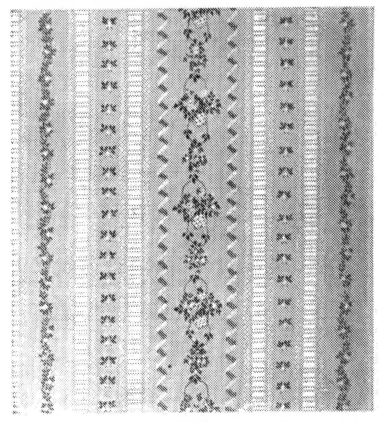

FIG. 23

a narrow white, cream, or gold wood strip molding. Sometimes such papers are topped by a dainty frieze of garlands or swags of flowers coming down over the stripes, the lower undulating edge being cut out before being pasted onto the side wall paper.

35. In Fig. 24 is shown a striped paper that is more pretentious than the ones already shown; such a design as this would be most suitable for a parlor, reception room, or drawing room

Fig. 24

of pretentious size. It will be noted that plain stripes serve as a background for the important stripes composed of floral elements and rococo scrolls. The chief characteristic of this

FIG. 25   44

paper is the rich device at the top of each floral stripe, serving as a crown or finish. Thus the crowns, repeating side to side, serve as a frieze or finish all around the room.

36. Plain Panel-and-Crown Effects.—All-over floral effects, and vertical-striped effects, by no means exhaust the decorative possibilities of wallpaper designs. Following the

FIG. 26

structural arrangement of building interiors, ancient and modern, where by marble, stone, or wood, the wall surfaces were divided into friezes, panels, and dados, the modern wallpaper designer also plans friezes and panels, which, in the wallpaper trade, are known as panel-and-crown effects.

It is in the designing of effects of this kind that the designer has opportunity to use, and must bring into play, what he has learned about historic styles of design and decoration. He may be called upon to design panel arrangements in Greek or Roman proportions; or perhaps Moorish, Renaissance, or modern decoration must be used. Thus the modern wallpaper designer is not merely one who evolves geometric repeats for certain flat spaces, but he must be, in a sense, an interior decorator who must know how to harmonize for special uses form, proportion, and color, sometimes in definite historic styles.

37. In Fig. 25 is shown perhaps the most simple form of a paneled paper that can be imagined. It is designed in imitation of wood paneling in antique oak. The use of paper of this kind is of course limited to positions and conditions where such an imitation is permissible. With the light falling on the wall from above and to the left, this paper presents the appearance of raised panels against a flat ground; whereas, by inverting it, the appearance of sunken panels with raised stiles and rails is obtained. In the former position the crown shown in Fig. 26 is used as a finish at the top, but in the latter position another style of crown is necessary. Such a paper would be suitable only for a dado treatment, another paper, say a tapestry effect, being suitable for the field above the dado.

38. The crown-and-panel effect shown in colors in Fig. 27 is a design made in imitation of leather. That the designer of such a paper would have to be familiar with historic styles, particularly the Persian and the Moorish styles, is very evident. A design such as this is printed and heavily stamped upon a very heavy paper, in an embossed effect. The characteristic markings of the hide are also impressed in the surface of the paper, so that the imitation is very deceptive. For a library, den, or lounging room, the paper shown in Fig. 27 is very effective, and it lends itself to an Oriental and luxurious treatment with plenty of brass work, Oriental implements, antique daggers, and other accessories.

39. In Fig. 28 is a reproduction of another panel-and-crown effect executed in imitation of leather. This design is very conventional, and extremely graceful in its lines, again illustrating the necessity for the wallpaper designer being

FIG. 27   § 19   289

47   Fig. 28

FIG. 29

familiar with historic styles. The design suggests the Art Nouveau, or Austrian Secession, types of Modern ornament.

40. Fig. 29 shows the central portion of a simple crown-and-panel design that was frankly made for wallpaper and not as

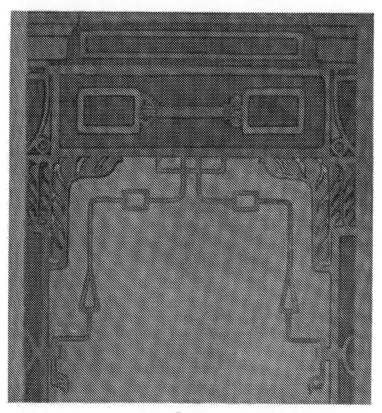

FIG. 30

an imitation of anything else. Such a panel design could be cut to any length and finished top and bottom with the crown and foot-piece shown in Fig. 30. It is a very conventional design, the forms being based on Gothic details, especially those at the upper right and upper left corners of the rectangular panels. This design is printed in three values of olive green,

51　　　　　　　　　　　　　Fig. 32

FIG. 33

and is appropriate for a hall, a library, or a dining room that is to be decorated in the Modern style of decoration.

41. In Fig. 31 is shown a simple conventional crown effect, with heraldic devices. This crown effect is printed in four values of the same color, and is suitable for a side wall over a plain ingrain or oatmeal paper, of the same value as the ground

FIG. 34

color, on which shields, crests, spot patterns, or other suitable devices may be stenciled. Simple tapestry effects may also be used under this design as a field filling, or, in some extreme cases, panel devices with the frieze omitted and the panel work carried out symmetrically at top and bottom, may be employed. The frieze is appropriate for a modern Gothic interior, or one in which furniture and fittings of the rather severe "craftsman" type have been used.

42. Papers showing simple stripes in two shades of blue, buff, or pink, often provide a suitable treatment for a small reception room, particularly where the ceiling is low and a deep frieze cannot be considered. In Fig. 32 is shown a combination of this character, in which the stripes are laid first and the crown effect is applied above. The stripe effect can be varied by sub-dividing the wall into panels, as in Fig. 33, and if a deeper crown is desired, additional designs can be obtained, one of which is shown in Fig. 34.

43. In Figs. 35 and 36 is shown a most ingenious design, with a crown effect instead of a frieze. The hanging consists of a naturalistic rendering of swamp grasses, Fig. 35, in a tangled growth that completely fills the field. Over this design two crowns are hung, the one shown in Fig. 36 (*a*) providing the tops of the grasses and introducing a pair of flying ducks, and the other in (*b*), simply topping out the grasses. When arranged judiciously, this design makes an attractive decoration for rooms, in which it is considered suitable.

44. Special Decorative Frieze Effects.—The old-fashioned frieze effects, 12, 15, or 18 inches deep, consisting of a pattern of running or repeating ornament to match the design in the field, are no longer employed. A special kind of decorative frieze, however, very often purely pictorial in character, is employed for certain classes of rooms.

The frieze reproduced in Fig. 37 is one that would be suitable for a room that is finished in any severe style of woodwork. This design is made in three sections, so that variety can be obtained in the procession of the knights as seen from different points in the room. These sections can be united so as to make the groups of figures vary in number and extent, with sections of conventional landscape between. Another arrangement is to have the landscape section repeat with another landscape piece that is designed to fit it so that the figure groups may occur only once or twice in a room frieze, or even be omitted entirely. With skilful handling, many different combinations that will afford a variety of design can be effected with this frieze or with any of the simple repeating friezes.

Fig. 35.   § 10. 280

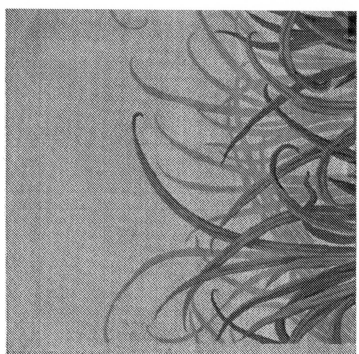

(a)

(b)

Fig. 26

(a)

(b)

(c)

FIG. 37

45. In Fig. 38 is shown another frieze design in sections that can be put together in various combinations as described for Fig. 37. This frieze is of a somewhat lighter and more frivolous character than the preceding one, and would there-

(*a*)

(*b*)

FIG. 38

fore be most suitable for a dining room or breakfast room, or for a child's bedroom or nursery. As in the case of the frieze design previously considered, there are other sections that can be fitted in between the ones shown in (*a*) and (*b*). These will permit the landscape or the procession of geese to be extended, and thus make it possible that the entire frieze shall be of either subject by itself, with the other as an incident here and there.

Fig. 39

46. In Fig. 39 is shown another interesting frieze that would be suitable for a child's room. Such a frieze, repeating around the nursery walls, is not only a clever design, but adds a spirit of jollity and merriment to such a room.

Fig. 40

47. The frieze in Fig. 40 is another example of the continuous repeating decoration in a frieze suitable for a child's room. This one portrays characters from the legend of The Pied Piper of Hamelin.

48. In all of these friezes, Figs. 37 to 40, the elements are all pictorial; there is nothing in the nature of decorative design. But the decorative designer who has been thoroughly trained in drawing should have no difficulty in drawing such figures. However, he will be assisted thereto by reference to books on figure and animal drawing, the names of which will be recommended to him upon request.

49. Geometrical and Other Patterns for Glazed Papers.—A certain class of wallpaper is made by coating it—after printing—with a hard varnish, which protects the surface of the paper and the pattern printed on it in such a way that the paper, when it becomes dusty and dirty, can be wiped with a damp cloth. Such paper is used in kitchens, bathrooms, etc., and, since it really serves as a cheap substitute for real tiling, is usually designed in more or less geometric patterns, as square, rectangular, etc., suggestive of the shapes of real tiles. However, certain liberties are taken with the extreme geometric shapes and sizes of the tiles in these designs, they being usually made smaller than actual marble or vitreous tiles and being relieved by symmetrically arranged conventionalized floral forms.

50. In Fig. 41 (*a*) is shown a plain rectangular-tile pattern in blue and white, with little vertical spot ornaments introduced as shown, that would be very suitable for a bathroom. In (*b*) is shown, in blue and white, a checker effect of large squares, alternating decorative and plain, that would be suitable for a kitchen wall. Note that, although the general plan of repeat of the squares is geometric, the rosette decoration in the darker square consists of a very cleverly designed floral motif based upon the acanthus in the center surrounded at the four corners by smaller floral forms. In (*c*) the tile arrangement is cleverly devised vertically and horizontally so as to form or surround a small square that is then filled with conventionalized leaf and berry ornament, thus making a dark spot of accent. In (*d*) is shown another tile effect based on the geometric repeat, every alternate square, in checker effect, being decorated by a curved-line motif showing the Art Nouveau

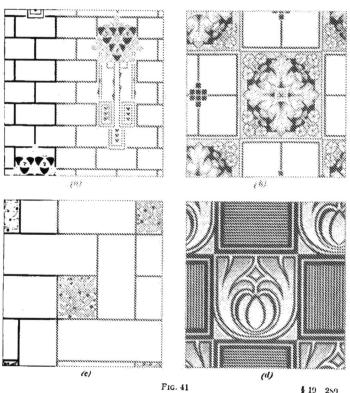

(a)

(b)

(c)

(d)

FIG. 41

influence. In the original of this pattern only the dark blue parts are glazed, the lighter parts being of dull surface. This alternating of glazed and unglazed surfaces produces a satiny effect that is very pleasing.

In Fig. 42 a portion of the pattern shown on a small scale in Fig. 41 (d) is reproduced full size, so that the scale upon which such designs are drawn may readily be seen, as well as the method of drawing the lines, dots, and masses, to get the effect.

_____

SPECIMEN ARRANGEMENT OF WALL SURFACES

51. Diversity of Arrangements.—The plan of papering a wall surface so that it presents one unbroken expanse composed of a more or less intricate all-over pattern may be the easiest plan (and the most monotonous), but is by no means the only one that can be employed. The most satisfactory method of securing variety and interest, with the simple materials available, is to use the system of paneling. This may be accomplished by using only wallpaper itself, or by combining wood moldings and battens, or strips, with the wallpaper.

52. Paneling With Wallpaper Only.—When the subdivision of the wall surface is effected *in the flat*—that is, without projecting pilasters or columns—certain combinations of wallpaper will give interesting results.

In rooms where the ceiling is low, where there is little or no room for a frieze, panels can be formed of such designs as those shown in Figs. 27, 28, 29, 30, and 32. Another good arrangement would be to use the frieze illustrated in Fig. 31 with panels composed of the designs shown in Figs. 29 and 30. These were designed to be used in such a combination or to be used separately, as desired.

However, it is not always necessary to use only stock panel designs for the field. The wall-paper hanger or decorator can work up many unique effects by using a paper with broad stripes, and then cutting out the stripes and mitering them, thus forming panels over a plain ingrain field paper. This can then be topped by a stock frieze. Such an arrangement is shown in Fig. 43.

Where a conventional landscape frieze is used over a plain, striped ingrain paper, pieces of the dark stripe may afterwards be cut out and inserted, both at the top and at the bottom,

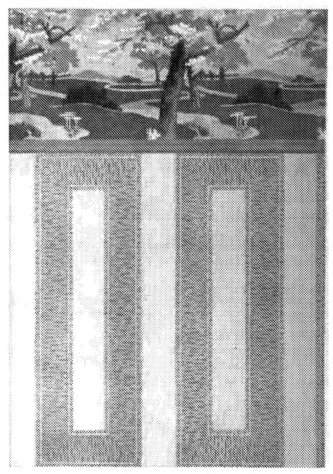

Fig. 43

to form panels. Almost any stripe can be used in this way if a little ingenuity is exercised to fit it to the style and condition required.

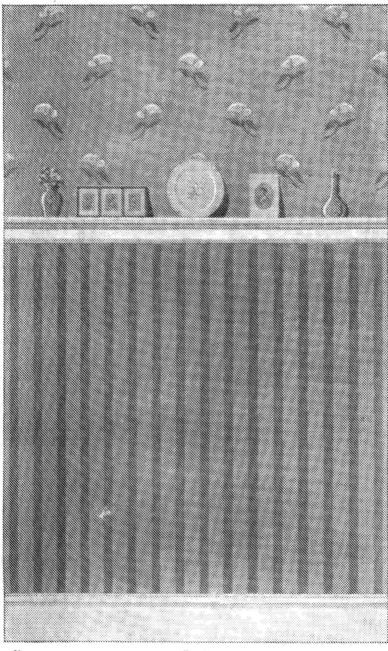

Fig. 44

53. Paneling With Wallpaper and Wooden Rails and Battens.—The proper arrangement of different wallpapers in frieze, dado, and panel effects, is greatly assisted by the proper use of horizontal wooden chair, picture, or plate rails and vertical strips or battens. The kind and color of the wood used in these rails and battens must, of course, harmonize with the wallpaper that is used.

A common treatment for bedrooms is to divide the wall two-fifths, or one-third, from the top and then paper the upper sections with a large figured floral pattern, and fill the lower portion with stripes, as shown in Fig. 44, or with a plain ingrain, burlap, or grass cloth, if the height of the ceiling will permit. In either case, the two sections should be separated by a prominent picture molding or a plate rail. A *picture molding* is grooved or rounded at the top edge, so that picture hooks supporting wires and pictures may be hung thereon. A *plate rail* consists of a shelf from 4 to 6 inches in width with a picture molding below, as shown in Fig. 44. The shelf may be used to support small pieces of bric-à-brac, etc., but no pictures should be hung above it. The upper surface of the plate rail is grooved near its outer edge, so as to catch the rims or edges of plates, or plaques, supported on it, from which it derives its name. Such a system of wall arrangement is frequently used for unpretentious dining rooms by making the woodwork dark oak, or Early English or Flemish oak, and the paper above the plate rail a tapestry effect, with the paper below the plate rail a plain ingrain, burlap, or grass-cloth.

54. Another system of panel treatment is carried out by papering the entire wall with a plain ingrain or burlap paper, and then fastening over it wooden battens, or stiles, to form panels under a wide shelf, or plate rail, as shown in Fig. 45. Another method is to have the battens or stiles built in on grounds made flush with the plaster when the house is built, and then to paper the wall surface in between these battens. The former treatment lends itself to the decoration of an old room, while the latter would be the method to follow in a new building. This scheme of decoration is suitable for a library,

FIG. 45

a dining room, a studio, or a den, and is inexpensive and very effective. If desired, the upper part can be treated with a frieze paper showing heraldic devices or Gothic figures, or the panels can be filled with leather patterns.

This scheme of wall treatment shows that even the simplest ideas can be worked out to result in a most satisfactory manner without adding greatly to the expense. The few extra dollars required for the woodwork would be offset by the money saved through the omission of a more elaborate paper on side wall and ceiling. An endless variety of subdivisions can be attained by this simple use of battens and a decorative scheme based on this idea can be made as inexpensive or as costly as the designer may desire. The idea should not be looked upon as a cheap subterfuge, as the decorative value of the design depends on the artistic handling of the details, and not on the value of the materials.

The substitution of quartered oak or mahogany would run the cost up and at the same time require a more elaborate fabric for the panels and frieze. The battens could be treated as pilasters with molded capitals and bases. This would change the character of the projecting shelf and with the other dependent details an ornate and expensive composition would result. Thus, while it can be seen that a simple idea can be worked up either as an inexpensive or a costly design, it should ever be remembered that the elaborate composition of pilasters, columns, pedestals, and entablatures should never be attempted with the simple, inexpensive materials. An elaborate design rendered in the most inexpensive materials will always look cheap, while a simple design in the same materials will always appear suitable and proper; and a simple design in expensive material will be dignified and luxurious.

NECESSITY FOR DESIGNER KNOWING SCHEMES OF WALL ARRANGEMENTS

55. While the work of the wallpaper designer and that of the decorator are separate and distinct, yet the designer who learns how the wallpapers of various patterns can be combined in different ways can then prepare special designs for frieze, dado, and panel effects, and thus make his work more suitable to commercial conditions.

The wallpaper designer must have a broad general knowledge of the entire field of interior decoration, and must know what has been and is being used. It is only by keeping in touch with the commercial field in this way that he can make designs that are salable.

WALLPAPER DESIGNING EXERCISES

GENERAL INFORMATION

56. Required Work in Wallpaper Designing.—As a test as to whether or not the student can apply to practical work what he has learned about wallpaper designing, and as a preparation for commercial work in this line, he will be required to prepare original designs for various kinds of wallpapers, following out the general methods of working as described in this Section.

These required drawings and designs, which, as before, are to be in the form of drawing plates, are to be submitted to the Schools for examination and advice.

57. Character of the Drawing Plates.—In this subject the required work will cover six drawing plates, five of them each about 10 inches wide and 15 inches high, and the sixth plate consisting of two sheets each 10 in. × 15 in., placed edge to edge, thus making a 20 in. × 15 in. shape, as will be described in connection with the plate. The plates comprise designs, all of which are to be executed in color; for this reason a smooth water-color paper, properly stretched on the drawing board, and over which a flat background wash of the desired color has been placed, should be used. In some cases wallpaper designers use a good quality of flat-color wallpaper, working thereon with opaque or distemper color. The designs in this present Section, however, are to be made in water colors on stretched water-color paper.

These plates are to be sent to the Schools, one by one, for examination; and, while the first plate is being examined and returned, the student will be working on the following plate, pursuing this method until all plates are satisfactorily completed.

_____

PLATE 1

58. Exercises for Plate 1.—On a 10″×15″ sheet lay out a collection of floral motifs suitable for wallpaper work, similar to, but not copies of, the collection shown in Fig. 4. Special studies may be made direct from nature, or floral motifs that were arranged for previous plates of the Course may be used again here.

The important feature, in preparing these floral motifs in color, is that the rendering must be in flat masses of color, appropriately placed as shown in Fig. 4, with no blendings as there would be in naturalistic water-color painting. If desired, a certain amount of opaque quality may be added to the water colors by an admixture of Chinese white. A careful study should be made of the method of placing masses of flat color in Fig. 4, before the rendering of the studies on this plate is attempted.

59. Final Work on Plate 1.—Letter or write the title, Plate 1: Wallpaper Designing, at the top of the sheet, and on the back place class letters and number, name, address, and date of completing the plate. Roll the plate, place in the mailing tube, and send to the Schools for examination. Then proceed with Plate 2.

_____

PLATE 2

60. Designing an All-Over Pattern for a Parlor Paper.—Prepare a sketch design 9 inches by 12 inches high, which will be just one-half of a full-size 18 inches wide by 25 inches high wallpaper repeat, for one repeat of an all-over-pattern wallpaper suitable for a parlor or reception room. The all-over repeating pattern or design may be of a more or less conventionalized character, as shown in Figs. 8 to 14, or of a decidedly naturalistic character, as shown in Figs. 15 to 21, but not in any respect a copy of any one of these examples; the design must be entirely original.

Although the work on this plate is to be a half-size sketch, yet every detail of ornament and background must be drawn and rendered with the highest degree of accuracy and precision. No rough sketch will be accepted.

Before starting the design, great consideration must be given to the particular room in which this paper is to be placed, and the pattern must be designed so as to be suitable for that room, as well as being artistically and technically correct in itself.

61. Final Work on Plate 2.—Letter or write the title, Plate 2: Wallpaper Designing, at the top of the sheet, and on the back place class letters and number, name, address, and date of completing the plate. Roll the plate, place in the mailing tube, and send to the Schools for examination. Then proceed with Plate 3.

PLATE 3

62. Designing a Vertical-Stripe Pattern for a Bedroom Paper.—Prepare a sketch design 9 inches wide by 12 inches high, which will be just one-half of a full size 18 inches wide by 24 inches high wallpaper repeat, for one repeat of an all-over pattern wallpaper suitable for a bed room. The pattern may be designed similar in arrangement to, but not a copy of, any one of those shown in Figs. 22 to 24. As in the case of the design on Plate 2, every detail of ornament and background must be drawn with exactness, preceded by a careful consideration of the requirements of the specific kind of room in which the paper is to be used.

63. Final Work on Plate 3.—Letter or write the title, Plate 3: Wallpaper Designing, at the top of the sheet, and on the back place class letters and number, name, address, and date of completing the plate. Roll the plate, place in the mailing tube, and send to the Schools for examination. Then proceed with Plate 4.

PLATE 4

64. Designing a Panel-and-Crown Pattern for a Library Paper.—Prepare a sketch design 9 inches wide by 12 inches high, which will be just one-half of a full size 18 inches wide by 24 inches high wallpaper repeat, for one repeat of a panel-and-crown pattern, or side-wall-and-frieze pattern, wallpaper suitable for a library or den. The wallpapers illustrated in Figs. 24 to 40 show diverse arrangements of panel-and-crown effects, and side-wall- (or panel) and-frieze effects, which will serve to give an idea of what is wanted. The student should also seize every opportunity to look over the stock of panel-and-crown effects displayed in wallpaper stores and interior decorator's shops; for new arrangements of panels, crowns, friezes, etc., are being made every season.

The same care in considering the use to which the wallpaper is to be put and in drawing and rendering the details, as advised for the designs on previous plates, must be exercised in the case of this one.

65. Final Work on Plate 4.—Letter or write the title, Plate 4: Wallpaper Designing, at the top of the sheet, and on the back place class letters and number, name, address, and date of completing the plate. Roll the plate, place in the mailing tube, and send to the Schools for examination Then, if all required work on previous plates has been completed, proceed with Plate 5.

PLATE 5

66. Designing a Geometrical Pattern for a Glazed Bathroom Paper.—Prepare a sketch design, following sizes as described in text, for a geometrical pattern for a glazed paper suitable for a bathroom or hallway; after the same general style, but not a copy, of the patterns shown in Figs. 41 and 42.

Observe the same care in designing, drawing, and rendering this pattern as was used in the case of the sketch designs on previous plates.

67. Final Work on Plate 5.—Letter or write the title, Plate 5: Wallpaper Designing, at the top of the sheet, and on the back place class letters and number, name, address, and date of completing the plate. Roll the plate, place in the mailing tube, and send to the Schools for examination. Then, if all required work on previous plates has been completed, proceed with Plate 6.

PLATE 6

68. Laying Out a Full Size Wallpaper Design.—This plate will comprise two $10'' \times 15''$ sheets placed edge to edge, so as to make a shape 20 inches wide by 15 inches high, and will consist of a full size drawing and rendering of the upper half of an $18'' \times 24''$ wallpaper repeat. Any one of the original designs used on Plates 2, 3, 4, and 5, and there laid out half size, may now be selected for Plate 6, and the upper half laid out full scale; that is, in a space 18 inches wide by 12 inches high.

The two $10'' \times 15''$ sheets may be placed edge to edge, and within the resulting $20'' \times 15''$ space, a size 18 inches wide by 12 inches high may be laid out. Thus there will be white margins at only the top, left, and bottom edges of the left-hand sheet and at the top, right, and bottom edges of the right-hand sheet, the design extending across the joining edges of the two sheets. The design must be drawn and rendered with absolute accuracy, and must appear just like the finished wallpaper is expected to look. Transparent or opaque colors may be used as preferred.

The two sheets are *not* to be pasted together, but are to be left separate so that they can be properly rolled when placed in the mailing tube.

69. Final Work on Plate 6.—Letter or write the title, Plate 6: Wallpaper Designing, somewhere on *each* one of the two sheets, marking the left-hand sheet Plate 6 (*a*) and the right-hand sheet Plate 6 (*b*), and placing on the back of *each* sheet class letters and number, name, address, and date of completing the plate. Roll both sheets, place in the mailing tube, and send to the Schools for examination.

If any redrawn work on any of the plates of this Section has been called for and has not yet been completed, it should be satisfactorily finished at this time. After all the required work on the plates of this Section has been completed, the work of the next Section should be taken up at once.

STAINED- AND LEADED-GLASS DESIGNING

INTRODUCTION

PURPOSE

1. Necessity of Specialized Training.—The colored windows seen in churches, public buildings, and private residences, made of mosaic patterns of colored glass and lead strips, are known as **stained and leaded glass.** Not only the average person, but the decorative artist himself, has a rather vague idea as to what a stained-glass window is, how it is made, and how it must be designed. The average churchgoers, or frequenters of public or private buildings where there are leaded-glass windows, are vaguely aware, if they notice the windows at all, that the windows keep out the inclement weather, that bright colors are used and that these become intensified and sparkling when the full sunlight strikes them. Perhaps a few observers may also notice what picture subjects are used, but beyond these points their knowledge and opinions do not go.

In the case of the designer, no matter how well as a decorative artist he may understand his draftsmanship and his principles of design and color, he is confronted by an entirely new problem when he attempts to design for stained- and leaded-glass work. Stained glass is, to an unusual degree, a technical art. One may write a poem or a musical composition, paint an easel portrait or landscape, or even do certain kinds of designing, and not be hampered by any restrictions of men or materials. But in the case of the strictly technical arts, such as stained glass, limitations of men, materials, and processes enter, which need consideration before the designer's ideas and sketches can be completely expressed in the actual material.

The purpose of this Section, therefore, is to give the designer a history of the craft of stained- and leaded-glass work, the technical points of its manufacture, and the principles of designing for it, so that his designs may not only be truly artistic but may also be technically correct.

2. Scope of Training in This Section.—It must be understood that this Section is not intended to teach the trade of the leaded-glass worker. Descriptions of the materials and processes used in making leaded-glass windows will be given, but only to the extent that these should be understood by the designer in order to enable him to prepare designs that are technically correct.

First will be presented data regarding the evolution and development of stained- and leaded-glass work from earliest times up to the present day; then will be discussed the materials and processes of making stained- and leaded-glass windows; after which the designing of leaded-glass work will be taught. As in the case of the other Sections on technical design work, the tests at the conclusion of the Section will take the form of practical problems in stained- and leaded-glass designing, requiring in answer thereto original designs in the form of exercises on drawing plates.

EVOLUTION OF STAINED AND LEADED GLASS

3. First Use of Glass for Windows.—The use of glass dates back to a very remote period. It is definitely known that the ancient Egyptians used glass, for examples of their use of it are to be seen in museums; even colored glass was known to them. The Phœnicians, and other races following the Egyptians, continued the use of glass. The very earliest recorded use of colored glass for the purpose of filling window openings was that made by Singhalese artists about 306 B. C. This was the combination of small gem-like pieces of colored glass, which had all the brilliancy of precious stones, set together in a mosaic window.

The natural causes leading up to the use of colored glass for window openings are interesting. As civilization moved northward from Egypt, Phœnicia, Greece, and Rome, the character of the buildings changed. Instead of the classic styles, with open apertures to admit light, high pointed roofs and buildings that would keep out the weather became necessary. The openings for the admission of light could not be filled merely with clear glass, for this would admit the light in such a manner as to be dazzling and blinding. To reduce the size of the apertures would have been unsatisfactory, thus causing the lighting to be unequal. Consequently, the most natural solution of the difficulty was to use toned or colored glass, which would subdue the light, and at the same time not make necessary the reduction of the size of the window. These colored glasses at once presented an opportunity for decorative treatment; and it followed naturally that the mosaic pictures and decorative work previously used on walls and floors of churches were simply carried out in spirit in the translucent glass of the windows.

4. Historic-Period Styles of Stained and Leaded Glass.—It is absolutely essential that the designer of stained and leaded glass should have a clear idea as to the historic periods and styles of glasswork. This knowledge will show him what is correct and what is inappropriate, and the reason therefor, when he comes to design windows that are to be suitable for a certain style of building or a certain religious sect or denomination.

To say when stained and leaded glass was first used for filling window openings would be to speculate. There is no existing glasswork of this class which can be proved to have been done previous to the 13th century; but the stained-glass work of that date shows evidences of development that indicate that even in the 12th century the art had been long in practice.

As early as the 6th century colored windows were used in the basilica of St. Peter's, at Rome, and in the Church of St. Sophia, at Constantinople.   In 709 A. D., the Bishop of York, England, imported glass workers from France.   Indeed, the French claim to have invented the process of painting on glass, and to have carried it to the English, who in turn instructed the Germans in the art.

It will be of help to the student and designer to divide the development of the stained- and leaded-glass art into periods, and to note in a general way the characteristics that distinguish the glass of each period.   Stained and leaded glass, being a technical art, naturally followed the trend and development of building construction and styles of buildings, the artist, glass painter, and glazier simply working in the style of their particular period because they knew no other.   They naturally designed their window patterns to fit the shape of the opening in the masonry which the builder had provided.   Stained and leaded glass is distinctly a Gothic art, and the periods and styles of the art naturally follow the periods and styles of Gothic architecture.

The classification of these periods as made by Winston has been accepted as standard, and—amplified somewhat and brought up to date—is as follows:

Pre-Gothic Period........... 600 A. D.? to 1000 A. D.
Early Gothic Period.........1000 A. D. to 1280 A. D.
Decorated-Gothic Period.....1280 A. D. to 1380 A. D.
Perpendicular-Gothic Period..1380 A. D. to 1530 A. D.
Renaissance Period..........1530 A. D. to 1700 A. D.
Period of Decadence.........1700 A. D. to 1800 A. D.
Gothic Revival Period.......1800 A. D. to present day

It will be interesting to study the kinds of material and the methods of designing and setting the glass that were employed in the various periods.   There were no sharp and distinct lines of demarcation between the various periods; one encroached upon another and the advance was not regular; sometimes it took a spurt ahead, sometimes it lagged.

5. Pre-Gothic Period (600 A. D.? to 1000 A. D.).
The earliest way of filling window openings was probably by

the use of large sheets of glass joined by lead strips, the whole being supported by iron bars. As this was found to be weak, the pieces were reduced in size, thereby not only strengthening the window, but giving opportunity for brilliant mosaic coloring. The earlier mosaic windows were distinctly geometric in pattern, with no paint upon them.

6. Early Gothic Period (1000 A. D. to 1280 A. D.). The patterns in the glass of the first windows of this period were of the square and diamond shapes, regular polygons, or mosaic effects not geometrical. Later in this period there were practically four separate kinds of windows: *pattern windows, figure windows, medallion windows,* and *Jesse windows.*

1. *Pattern Windows.*—The windows made of clear glass and devoid of paint were known as pattern, or *grisaille,* windows. The designs were geometric, interlacing bands being employed, and were characteristic of the Byzantine style. Later, windows of this class employed bright colors and some painted work.

2. *Figure Windows.*—Windows in which human figures were combined with structural canopy work, the whole being very richly colored, were known as figure windows. The drawing of the figures was very archaic, and in many cases very stiff and unnatural. The figures, owing to the long lancet shapes of the English Gothic windows, were usually portrayed in a standing position. Flesh could not be satisfactorily expressed, because the glass maker could not produce a pot-metal glass of a flesh tint. The nearest he could come to a flesh tint was a reddish brown.

3. *Medallion Windows.*—Those windows where the pictures were arranged in medallions and surrounded by decoration were called medallion windows. These are typical of the Early Gothic period. The spaces between and surrounding the medallions were usually of brilliant colors, filled by decorative details in strong contrast. The strong supporting bars were usually so fashioned as to help outline the medallion, and this was also characteristic of the windows of this period.

4. *Jesse Windows.*—The pictorial windows in which the genealogy of the Savior was decoratively portrayed were called

Jesse windows. The colors used were few but rich; and deep ruby hues, sapphire blues, pure greens, strong deep yellows, all combined to make brilliant effects—owing frequently to the fortunate accidents of the melting pot.

At first all the decorative details used in windows of the Early Gothic period naturally partook of the Byzantine style, but later became simpler.

7. Decorated-Gothic Period (1280 A. D. to 1380 A. D.).—The period styled the Decorated-Gothic was characterized chiefly by the prominence of the canopy effect used to enclose the figure subjects, in conjunction with elaborate foliated decoration; and the spreading of the design across several window openings. The desire for more illumination caused new shapes of windows to be designed, and the canopy and bands solved the design problem. Tracery windows—that is, windows in the upper part of which the mullions or dividing bars spread out and were split up into decorative shapes—came into use in this period, thus giving opportunity for more elaborate design. The use of yellow, or "gold," stain arose also in this period—the 14th century.

8. Perpendicular-Gothic Period (1380 A. D. to 1530 A. D.).—The canopy and the long perpendicular bands continued to be used in the 15th century for enclosing figure subjects, and the period is thus known as the Perpendicular-Gothic period.

The plan of using the structural canopy, suggestive of stonework and yet done in glass and set into a niche of stone or wood, does not seem natural, but yet it appears to be an effective way of designing the filling of the window space. In this way the picture grouping is properly included. No better means of designing a window to fill such a space has ever been devised, even by modern designers.

In this period both the structural and the foliated decorative details were so twisted and elaborated as to be far removed from the naturalistic.

9. Renaissance Period (1530 A. D. to 1700 A. D.). The chief characteristic of the best work of the Renaissance period was the portraying in glass of a picture unrelated to the stonework of the window sides or mullions. In the early part of the period the trend of the decoration was toward the arabesque, and later the cartouche and strap work. The canopy work of the Renaissance period, while following on general lines the Gothic, was totally different from it in detail of drawing and in manner of execution. The art of glass painting came to be more perfect; new means of obtaining naturalistic effects, both by kinds of paint and by methods of execution, came into use; pictures were built up in elaborate detail, and the leaded-glass idea was kept more and more in the background. Draftsmanship and expert painting reached such a consummate stage as to finally lead to the period of decadence, in the latter part of the 17th century.

10. Period of Decadence (1700 A. D. to 1800 A. D.). In the transition period, which has come to be called the period of decadence, the splendid effects secured by painting on glass were carried to such a degree that the painting was overdone. The beautiful effects to be secured by the translucent glow of the glass itself were hidden by the paint; and the effect of leading, the chief characteristic of stained glass, was minimized. This at once marked the decline of the art, for craftsmanship was lost sight of, and the glass painter held full sway, producing naturalistic pictures that were more suitable for easel pictures and mural decorations than for the noble medium of stained glass.

11. Gothic Revival Period (1800 A. D. to Present Day).—After a period of decadence, the art of stained and leaded glass began to be revived with the advent of the 19th century. ' The old secrets have been discovered anew, and today better work is produced than ever before. In England Lewis F. Day, Walter Crane, Henry Holliday, and others have helped to bring the art back to its high plane; and in the United States John La Farge, Louis Tiffany, and others have done even more, along certain lines. The tendency of English glass is to be staid and conservative; while the American tendency is to strike out along bold and untried lines.

Opalescent glass, as it is called, is practically an American invention, being the result of John La Farge's studies and experiments. Mr. La Farge, an artist and mural decorator of high artistic ability, turned his attention to working in stained glass and, being unable with the glass on hand to get the effects he wanted, experimented upon the glass itself; that is, its manufacture from the raw material. By introducing opalescent qualities, by having one color run into another, and—while the glass was still soft—twisting it about and manipulating it with the ladle, he obtained a variety of colors in his material, and a surface ridged and corrugated resembling in some cases flowing drapery. Mr. La Farge's idea was to produce a window, either decorative or with a picture subject, by simply using the accidental effects obtained in the glass itself; doing away with the painting altogether, thus preserving the transparency and brilliancy of the colors, and retaining the light and shade values.

Some remarkably beautiful windows have resulted from using this opalescent method in their construction, but where one has the opportunity of seeing such an opalescent window side by side with an antique window done upon the lines of the English mosaic style, one cannot help preferring the window of the antique, or painted mosaic, style.

STAINED- AND LEADED-GLASS WINDOWS

MANUFACTURE

MATERIALS

12. Nature of Stained and Leaded Glass for Windows.—In the term stained and leaded glass the word **stained** is used to refer to the color of the glass, because the pieces of glass used must either have their coloring matter diffused throughout, forming a part of the glass itself, or the colors must be painted onto the surface of the glass with vitrifiable pigments and then burnt in by the action of heat. The word **leaded** is used because the pieces of glass are held together by lead strips and thus formed into a mosaic pattern.

Stained and leaded glass finds by far its widest application in the construction of decorative windows such as are used in churches, public buildings, and private residences. The principles of designing such a window are the same as those governing the designing of any other kind of decorative work or the painting of a picture, except that in the case of stained and leaded glass the limitations of materials and processes must be considered.

13. Materials Required.—The chief materials required in constructing a stained-glass window are: pieces of colored glass, strips of lead, and pigments for painting the glass.

For this reason the resulting design cannot be expected to rival an easel picture in the matter of realism and fidelity of detail; in fact, the intention should not be to do this. The chief beauty of a stained-glass window lies in its colors, and the success of the design depends mainly on the arrangement and harmony of the colors, and the proper use of the strips of lead to serve as an essential part of the design.

14. Composition of Colored Glass.—Although the artist and artisan designing and constructing the window do not need to be familiar with the composition of the glass, because the glass is already made and ready for use when it comes to the designer and the leaded-glass worker, yet it will be of interest to know its composition.

Like plain sheet glass, or plate glass, colored glass consists of a double silicate of lime and soda, the coloring being accomplished by the application of metallic oxides which are soluble in the fused glass. The basic materials—sand, limestone, and soda—are mixed in the proportion of 30 parts of lime and 40 parts of soda to every 100 parts of sand, and are fused in the glass furnace, fireclay crucibles being used. The coloring matter is added at different stages of the process. The best shades of violet are produced from manganese or from weak cobalt. The blues, from light to dark, and from purplish to green blues, are produced from different proportions of cobalt. Peacock blue comes from copper, which, with chromium, is the source of the finest greens. The dull water-green comes from ferrous oxide; and the brilliant emerald green comes from oxide of copper. The yellows in glass are of many kinds; permanent yellow stain is made by applying oxide of silver to the surface of the glass; the pale yellow comes from oxide of lead; the fine sparkling yellow comes from sesquioxide of uranium; orange color is made by the higher oxides of iron. In the case of the reds in glass, manganese gives a variety of pinkish reds, and copper gives the blood reds that make a window appear so brilliant. The fine ruby glass gets its quality from the proportion of gold used in it.

In commercial use, the glass employed for stained and leaded windows may be classified in four groups: *antique glass*, *cathedral glass*, *opalescent glass*, and *white* (or *fancy*) *glass*.

15. Antique Glass.—In making the glass that is known as **antique,** a bubble of glass is first blown from the molten glass. This bubble is then opened at the ends and manipulated, while still hot, until it takes the form of a large tube. The tube is then cut down one side, parallel to the axis, and then opened, spread out, and flattened into a sheet on the surface of a stone slab. The side of the sheet of glass that comes in contact with the stone receives slight indentations and wave-like streaks, but it is on the upper, or smooth, surface that subsequent cutting and painting should be done.

Antique glass is transparent as well as translucent, and is the clearest and purest in its colors of all the glasses. The finer varieties have many minute surface bubbles that relieve the even tone of color, and give it a sparkling brilliancy. This glass may be of one solid color throughout, and made as already described, in which case it is called *pot-metal* antique. Or, it may have the color on only one side, and be known as *flashed antique*, or simply *flashed* glass. Most ruby glass, and some blue glasses, belong to the flashed glasses. A bubble of white glass is first blown, and this is then dipped into molten colored glass of the desired hue, the bubble thus becoming covered with a layer of colored glass. The blowing is then continued, the bubble opened and rolled to cylindrical shape, and then cut and flattened, resulting in a sheet composed of white glass with a superimposed film, or flashing, of color.

This flashed antique glass is very valuable for use in etching, when the glass painting is done, whereby delicate embroidery on drapery, or minute decorations on heraldic devices, may be portrayed.

16. Cathedral Glass.—As far as manufacture is concerned, cathedral glass is practically antique glass, but its quality is such that, in the trade, it bears its special name. It is not so pure in color, nor so transparent and translucent as is antique glass; in fact, in some cases it is not at all transparent. In some cases one side of the glass is very rough, like extremely rough leather. The varieties of color obtainable in cathedral glass are many; and the comparative cheapness of cost makes it very satisfactory for general use.

17. Opalescent Glass.—The glass classified as opal-escent, because it looks like the opal, is the least translucent of all stained glass, but gives the richest effects of coloring, because of the great variety of colors and their harmonious blending in single sheets. While the details of the processes of making the various kinds of opalescent glass are kept secret, yet the general principle upon which it is done is to blend the colored glasses while molten. The various colors of molten glass are kept in separate pots or crucibles and the glass worker with his ladle throws the different colored molten glass out along the stone slab or table, blending the colored glasses in long valleys or ridges which fuse together, the colors blending and mixing as the glass hardens. The result is a creamy white ground in which are beautiful streaks of gold, green, amber, pink, etc., all softly blended.

18. White, or Fancy, Glass.—Another variety of glass which, although not stained, must be included under the head

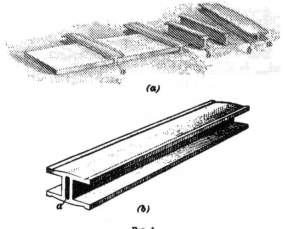

(a)

(b)

Fig. 1

of leaded glass, are the so-called **white** glasses which are used commonly in banks, cafés, and private residences. These are chiefly the Florentine, muffled, chipped, ruffled, fluted, Etruscan, and similar glasses. Nearly all these glasses are semitransparent, obtaining their names from the character of their surfaces.

19. The Leads.—The lead strips used in stained- and leaded-glass work are very much alike in form, but differ in size. In Fig. 1 are shown several forms and sizes of **leads,** indicating the manner in which the pieces of glass fit into them. The core, or heart, a is made of different depths or thicknesses in order to accommodate pieces of glass of different thicknesses, while the flange, or leaf, b is made of different widths, varying from ⅛ to ½ inch. The different widths may be used to advantage in the same window, the designer selecting whatever he thinks preferable for a particular position. A special form of lead is shown in Fig. 1 (b), consisting of a wide-leaved lead having a steel strip a inserted in the core. The object of the steel strip is to add lateral stiffness when in place in the window.

20. Ironwork.—The window, after being leaded and cemented, has considerable rigidity, but not sufficient to make it strong enough to withstand the elements; therefore, it is supported by ironwork. This ironwork takes the form of horizontal brace bars or rods, either flat or cylindrical, and upright stanchion irons, or T bars, in very large or wide windows.

21. Pigments for Glass Painting.—The pigments used in glass painting will be discussed more in detail when glass painting is described. It will be sufficient to mention here that the pigments employed consist very largely of iron oxide. This oxide is very red and is an extremely ugly color, so that it is seldom used by itself, but is modified in color by the addition of various other mineral oxides. The colored mineral pigments have the property of being soluble with the molten glass, and become part of it. The method of using these pigments will be discussed fully when glass painting is taken up.

MAKING WORKING DRAWINGS AND PATTERNS

22. Making the Working Drawings.—The processes now being described concern only the actual manufacture of the window. The designing of a window, although it comes previous to the manufacture, must, in this treatise, be considered after the description of the window's manufacture because no one can design stained- and leaded-glass windows intelligently until he knows how they are made. Therefore, it will be assumed that the small-scale water color sketch for the window, and also the full-size cartoon or picture, have been designed properly and drawn completely. The first stage, therefore, in the actual making of the window is the making of the working drawings.

A piece of tracing paper is pinned over the face of the full-size picture or cartoon of the window. Then with soft lead pencil, or with conté crayon, a clear line is drawn on the tracing paper exactly in the middle of each lead line on the cartoon. The designing and placing of the lead lines will be fully discussed when the designing of a window is taken up. The proper border lines denoting the sight size and the full size (to be fully described later) should then be drawn. The resulting network of lines will then indicate the shapes of the glass pieces. The tracing paper should then be removed from the cartoon and studied to see whether the abstract arrangement of lines is pleasing, as it should be, and whether any of the pieces of glass are of inharmonious shape and need to be altered. These points can more easily be determined by having the tracing of the lead lines disassociated from the design on the cartoon. All lines must be very accurate, squared-up and trued, and especial care must be taken that the decorative details or figures do not run into and become hidden by the stone or wooden border strip forming the flange of the groove into which the window fits, called the *rebate* (to be described later).

23. Cutting the Patterns.—The shapes of the pieces of glass as outlined on the tracing paper must now be transferred into patterns to be used in cutting the pieces of glass. A sheet of heavy cartridge paper, larger than the proposed window, is laid flat on a large drafting table and a sheet of black carbon paper or carbon cloth is laid on it, face downwards. Over this is stretched the tracing paper with the lead lines, or cut lines, marked on it, the object being to transfer the lines from the tracing paper to the heavy cartridge or pattern paper. However, the lines on the tracing paper show the shapes of the pieces of glass as fitted edge to edge in contact; whereas, when the leads are introduced, the core, or heart, of the lead strip separates adjacent pieces. Consequently, each piece of glass must be cut a little smaller than indicated by the lines on the tracing paper, to allow for the core, or heart, of the lead. A simple method of allowing for this core is to take an ordinary ruling pen and set the points of its blades to the width of the core, as illustrated in Fig. 2. Then, holding the pen so that its points lie equidistant on each side of the line, each line on the tracing paper should be traced over with a firm pressure. The result will be a copy or transfer of the lines on the tracing paper, except that the cartridge paper will show a series of double lines instead of single ones. Before removing the tracing paper from the carbon paper and cartridge paper, all the separate pieces

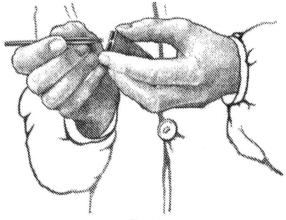

Fig. 2

of glass shown on it should be numbered. These numbers will be transferred to the cartridge paper. After removing the tracing paper and the carbon sheet, the sheet of cartridge paper should be placed on a sheet of glass and cut with a sharp knife along all of the lines shown on it. The result will be a numbered paper pattern of each piece of glass to be used. The narrow strips of paper between the double lines representing the cores of the leads may be thrown away.

24. Glazier's Drawing and Pattern Drawing at One Operation.—Sometimes, if the full-size cartoon is for a simple window and is not too valuable on account of containing fine figure and ornamental work, there may be made, at one operation, the glazier's drawing and the pattern drawing. First, a sheet of cartridge pattern paper is laid on the table, over it a sheet of carbon paper or cloth, over that a sheet of thin manila detail paper, over that another sheet of carbon paper or cloth, and over top of all the full-size cartoon with the lead lines, or cut lines, marked upon it. Then, with a steel stylus, or even with a hard lead pencil (as a 6H), the lead lines of the full-size cartoon should be gone over, thus transferring the lead lines to the thin manila paper, for the glazier's drawing, and to the heavy cartridge paper, for the pattern drawing. The pieces of the pattern for the glass may be numbered as previously described.

25. Patterns Cut With Special Pattern Scissors. Instead of marking off double lines on the cartridge pattern

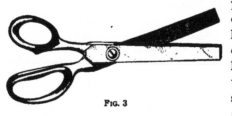

paper, to allow for the core, or heart, of the lead, the pattern paper can be cut up into the little individual patterns by means of scissors of special design, devised particu-

FIG. 3

larly for this work, as shown in Fig. 3. One blade of these special scissors is constructed like the blade of any common scissors, namely, in one strip of steel, but the other blade is in reality composed of two blades kept parallel and a distance apart corresponding to the width of the heart, or core, of the lead strip. The edges of the blades are all square and sharpened, the single blade coming down between the double ones and cutting out from the pattern paper a thin strip of paper corresponding in width to the width of the heart, or core, of the lead strip. There are scissors of various sizes to suit the leads of different-sized cores. When the pattern sheet is cut apart the little individual patterns thus become the proper size to which the pieces of glass should be cut.

After the individual patterns are cut they should be laid in place upon the original tracing of the lead lines or upon the glazing drawing, spread out upon the work table or upon a sheet of glass, or upon the plate glass painting easel (to be described later).

CUTTING THE GLASS

26. Selecting the Glass.—This very important part of the process is frequently left to the skilled workmen or glaziers in the shop, the designer merely furnishing them with a colored sketch to scale, showing where the different colors of glass are to go. The most careful method, however, and that which results in the most artistic window, is for the designer and the glass painter to super-intend the selection of the glass, or to select it themselves. One method is as follows: The glass easel is lowered to a horizontal position, the cartoon or the glazier's drawing is pasted or pinned underneath, and each little paper pattern is mounted by wax on the top side of the easel, which is then pushed up into a vertical position, and set up in a good light. Any special place is determined on, as, for instance, a large section of the colored

FIG. 4

robe of a saint in a figure window, the paper pattern is removed, a large sheet of glass of suitable color is obtained from the racks in the store room, as shown in Fig. 4, and is held over the vacancy left by taking away the pattern. The most suitable portion of the sheet of glass is then chosen and a shape is cut out therefrom to conform with the shape of the paper pattern. It may be necessary to look over a number of sheets of glass in the racks before the right piece is found. The accidental color effects in the glass thus aid the artist.

27. The Glass Cutter, or Cutting Tool.—The tool with which glass is cut, and the manner in which it is held, are shown in Fig. 5. The tool consists of a small steel wheel *a*, having a **V**-shaped edge, mounted on a pin so that it will rotate, and held in a slot in the end of the metal head *b*, which is attached to the handle *c*. On the under side of the head are three rectangu-

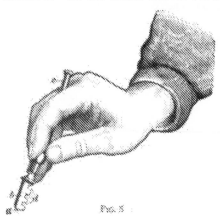

Fig. 5

lar slots *d*, of different widths. These are used only in breaking off very narrow edges in cutting plain sheet glass, and when the fingers cannot be used to advantage in breaking off the glass. The slot that will fit the thickness of glass being cut or trimmed is slipped over the edge of the glass, and the handle is swung around, thus twisting the edge of the glass and breaking it off in a sharp line.

A diamond point mounted on a tool is sometimes used for cutting glass, but the steel-wheel cutter just described is just as satisfactory for ordinary purposes, and is much cheaper.

28. Cutting Simple Shapes.—A straight cut is the simplest and easiest to make. The cutting tool is held as in Fig. 5 and the wheel *a* is rolled along the line, on the surface of the sheet of glass, the forefinger guiding the cutting tool and supplying the necessary pressure. The tool must be held square with the surface of the glass, in a lateral direction, although the top of the handle may be inclined considerably toward the workman, in the direction of the line of cutting.

The cut is made by drawing the cutting tool toward the workman, and pressing just hard enough to cause the wheel to bite

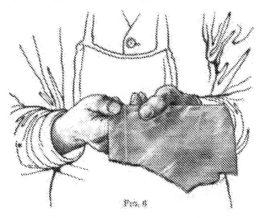

Fig. 6

into the glass. The scored line thus made should not show that the glass has been splintered; in fact it should scarcely be visible except when the sheet is held up to the light, and then it should show as a clean, silvery line. The sheet should then be held as in Fig. 6, and an upward pressure should be exerted by

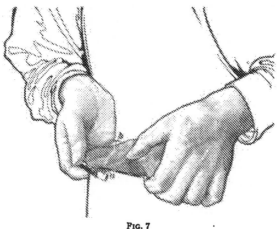

Fig. 7

the fingers underneath the cut, when the glass will break smoothly along the line.

The manner of breaking the glass along the cut, as illustrated in Fig. 6, will do very well for straight cuts, but will not be applicable if the line is irregular. For example, suppose that the glass is to be cut along a curved line like that indicated by ab, Fig. 7. The cut is made in the usual way. Then, holding the glass as shown in the illustration, the head of the cutter is rapped sharply, but not heavily, against the under side of the sheet, following along directly under the cut. The result will be that a crack will spring through the glass from the cut above to the surface beneath. When this crack shows all along the line of the cut, the glass is grasped on each side of the line and bent upwards with a gentle pressure of the fingers, when it will break cleanly along the desired line.

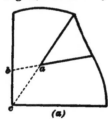

(a)

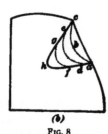

(b)

FIG. 8

29. Cutting Difficult Shapes. There are some shapes that cannot be cut in glass. For example, if an attempt were made to cut the shape shown by the heavy lines in Fig. 8 (a) by removing the triangular piece, the glass would certainly split across from the sharp angle a, probably along ab or ac. In such a case, an approximation to the desired shape would have to be used, such as that indicated by the heavy lines in (b). Furthermore, this shape could not be formed by a single cut. Instead, a first cut would be made along abc, and the segment broken out. Then a second cut would be made along $adec$ and the segment taken out, followed by a third along $dfgc$, and a final one along fhg. The deeper the curve extends inwards, the greater is the danger of splitting; therefore, in taking out the segments formed by the successive cuts, the cuts are first deepened by rapping, and the pieces then carefully removed by using the pliers. This tool is illustrated in Fig. 9,

FIG. 9

and the method of using it is shown in Fig. 10. The margin
to be broken off is gripped by the pliers. Then, by pressing

Fig. 10

downwards on the handles of the pliers, the glass may be broken
away bit by bit, gradually approaching the line of the cut.

30. Precautions in Cutting.—In cutting a piece of glass
to a certain shape, it is not advisable to cut entirely around the
pattern at first. One side should be taken at a time, and it is
an excellent plan to cut the most awkward and difficult edge
first of all, since, if the piece breaks during the operation, the
time of cutting the other edges will not
be wasted. For example, suppose that
the square of glass shown by the outer
dotted lines in Fig. 11 is to be cut to the
shape indicated by the shaded portion.
The cut $abcd$ would first be made, removing the corner, and enabling the
segment bec to be cut out as previously
described. Then the side bf would be
cut out, extending the cut to g so as to

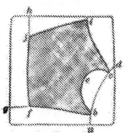

Fig. 11

facilitate the breaking off of the strip. Next the cut fh would
be made, and then the cut ci, after which the cut ij would
finish the piece.

When cutting the glass, the pattern is held on the surface of the glass as in Fig. 12, and the wheel of the glass cutter is kept in contact with the edge of the pattern.

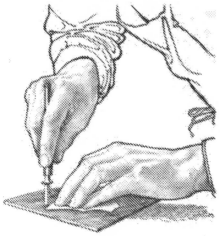

FIG. 12

31. Sharpening the Glass Cutter.

The wheel of the glass cutter may become dull after a time, and begin to scratch. It then becomes necessary to sharpen the edge. The cutting disk, or wheel, is set so as to project very slightly beyond the shoulders between which it rotates, as may be seen in Fig. 13 (a); consequently, to get the wheel at the proper angle on the oil stone, one of the thick shoulders must

have its corner ground off, as shown in (b) at a, so that the bevel of the shoulder corresponds to that of the wheel. When this has been done, the sides of the wheel can be brought in contact with the stone and rubbed to and fro, the motion serving to turn the wheel and thus cause it to be ground evenly. The spindle should be oiled to enable the disk to turn evenly. The wheel does not need to be very sharp; and the sharpening consists rather in repairing uneven spots on the edge than in putting a keen edge on it.

It is very important that this sharpening be done; for, otherwise, not only does

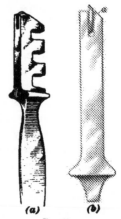

(a)   (b)

FIG. 13

the process of cutting glass become burdensome, but the dull tool may spoil and ruin a carefully-selected piece of expensive glass.

PAINTING THE GLASS

32. Styles of Painted Windows.—It is well at this stage to refer again to the chief styles of painted leaded-glass windows. One is known as the **antique**, or **English,** style, in which the effect is obtained by a mosaic treatment of many little pieces of antique glass of clear pure colors, without paint or stain except on the flesh parts, as the face, hands, and feet, and on parts of the drapery. A second style is known as the **cathedral,** or **German,** style, in which paint or stain is used over practically the entire window surface; that is, not only for flesh and drapery, but also for all parts of the picture—landscapes, decorative features, etc. Cathedral glass is very generally employed; except for the flesh, for which *flesh* glass, or *milk* glass, is generally used. If red drapery, for instance, is to be represented, it will be painted on red glass, the shadows being painted in brown or black. A third style is the **opalescent,** or **American,** style, in which practically the only portions painted are those parts representing flesh, the effects of draperies, landscapes, etc., being obtained by selecting pieces of opalescent glass to represent them. A special opalescent glass is manufactured, termed *drapery glass,* whose surface consists of heavy ridges or folds, the effects of drapery being portrayed thereby in a very realistic manner.

If the window is to be made in the antique style or the opalescent style, the workmen may retain in the shop all glass cut except the flesh glass, which is sent direct to the glass painter. But if the window is made in the cathedral, or German, style, all the glass when cut will be sent in on trays from the shop to the glass painter. Flesh is usually painted on white ground-glass, or on white milk glass for the finest work.

33. Pigments for Glass Painting.—Reference has already been made to the iron oxide that forms the basis of the pigment for glass painting. This oxide is modified in color by the addition of various other mineral oxides. In preparing the pigment for painting, red tracing color and intense black are taken in equal quantities and put on a palette of ground

289—32

glass; or, if desired, there may be a little less of the black than of the red, as the black is used merely to modify the red. Cold water is then added, and the whole is worked into a paste with a palette knife. Next some pure white gum arabic is dissolved in cold water, and two or three drops are added to the paste and thoroughly mixed with it. A portion of this paste is then cut off with the palette knife, placed in the middle of the palette, and more water is added, after which it is mixed well. The paint is then ready to be applied to the glass. It is advisable to keep the major portion of the pigment moist, at the edge of the palette, and to draw from it as required, for it will become unmanageable if it is all thinned out at once.

34. Introductory Practice in Painting.—In painting on glass, a long-haired brush, known as a **rigger,** like that shown in Fig. 14, should be used. It is dipped in the little pool of pigment on the palette, and in lifting it from the palette it is given a twirl so that it gathers to a point with which a clean line can be drawn. It will be advisable to practice making clean strokes or lines on a piece of glass to learn the making of manageable strokes that are neither too wet nor too dry. After some practice, the consistency of the pigment required to produce a sharp, clean line will be found. The lines on the glass, when dry and held up to the light, should be an opaque black, and this gives another test as to whether or not the paint is of the required consistency to be sufficiently opaque. The gum arabic is added to the paint to make it adhere to the glass, and when dry it should stick so tightly as to require a fairly hard rub with the finger to remove it.

FIG. 14

35. Tracing the Outline on the Glass.—In starting the work of painting on glass, the glass painter spreads the full-size cartoon out flat and places the little pieces of glass in their proper positions on the cartoon. The main outlines of the picture or design are traced with opaque pigment, and certain lines which are not intended to be so prominent are allowed to be semitransparent.

The contours of faces and figures, the folds of draperies, etc., are usually outlined in black. When tracing, the glass painter should lean well over the work, as shown in Fig. 15, with his hand and arm supported by a wooden rest *a*. When finished, the tracing should be held up to the light and compared with the

FIG. 15

original. If well done, it should require very little altering to get it correct.

In order to determine whether all cutting has been properly done the glass must be mounted in such a way that it can be held up to the light. To accomplish this, an easel like that shown in Fig. 16 will be found useful and convenient. It consists of a small wooden frame *a* in which is fixed a piece of plain sheet glass *b*. The piece of glass *c* on which the outline is traced is fixed on the sheet *b* by four small drops of beeswax, as at *d*.

This plan of fixing up the glass to the light saves time in the long run. Also, it removes the temptation to hold the glass up in one hand and make alterations with the other, which is a very slipshod and unworkmanlike method.

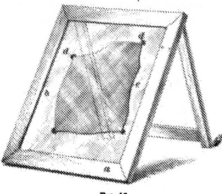

FIG. 16

36. Etching Work With Acids. Certain kinds of colored work in stained-glass windows are done by etching out the color of the glass at places with acid. This can be accomplished only with *flashed* glass, where the color is simply a thin film on one side of the glass. Suppose, for instance, it were desired to show a white lace-like embroidery on a red robe. Red flashed glass (ruby glass) would be selected, and the pattern then secured by etching off the ruby film, allowing the clear white glass to show. If it were desired to show gold embroidery instead of white, the open, or clear-glass, portions could then be stained with gold (yellow) stain. The process of etching is as follows:

The parts of the piece of ruby glass that are to remain red are first painted with asphaltum paint, which resists acid, leaving uncovered those portions which are to be etched or eaten away by acid. When the asphaltum paint is dry and hard, the glass is ready to be treated with acid. The piece of glass is

FIG. 17

first laid on the bottom of a shallow tray made of lead, shaped like that shown in Fig. 17, and over it is poured hydrofluoric acid. A small quantity of water is then added to dilute the acid somewhat, so as to prevent the glass from festering and losing its brilliancy. When the red flashing, or film, on the unprotected parts of the surface has been completely eaten away, the piece of glass should be removed from the tray and washed repeatedly in water, so as to remove every trace of the acid; for, as long as any acid remains, it will eat into the glass.

Rubber finger stalls should be worn to protect the fingers from the acid while working, otherwise, very painful burns may result. The hydrofluoric acid should be kept in gutta-percha bottles.

These directions for etching have been given at this time because the process appropriately comes previous to the work of painting the glass.

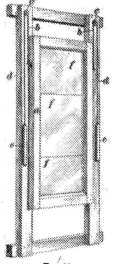

Fig. 18

37. Mounting the Glass on the Painting Easel.—When glass is being painted, it is necessary to fix it up to the light so as to have it as nearly as possible under the same conditions as will prevail when the window is in place in the building. An adjustable frame like that shown in Fig. 18 will be found useful for this work. It consists of a heavy sash *a* suspended by cords *b* that pass over pulleys *c* fixed on the uprights *d* of the main frame. The cords are weighted with heavy iron weights *e* to serve as counterbalances of sufficient weight to hold the sash in any desired position. The glass *f* may be plain sheet glass for small work; but for easels to be used in mounting large windows, plate glass should be used.

38. Painting the False Lead Lines.—The adjustable sash should be unhooked from the frame and laid flat on the work bench. Then the first drawing, made on tracing paper or cloth and showing the cut lines, or lead lines, should be placed over the glass and stuck fast to it at the corners by means of drops of beeswax. The frame should be reversed, and lines

representing the lead lines should be painted on the back surface of the glass in the frame.   These lines may be seen very
clearly on the lead-line, or cut-line, drawing pasted on the other
side of the glass.   These false lead lines should be painted with
a mixture of lampblack and water to which a few drops of gum-
arabic solution has been added, and this paint should be well
mixed so as to flow readily.   These false lead lines drawn on
the back of the glass should be $\frac{1}{4}$ inch wide, except those surrounding the entire window, which may be $\frac{1}{2}$ inch
wide.

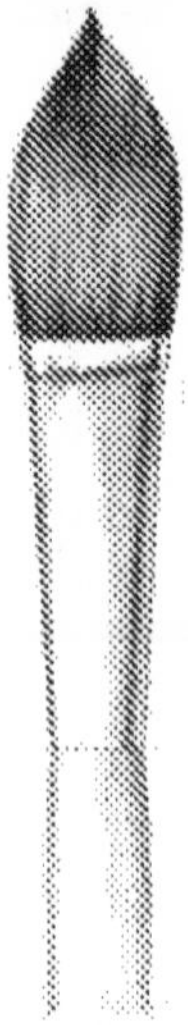

FIG. 19

**39. Mounting, or Waxing Up, the Pieces of
Glass.**—The next step is to mount the pieces of
glass on the easel, to get them ready for painting.
To do this, the painting frame or easel should be
turned over, and the lead-line drawing removed.
Then the various pieces of glass are fixed on the front
of the plate-glass sheet of the frame, each in its
proper place with respect to the lead lines painted on
the back.   The pieces are fixed in place by drops of
beeswax, and the operation is consequently known as
waxing up.   One drop of wax at each corner of a
piece of glass is sufficient to hold it.   There is nothing
to be gained by smearing wax all along the edges.
After the work of waxing up has been completed, each
individual piece of glass should be tapped lightly with
the fingers, to discover whether it is held tightly.   If
it is not tight, the sound given out when it is tapped will betray
its looseness.   After all the pieces have been made tight, the
sash frame is attached to the counterbalances and the whole is
hung vertically on the uprights, as in Fig. 18.   The pieces of
glass are now in position ready to paint.

40. First Step in Painting—Matting.—After the window is waxed up, it is necessary to go over each piece on which
the design is traced and to spread over it a thin wash, or film,
of pigment; this film is known as the **matt**.   The purpose of
the matt is to produce the effect of shading in the design.
Gum is added to the wash of pigment used for the matt, to

cause it to adhere, but the amount added is small. A camel's-hair brush like that shown in Fig. 19 should be used, and the matt should be applied in vertical strokes, beginning at the upper left-hand corner, the brush being held and manipulated as indicated in Fig. 20.

The pigment should be laid on as uniformly as possible, but the desired uniformity cannot be obtained without further treatment, which additional treatment is given by the **badger** or the **stippler**, two forms of brushes shown in Fig. 21 (*a*)

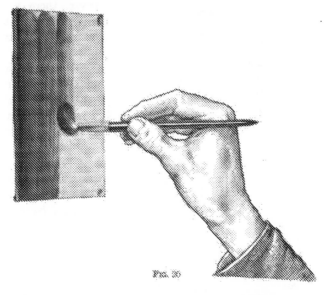

Fig. 20

and (*b*), respectively. In using the badger to obtain a flat tint, only the tips of the delicate hairs must touch the pigment, the brush being swept to and fro in every direction to distribute the wet paint and remove all brush marks. When finished by the use of the badger, the surface will be perfectly smooth and even in tone value, and without any pronounced texture. This absence of pronounced texture may not always be desirable, in which case the surface is *stippled* by the use of the stippler, shown in Fig. 21 (*b*), in the manner indicated in Fig. 22. The stippling is done by gently stabbing the matt with the brush, stabbing hardest where the matt is darkest. The result of the stippling will be to gather the paint into minute little heaps or dots, giving a rough or grained texture.

Sometimes, in putting on the matt the outline tracing of the design may be obliterated, and this difficulty increases rapidly as the size of the piece of glass grows greater; but after considerable practice it will be possible to put on a flat even matt without erasing the tracing. Sometimes, to prevent erasure, the outline is fixed by firing before the matt is applied. When this is done, however, there is no chance of altering any line, and if it is wrong, the error must stay; whereas, if not fired, the line may be modified at any time.

When the matt has been properly placed, and is of the desired thickness, it simply remains to do the required modeling or grading of tone values, partly by scrubbing out to get high lights, and partly by overpainting to get dark values. The matt, therefore, must originally be of the depth of the half tones, and is lightened by being brushed away by means of the hog's-hair brushes like those shown in Fig. 23 (a) to (e), known as scrubs. These should be of different degrees of softness, the most useful being those that have been much worn. The darker shadows are produced by painting over the half tones, thus deepening them. Before beginning to brush out the matt, it may be well to rub it with the finger, as this serves to loosen it and makes it readily workable by the scrubs, and brings out any texture the glass itself may have. The scrubbing out must be done carefully, working from the half tones toward the high lights. There is some danger of getting the latter too open, as the light passing

(a)   (b)

FIG. 21

through them diffuses and thus produces an effect of expanding, when viewed from a distance.

41. Glass Staining.—Beautiful effects are sometimes

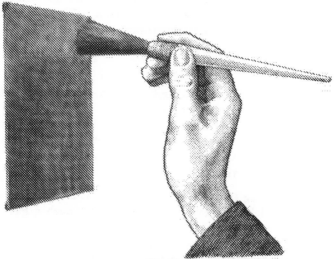

FIG. 22

secured in windows by staining with a transparent stain such white or clear glass portions as it is desired to color. The stain used for this purpose con-tains silver, and is put on the glass in the same manner as pigment, but on the opposite side of the glass. This .is done because the stain gives off fumes during the process of firing, and these fumes would prevent the pigment on the painted surface of the glass from fusing and fixing properly if the stain were put on the same surface as the

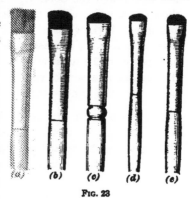

FIG. 23

pigment. Further, the stain is not added until just before the second firing.

To assist in determining the color values of the window during the process of painting, a mixture of gamboge with a touch of red ink may be used as a paint, and may be painted on the *back* of the heavy plate glass of the easel on which the window is waxed up. This does not show so fine a yellow as the fired stain, but it is a very good temporary substitute.

FIRING THE GLASS

42. Necessity for Firing the Glass.—Permanence of the colored pigments placed on the surface of the glass during the process of glass painting is secured by subjecting the glass to very great heat, which causes the pigments to become fused into the glass itself, and thus they cannot be erased. This process is called **firing** the glass.

43. Firing Ovens, or Kilns.—Glass is usually fired in a kiln of special construction, heated by gas. Such a gas-fired kiln is illustrated in Fig. 24. The gas-supply pipe *a* has two branches *b* and *c* that extend into the pit beneath the kiln *d*. From each branch there are risers, as at *e*, that extend upwards into the kiln and supply gas to separate burners. The kiln is lined throughout with refractory material, and the glass is put in through the doors *f*. The upper of the two chambers shown is a preparatory chamber, which never gets very hot, and in which the glass is heated before being put into the hot lower chamber. The waste gases are led off through a chimney not shown in the illustration. The receptacle *g* at the side of the furnace is a sort of rack in which the glass that has been taken from the kiln is placed to cool.

44. The First Firing.—The first firing is applied to the pieces of glass on which the outline tracing has been made. The kiln must be heated gradually to the proper temperature. A trayful of glass is then placed in one of the compartments of the kiln and the temperature is raised slowly so as to simply drive off all moisture from the glass before it is put in the hottest part of the kiln; otherwise the sudden heat of a high temperature would crack the glass. The firing will occupy from 15 to

25 minutes. When the glass begins to soften, the heating process should not be carried on so rapidly, but should from that point on be continued slowly.

Precaution is required to watch the kiln constantly and to see that no portion of any of the trays of glass becomes too hot. This can be regulated by turning the gas cock leading to the particular compartment that is receiving too much heat. If the glass has been properly fired it should show, when cold, a smooth shiny surface, but not too shiny. A peep hole is

Fig. 24

provided in the kiln through which the glass in process of firing may be watched, and when its surface has become glossy it has had enough firing and should be removed.

45. Repainting and Refiring.—The first firing eliminates some of the freshness and crispness of the first painting, as will be discovered when the pieces of glass are remounted on the glass easel and looked at against the light. Some repainting and additional painting is therefore necessary, and after that a second firing.

It might be thought that the *firing out*, or dimming, of the paint that occurs from the first firing could be avoided by making the first painting quite thick and heavy. However, this would not work well because the paint (being so thick) during the process of firing would only fry and bubble and would not become fused into the glass.

The second painting consists of strengthening the outlines that were dimmed by the first firing and putting on the required *matts*, as previously described. Some of these matts may be put on and worked, quite wet, with the stippler, or may be left until nearly dry for stippling. In this second painting, if the matts are not satisfactory to the glass painter they may be removed and new ones painted on, without disturbing the lines underneath.

The repainted pieces of glass are then put on trays, placed in the kiln, and fired again. Even after this second firing the glass should be mounted on the glass easel and both the general effect of the window as a whole and the firing effects on the individual pieces should be carefully scrutinized. It may be necessary, even, to repaint and fire again certain portions of the work.

The designer should endeavor to master the technique of glass painting and glass firing, but where this cannot be done he should constantly personally supervise the work of the glass painter, for only in this manner can he expect to obtain a result satisfactory to himself. ——

LEADING UP, OR GLAZING, THE WINDOW

46. Laying Out Glass on Glazing Drawing.—After all the pieces of glass have been properly painted and fired, the next process in making a stained-glass window is to assemble these pieces in their proper arrangement and fasten them together by lead strips and cement so as to form the window. This process is called **leading up, or glazing,** the window.

First of all the glazing drawing (that is, the large sheet of manila detail paper on which a tracing of the lead lines, or cut lines, and the shapes of the pieces of glass, was previously made) is laid out on the workman's large flat table or bench, so that the *side* of the window is nearest the workman. The glazier then trues up, or squares, the glazing drawing with a steel square to be sure that the angles are accurate. Next he nails horizontally a wooden strip or lath at the side of the table nearest him and another strip vertically at the end of the table to his left. These strips will then be at right angles to each other, as in Fig. 25 at *a* and *b*. The inner edges of these strips should be exactly on the full-size lines, or outside-edge lines, of the window as marked on the glazing drawing. The glazier then proceeds to assemble the window.

First a heavy wide lead, about ½ inch wide, is laid snugly against the inner edge of strip *a*, as shown at *c* in Fig. 25, and

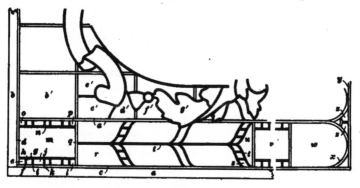

Fig. 25

another lead *d* of the same width is placed against strip *b*, the end of lead *d* fitting against the core, or heart, of lead *c*. The leads come in long flat boxes, and before being in condition to use for glazing must be stretched out straight, by the method shown in Fig. 26, and the leaves of the lead separated by the method shown in Fig. 27, the tool *a* being a piece of hard wood shaped to a point. For cutting the lead a palette knife, or a putty knife ground down, as shown in Fig. 28, will be found useful. The blade of the knife is forced downwards at right angles to the core of the lead, as shown in Fig. 29.

47. Order of Assembling and Leading the Glass. First the piece of glass marked *e*, Fig. 25, is pushed firmly into the corner formed by the leads c and d. Then a strip of $\frac{1}{4}$-inch round lead f is fitted at the right, the end of strip f going right up to the core of strip c. At the other end, the piece f is cut off somewhat shorter than the side of the piece of glass e, since it is just to meet the leaves of the strip g when the latter is in place. The piece of glass h is then put in position, followed

by the lead i, and then the piece of glass j and the lead k, and so on until the piece of glass l is reached. It will be found that the piece of glass e will tend to work loose while h is being inserted. To prevent this, a nail should be driven into the bench against the upper edge of e, and when the piece h is inserted it should be held in a similar manner.

Before lead g can be put in place the nails holding the squares of glass must be removed. The end of the strip g should be pushed up to the heart of the lead d and the strip then forced down so that the pieces of glass e, h, j, etc., fit firmly into it. It should then be held in place and the piece m fitted into it, followed by the lead n, and then by the series of small glass pieces from o to p, which are put in place in the same manner as are those from e to l.

Next, the $\frac{1}{4}$-inch lead q should be fitted, cutting it off about $\frac{1}{4}$ inch inside the outer corner of the piece p. The several pieces from r to s should now be fixed in position, using round leads, and the lead t should then be added, bending it down over the piece s to meet the lead c. The similar pieces on the other side of the lead t are then put in place, followed by the piece u. Then the piece v and its bordering squares are set in, and finally the piece w. The curved lead x is placed so that it fits right

Fig. 26

up against the heart of the top lead y, but the lead y and the small pieces s are not put in place at this stage, as they can be added more easily when the window is finished.

The next step is to fit into place the long straight lead a', which is continuous from the lead d down through the window. The reason for placing the glazing drawing lengthwise of the bench now becomes apparent, since the lead lines that are to be vertical when the window is put in place are continuous along

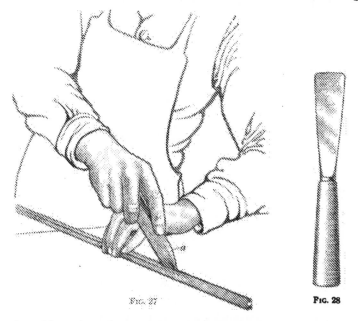

FIG. 27   FIG. 28

the table and can be worked upon most conveniently, and with the best saving of time, for there will be fewer joints to be soldered.

The pieces of glass b' to g' should next be set in place in alphabetical order, and the process continued throughout the remainder of the window, working always from left to right.

48. Practical Hints on Leading.—Great care should be taken to see that each piece of glass fits exactly on the space marked out for it on the glazing drawing. If the pieces have been cut accurately they will fit properly in the alloted spaces; but if a piece has been cut too large it will be necessary to break away the edge, bit by bit, with pliers.

The leads with flat leaves should be allowed to overlap, but

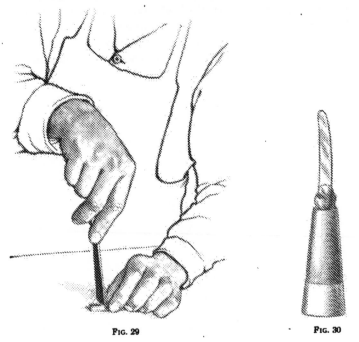

FIG. 29 · FIG. 30

the round leads should just touch, as the leaves of the latter are not sufficiently pliable to lap well.

In putting on the outside leads to finish the window, a wooden strip should be laid against each, and pounded inwards slightly so as to knock the pieces firmly together.

A very useful tool for doing the leading is shown in Fig. 30 and is called a **stopping knife.** The blade of this tool may be used to lift the leaves of the leads, and assist in putting the glass into place; the heavy lead end on the handle makes an excellent hammer for driving nails to hold the pieces of glass in position.

FINISHING THE WINDOW AND FIXING IN PLACE

49. Soldering the Lead-Strip Joints.—Although the window appears to be completed as it now lies on the work bench, it would fall apart were an attempt made to lift it. Therefore, the joints of the lead strips must be soldered together by melting solder over each joint. The strip of solder is held in one hand and the specially devised soldering tool with a heated tip held in the other. The end of the solder is placed successively over each joint of the leads and is touched with the heated tip so as to melt off a piece of molten solder, which is then spread smoothly over the joint of the lead. All joints on one side of the window must be soldered first, after which the window must be turned over and the joints on the other side soldered.

To turn over a window light successfully great care is required. After knocking away, or prying off, the wooden strips around the window the window light should be pulled forwards until it balances on the edge of the bench or table; that is, so that one half of it lies on the bench and the other half projects over the edge. The projecting part should then be swung downwards, supported by one hand, until the window light assumes a vertical position, and it should then be lifted and set on edge on the bench on which it should be turned halfway around, still being kept vertical. Then, still in a vertical position, it should be lifted off the bench and lowered until the middle is level with the edge of the bench. It should then be tilted, on this edge as a fulcrum, until it is horizontal, when it may be pushed back on the bench, and the joints of the leads on this new side soldered.

50. Cementing the Window.—In addition to soldering the lead-strip joints the window must also be cemented in order to fill up all the crevices under the leads and to make the window water-tight. The cement, which is composed of plaster of Paris, whiting, boiled linseed oil, and turpentine, is rubbed over the glass and leads with a stiff brush, scrubbing the cement well into the crevices and under the leads. Both sides of the window should be subjected to this cementing process.

51. Fixing, or Setting Up, the Window in Place.
Before setting up the window light in place in the church, residence, or other place where it is to go, it must be strengthened by fastening iron or copper bars horizontally across its outer surface. Small cylindrical rods are used for ordinary-sized window lights; but, if the window is very wide, heavy iron T bars are also employed.

For a window that is 2 feet or more in width the horizontal strengthening rods should not be more than 1 foot apart.

If the window light is to be placed in a carved stone setting there is always provided a groove, or rabbet, carved in the stonework to receive it. To get the window in place, the leaves of the outside wide leads must be bent back somewhat. The position of the strengthening rods should then be marked off on a wood strip from the window itself and then transferred to the stone framework or mullions on the inside of the opening. Holes should then be cut and the rods put in position. Then the base of the window light should be set in the lower groove and the window pushed into place in the opening, after which the leaves of the outside leads are straightened out so as to fit into the grooves. The wires, previously soldered onto the lead strips, are next twisted round the strengthening rods. It simply remains to fill up the crevices in the grooves of the stonework with good cement, in this way fastening the window light tightly in place.

If the window light is to be fastened in a wooden frame or sash the operation will be more simple; for all that is required is to remove the beading from one side of the frame or sash, place the window light in position, and replace the beading. Usually a bed of putty is placed in the groove on which the window light is to rest, so that the window will be water-tight.

DESIGNING

GENERAL PRINCIPLES OF LEADED-GLASS DESIGNING

52. Making the Most of Technical Restrictions. Designing for stained glass presents problems to be solved and difficulties to be overcome such as the artist will meet in no other field of design work. He must therefore understand fully the restrictions and limitations that will be placed upon him, as concerns the material and its manipulation, and not try to evade them, but frankly admit and conform to them.

Sometimes indolence or carelessness may lead a young designer to underestimate or ignore these technical restrictions imposed by stained glass, but most frequently he ignores them because of the generally prevalent idea that all historic specimens of stained-glass windows, as seen in cathedrals, etc., are too stiff and formal. Swinging to the other extreme, the young designer therefore attempts to produce, in leaded glass, naturalistic pictures elaborately executed. He thus tries to make of his sketch a pretty picture, with the result that his picture cannot be carried out practically in the actual glass. Even among a certain class of manufacturers this overly-naturalistic style finds favor, and one sees many churches today with very realistic pictures in the window openings, where the whole attempt seems to have been to make them look "natural as life," and to disguise the fact that the window is leaded.

On the other hand, an overly-conscientious designer will follow all the restrictions imposed by materials, thus unduly accenting the mechanical features. Thus, there may be seen countless examples of windows composed largely of diamond-shaped pieces, polygons, odd and inartistic pieces, etc., used simply because they are easy to cut and to lead. Even many picture windows bear this fault, having stiff, severe, unyielding lines; whereas, graceful sinuous lines would have been far more artistic and just as easy to lead.

The happy medium between these two extremes must always be sought. The lead lines must not be entirely disguised by

deep shading and dark glass in order to present a "natural
looking" picture; the leads must be frankly admitted, but so
arranged as to add artistic grace. However, the leading must
not be overdone, thereby producing an awkward and archaic
effect in this age when figures and decorative work have
acquired perfection in draftsmanship.

53. Situation and Purpose of the Window.—The problem that is presented to the designer of stained glass is as follows: The builder has left an aperture in the side of the wall,
for illumination, which must be filled with glass in order to
keep out the elements and admit the light. Tradition teaches
the designer that this glass is not inserted in the window opening in a thoughtless, haphazard manner. The problem is, how
shall this glass be treated and arranged?

From the structural nature of the window opening, the most
logical conclusion is that the glass also should be arranged so as
to introduce some structural treatment; and from the fact that
the glass is to be seen constantly in a strong light, it follows that
it should be decorative. On this account a mere picture, or a
series of pictures telling a story, would be inappropriate and
unsuitable. As soon as structural features and decorative details
are introduced, the treatment becomes more decorative and
therefore more fitting. This principle applies even more closely
when the window is very large and wide; an elaborate picture
stretched across such a window, supported by iron **T** bars
and stanchions, may be mechanically and structurally strong
enough, but it *does not appear so*. For this reason structural
details introduced into a design not only add to the apparent strength of the window and its glass design, but also make
the design more decorative, less tiresome, and of more permanent interest than a simple figure grouping, which one soon
learns by heart and soon tires of. The decorative treatment
becomes absolutely necessary where small mullioned windows
are used, or where elaborate Gothic tracery is employed.

54. Importance of Form in a Window Design.—The
designer of stained-glass windows is practically unrestricted as
to the forms he may include in his design; he may use anything,

from the boldest and broadest treatments to the very elaborate treatment with intricate details. For this reason it is absurd to deliberately employ bad drawing, as is sometimes done by some modern makers of windows, to imitate antique effects. It is absolutely devoid of any artistic reason or common sense to place in a modern church a window in which the drawing of a figure of a saint, for instance, is done in the archaic style of the 12th or 13th century. On the other hand, the excellent draftsmanship that is permissible, should not be carried so far as to become soft and effeminate, and lacking in that dignity that should characterize all stained-glass work, whether for church or secular use.

55. The Place of Color in a Window Design.—While form is absolutely indispensable in a leaded-glass window, color is not. It is perfectly possible to make a very attractive leaded-glass window where not a bit of color is employed, the whole effect being obtained by the lines of the leading, and the variegated effects of the different white glasses. Nevertheless, it is color that gives to stained glass its most beautiful effects—the colors imparted in the melting pot, whether deliberate or accidental; the sparkling effects obtained by the use of shading and coloring pigment; and the richness of gold and orange stain.

While ancient glass was limited to a few gradations of the primary colors, the palette of the modern glass worker is practically unlimited, owing to the perfection of modern glass manufacture. Therefore, the designer when making his sketch has practically unrestricted freedom to employ what colors he wishes; but he must become acquainted with just the sparkling brilliancy of a color *in the glass*, as distinguished from the same color in some other material or fabric, as a rug, a wallpaper, etc.

Color, as used in stained-glass windows, must of necessity be decorative and not naturalistic and imitative. This consideration must always be kept well in mind by the designer of stained glass.

Strong contrasts of brilliant hues, such as will not be met with in other fields of industrial design work, must be skilfully handled by the designer of stained glass; and a general warmth of tone, whether in a bold or in a delicate treatment, must be employed.

56. The Element of Transparency in a Window Design.—One of the chief characteristics of a stained-glass window is the effect produced on the beholder by the transparency of the glass. In the design this must be properly brought out by the correct proportioning of high lights and shading when applying the surface pigment. This applies to both the preliminary water color sketch as well as the painting on the actual glass. Any painting that becomes so overly-naturalistic as to obscure or hide the transparent brilliancy of the glass itself, is out of place, and robs the window of its chief element of beauty.

57. Figures and Costumes in a Window Design.—In portraying figures, costumes, drapery, and other accessories to the figure the very best draftsmanship is required on the part of both the designer and the glass painter, for the window is seen in brilliant light, and all forms stand out very distinctly on account of the lead lines.

The composition should show strength and dignity of draftsmanship, and an intelligent understanding of the appropriateness and suitability of the particular figure or Biblical subject to the particular window. Excellent draftsmanship is also necessary in managing the drapery effects. An important point is to see that the correct historic period is adhered to in the costumes and other figure accessories. While it is true that many old German and Italian masters painted the Biblical characters in their windows wearing German and Italian costumes, yet this is an affectation that the modern designer of stained glass must avoid. Therefore, the costumes must be archeologically correct; for example, a figure group portraying the Old Testament incident of the selling of Joseph by his brethren requires a treatment of costumes and accessories far different from the costume treatment of the New Testament incident of the marriage feast where Christ turned the water into wine.

58. Treatment of Backgrounds and Perspective in a Window Design.—A window, being distinctly decorative, must not express, in too frank and apparent a manner, effects of distance or perspective depth. While it is permissible, of course, for the filling of backgrounds, to suggest distant hills, sky, clouds, etc. in the upper background where figures cover largely the foreground, yet it is not in the best taste to use subjects that require buildings or people seen in long and distant perspective. The reason for this is plain; atmosphere and distance, if made too naturalistic, are incongruous when portrayed in stained glass.

59. Importance of a Consistent Style in Window Designs.—Designs for stained glass must be distinctly decorative. If they were to be naturalistic, it would be a simple matter for the designer to cut a picture out of some book of Biblical illustrations, fit it into a scaled drawing of a window opening, and call it a window design. But it must be remembered that the design is not merely a drawing on a sheet of paper, but is the plan for an arrangement of a decorative or pictorial effect in glass to suit a particular window.

Therefore, if the church in which the window is to be placed is built in the Gothic style, it will be most natural to include some Gothic canopy work and columns at the side, executed in the glass itself, and then, within this decorative work as a frame, to place the pictorial or decorative features that constitute the chief part of the window design. A conscientious study should always be made of the particular period represented in the church construction, and the leaded glass should be designed in harmony with this period style. As an example, it would, obviously, be inappropriate to use bands of decorative Romanesque leaf form in a design for a window to be placed in a church which is wholly in the perpendicular Gothic style. Neither is it permissible to use several different styles or periods of decoration in any one window or group of windows. The designer should be thoroughly trained in the period styles, particularly those of the Gothic period and the Romanesque and early Renaissance periods.

PREPARING THE SKETCHES

60. Securing Preliminary Data.—The first step to be taken by the designer of stained-glass work will demonstrate clearly to him that other requirements exist in addition to ability to draw, to paint, and to design, one of which is that he shall be familiar with certain necessary commercial aspects.

Most of the designing for modern leaded-glass work is competitive. For this reason the wide-awake designer will learn from building trades journals, or journals devoted to

Fig. 31

real estate news, or from builders' offices, what new churches, public buildings, residences, etc. are to be erected. His next step will be to call on architects and builders and secure data regarding the proposed amount of leaded glass to go in the building. Most builders are perfectly willing to give out such information to designers and representatives of reputable firms; although there are certain snobbish and vain architects who may at times refuse to give such information, in which cases there are always ways of securing this data from other sources. In the offices of the larger building and architectural firms a room is usually set aside where these blueprints are posted on the walls, and the accredited designer or representative is always welcome to look them over and make tracings of the shapes and sizes of the windows that are to receive leaded glass.

These tracings should be made accurately from the front-, rear-, and side-elevation drawings, and the sizes should be verified from the floor plans, if necessary.

61. In church work the designer will be called upon to make designs for various kinds of windows, which are named according to their positions in the church building. In Fig. 31

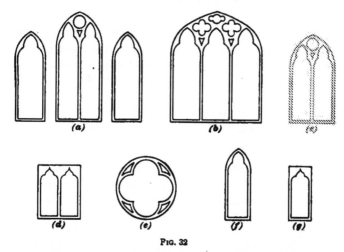

FIG. 32

the locations of the various windows are shown. At *a* are the transept windows, there being two sets of these; at *b*, the main front windows; at *c*, the main side windows; at *d*, clerestory windows; at *e*, rose window; at *f*, tower windows; and at *g*, the vestibule windows. The outlines of these several windows are shown in Fig. 32 (*a*) to (*g*), respectively.

Where there is a group or series of similar windows, only one window of the series need be traced, and a notation can be made of the number of such windows in the series. In the case of a group of odd-shaped windows, as in a transept group such as in Fig. 32 (a), it is advisable to trace the whole group.

The scale appearing on the plans, or blueprints (usually ¼ inch to the foot), must be carefully noted on the tracing; and free-hand sketches and memoranda should be made of any especially characteristic features of style in the stonework or interior features.

62. Special Information to Be Obtained by the Designer.—The far-seeing designer for glass in church work will supplement the above data by ascertaining from the minister, pastor, or other high dignitary of the church, or from the chairman of the building committee, what special decorative features—such as emblems, insignia, and the like—they would like to see used in the windows, and what general scheme of color they prefer. The designer must be sure to learn what amount of money has been reserved for the leaded glass; or what price per foot they will be willing to pay. · Next, he should visit the building site, study what kind and degree of lighting each one of the windows will get, and note whether any neigh-boring buildings are so close as to obstruct or interfere with the light at any point. Other features may require attention, as circumstances arise.

63. Laying Out the Window Shapes.—First, the exact shapes and sizes of the window openings should be laid out on tough but transparent tracing paper, to the scale of 1 inch to the foot, which scale will be found the most convenient for the working up of details. Great care should be taken in enlarging the mullion and tracery work with the greatest accuracy.

When such layouts have been made for the average church job the designer will have a series of window shapes about as shown in Fig. 32; two groups of transept windows, as in (a); one main front window, as in (b), and perhaps a similar one at the other end of the church; seven main side windows, as in (c); six or seven clerestory windows, as in (d); two rose windows, as in (e); eight tower windows, as in (f); and perhaps two vesti-bule windows, as in (g). In larger churches the number and kinds of windows would differ somewhat from this classification.

64. Amount of Detail Dependent on Cost of Work. Before designing any decorative features for the window shapes so far laid out, the designer must ascertain what grade of work he dare use; that is, the amount of detail he may use in order that the expense of making the windows may not exceed the price specified in the contract.

To obtain this data the designer must first of all secure the "footage" of the whole job; that is, the total number of square feet of leaded glass to be furnished. For example, if a window is 5 feet wide and 7 feet high there will be 5 times 7, or 35, square feet of glass in it. If there are eight of that kind of windows in the building, the total footage of that particular job will be 8 times 35, or 280, square feet of glass.

Gothic arched windows (pointed), and Romanesque arched windows (round-topped), as well as circular rose windows, are all computed on the square. Thus, if a window is 5 feet wide and only 5½ feet to spring of the arch, but 7 feet to point of arch, it is considered as containing 35 square feet of glass. A circular rose window 4 feet in diameter will be counted as having 16 square feet.

Let it be supposed that the designer has ascertained that, for a particular church building, the total footage is 1,200 square feet and that the church committee are willing to expend $1,800 for the glass. By dividing $1,800 by 1,200 it is found that the price allowed per square foot is $1.50. Therefore, the designer may draw, in his window sketch, only such decorative work as will not exceed in cost an average of $1.50 per square foot. It is well known, however, that in average church work the clients and the public want a better grade of work in the large front windows and in the transept windows than is required in the other windows. For this reason the designer arranges a sliding scale of costs, and therefore of degree of decorative detail allowed; that is, he arranges the front windows and the transept windows to cost *more* than the average price allowed and the rest of the windows to cost *less* than the average price. Thus, he may have 600 square feet of front and transept windows at $2 per square foot, making a total of $1,200, which leaves $600 for the remaining 600 square feet. But a better grade of work will also be required in the rose windows, clerestory windows, and side windows, which are constantly seen, than in the vestibule and tower windows, which are rarely seen. Thus, if there is allowed $1.25 per square foot for the 400 square feet of rose and side windows, the total for those windows will be $500; which leaves $100 for the 200 square feet of miscellaneous windows—vestibule, tower, etc.—or at the rate of 50 cents per square foot. The sliding scale of costs per foot will then be as follows:

600 square feet of front and transept windows at $2.00 = $1,200
400 square feet of rose, side, and clerestory
     windows at........................ 1.25 =   500
200 square feet of vestibule and tower windows
     at .... .50 =   100
1,200 $1,800

There may be, of course, other kinds of windows, other arrangements of footage costs, etc., but the principle of calculating and apportioning the costs will always remain as described above.

FIG. 33

65. Planning Decoration to Conform to Allowed Footage Costs.—It is not an easy matter to lay down general rules and principles for determining just the kind and grade of leading and detail that may be allowed for certain footage costs. Although it comes as second nature to the experienced designer or worker in leaded glass to decide very readily the decorative work that may be used for a given price, it is difficult to explain this to the novice or the uninitiated. Such an explanation would involve so much that is foreign to artistic matters, such as the plotting of local rates and schedules of labor and overhead costs in different cities and the calculating of percentages of profits, that such detail will be omitted here, and only a general basis of planning suggested.

The cost per square foot of a leaded-glass window is estimated by the expenditure necessary for shop wages, transporta-

tion, and office expenses, plus the percentage of profit. In this
case only the shop expenses will be considered. Thus, if the
designer makes a
sketch and after-
wards turns into the
glazier's shop a draw-
ing of it showing a
great deal of com-
plicated detail, diffi-

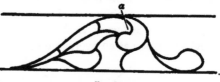

FIG. 34

cult to cut and lead and requiring numerous splicings and
much mitering, the foreman, the cutters, and the glaziers
will be obliged to spend more time on the job, and thus materially increase the cost of the whole. Square, rectangular, or
diamond-shaped pieces of glass, as in Fig. 33, are easiest to cut
because they can be rapidly cut by a gauge, or cutting machine,
an apparatus with a sliding, measuring edge, that can be set
to any definite width or length, and the pieces can be cut
rapidly and mechanically at a computed rate of 50 cents or
less per square foot. Thus, a leaded pattern such as that in
Fig. 33 may be classed as costing 50 cents to $1.00 per square foot.

However, when the designer uses in his sketch scrolls, long
sweeping curves, or simple-shaped leaves, he is making very
much harder work for the cutters and glaziers. In such work,
the pieces of glass must be cut freehand, and any little kinks,

FIG. 35

as at *a* in Fig. 34, must be gently tapped
with the cutting tool until they are brit-
tle enough to break away. Then, in the
process of glazing, the leads must be
curved around such difficult places,
which in some cases means making ser-
rations on the edge of the lead, and great
care must be exercised that the delicate
pieces of glass do not break.

All this requires the *time* of the workman, which means the *money* of the firm;
hence, the production costs rise suffi-
ciently to force the footage cost up to $1.50 to $3.00 per square
foot for this class of work, an example of which is shown in Fig. 35.

It is evident that if these two grades of work are combined, an average can be struck between 50 cents to $1.00 and $1.50 to $3.00 and yet show decoration in the leaded-glass work; thus, by a suitable combination of comparatively plain work relieved by scroll and leaf work, as shown in Fig. 36, an attractive window might be made at an average cost of $1.00 to $2.00 per square foot, depending on the wage scales, etc., in force in various sections of the country.

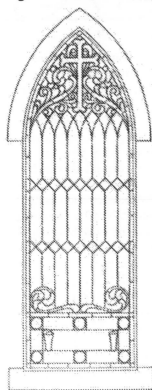

These general considerations will give the designer a basis from which to estimate costs. He understands that the more elaborate the decorative forms he introduces, the higher will be the footage price. Thus, if instead of simple scrolls he uses Gothic leaf work, as in Fig. 37, or emblems entirely leaded, it is evident that the price will mount even higher; sometimes to $3, $4, and even $6 per square foot.

66. Drawing the Details in the Sketches.—With the above data secured, the designer is ready to draw his sketches in detail. Inasmuch as he is allowed to use "$2 work" in his front and transept windows, the designer may use geometrical shapes in the background, which, though interesting in appearance, may be cheaply cut

FIG. 36

with a gauge. Upon, or across, this background may be introduced interesting features, such as Gothic ornament or bands. The tops may have a simplified Gothic canopy effect, with conventionalized Gothic leaves and scrolls; and perhaps a leaded emblem introduced, such as a cross and a crown, or an Alpha and Omega device, allowing $10 or $15 extra for each leaded emblem

Next should be estimated the grade of work that can be used in the rose window, the main side windows, and the clerestory windows, for $1.25 per square foot; and also the grade of work for 50 cents per square foot that can be used in the vestibule and tower windows, consideration being given in each case to the frequency with which the window will be seen, whether mostly from inside or from outside, and at what times of day.

Having decided upon each scheme and having blocked it in in a bold way on the left of the center line of each window opening he has previously laid out, the designer will (on the reverse side of the tracing paper) carefully draw in the design of the left half, using a comparatively soft pencil with a sharp point. Then, folding the tracing paper on the vertical center line, he will draw in carefully all the details of the other half of the window, being sure that both of these halves are

Fig. 37

drawn on the same side of the tracing paper. The tracing paper is then spread out flat and the design is rubbed onto the bristol board or illustrators' board in the following manner: The tracing-paper drawing, with the penciled design face downwards, should be laid on the bristol board, and another piece of tracing paper laid over the first one, the two pieces of tracing paper being held in proper position by means of thumbtacks or weights, so that there will be no chance of their slipping. Then a well-sharpened, but not pointed, 4H or 6H lead pencil should be rubbed back and forth over the top piece of tracing paper with firm even strokes close together, first vertically, then horizontally, care being taken to prevent even the slightest displacement of any of the sheets. Upon lifting the two sheets of tracing paper it will be found that the design has been properly transferred to the bristol board.

This transferred pencil design will then need to be touched up, or strengthened, by soft pencil lines. This should be done with firm pencil strokes occasionally relieved by little breaks in the lines, as shown in Fig. 38 (*a*), in order to imitate lead lines, rather than in firm, even, mechanical-looking lines, as in Fig. 38 (*b*). The sketches are now ready for coloring.

67. Coloring the Sketches.—The important point to remember in coloring a window sketch is that, when finished,

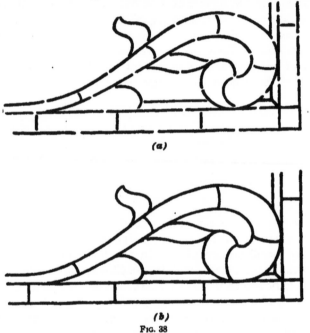

(*a*)

(*b*)

Fig. 38

the sketch must appear, as nearly as possible, exactly like the completed window would look to a spectator from the inside of the church. To obtain this result, the colors applied to the design must portray colored glass, as that glass appears when there is sunlight, direct or reflected, on the side opposite to the eye of the spectator.

This is no simple matter to accomplish, and it is necessary that the designer must first become familiar with the various kinds of glasses that are used in leaded-glass work. He should himself go the rounds of the racks and see how each kind of glass appears when held up against the light, and become familiar with all the characteristics of each variety. Finally, he should have made for himself a color chart of samples, consisting of little pieces of glass about 2 inches by 3 inches, each different, and leaded together in harmonious combination. There should be one chart for antique glass, one for cathedral, and one for opalescent, and each chart should consist of some 15 or 20 pieces, as shown in Fig. 39. These charts should be hung in a window, with a good light, and be constantly before the designer as he works.

In the actual application of the water colors to the sketches the designer must use his own individual method. While no two artists work in the same manner when coloring their sketches, yet a few general hints and suggestions as to technique may be of aid to the inexperienced designer.

Let it be assumed that the window is to have a prevailing golden tone, with the

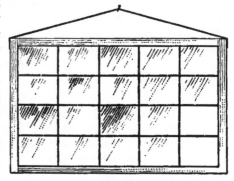

Fig. 39

decorative details in rich greens and ambers, with some warm red introduced. The designer will turn his sketch upside down, and, starting at the base of the window, will wash in, very wet, a light amber tint, gradually deepening the tint as the wash approaches the top of the window, by introducing touches of yellow ocher, brown pink diluted, and even a little gamboge. Before this wash is entirely dry he will *take out*, or lift off, with a clean brush, those places which are to be green, or red, etc., and also certain squares or rectangles at odd places, if there is a geometrical background, so as to relieve any monotony of hue or value. The introduction of deeper values of amber, or even emerald green, or warmer tints of green, into others of these rectangular pieces will assist in obtaining this variety of background desired. A study of a *single sheet* of amber opalescent glass will furnish a marvellously complete color scheme for such work. No two pieces of glass are alike, even if cut from the same sheet, and, consequently, in coloring, no two adjoining parts should be fused together in a flat dead value; the more of this that occurs, the less will be the brilliancy and the transparent effect. Thus, if the background of the tops of the windows is to be a rich blue, it should not be painted in one solid blue, but one part of it should be new blue, another part Prussian blue, another purple, with even a touch of carmine introduced. The depth of color should also be varied, allowing some parts to be deep blue, and at other parts *lifting off* the color, or taking out high lights, with a clean, semidry brush, the whole being an effort to obtain transparency. It is evident that written directions alone will not enable the designer to obtain these brilliant results; it is only after practice, and numerous disappointments and failures, that the designer can put *transparency* into his work.

68. Examples of Rendered Sketches for Leaded-Glass Work.—In Figs. 40 and 41 are shown photographic reproductions of sketches for leaded-glass windows, one in monotone and the other in color.

The purpose of the reproduction in Fig. 40 is to show, at almost full scale, how the designer uses the brush and the pigments to get the sparkling effect and brilliancy of glass in the sketch. The pigment is not spread on in smooth even washes, but is applied in *patches*, some of them blended evenly into contrasting values, and others abruptly and sharply contrasted with lights or darks as the case may be. No two adjoining rectangles or diamonds are of the same value; they are purposely contrasted, for this is exactly what occurs when pieces of glass are leaded up in this way; therefore, the sketch is so made as to produce this effect.

Fig. 41 is introduced to show, on a somewhat reduced scale, the appearance of the completely colored sketch. The original

Fig. 40

was about twice the size of the reproduction in Fig. 41. A careful inspection of this color reproduction will reveal the same effect of rendering the individual pieces of glass so that effects of marked contrasts, rather than of smoothly blended gradations, are produced. The contrasts here are both of values and of hues, as can be seen particularly in the rectangular pieces of glass in the lower parts of each of the three large sections. Contrasts of strong hues are also used in the upper three kite-like sections. In the one on the left, for instance, a purplish-red is used on one side for the background and a distinct blue on the other side for a similar background. This does *not* mean that, in leading up the window, pure red glass would be used for one part of the background and pure blue glass for another part; such an effect would be inartistic and decidedly odd. It means, however, that when the window is completed and viewed from the inside, the variegations of hue and color in any one sheet of glass of the same variety (due not only to the composition of the colored glass itself, but also to lighting conditions) will cause the window to possess these marked contrasts. In this case a purplish or blue-purplish opalescent glass would be used. Therefore, the sketch, in order to show what the window is to look like when completed, must contain these contrasts.

69. Drawing and Coloring Sketches for Painted Windows.—Similar preliminary directions apply to the preparatory work of preparing the sketches and cartoons for stained-glass windows as have been described for leaded-glass work. However, in making estimates, it is customary to quote a lump sum per figure rather than a footage price. No firm would guarantee a good picture window for less than $80 per figure, which includes the painting of one head, two hands, and two feet. Satisfactory work should command a price of $100 to $150 per figure; and really artistic productions run to eight and ten times that sum.

The designer in making his sketches for stained-glass work, and the firm in quoting their price on it, must consider not only the amount and grade of decorative details that may be used

FIG. 41 $20 289

(as explained under leaded-glass work), but must also consider the amount and grade of glass painting that is to be done; which means the time of the glass painter, which is worth from two to three times that of the cutter or glazier. Thus, if a close

(a)

Fig. 42

(b)

figure has been quoted on a picture window—barely enough to allow for the painting of one head, two hands, and two feet—it is evident to the designer that, for his window, he dare not take as his subject the Nativity, for instance, where there are groups of figures surrounding the Christ child in the manger, and decorative angels in the background. A single figure, say of the Savior with extended arms—the "Come Unto Me" subject—is as much as can be allowed. But if unbridled liberty has been given, and a large sum of money provided, the designer may make his subject as elaborate as he wishes; as, for instance, the marriage of Isaac and Rebecca, where camels, slaves, decorative draperies, minutely detailed embroideries, all may be introduced.

In making the picture part of the sketch the designer need not give great concern to the matter of leading, except in the decorative part, as before noted, for the proper placing of leads will be attended to in the making of the cartoon.

70. Examples of Colored Sketches for Painted Windows.—The representations of sketches of leaded-glass windows in which painting is used, shown in Fig. 42, are introduced more to show types of such sketches than color, for here they are in black and white. These two windows represent styles suitable for residence work. The window in (a) is a design that represents, at the top of the window, a medieval knight dressed in full armor and mounted on his charger with full trappings. In (b) is shown a companion window to this, representing a medieval lady arrayed in gorgeous robes and seated on horseback. The general color scheme for these two windows in the originals was somewhat cold, being chiefly in green and white, with a slight touch of red to give snap to it.

The colored sketch for a painted window shown in Fig. 43 gives a clear idea of how sketches for high-grade figure windows should be painted. It is a design for a three-light window in a church. The central light represents the Ascension, the coloring being quiet, and interest in the design being centered by the picking out in red and purple of the under robes. The two side lights represent the Biblical subjects of the angel with the sword, on the left, and the angel with the keys, on the right. The coloring throughout these sketches is of the very highest type, and is of the kind that the beginner will do well to imitate. It is quiet and refined, the figures in each case being the prominent and central portion of the design. The method in

Fig. 43

which the leads are worked into the lines of the design, and are subservient to the general scheme, should be noted particularly.

By examining this sketch with care, the beginner can not only see very clearly how harmonious color schemes can be secured in a sketch for a stained-glass window, but can observe just what pigments are used, how they are applied, how deep, rich hues are strongly contrasted with pale and delicate hues, and, in short, how the professional designer of stained glass works to get his effects.

71. Mounting the Sketches.—After all the sketches for a particular church or residence job have been carefully colored and cleaned, they should be mounted on dark gray or green cardboard, or mat board, leaving a margin of 3 or 4 inches all around. Black cardboard or paper for mounting is too severe in value, bringing out light parts in the sketch too prominently and killing any soft semitones in the sketch.

The designer is justified in using whatever artificial aids he judges best for giving his sketches the most attractive appearance, and therefore for being most acceptable to his prospective patrons. In no cases, however, must it be assumed that careful·mounting can atone for bad qualities in the sketch itself.

72. Submitting Sketches to Clients.—Frequently the designer connected with a stained-glass establishment will be called upon to be the *outside man;* that is, the representative of the firm who is to meet with the customers, the pastor, the church committee, etc., and explain the sketches and the proposed method of making up the leaded-glass work. Instead of avoiding such a "commercial" undertaking, the designer should be very anxious to accept such opportunity, for not only will he benefit himself, but he will be more likely to obtain the contract for the work. Consequently, he should explain to the committee what each part of his sketches means, how it is to be carried out, what glasses are to be used, where ventilators are to be placed, and so on. He should also be prepared to answer any searching questions that are put to him. If dissatisfaction is expressed with any of the sketches, he should learn wherein this dissatisfaction consists, and revise his sketches accordingly.

When the sketches have been found satisfactory, the designer should have each one approved by the customer or committee, and have the contract properly signed, after which the firm is then ready to make up the windows. The final stage of the designing of the window, and the introductory stage to its manufacture, is the making of the full-sized drawing or cartoon, which will now be described.

PREPARING THE CARTOON

73. Preliminary Work.—While the water color sketch was merely a suggestion, a color map, as it were, of the proposed leaded-glass window, it is necessary to make a full-size drawing in charcoal or crayon of the window, which drawing is called the **cartoon**. Although the small color sketch is drawn to scale and the general proportions given, yet the designer must obtain an accurate pattern of the full size of the window (that is, from inside of left-side rebate to inside of right rebate), and then outline the window shape at full size. Within this full-size outline, the full-size details of the window must be drawn, using the small sketch as a scaled chart or guide. The cartoon must include all details of light, shade, and shadows, modeling of flesh, drapery, and such other pictorial details as may be included—even the leads and the strengthening bars must appear at their proper places. In fact, the cartoon must be practically a full-size photograph of the window as it would appear when completed. The cartoon should be drawn with charcoal or crayon on heavy cartoon paper or manila detail paper, in large sheets, or hanging from a roll fastened up on wall or ceiling, and hanging against a large drawing board supported vertically.

The careful designer will find it advisable to make preliminary studies of figures and drapery, from models if possible, and do all in his power to produce accurate draftsmanship. He must bear in mind constantly that he is working in glass; therefore, he must not only keep in mind as he works the general shapes and sizes of the pieces of glass, but must likewise draw the details so that the cut lines, or lead lines, and the supporting bars, can be put in at their proper places without conflicting with the lines and masses of the picture.

74. Putting in the Lead Lines.—An artist who may be able to draw with great skill the pictorial features of the cartoon, may find it very difficult to arrange the lead lines properly. It is only after investigating for himself how glass in differently shaped pieces acts when cut with the tool, when fired in the kiln, or when put through the process of leading, that he can intelligently arrange the lines for leading in his cartoon. This is the feature of drawing the cartoon that demands the utmost care and investigation; and it is at this point that the success or failure of the effectiveness of a window may be decided.

FIG. 44

No hard-and-fast rule can be made for drawing these cut lines; but, in general, it may be said that they should be so drawn as to include in one piece each separate color, and that the lines, as far as possible, should keep in the deeper shadows. Thus, where there is a red drapery over which another piece of drapery or a sash of yellow is folded, there must, of course, be separate pieces of glass for the yellow and for the red; consequently, the cut lines must be drawn accordingly. The glass painter cannot paint yellow onto red. It may be noted here, however, that golden jewels on a velvet drapery are sometimes indicated by etching out the outlines of the jewels from ruby flashed antique glass and then afterwards staining the etched-out parts with gold stain as previously explained.

The cut lines, or lead lines, should be subservient to the pictorial effect of the design, following dark places, deep shadows, etc., as shown in Fig. 44 at *a*. However, when a lead must cut across solid drapery, as shown at *b*, it should be frankly admitted and no attempt made to hide it or disguise it. Where a head, as of a saint or an apostle, for instance, is so drawn that a lead must surround it, the introduction of a halo, as at *c*, will help to simplify the matter of the lead line. The size of the individual pieces to be arranged for depends on what kind of glass is used, and how many firings it is to receive. On the average, no piece of glass should be over 14 inches long, certainly not as long as 18 inches. Pieces 10 inches square, or a foot square, are safe enough to handle. Antique glass will stand more strain, when fired, than opalescent glass. Drapery opalescent glass, if not fired, can be used in quite long pieces, for its strength insures it against danger of breakage. The designer must himself carefully investigate this matter of the strength of glass, unfired and fired, the sizes and shapes of pieces allowable, before he can intelligently put in the lead lines on his drawing. In many studios of firms making stained glass the drawing of backgrounds, draperies, etc., is given over entirely to∙ young draftsmen earning small salaries, while no one is allowed to draw the skeleton, or lead lines, also called *cut lines*, except the designer of the window, or the glass painter.

When the cartoon is entirely completed it is fixed by spraying it with fixatif, a combination of shellac and alcohol, as previously described.

The making of the working drawings, the cut-line drawing, and the glazing drawing can then be done direct from the cartoon, as described in the first part of this Section, when the making of working drawings and patterns was discussed.

STAINED AND LEADED-GLASS DESIGNING EXERCISES

GENERAL INFORMATION

75. Required Work in Stained- and Leaded-Glass Designing.—The required work in stained- and leaded-glass designing will consist of making drawings and designs for leaded glass, and not practice work in actually cutting and leading glass. Therefore, this test work will be arranged as drawing plates to be prepared and submitted to the Schools for examination and correction, these plates to comprise original designs for various styles and types of windows.

76. Character of the Drawing Plates.—There will be eight drawing plates, each about 10 inches wide and 15 inches high, depending on the kind of paper or board on which the designs are made. Whatman's smooth white water color paper, bristol board, or illustrators' board, will be suitable. Four of these plates, 1, 3, 5, and 7, are to be copies, on an enlarged scale, of certain illustrations in the text, and four, 2, 4, 6, and 8, are to comprise original designs, in accordance with directions given.

The designer is expected to do his or her very best in getting up these window sketches. No haphazard, indefinite sketches, or ones that simply resemble rough pictures of windows, will be accepted. They must be definite designs for windows to be used in definite buildings, as churches, residences, etc.

Upon completion, the plates are to be sent to the Schools one by one for examination, the student working on the plate in advance while each succeeding one is being examined.

PLATE 1

77. Technique of a Simple Window.—On a sheet about 10 inches wide by 15 inches high, lay out the window shown in Fig. 40, copying exactly the window shape and the design shown therein, making the design twice the size of the text illustration. The geometrically arranged lead lines must be laid out accurately, and spaced with absolute uniformity, and the curving lines drawn accurately—rough freehand sketching cannot be accepted.

When the patterns in each window have been carefully copied and portrayed with bold broken strokes of a soft lead pencil, they should be rendered with water colors, as described in the text directions. Thin washes of color must be used, allowing little *lights* to show, no opaque washes being employed, the entire effort being to produce on paper the effect of a colored leaded-glass window seen from the inside of the building when daylight is coming through the glass.

78. Final Work on Plate 1.—Letter or write the title, Plate 1: Stained- and Leaded-Glass Designing, at the top of the sheet; and, on the back, place class letters and number, name, address, and date of completing the plate. Send the plate to the Schools for examination (rolled or packed flat, as circumstances may require), and then proceed with Plate 2.

PLATE 2

79. Original Design for a Simple Window.—Lay out on the usual size sheet a window of exactly the same size and shape as the one used on Plate 1. Prepare original designs for the geometric shapes and the curved-line work to fill these window openings, the general grade of work being about the same (from standpoint of cost) as that used in the copied design for Plate 1.

Before starting to design these simple window patterns it would be well to study very carefully the specimens of reproduced window designs shown in the text illustrations, and, better yet, to make special trips to nearby churches, public buildings, and private residences to see the appearance and general arrangement of the patterns in the leaded-glass windows in those buildings. All such preliminary data will be of great assistance in designing original patterns of such simple character.

In coloring the design, the method described in the text should be carefully followed, and the same painstaking attention as to accuracy of detail observed as was employed in rendering the sketches for Plate 1.

80. Final Work on Plate 2.—Letter or write the title, Plate 2: Stained- and Leaded-Glass Designing, at the top of the sheet; and, on the back, place class letters and number, name, address, and date of completing the plate. Send the plate to the Schools for examination (rolled or packed flat, as circumstances may require), and then proceed with Plate 3.

PLATE 3

81. Technique of a Decorative Window.—Lay out on the usual size sheet the window opening with triple divisions and tracery at the top shown in Fig. 41. Copy exactly the design shown therein, making the sizes and shapes of the openings, and the details of the ornament therein, two or three times the size of Fig. 41. The geometrical shapes must be laid out with great accuracy, and the decorative work must be drawn therein with great care, being proportioned and detailed as shown in the sketch, but on an enlarged scale.

The design, thus carefully drawn with a soft, sharp pencil, must then be rendered with water colors as shown in the text illustration, and with the greatest care, as previously advised.

82. Final Work on Plate 3.—Letter or write the title, Plate 3: Stained- and Leaded-Glass Designing, at the top of the sheet; and, on the back, place class letters and number, name, address, and date of completing the plate. Send the plate to the Schools for examination (rolled or packed flat, as circumstances may require), and then proceed with Plate 4.

PLATE 4

83. Original Design for a Decorative Window.
Lay out on the usual size sheet a window shape with triple
divisions and tracery at the top of exactly the same size and
shape as those used on Plate 3. Prepare an original design
for this triple window, the general grade of work being about
the same, from standpoint of cost, as that used in the copied
design for Plate 3; that is, decorative details of appropriate
Gothic character for the upper parts and tracery, and more
simple geometric forms for the lower parts.

In this case, also, it will be of advantage, in fact necessary,
for the young designer to first look about him—in churches, public buildings, etc.—to see the character of the work used in such
windows. With such data well in mind the designer can prepare
more intelligently the original design required for this plate.

84. Final Work on Plate 4.—Letter or write the title,
Plate 4: Stained- and Leaded-Glass Designing, at the top of
the sheet; and, on the back, place class letters and number,
name, address, and date of completing the plate. Send the
plate to the Schools for examination (rolled or packed flat as
circumstances may require), and then proceed with Plate 5.

PLATE 5

85. Technique of Drawing Lead Lines.—As practice
in the proper placing of lead lines, or cut lines, in a full-size
cartoon of a picture window, make a copy of the right-hand
window opening of the group in Fig. 43, making it two or two-
and-one-half times the size of the text illustration, and so that
it will fit nicely on the length of a 10″×15″ sheet. The drawing need not be made in colors, but in shaded pencil work, the
faces and drapery being carefully rendered with softly blended
values. The lead lines, showing brown in the illustration, may
then be put in with a very black, soft lead pencil, or with ink
and a pen, the greatest care being observed in the placing of
these lines.

86. Final Work on Plate 5.—Letter or write the title, Plate 5: Stained- and Leaded-Glass Designing, at the top of the sheet; and, on the back, place class letters and number, name, and address, and date of completing the plate. Send the plate to the Schools for examination (rolled or packed flat, as circumstances may require), and then proceed with Plate 6.

PLATE 6

87. Original Work in Drawing Lead Lines.—As further practice in the proper placing of lead lines, or cut lines, in a cartoon of a picture window, select any picture of a religious nature, make a carefully rendered pencil drawing of it, well filling the 10″×15″ sheet, and then place the lead lines properly thereon.

A suitable religious picture can be selected from current magazines, from old prints, or from among the Perry or Copley prints that sell very cheaply; from 1 cent to 50 cents (or more) each.

In placing the lead lines the principles of cut-line work, as explained fully in the text, and as illustrated in the examples given, should be put into practice.

88. Final Work on Plate 6.—Letter or write the title, Plate 6: Stained- and Leaded-Glass Designing, at the top of the sheet; and, on the back, place class letters and number, name and address, and date of completing the plate. Send the plate to the Schools for examination (rolled or packed flat, as circumstances may require), and then proceed with Plate 7.

PLATE 7

89. Technique of a Complete Figure Window.—Lay out on the usual size sheet the group of window openings, with triple arrangement of picture subjects, shown in Fig. 43, making it about twice the size of the illustration, and so that it will fit well on a 10″×15″ sheet, copying exactly the pictorial work and accessories as shown. The details of this pictorial window must be copied with great care.

The design must then be carefully colored with tints of water color to reproduce as closely as possible the effect shown in Fig. 43. Carefully detailed rendering must be employed. No rough, hastily executed, sketch will be accepted.

90. Final Work on Plate 7.—Letter or write the title, Plate 7: Stained- and Leaded-Glass Designing, at the top of the sheet; and, on the back, place class letters and number, name, address, and date of completing the plate. Send the plate to the Schools for examination (rolled or packed flat, as circumstances may require), and then proceed with Plate 8.

PLATE 8

91. Original Design for a Complete Figure Window. Lay out on the usual size sheet a group of window openings, with triple arrangement of picture subjects of exactly the same size and shape as those used on Plate 7. Prepare an original design for this triple window, the grade of work being as used on Plate 7; that is, pictorial work showing figure subjects carried across the entire group of three lights.

Before preparing this pictorial window design, the young designer should seize every opportunity to visit churches and see just what picture subjects are used for moderate-priced work and what subjects are used for elaborate work; how they are treated; how the lead lines are arranged; what kinds of glass are used; how the colors are harmonized, etc.

92. Final Work on Plate 8.—Letter or write the title, Plate 8: Stained- and Leaded-Glass Designing, at the top of the sheet; and, on the back, place class letters and number, name, address, and date of completing the plate. Send the plate to the Schools for examination (rolled or packed flat, as circumstances may require).

If any redrawn or rerendered work on any of the plates of this Section has been called for and has not yet been completed, it should be satisfactorily finished at this time. After all required work on the plates of this Section has been completed, the work of the next Section should be taken up at once.

SELLING DESIGNS AND OBTAIN-
ING A POSITION

INTRODUCTION

1. The Desire to Earn Money at Designing.—Experience has shown that, while many students take up the study of decorative design for the pleasure and fascination it affords in giving them definite forms in which to express their artistic inclinations, a certain proportion are eager to apply such training commercially.

No matter how well trained technically the design student may be, it is very rare, unless he is already engaged in some industrial field, that he is familiar with the methods he must use to sell work or obtain a position in the field of decorative designing.

2. Extent of Art Instructor's Duty to Student.—It is not unnatural that students, upon completing a course in some line of decorative design work (or even before), should turn to their instructors for information and help on the matter of marketing the training they have received.

While inquiries for information on this question are not entirely out of place, it is neither reasonable nor fair for a student to expect his instructors to help him to sell designs or obtain a position. No reputable resident training school in decorative design obtains its students by promising to secure positions for them when they graduate; for a high-grade art school is an educational institution, and not a training school for apprentices or an employment agency. It furnishes a training for practical commercial work in designing just as

§ 21

colleges furnish a training in letters, sciences, and languages; and the matter of making commercial use of this training (that is, selling designs and obtaining a position) rests entirely with the individual student.

Because a school furnishes the training by correspondence does not in any way change conditions; the responsibility for making a practical application of his training rests at all times with the student himself.

3. Importance of Practical Experience.—The proper stepping-stone from a training course in some technical line of decorative designing to the practical work of making and selling commercial designs, or of occupying a salaried position as designer, is practical experience. In the industrial world no designer is considered as being thoroughly trained until he has a certain amount of commercial experience, and thus becomes adapted to local conditions in his particular field.

For instance, a wallpaper manufacturer takes a great risk when he experiments with a "greenhorn" designer. A certain design as turned out by such novice may be of pleasing appearance and, being passed by the head designer and the head of the firm, may be made up into rolls, yet may prove a poor seller because not designed in accordance with the popular demand. Experienced designers are less liable to make such errors, therefore manufacturers are inclined to avoid taking risks with designs made by those without commercial experience. Similar conditions exist in other fields of commercial designing, for manufacturers and other users of designs have a certain standard that their patrons and the public expect them to maintain. In some cases they buy designs from free-lance artists and in other cases they employ regular staffs of high-grade designers to do the required work, but from their viewpoint there is little reason why they should experiment with unknown and commercially inexperienced designers.

4. What the Young Designer Must Know.—The conditions existing in the commercial world have been frankly outlined to show the student that a technical design training unaccompanied by experience will not enable him at once to sell designs at high prices, or to step at once into a position paying a high salary. The student must first learn what lines of work are comprised in the field of commercial designing, and then decide for which one of these many lines his training has fitted him or local conditions make it seem best for him to follow. If his design training has been such as to make his method of marketing it take the form of selling designs on a free-lance basis, he must learn where to sell designs and how to sell them with the best results. If he has been trained in one of those lines in which the designers do their work as salaried staff-designers, he must learn where to look for a position as designer and how to obtain such a position. He must learn how to approach properly the men who have charge of establishments that can use his services, and to convince these men that his services will be valuable to them. All this is practical experience; and every seeker of a position *must* pass through practical experience. He cannot evade or avoid it. Experience comes only by daily living and learning, constantly applying whatever is valuable in increasing one's usefulness and furthering one's interests.

5. Value of Professional Advice.—While practical experience, sometimes in the form of a long and arduous apprenticeship, is the only method of approach to an established place in the commercial design field open to some novices, the next best thing is professional information and advice from experienced men in the art world.

It might naturally be supposed that there would be in existence handbooks or manuals of information telling students and graduates of training courses of the opportunities in the commercial world for well-trained designers, and how to find and take advantage of these opportunities. A careful search, however, fails to reveal any such handbooks. It is true that the advertising literature of certain "short-cut" schools gives the impression that positions are easy to get, but such statements are generally issued with a business-getting motive, and are harmful, because they deceive the student as to actual commercial conditions and arouse false hopes in his mind.

The purpose of this Section, therefore, is to tell the graduate student of designing where and how to sell designs, where to look for a position, and how to obtain it. The information presented is fully in accord with facts, and is therefore entirely reliable.

The information and advice given is particularly dependable and authoritative because it has been compiled from information furnished by commercial designers who have been through the stages of student, amateur, and semiprofessional, and are now holding positions of prominence in the practical field of industrial designing, and are the head designers for prominent Eastern manufacturers of wallpapers, carpets, stained-glass windows, etc. It represents such honest and candid information and advice as would be given personally by the art managers of large companies if they had the time to do so. The student reading these pages may therefore consider himself fortunate, in that he has presented to him facts and advice on the matter of entering the commercial designing field that many designers now prominent would have been glad to receive (but did not) when they were starting their careers.

SELLING DESIGNS

WHERE AND HOW TO SELL DESIGNS

FIELD OF HANDICRAFTS DESIGNING

6. The Two Methods of Marketing a Design Training. There are two methods by which the student who has had a systematic training in artistic designing can market his training; that is, make money at designing: One is to prepare designs and sell them on a free-lance basis; the other is to get a salaried position in some commercial designing studio. Usually, the young commercial designer, especially for industrial products, begins his career by taking a salaried position; for by this method he learns most thoroughly the professional tricks of the trade, technique, business practices, etc., of that particular design field. If, later, his inclination is toward the free-lance work of setting up his own studio and selling designs independently, he is then best fitted to do so.

Often, however, circumstances of location, as well as of a personal nature, make it necessary for the designer to do free-lance designing first—perhaps as a side line to a regular position in some other line of work—and take up a salaried position as designer after his free-lance experience has established him. For this reason there will first be discussed in this Section the free-lance work of selling designs, and later the work of obtaining a regular salaried position.

7. Selecting the Proper Line of Handicrafts Designing.—The first step of importance to be observed by the beginner, in attempting to sell handicrafts designs, is to select and adhere to some definite line of handicrafts designing, and to specialize in that line. The training course just completed has fitted the student to prepare salable designs for stencils and block prints, for leather and metal work, for china decoration, etc., and this training has, of course, fitted him to design for other and associated lines of handicrafts work. A definite selection must now be made as to the line in which to specialize and all efforts should be bent to work for that line, and to investigation of that field. The decision as to what is the best line to take up may be strongly influenced by the opportunities.

8. Investigating the Demand.—The beginner in handicrafts design work should look about him and ascertain what are the opportunities in his or her own city, town, or locality, and just what demand exists, or could be created, for the design and sale of handicrafts work. There is hardly any town, no matter what the size, where opportunities do not exist for the designing, preparation, and sale of one or another article of handicrafts work. Just what this opportunity is, and what the demand is, must be investigated and determined by the young designer himself; no one can do it for him.

Perhaps the situation is such that suitably decorated china will be in demand, and sell well. Perhaps stenciled articles, well designed, will be popular. Or, perhaps, tooled leather will best meet the artistic inclinations and wants in the young

designer's particular locality. This can best be determined by
numerous personal interviews with proprietors and clerks of
dry-goods stores, jewelry stores, etc., in the town, and with as
wide as possible a circle of friends and acquaintances. One
of the most important requisites on the part of the novice in
handicrafts designing work is to make up his or her mind that
if such services or work are to be marketed there must first
be full and free personal intercourse and association with hosts
of people in the locality where designs are to be sold, in order
to learn the demand for handicrafts work and the possibility
of building up a clientele. The friendly advice and suggestions
of some well-known business man in the locality will greatly
assist one's efforts in this direction.

9. Necessity for Self-Advertising.—It is assumed that
the student has worked conscientiously at, and has successfully
completed, his design course and can make salable designs.
This fact alone, however, will not necessarily enable him to
sell them. Many a merchant has on his shelves standard
brands of goods that are salable, but which he does not sell
because he does not advertise his wares and his services. Similarly, the well-trained designer has an ability and a service
that can be sold, but unless he or she will advertise this ability
or this service, it cannot be marketed.

Those who are overly sensitive about mixing with the public
and about calling attention to their abilities and the kind of
design work they can do, must make up their minds to get rid
of their sensitiveness at once. The buying public is always
eager for something new and attractive in the art line, and will
always meet the artist half way in his efforts to market his
designs.

10. Methods of Self-Advertising.—Just how this self-
advertising is to be done in each case is purely a problem for
the individual designer. So many considerations enter; such
as the kind of design training the artist has had, the character
of the local demand, etc., that the designer must, in every
case, himself devise and carry out the details of his plans.
There are a few general suggestions, however, that may be given

for these publicity campaigns that will apply to any case. Some of them are as follows:

1. *The Display Room of Handicrafts Designs.*—If some line of handicrafts designing is being followed, the designer should conduct a permanent display of his or her work, changing the individual designs or articles from time to time. In small towns, or even in cities, such a display may be set up in one of the rooms of one's house. Or, if circumstances will permit, a small room may be rented in the business section of the town, and used as a combination workshop and display room. If this room is on the second floor of the building, a small upright show case containing specimens of work may be set up at the foot of the stairs, accompanied by a clearly lettered placard or sign explaining the kind of work being done and the name of the designer.

Branch displays of the designer's work may be set up in jewelry stores, department stores, drug stores, art stores, tea rooms, etc., by making satisfactory arrangements with the proprietors. Excellent opportunities are offered in this way during the summer season in those towns and localities frequented by summer tourists.

2. *The Portfolio of Industrial Designs.*—The industrial designer making designs for carpets, wallpapers, stained glass, etc., likewise needs to have displayed, in attractive form, specimens of his work. However, inasmuch as managers and head designers of mills, factories, and workshops do not make a practice of going shopping for the designs they need, the designer of industrial work must put up the display of his designs in portable form, and for this purpose the convenient portfolio is the best. A representative collection of such industrial designs, each attractively mounted, should comprise the contents of the portfolio, which should close with a snap fastener or be tied with tapes, so that it can be readily opened and closed during the personal interview.

3. *Business Cards and Letters.*—An interesting and convincing display room having been established for handicrafts work, or an attractive collection of original industrial designs having been prepared, the next step for the designer is to bring himself

and his work to the attention of possible purchasers. To this end, the designer should have engraved, or printed, an appropriate business card, giving his name and address, and indicating clearly the character of designs he prepares for sale. In addition to this card, there should be prepared some sort of letter or message to go to the prospective patron; this, depending upon local circumstances, could be written in longhand, typewritten, mimeographed, or printed. The neatly printed letter or circular of information will, of course, be the most attractive and compelling, and will be most likely to lead to a sale of designs, particularly if it is accompanied by a specimen design or a reproduction of such a design. Such a letter or circular must be carefully written, setting forth the patron's or client's need for work of the kind offered and showing clearly the designer's ability to prepare such work. If in the form of a letter, the communication should make a request for an opportunity to call in person with samples of work. It would pay the young designer to have this letter or circular prepared by some young advertisement writer who would probably not charge too highly for his services.

4. *Enrolling With a Women's Exchange.*—Girl and women designers living in or near the large cities are already familiar with the Women's Exchanges in their city, and the system of taking designs or handicrafts work there and displaying it for sale, the only stipulation being the payment of a small fee, say $2. This fee is necessary in order to assure the sincerity of the applicant, and to guarantee a sufficiently high quality of work to make it worth while for display purposes.

The city girl or woman can readily learn the address of the Women's Exchange in her city by consulting the city directory, or by inquiring at the office of the city Young Women's Christian Association. The girl or woman living in the small town or country districts, and desiring to display designs or work for sale at one of these Exchanges, need simply write to "The Director (or President) of the Women's Exchange" in the city nearest to which she lives, asking for the rules and regulations of that Exchange, and enclosing a stamp for reply. Such a letter will be sure to bring an answer, and then further correspondence on the matter can be conducted, and a personal visit made to the Exchange, if desired. It is understood, of course, that the work submitted to this Exchange for display and sale must be high grade in every particular in order to be salable. Further, these Exchanges are only for the marketing of work done by women.

5. *Enrolling With an Artists' Syndicate or Agency.*—A very businesslike avenue through which both men and women designers of handicrafts work or industrial products may secure publicity for themselves and their work, is the artists' syndicate or agency, generally to be found in any large city. It is true that these agencies specialize on disposing of pictorial illustrating work, manuscripts, songs, poems, etc., but they will also perform a service for the young designer if the proper negotiations are made. The entrance fee is usually $5 or $10.

The names of such syndicates can be obtained from the advertising pages of monthly fiction, or so-called popular, magazines, or from art magazines, and trade papers of printers and publishers.

6. *The Personal Canvass and Solicitation.*—No matter how carefully and thoroughly a preliminary campaign of self-advertising has been conducted, there must eventually occur the personal interview with the one who is to purchase one's designs. The young designer must get rid of the idea that his entire business experience of marketing his designs can be done by mail. No such easy and reserved course of procedure will accomplish the desired result; the young designer must actually get out and meet personally, face to face, those to whom it is desired to sell the designs.

This matter of the personal interview is of such importance that it will now be discussed in detail, in connection with building up a clientele, and will later be treated when "The Personal Interview" is discussed.

11. Building up a Clientele.—When the young handicrafts designer has gotten up his material to show the kinds of designs he can prepare, he is ready to approach those who can use them. The problem is, now, to find these possible patrons or clients and to sell the designs; in other words, the building up of a regular class of patrons, or a clientele.

The questions are frequently asked by graduates of handicrafts design courses: Where can I sell my designs? To whom must I go to dispose of my work? Where can I get a list of names of possible buyers of designs? First of all, the young handicrafts designer must realize that he or she must furnish the answers to these questions. The problem of securing names of possible buyers of such work is an individual personal problem; because the local circumstances surrounding one designer are in no case exactly the same as those surrounding another, therefore, no instructor, or other person, at a distance can direct the student where to sell his designs.

The situation to be faced squarely by each design graduate is this: He or she has been trained to make something that somebody somewhere wants. The problem is to find this somebody. It is evident that not all the persons, whether in a town or in a city, are in need of or would be interested in artistically designed handicrafts work, but there will always be *some* persons who are interested. By a process of elimination those people may be set aside who, it is easily known, do not want artistically designed articles. There would then be left such persons as women of culture and means; society and club women who entertain a great deal and want their home furnishings and gowns distinctive; daughters of such women who are attending school or college; girls about to be married, or friends of those about to be married, etc. The possibilities of extending such a list are readily seen. Nor is the field in which well-designed handicrafts articles may be sold limited to women; professional men—doctors, teachers, etc.—who appreciate the artistic and unusual in home furnishings; library, study, and studio accessories, etc., may also be approached.

A very effective entering wedge for opening relations with this class of prospective patrons is to show them how distinctively designed handicrafts articles make even better (because they are original and not to be duplicated) presents for special occasions, or favors for parties, etc., than do the stereotyped silver, cut glass, and china sold in jewelry and china stores.

These occasions when presents or favors of handicrafts work are distinctive and appropriate are spread throughout the entire year, so that the opportunities are not limited to any one season. There are New Year's gifts; favors at Washington's birthday and St. Patrick's Day events; Easter gifts; Memorial Day and Independence Day favors; gifts for those leaving on vacation trips (especially by boat); gifts for the daughter or friend going away to school or college in September; Thanksgiving Day favors; and, most prolific of all, Christmas gifts. Besides these, scattered throughout the year are bridge and other parties at which prizes and favors are used. It is therefore readily seen that opportunities to dispose of artistically designed handicrafts articles for the gifts, prizes, and favors of these affairs are practically unlimited.

These do not constitute all the opportunities, by any means, whereby the handicrafts designer may sell work; they are simply offered in the line of suggestion and to lead the way to the consideration of other opportunities that will be presented to each individual designer.

Now, how shall these people be approached? The matter of the business cards and letters has already been presented. These will pave the way for a call from the patrons or for an opportunity for the designer to call upon the possible patron with specimens of work. The characteristics of the person called upon, and the nature of the designs it is desired to sell or to prepare, will indicate the "line of talk" to employ. Suppose, for example, persons were being interviewed sometime previous to the June-commencement season, or the June-bride season, the young designer can point out how much more appropriate and distinctive, as commencement or wedding gifts, are suitably designed handicrafts articles, such as stenciled goods, wrought leather, or metal articles, etc., than the conventional and stereotyped articles of silver, glass, etc., usually given to graduates and brides. If to this tactfully worded statement is added, with similar tact, a clear explanation of what kind of work the young handicrafts designer is prepared to furnish, there should be no difficulty encountered in selling designs and in building up a regular clientele of patrons.

Further details regarding the matter of getting in touch with possible patrons, and conducting successful interviews with them, will be brought out in connection with the discussion of the personal interview when, later in this Section, obtaining a position is treated:

12. Reasons for Failure to Sell Some Designs. Excellence of design, execution, and drawing alone will not necessarily sell work. The design may be entirely satisfactory from the standpoint of the art instructor's criticism, and yet the designer may be unable to sell it. There are certain causes, aside from artistic reasons, why designs sometimes cannot be sold, a consideration of which will help the young designer to avoid such faults when getting up and submitting handicrafts designs to prospective patrons. Some of these causes are as follows:

1. The design, although artistically planned and well carried out in the piece of crafts work, may be for some very unusual and obscure article for which there is little demand. Such a design will of course remain long unsold, unless some fortunate chance brings an unexpected purchaser. It is not good business, however, to depend upon the uncertain element of chance.

2. The design may be artistic, well drawn, etc., but may be unsuited for being carried out in the particular material or on the particular surface desired. For example, an elaborate and intricate design may be prepared, which would do very well for decorating china, but which would be wholly unsuited for tooled leather or metal work. The attempt to carry it out in leather or metal spoils it, and the discriminating patron, recognizing this, will not buy the design.

3. The design, although suitably prepared and executed, is rejected by the prospective buyer because the method pursued by the designer-salesman in attempting to dispose of it is not businesslike, is not refined, and is perhaps so tactless as to be almost offensive to persons of refinement, such as are usually the class of patrons buying handicrafts designs.

4. Designs for handicrafts work in many cases remain unsold because the designer did not first of all carefully study

the demand in his or her particular locality. The result was that money, time, and effort were spent in getting up a collection of handicrafts designs for things that were not wanted by patrons in his city, town, or locality. For example, there are localities in which people are enthusiastic over stenciled articles of all kinds—portieres, table covers, pillow tops, etc., while in certain other localities the people consider that stenciled work is out of date and they are going in for tooled leather or metal. In other localities designers for china decoration are greatly in demand, while in still other localities nobody wants hand-painted china, but they are enthusiastic over hammered-brass desk sets, etc. It thus becomes the duty of each handicrafts designer to prepare designs for those things that are in demand, and for nothing else, if he would sell his work.

FIELD OF INDUSTRIAL DESIGNING

13. Free-Lance Industrial Designing.—As has already been indicated, the normal procedure in the industrial world is for the designer to start his career as a salaried employe in some factory or designing room where industrially designed articles or fabrics are produced. However, the young graduate of a course in industrial design is usually in such circumstances that he desires to prepare and sell industrial designs "on the side," without interruption to his regular occupation. This class of work is known as *free-lance* industrial work, and the designer doing it is known as a free-lance designer.

The student having been trained by the industrial design course just completed has had the opportunity of learning the artistic and technical sides of designing for stained and leaded glass, carpets and rugs, wallpapers, linoleum and oilcloth, tile and parquetry, etc., and therefore the industrial fields open to him as a free-lance designer are wide and varied.

14. Choosing the Proper Field.—As in any other line of endeavor, whether or not it is art work, the designer must specialize. He must decide whether his talents and training, as well as the conditions in his locality, make wallpaper designing, or stained- and leaded-glass designing, or perhaps carpet and rug designing, the one line on which to specialize. Such a specialty must be chosen by the novice if he wants to do good work, in spite of the fact that professional free-lance designers sometimes carry on several associated lines of designing, as wallpapers and carpets, for example.

Such a choice must be influenced not only by the student's personal liking or aptitude, or his individual preference, but also by the opportunities and demands in certain lines in his locality. For a student to select wallpaper designing as his specialty simply because he may think he likes that work in preference to some other line, when there are no wallpaper mills in or near his locality, and when he does not know where there are such mills, is a very foolish procedure indeed. The only remedy for such a condition is for him to move to a locality where there are wallpaper mills.

15. Studying the Public Demand.—Having selected the design specialty to follow, the free-lance designer must first of all study the public demand for that specialty. This means that he must not only investigate the volume of the demand, but especially the character of the goods (in that particular design field) demanded and bought by the public. It is upon such a demand, in both quality and quantity, that the free-lance designer must base his designs.

No matter what specialized line may have been chosen, there are certain general lines of procedure that apply in studying the public demand. If the designer is located in a city or large town, the city directory will reveal the names and location of factories, display rooms, large dealers, etc., making or selling the particular product for which he wants to make designs. If he is not so located, he should go to such manufacturing or marketing centers, visit the factories, ask permission to go through them, make personal calls on and obtain interviews with proprietors and clerks in stores handling these goods, and should ask questions freely as to how such goods sell, to whom they sell, what patterns are most popular, under what conditions free-lance designs are bought, etc. A request for old sample books, of a previous season's patterns, if tactfully made, will usually be granted, and these will prove very useful.

It is thus seen that the young designer cannot expect to get this information entirely from books and trade papers, but must depend upon his personal investigations.

16. Importance of Self-Advertising.—If, as has been pointed out, it is necessary for the handicrafts designer to advertise himself and his ability, so that prospective patrons will know of him and his work, it is even more necessary that the industrial designer should so advertise himself. The reason for this is that manufacturers of these artistically designed fabrics and products are a very self-contained and self-satisfied class of people. By this is meant that they are pretty well pleased and satisfied with the work of their own designers and with the products turned out in their mills and factories, and are not going to spend much time in looking up unknown designers and their work. It is therefore the duty of the novice in industrial design work to look up the manufacturers and dealers, and acquaint them with himself and his work.

The preliminary campaign for this publicity has already been pointed out in connection with handicrafts designing; namely, the use of business cards and letters. What has already been said about these cards and letters and their use will apply particularly to the selling of industrial designs. The details of the approach to manufacturers and the selling of the designs will now be considered.

17. Getting in Touch With Manufacturers and Selling Designs.—No two individuals would use the same method of procedure in getting in touch with manufacturers and dealers in artistic products. There are certain helpful suggestions, however, that may be made, and these will be here presented. Inasmuch as the young designer will first select a design specialty, these suggestions will be classified according to the particular field selected; whether tiles and parquetry, linoleums and oilcloths, carpets and rugs, wallpapers, stained and leaded glass, etc.

1. *Tiles and Parquetry.*—Let it be assumed that the designer has chosen the work of free-lance designing for tiles of various

kinds and hardwood flooring (parquetry), and that there are
in his locality, or that he has located in a section where there
are, companies manufacturing these products or large dealers
handling them and using designs therefor. His first duty
is to call upon the managers of these manufacturing concerns,
or upon the dealers handling these lines of goods, and to acquaint
them with himself and his ability for making designs for these
purposes, showing specimens of his work, and requesting the
opportunity to make up designs on assignment for goods in
their line, such as designs for mosaic tiling for vestibule, bathroom, restaurant, and theater-lobby floors; designs for hearth
and mantel tiles; designs for parquetry flooring; etc. The
details of arranging for and properly conducting such personal
interviews will be discussed later. When once opportunity has
been given to make up such designs on assignment, it is then
a simple matter for the well-trained designer to demonstrate
the kind of work he can do, and to dispose of it.

2. *Linoleums and Oilcloths.*—What has been said about tile
and parquetry manufacturers and the methods of reaching
them and selling designs to them applies likewise to makers of
linoleums and oilcloths. In these fields, however, the opportunities are wider than in the tile and parquetry field, for there
is a great diversity of patterns for these fabrics. Every opportunity should be seized to call upon the proprietors and clerks
of carpet and linoleum stores, furniture stores, or department
stores, and to talk over with these men the conditions in the
linoleum and oilcloth trade; namely, whether there is an increase
or decrease in the amount of linoleum and oilcloth used this
season as compared with other seasons; what kinds of patterns
are selling best; what manufacturers are most likely to give
free-lance designers an opportunity to make designs for them,
etc. Sample books of this and former season's styles in linoleum
and oilcloth are always available, and are worth looking over
to see what kinds of patterns the public likes and what kinds
are therefore put on the market by the manufacturers.

When names and addresses of prominent manufacturers have
been secured from a local factory or local dealer, it will pay
the young designer to write letters to each one explaining his

qualifications to make linoleum and oilcloth designs and requesting the privilege of a personal interview with the manager or head artist, at which time the designer should be able to show specimens of his work. When negotiations have once been carried this far, it then simply remains for the designer, by his personal tact and persistence, to secure the assignment to make up some designs and, to then do his best in preparing suitable ones to meet the conditions laid down by the manufacturer. If this is done, the designs, of course, can be sold without any trouble.

3. *Carpets and Rugs.*—The field of designing for carpets and rugs is wider and possesses greater opportunities than any so far discussed, but the designer entering it must preface all his work by repeated visits to various carpet mills. These visits must not only be for the purpose of obtaining the usual preliminary design requirements from the manufacturers, but chiefly to make a close study of the machinery in that particular mill and how it weaves the particular class of carpet turned out by that mill, and for which the student wants to make designs. This is absolutely necessary, for the student cannot hope to make a carpet or rug design technically correct in every particular without such a personal investigation of the weaving process.

Most of the large carpet and rug factories are grouped in certain special sections in Connecticut, New York, Pennsylvania, New Jersey, etc. If, therefore, the student does not live in any of these sections, the names of the best makers of carpets and the location of their factories must be obtained as previously suggested, by personal inquiry among local carpet and rug dealers, and their salesmen and clerks. When this information has been obtained, letters of inquiry requesting personal interviews may be written to these firms, and through the interviews so obtained opportunities can be secured to make carpet and rug designs on assignment, as before described.

4. *Wallpapers.*—There is perhaps no industrial art product with which the student has greater opportunity of becoming familiar than that of wallpapers. There is hardly any city, town, or village, no matter what its size, that does not contain a store that displays prominently and sells wallpapers of various kinds. It thus becomes a simple matter for the free-lance

designer who is specializing in wallpaper designs to have repeated personal interviews with proprietors and clerks in these stores, and learn the conditions in the wallpaper industry; such as the quantity and quality of wallpapers being sold this season as compared with previous seasons, the kinds of patterns that are the best sellers, the names of the best wallpaper factories nearest the student's home, etc. When once this information has been gathered, the usual steps of arranging for and conducting the personal interview, securing the assignment, and preparing and selling the designs, can be carried out as previously described.

5. *Stained and Leaded Glass.*—The industrial designer taking up stained and leaded glass as his specialty has undoubtedly done so because he is already familiar with the work of some stained-glass factory, studio, or workshop in his vicinity. Perhaps he is an employe of one of these concerns, or lives near one and visits it. While one or more such leaded-glass establishments is to be found in every city or large town, their number is not so great that one can get lists of their names from trade papers, or through dealers. Their names, however, can be learned by consulting the city directories, where such concerns may be listed as stained-glass companies; leaded-glass companies; art-glass companies; decorative-glass companies, etc.

Opportunities to make up, and sell, on assignment, designs for these concerns must be secured by personal calls on the proprietor or head designer and submitting to them specimens of designs. Designs for stained and leaded glass made by these concerns are always special designs made especially for a certain individual job or contract, and are not made to be reproduced in multiple or in quantities, as are wallpaper designs or carpet designs, for example. For this reason, the free-lance stained-glass designer must keep well informed, by reading the real-estate sections of newspapers and the building-trades journals, as to what private residences, banks, churches, etc., in course of erection are in need of leaded glass, and when the bids and sketches are to be submitted. If he is alert, he will make up a set of sketches for the glass for the particular building in question, take them to some stained- and leaded-glass shop and sell them outright. If he does not care to do this, nor feel able to do it, he may simply take specimens of his work there, and endeavor to obtain, in the usual way, an assignment to prepare sketches. From this point on, the success with which he may meet in disposing of the sketches will depend upon his care and throughness in doing the designing and rendering.

18. Selling Designs by Mail.—No matter how well-trained may be the free-lance industrial designer, the method of attempting to sell designs entirely by mail to firms or dealers in a distant city or town is a very uncertain and precarious one. From the standpoint of the designer himself it is absolutely necessary that he should meet and talk with the man to whom he desires to sell designs, and that he should visit and look over the operations of the factory, mill, shop, or studio where his designs would be worked out, for the reasons previously explained. Otherwise he would not be able to design intelligently for that particular field and, of course, could not sell his designs. From the standpoint of the manufacturer, it is especially necessary that he should have personal relations with the designer, should know what he is like personally, and should have him ready of access when a design is to be made or talked over.

However, there are occasions when some novices in the design field must depend on negotiations conducted by mail when attempting to sell designs. This simply means that the designer must apply the same principles of investigating the demand, self-advertising, reaching manufacturers, getting assignments, etc., as described above, but must do so through the medium of writing letters. To write letters of such a kind is not an easy task; it requires a good foundation knowledge of and training in the English language, and in the writing of business letters. The reading of good practical manuals on the writing of business letters, or taking a course of training in such work, is almost a necessity. The young designer will be very fortunate indeed if he knows, and can count on the assistance of, a friend who is an advertisement writer or solicitor, or a salesman.

It would be useless to write out for the young designer sample forms of such letters that could be used to solicit assignments and sell designs by mail, for no such forms would meet the conditions of any two cases. Therefore, the designer must get up such letters himself, remembering all the while that the same program or course of procedure must be followed as has been laid down for the designer that sells his work in person.

19. Inadvisability of Furnishing Names of Manufacturers.—The intention has been, so far, to make clear to the student, about to start his career as a free-lance designer, that it is only the general principles of selling designs and obtaining a position that can be given. It would be impossible, for example, for a treatise of this kind to tell individual student John Smith, living, say, in Smithville, Ohio, all the details of how *he* should proceed step by step to get a position in *his* selected specialty in *his* town or vicinity. John Smith must work out for himself the details of his own problem, applying to his individual case the general principles of procedure brought out so far in this Section.

For this reason it is obvious that it would be impracticable to furnish to individual student-designers lists of firm names and addresses with the statement that they could sell designs to these particular firms. For, though these firms were in the habit of buying designs from free-lance designers, it might happen, for one of many reasons, some of which will be pointed out later, that the particular young designer to whom these firm names were recommended could not sell his designs to them. The result would then be that he would unjustly feel aggrieved and resentful toward those who furnished him the list of names. For this reason, there are here given only general suggestions for securing firm names and addresses in the various lines of industrial design work. Some of these methods are looking through city directories and the advertising pages of trade papers of the tile, parquetry, linoleum, carpet, and wallpaper industries, etc. Also, there are firms who make a business of compiling and selling mailing lists of names of all kinds, and from these firms certain lists can be purchased. The best plan, of course, is for each individual student-designer personally to investigate the field, and make out lists of firm names, in his own town or city, or in neighboring towns and cities easy of access. He is much more likely to sell designs to such near-by firms than to firms at a distance, particularly if he is obliged to depend on orders and sales by mail alone.

20. Reasons Why Some Designs Are Rejected.—Even earnest personal work and a careful following out of the suggestions already given may not always result in the sale of industrial designs; for such failures may be due to one or more of many causes, some of which are mentioned below so that the student-designer, by careful study of them, may be able to avoid similar ones in his own experience, and thus meet with fewer rejections of his submitted designs. The following are some of the causes:

1. Designs may be rejected because the manufacturer to whom they are submitted has no immediate use for them. This does not necesarily imply that the designs are not good ones; it may simply mean that the particular manufacturer has all the designs he needs, or that, perhaps, the designs submitted do not exactly meet the requirements of his particular weaving machinery, printing rollers, etc., and that they could not be used thereon, without considerable expensive alteration. From this it can be seen that the young free-lance designer, especially in the carpet and wallpaper industries, should not rush into the manufacturer's presence with a miscellaneous assortment of designs and expect to sell them; but, before submitting any designs at all, should first get from the manufacturer a statement as to whether any designs at all are wanted and, if so, specifications of the kind of fabrics turned out in that mill. Then, and only then, can the designer stand a chance of preparing designs that will not be rejected.

2. Designs, however beautiful artistically, may also be rejected because they are not sufficiently correct in a technical sense to enable them to be carried out in the actual fabric or material. For example, the designer may have secured the

assignment to prepare a design for a body Brussels carpet, but, through inertia, haste, or some other inexcusable reason, he may have failed to make a careful inspection of the machinery in the factory where his carpet is to be woven, and may not have secured from the manufacturer the specifications and data as to number of colors allowed, methods of planting, etc., with the result that, while his design might look very well on paper, it could not be woven, which would therefore make it useless to the manufacturer.

3.   Designs submitted—although pleasing and harmonious from the standpoint of artistic form, mass, color contrasts, etc.—may not be in accordance with the public demand. Emphasis has been placed very strongly on the necessity for a full investigation by the designer in regard to the quantity and quality of the demand for certain patterns, what are the best sellers, etc.   Unless the designer fully acquaints himself with these points, and prepares his designs in conformity therewith, he may expect them to be rejected.

Many other reasons could be listed why designs, apparently artistic, are sometimes rejected.   However, the designer who is careful to observe the artistic, technical, and commercial requirements so far pointed out will not be so likely to encounter such rejections.

21.   Avoiding Discouragement.—It is hardly necessary to tell the young designer that he must expect to meet with refusals and rejections in attempting to sell designs.   To state it frankly, he may expect to sell designs in only a small proportion of the cases where attempts are made.   This, however, is true in all lines of salesmanship; the automobile salesman sells only a few cars each month, although thousands of people pass his display rooms, look at his cars, and are solicited to buy. The book publisher solicits thousands of people to buy his encyclopedias, dictionaries, histories, etc., and sells probably a few hundred sets among these thousands.   Thus it goes, in all lines.   No dealer, merchant, or advertiser allows himself to become discouraged or to get the blues because he does not sell to every one whom he approaches.   For this reason the young

free-lance designer has no cause for becoming discouraged if
he has two or twenty rejections of his designs. The twenty-
first one interviewed may buy his work, and thus compensate
for the twenty rejections. Further, from each interview,
whether or not it results in a rejection, he learns something
that will be of practical benefit in subsequent interviews.

It is admitted that, on the matter of avoiding discouragement, it is easier to give advice than to follow it. However, the
exercise of common sense, a sense of broad-minded humor, and
particularly of a firm will power (possessed, but not always
exercised by every one) will forestall discouragement.

PRICES PAID FOR DESIGNS

22. Handicrafts Designs.—When reference is made to
prices that should be asked for handicrafts designs, it is understood that this usually means the prices to be asked for the
handicrafts articles themselves, for it is not usually the case that
the handicrafts designer would sell his or her designs to another
craftsman or someone else to work out; except, perhaps, in
a case where designs would be sold to a publisher to be used as
reproduced illustrations for a magazine or book article on some
subject of crafts work. In such a case the publisher would
set the price, which would probably be from $2 to $5 or perhaps
up to $8 or $10.

Usually, however, it is the handicrafts article itself that is
sold, in which case it is not possible to quote any standard or
average prices. The designer, in setting a price, must estimate
the cost of materials used, and the valuation he or she places on
the time consumed, plus a reasonable margin of profit. The
character of the person to whom the specially designed article
is being sold must also be considered; a woman of means,
culture, and refinement, who really wants some of the work
turned out by the designer-craftsman, will be quite willing to
pay four or five times the actual production price of the designed
article if she recognizes it to be individual and distinctive.
For example, if the materials for an article cost 25 cents and
the time consumed in making it is estimated to be worth

7ȝ cents, the cost of the article is $1; but the class of patron described might readily pay $4 or $5 for it.

Therefore, although no standard prices for such designs can be quoted, the general rule for estimating charges, as estimated above, can be applied to all classes of specially designed handicrafts articles.

23. Industrial Designs.—In the case of industrial designs for tile, parquetry, linoleum, wallpaper, carpet, stained glass, etc., a standard price can more often be set than is the case with handicrafts designs; but it must not be thought that any regular schedules of prices for such designs can be given.

It is usually the manufacturer that sets the price in the case of work by the novice free-lance designer. For example, tile and linoleum designs generally run about $10 for each design, and it is rather unusual for any other price, either lower or higher, to be charged for such designs. In the case of the more artistic and elaborate wallpaper designs, $25 for a good design, if wanted at all, would not be considered excessive. Prices have been known to run considerably higher than that, depending on the reputation of the designer, the length of time required to prepare the design, etc. High-grade carpet designs, however, may run considerably higher than the figure for wallpaper designs; but, as in the case of wallpaper designs, there are no records of prices to be referred to, for the arrangements made by the wallpaper and the carpet manufacturers with the free-lance designers from whom they purchase designs are not public property; they must always be settled by the individuals concerned.

For good stained- and leaded-glass designs no figures are available as to prices. It is not unusual for a stained-glass shop to pay a free-lance designer from $100 to $200 for an elaborate figure-window design for a special purpose. Ordinary leaded-glass designs would, of course, sell for less. As previously stated, the prices for such designs are usually set arbitrarily by the manufacturer or shop manager, or individual arrangements are made in each case between the manufacturer and the free-lance designer.

TYPICAL EXPERIENCES IN SELLING DESIGNS

24. Advantage of Knowing Experiences of Others.
Even though one may have received the most detailed information as to methods of procedure in selling designs, the most human appeal comes when one has learned of the experiences of other designers in selling their designs. Some typical experiences are given below.

It is not an easy matter to get the average successful freelance designer to relate in minute detail the experiences he or she may have passed through in first attempting to sell work. Many such designers do not want the embarassments and setbacks of their earlier days to be revealed. But, it has been possible to locate a number of such designers who are honest, and who are only too glad to help the novice designer by recounting some of the experiences through which they passed in selling their designs. The cases cited below are literal transcriptions of actual cases of real people, and not in any respect imaginary. They should therefore prove of value to the student designer, not that they may be copied, or that any attempt may be made to imitate the details of these plans, but that they may serve as inspirations to each student to make the best of the opportunities he has or can create.

25. Experiences of Handicrafts Designers.—Miss C., a young lady who had studied a design course with a view to designing and executing china decoration, worked for a while in the usual way, painting roses on china in the conventional manner and trying to sell them; but the orders were few. She thought the matter over and came to the following decision: She knew that a summer resort is a place to make money, because people visit it to have a good time and are ready to pay for their pleasure in any form. She planned to let the summer resort visitors buy her decorated china. So she selected, from a wholesale dealer's stock, the oddest and queerest shapes in pitchers, bowls, cups, etc. Next, she planned out three sets of designs, quite different from the common and much used floral patterns, something unusual enough to attract people but not so freakish as to repel them. A great diversity of patterns was avoided, because such diversity is always confusing.

Then she made up complete tea sets; teapot and holder, sugar bowl, cream pitcher, cups and saucers, and sandwich plates to match; also bread and milk sets for children, marmelade jars, etc. She next selected a fairly large summer resort, patronized by the class of people who would be interested in well-designed handicrafts articles; and then made arrangements with the proprietors of a tea room to place some of her decorated china on exhibition there. The next step was to advertise her work by placing placards or posters in the various hotels and in the post office. Most important of all, she selected an attractive name for her china, calling it the "Blue Bird China," and painting the monogram *B. B. C.* at the bottom of each piece to identify it and give it distinction. She learned that nothing helped the sale of the china quite so much as a good name. Such a name strikes the attention; and a customer wants to know what to call his purchase, so that he can talk about it intelligently to his friends. The trade name and the monogram were a great advertisement for the china.

This young lady's sales were three times as great as she had expected. She says half the battle, in making money at art, is in giving people what they like, doing it well, and combining the ability with business management.

Another case is that of Miss P., who was trained to do stencil work on fabrics, and in the dyeing of artistically designed curtains, portieres, etc. She and a congenial as well as artistically trained girl friend, rented a little room in the quieter business section of a small city, on the second floor, over a restaurant, which they fitted up as a workshop, studio, and display room, combined. They made up, and placed on display, quite a number of articles of stenciled and artistically dyed goods, not only in their own room, but at the city Women's Exchange, at art stores, etc., throughout the city. They also put artistic, but very readable, signs on their windows and at the foot of the stairs leading to their room. Next, they started their self-advertising campaign; sending out business cards and letters not only to their friends and acquaintances, but to a carefully selected list of men and women who they believed would be inclined to become patrons. At first orders came in slowly, but they executed them faithfully and painstakingly, and, as satisfied patrons started showing their friends the quality of the work done by Miss P. and her associate, orders became more numerous, until soon there were so many orders that helpers had to be obtained and larger quarters secured.

26. Experiences of Industrial Designers.—Miss H., after completing a course in industrial designing, went to one of the larger cities in the attempt to sell work. Through an acquaintance she learned that a certain college society wanted some hand-lettering, engrossing, and illuminating done. She applied for and was given the commission to do this, worked on it a week and a half, and received $10. She then walked the streets of the city for several days with her portfolio of designs, trying to sell designs and get commissions and meeting with many rebuffs. Later, she obtained, by personal solicitation, assignments from a well-known firm making table and wall oilcloths to prepare designs for them, and received good prices for each design. She carried on as a side line artistic stenciling and dyeing of draperies, etc., which added considerably to her income.

Mr. S., after finishing a course in design, and trying for some time (but not trying properly) to sell work in the line for which he had trained—industrial design work on tiles, parquetry, etc.—finally succeeded in getting assignments to fill, in lettering signs or cards announcing the various departments in a city library and museum. Next, after several dozen calls on various publishers, advertising concerns, factories, etc., he was able to secure assignments from a designer of street-car advertisement illustrations, real-estate advertisements, etc., to hand-color outline prints for these cards. This work paid him little more than a living wage; so he resolved to rise above it by designing and selling to advertising agencies such cards himself. Not content with the limitations in this particular field, however, he kept up his search for something better. Through inquiries at tile and mosaic shops he learned of opportunities for selling

designs for mosaic-tiled floors to one of the large tile manu-
factories in the East. After making designs of this character
for a while, at moderate prices, he gradually improved his
work, by learning the technical and business practices thoroughly, so that now he arranges entire mosaic-floor schemes for
hotels, theaters, and public buildings all over the country,
and makes between $2,000 and $3,000 a year in this work alone.

OBTAINING A POSITION

WHERE AND HOW TO OBTAIN A POSITION

CHOOSING THE PROPER FIELD

27. Where Positions Are Found.—In treating the
subject of where to obtain a position, it must be understood
that the term *where* must not be interpreted by the student-
designer to mean that there are to be given to him lists of names
and addresses of manufacturers to whom he can apply for, and
from whom he can obtain, a position. To furnish such lists,
as has been pointed out already, would be impracticable for the
reasons mentioned.

The purpose here is to give only general suggestions as to the
kind of firms to approach, each individual student then applying
these general directions to the local circumstances and conditions in his own city, town, or locality.

28. In the smaller towns, the enterprising novice will
already know the names of every individual or firm that could
possibly use any one with drawing ability. In the larger towns
there are business directories that will reveal at once the names
and addresses wanted. In case the young designer has definite
ideas in regard to the line of work he wishes to take up, his best
plan will be to procure copies of the various trade papers in that
line and secure the desired names and addresses from the advertising pages, selecting those that are located in the city nearest
to him. When a visit is made to that city additional firm names

may be secured by referring to the city business directory. Carefully arranged lists of these firms should be made in a notebook, and so classified by streets and numbers that personal calls may be made upon them, if advisable, with the least expenditure of time and effort. These names can be made use of in any of the methods already described or that may seem best.

29. Advantage of Having a Regular Position.—The two methods of marketing a design training have already been discussed; namely, the free-lance method, and the salaried-position method, whereby the designer occupies a regular salaried position on the manufacturer's payroll, and works regular hours.

As has already been stated, there are reasons sometimes why the student-designer finds it more convenient to start his career with the free-lance method than to attempt to secure a salaried position. However, there are certain advantages in the salaried-position method, over the free-lance method, that make it perhaps the more satisfactory of the two. It is, of course, the salaried position that is eventually gone into by the designer. Some of its advantages are as follows:

The method of working in the salaried position, when once artistic, technical, and business ability has enabled the designer to obtain a position, assures him a steady and regular income each week or month. It also enables him to devote his entire energies to the artistic work of designing, as he is free from business or "bread-and-butter" worries, which is an important matter to the designer. Further, and perhaps most important of all, the designer in a salaried position is connected with, and has access at all times to, the printing and weaving machinery, or other methods by which the finished fabric or object is turned out in the factory, and can therefore be learning something every day about the technical processes of production, and can thus improve his work and eventually increase his salary or earnings.

30. Importance of Having a Definite Aim.—A training in designing, the ability to prepare usable designs, is just as much a commodity as a loaf of bread or a safety razor; and the matter of marketing it requires similar skill. The training the young designer must have before he can market his ability has been already discussed, and it has been shown that an important part of the training is to know what are the available fields of handicrafts and industrial designing. The beginner has been made acquainted with the fields, and the matter of selling artistic ability in these fields will now be discussed.

The first step toward getting a position as a designer is to decide definitely what kind of a position is wanted. If a person simply wanders around aimlessly, ready to do, as he terms it, "anything in the art line," it is quite unlikely that he will get any position that is worth while, if, indeed, he gets any at all. In the field of commercial art in general, there is a wide range from which to choose; in the case of handicrafts designing and industrial designing, however, the fields are more specifically defined. Whatever may have been the Course studied, the student-designer must carefully investigate and find the exact kind of position for which he is best fitted.

31. Initial Salary Versus Aptitude and Fitness.—The average art student, on being asked what line of practical design work he would select to follow, will reply that he will take the one that pays the most salary. However, to take the first step of one's life work for the flimsy reason that the reputed initial salary seems to be attractive, irrespective of one's liking or one's talent for that work, is an extremely unwise and short-sighted policy. Frequently, these attractive salaries demand exceptional ability, and if, through some influence or pretense, the young artist has secured such a position and cannot make good in it, he will not hold it long. It is far more sensible to get into a line of work for which one is suited, even if at first the salary is little or nothing, for here the desire of the novice to learn the details of the business is met by the opportunity to do so, and the result is eventual advancement.

32. Starting in Home Town Instead of Large City. The consensus of opinion, of those who know from experience what is best, is that the novice should first get some commercial design experience in his home town or vicinity before rushing away to the large city to try his fortune. The statement is made by one of the foremost artists in the United States that in New York City alone there are thousands of artists, and that among these the competition for work is very keen. They are constantly soliciting work from manufacturers and publishers. It can thus be seen how little chance an inexperienced outsider from a distant town stands in the matter of locating in a large city for the pursuit of commercial art work. Such outsiders are frankly advised not to go to New York City or other large cities unless they have definite assurance, from actual concrete experience, that they can make a comfortable living there.

The best plan for the beginner to pursue is to make his start in his own home town, or in one of the smaller cities, if possible; because living expenses are far less there than in the large cities, and there is little or no competition.

REACHING MANUFACTURERS AND HEAD DESIGNERS

33. Designer Must Make Himself Known.—If the popular conception about the designer were a true one, he might in the privacy of his own home or studio, or at his leisure, prepare designs for any purpose that might strike his fancy, and then have buyers come in scores to purchase. This conception, however, is quite contrary to actual trade conditions. Every commodity, whether it is a suit of clothes or an art training, must be properly advertised before it can be sold.

Manufacturers and other users of drawings are not going to go so far as to break down the door of the young designer's home or enter his private sanctum in their eagerness to have him make drawings for them. He must make himself known to these men and also convince them that he can be of sufficient business-getting value to them to justify their paying for his services. Such a state of affairs may be extremely unwelcome to students of decided "artistic temperament." In such cases, the first step should be to get rid of the "artistic temperament" and secure good business judgment in its place.

34. Methods of Approach.—It is very essential that the young designer desiring to obtain a position or sell work should go where a demand for such exists. It is unsatisfactory to conduct such negotiations by mail. There are cases where positions are secured by mail without the employer's seeing the designer, but they are rare and exceptional. Eventually, the designer must come face to face with his employer and conduct business on that basis. Therefore, when the young designer has settled in a town or city where there is demand for services such as his, it is important that he understand the various methods by which he may make himself known to manufacturers and other users of drawings. Some of these methods have already been suggested, but will bear repeating. They are:

1. *Personal letters, circular matter, follow-up letters, and business cards sent out to the trade.*

Whether the artist seeks a regular position at handicrafts designing or at industrial designing, he should prepare and send out special typewritten letters, signed with his pen signature, or artistically printed announcements, setting forth his qualifications and fitness for undertaking the commercial-design work of the manufacturers to whom they are sent, and requesting an opportunity to call, and to try some work on assignment. Business cards, and, if possible, reproductions of some of his work, should be sent with these letters. These should be followed by proper follow-up letters until some result is secured. If this plan is used on all possible employers of designers it will surely be productive of results.

2. *Enrolling with some artists' syndicate or agency.*

Syndicates and agencies, for an entrance fee of $5 or $10 and a 10 to 20 per cent. commission on all work sold, perform a valuable service in disposing of young designers' work to the manufacturer. There are a number of such agencies that are reliable and that, owing to their acquaintance with publishing houses and manufacturing concerns and the kind of art work needed by these concerns, are able to serve as agents for the beginner in getting his work accepted by manufacturers. Names of such syndicates can be obtained from the advertising pages of various art magazines, or even the popular fiction magazines.

3. *Enrolling with high-grade employment agencies.*

The system of high-grade employment agencies is somewhat similar to that of the artists' syndicates, although the service is not as sure of results. Only such employment agencies should be consulted as offer high-grade service, such as the securing of professional engagements for writers, artists, and department managers. The average employment agency devoted to the placing of unskilled labor will be of no service to the young artist.

4. *Advertisements in trade papers and newspapers.*

The experience of most designers has been that high-grade work is not usually secured through advertisements in the daily papers. There are many reasons for this, one of which is that such advertisements are usually those of unskilled labor. Manufacturers and managers do not usually have the time to search laboriously through such columns of advertisements. They know, too, that they would not find high-grade designers there. However, an advertisement placed in the classified columns of the trade papers of various manufacturing lines is sometimes productive of results.

5. *The personal interview.*

The various methods of approach that have been discussed are all subordinate to and must eventually result in that form of approach which is really the only sure one, namely, the personal interview, and this will now be considered.

THE PERSONAL INTERVIEW

35. Advantages of the Personal Interview.—Obviously, the advantage rests with the designer-applicant who can call on the manufacturer with specimens of his work. In fact, the majority of concerns insist on a personal call, and will not consider any application unless made personally. Most managers of art departments of manufacturing concerns make it a rule not to employ a man permanently before seeing him, talking to him, and trying him in the work. In the commercial world, a piece of design work is usually wanted in a hurry, and if there is a designer whom the art manager can call at once, that is the designer who will get that particular work.

36. Making the Appointment.—Personal interviews should be arranged for by appointment. Not only will the applicant stand a better chance of reaching the man he wants to see, but a better impression will thus be made. Little consideration is accorded to the applicant who rushes into a man's office or studio unannounced, in a manner suggestive of the cheap book agent. Appointments may be made in various ways; personally, through a friend, or by telephone, but the one that accords best with business courtesy and is most likely to bring good results is to make the appointment by personal letter.

The following form of such a letter is typical of what might be used for this purpose. No applicant should copy it verbatim, for it would probably not suit his individual case in every detail.

880 Main St., Jonesville, Pa.
October 1, 19—

Mr. James Hill,
Manager of Art Dept.,
The Bennett Co.,
Jonesville, Pa.
Dear Sir:
I greatly desire to connect myself with your firm in the capacity of designer in your Art Department, and I believe that my artistic training has been such that I can do work in your line that will be acceptable to you and in accord with the high standards of your firm. Will you give me permission to call and show you specimens of my work, with a view of demonstrating my ability to hold such a position?
Very truly,
Grant E. Harris

Letters of this character, asking for appointments, should be sent out to as many art managers, and manufacturers, as possible. Out of a dozen letters of this kind there should be several replies granting the desired interviews.

37. Preparing for the Interview.—First, the designer-applicant should prepare a portfolio, not a package (for packages are too hard to open at the critical moment) containing as many specimens as possible of his designs, along the particular line of work put out by the firm on which he is going to make the call. He should also include in his portfolio examples of other work he has done, not necessarily in line with that particular firm's needs. These examples of his work will serve to give to the prospective employer a comprehensive idea of the scope of the applicant's ability.

Second, he should prepare, to accompany these drawings, a "line of talk" that will be so skilfully arranged as to convince the art manager that he needs the services of the designer-applicant. This carefully arranged series of arguments and proofs should have as its ultimate purpose the immediate employment of the applicant, yet it should be remembered that there might possibly be no opening just then, so an additional "line of talk" should be kept ready in order to impress on the art manager the applicant's strong desire not only to have his name and address kept on file but to have his personality and the character of his work kept personally in the mind of the art manager, so that, when there is any hurry-up demand for work, the applicant may be sent for and given a chance.

Third, he should dress as neatly as possible, and pay unusual attention to his personal appearance before entering the office of the man to be seen. To look as prosperous as possible, even though one may not feel that way, pays, for the busy manager or head designer has no time to expend in sympathy on the run-down appearance or hard-luck story of the applicant.

And, last of all, the applicant should present himself *exactly* at the time appointed, neither before nor after. If the appointed time is 9 o'clock, he should not appear at 8:50 or 9:10; either would at once put him in a bad light in the eyes of the prospective employer. And he should take with him the art manager's letter in which the interview was promised; also a business card, to send in to the office if required.

38. The Interview.—Although a becoming modesty is essential, the applicant should not allow himself to become the victim of stage fright, which would probably cause him to forget all the carefully arranged points of his "line of talk." The art manager is a human being like himself and can be talked to with perfect freedom, as man to man; but he is busy and expects the applicant to come to the point at once. The applicant's remarks should thereupon be somewhat as follows:

"Mr. Hill, I have called, in accordance with your permission in this letter (showing it), to show you my qualifications as a designer, and to ask that you give me an opportunity, either by some work on assignment or by letting me start work modestly in your art room, to demonstrate that I can be of service to you, as I firmly believe I can.

"In this portfolio (opening it) I have some drawings, some of which were made during my course of art study and others made as practical work, along your line (mentioning it). I realize that perhaps few, if any, of these drawings could be utilized by you at the present time, but I want them to serve as concrete evidence that I feel a particular aptitude for the work of (here mention his line; also show the drawings, properly commenting on each).

"Here (showing the other set of work in the portfolio) I have some other drawings, not exactly along your line, which I have brought to demonstrate the carefulness of drawing and thoroughness of rendering I try to employ in all my work.

"Do you think my work indicates an ability on my part that would justify you in giving me an opportunity to try some work in your art room?" (Certain art managers deftly avoid looking at the applicant's drawings; therefore, every effort must be made to have the art manager actually *look at* the specimens the applicant brings along.)

The art manager will then probably ask: "What commercial-art experience have you had, Mr. Harris?"

The reply to this should be: "I have not been employed by any one in a salaried position, but I have some familiarity with the processes of manufacture of your line of goods, business conditions, and other practical features of preparing drawings for commercial-design work. Some of this information I received in connection with the concluding work in my regular course in designing, where I was required to do assignment designs of a practical character, some of which I have just shown to you. Further, some of my designs for (naming the purpose) have given me not only a knowledge of processes, but some insight into commercial conditions in that line. Of course, if I were given the opportunity to come into your designing room I would expect and would be willing to start right at the bottom and learn your requirements."

The next remark of the art manager will very likely be: "Well, Mr. Harris, your designs interest me, but I regret to say that we really have no need now of another designer. I'm sorry, but I'm afraid we can do nothing for you."

The reply to this should be very tactful and respectful, somewhat as follows:

"Mr. Hill, you will pardon me if I press the matter a little further, but I am very anxious to have an opportunity of convincing you that I can do work that will be of service to you. Could you not arrange to let me have desk room somewhere in your designing room and let me try small, unimportant things at first, or even be of service to your regular designers in helping them on details? Would you not be willing to make some such arrangement?"

In many cases the art managers, if the applicant's drawings show promise, are willing to try out a young designer in this way. When once this opportunity has been secured, the battle has been more than half won; and it then rests with the artist to take advantage of this opportunity and, by careful observation, close attention to orders, hard work, and a tactful demeanor, to prove his worth.

Should the applicant be told again, finally and definitely, that there is nothing for him, that there is no position vacant and that none can be created, nothing remains for the applicant but to make a courteous withdrawal. However, he should not lose the opportunity of impressing himself and his personality strongly on the man with whom he holds the interview, and of requesting this man to keep him in mind should any assignment work come up or should any position be vacant. To this end, the applicant should leave with the manager one of his business cards, containing his name and address, and a general outline of the character of his work.

If interviews of this character are held with all possible manufacturers and other users of drawings, and the list of such firms in every city is very large, there is every reason to believe that sooner or later the applicant will be able to place himself in a position. After that, his advancement and progress in the field of designing depends entirely on himself.

39. The Commercial Viewpoint.—The methods outlined for getting in touch with those who need the services of
designers will eventually result in positions secured. It must
be remembered, however, that the applicant will receive many
rebuffs before he is finally successful. To those applicants
who may be unusually sensitive or easily discouraged, it is
well to explain just why their propositions are sometimes
rejected by busy manufacturers. If such reasons are well
understood, not only will all cause for discouragement or
chagrin disappear, but the applicant may by this means be
enabled to be properly armed against future rejections.

These prospective employers of designers are really merchants
who sell goods. In considering whether or not to take on a new
assistant or helper, it is not alone the artistic ability of the
applicant that must be considered. The chief consideration
is whether or not the proposed services of the artist will enable
them to increase the sale of their tiles, parquetry, linoleum,
carpets, wallpapers, etc. The following reasons may help to
explain the rejection of the applicant or his work.

40. Services Not Needed.—No matter how capable the
young designer may be, it frequently happens that the man or
the firm to whom he applies for work does not need him. The
question is not one of ability but one of the economic law of
supply and demand; the supply exists but not the demand.
The reason may also be that the condition of the volume of
the employer's business, either in its present state or its future
prospects, makes it inadvisable to take on more help at the
time, or that the artist-applicant's line of work is such that it
could not be made use of by that particular employer.

As an illustration, the artist could not expect to secure a
position in the designing room of an establishment that had
just laid off a number of its experienced artists on account of
hard times, or because of the adoption of a policy of retrench-
ment. Again, it would be useless for the applicant to try to
interest a wallpaper manufacturer, for instance in carpet

designs; or, as another instance, to try to secure a position as
stained-glass designer, on the strength of mosaic tile designs
he might submit.

41. Personality Objectionable to Employer.—The
designer as an individual will be closely scrutinized and will be
considered from the standpoint of personality, what kind of
an impression he makes on his prospective employer. His
appearance, his manner, his disposition, and his apparent
character, as well as his artistic ability, will be taken into consideration. It is the employer who is going to pay the salary.
No resentment, therefore, is justifiable when the employer, in
exercising his right of choice, decides that the applicant would
not make a congenial or helpful employe, and therefore rejects
him.

42. Drawings Not Needed Because of Overstock.
There are certain kinds of work that all young designers think
are easy to do; and they do quantities of it. Such work also
can be readily done in the manufacturer's own designing department and he is likely to have a good supply of it on hand at
most times. If, therefore, the applicant's specimens are of
these kinds and give no marked indications of ability to do work
out of the ordinary class, his chances of obtaining a position
are remote.

43. Designs Not Satisfactory.—The applicant may consider his own work very good, but it may not be sufficiently
satisfactory to the manufacturer to warrant him in employing
the artist, for the following reasons:

1. The designs submitted may not have been made for
definite commercial uses. The designs carried in the portfolio
should be designs for the specific line of industrial art work
turned out by the manufacturer being interviewed, and not
simply some ingenious pattern arrangement, plant study, or
color arrangement.

2. Submitted designs, although apparently made for the
trade, may have been prepared without a thorough knowledge
of technical processes of manufacture, all very evident to the
discerning eye of the manufacturer inspecting them.

3. The designs that are shown to the prospective employer may be good in line and mass, but poor in color. Examples of this fault are very common; and designers submitting such designs are very reluctantly rejected by manufacturers. In such lines as carpet designing, wallpaper designing, and stained-glass window designing, it is absolutely necessary that the harmony and beauty of color schemes must be very pronounced. If the designer cannot show these he is very likely to be rejected.

4. Submitted designs may sometimes be overloaded with useless details instead of being well designed from the standpoint of good space distribution; and this will cause the rejection of the designer.

5. Designs submitted, in which historic period styles are incorporated, may be not correctly drawn, not appropriate or not consistent. Designers submitting such careless designs (for which there is no excuse) are usually rejected.

It would be possible to enumerate other reasons why applicants for positions as designers are sometimes rejected, but those already given are ample. The student has received a sufficiently thorough training in artistic designing to enable him to avoid making the mistakes enumerated. It is, then, simply a matter of ordinary care on his part for him to be able to avoid many of the reverses and rejections experienced by the careless designer who applies for a position.

* * *

SALARIES PAID TO DESIGNERS

44. Earnings of Handicrafts Designers.—No exact figures can be given as to what any class of designers can or do earn. The question is frequently asked by the design student, "What line of designing pays best; what line will enable me to earn the most money?" Such a question cannot be answered with definiteness. Personal ability, local and business conditions, and a score of other matters influence money earned by designers. As previously stated, there is no union wage scale for artists; they can earn just as much as their technical ability, business enterprise, tact, and energy, will bring.

It cannot be said that an artist can earn more at one line than at another. For instance, Mr. A. might be able to earn $40 a week in the designing rooms of a carpet factory, and Mr. B. might not be able to earn $15 in the same work, because he is not particularly adapted to it. But Mr. B. may be making $50 a week as designer and solicitor for stained-glass window work, in which line Mr. A., the $40-a-week carpet designer might not be able to earn even $15 a week as assistant designer. Further, Mr. M., a professional stained-glass designer and sales agent, with strong natural aptitudes for, and with thorough artistic training and experience in, stained-glass work, may earn $75 or $100 a week; but this fact cannot furnish any absolute proof to student N. that he, too, can earn $75 or $100 each week, even though he has taken a training course in that same line. His opportunities, the customs of the particular locality and firm, and even his own energy and enterprise may be far different from those of Mr. M.

45. In the case of handicrafts designing done on the free-lance basis, the designer's earnings cannot be even estimated. Of course, the more business the designer gets for himself, in the form of commissions, and the harder he works, the greater will be his earnings. What is paid for individual designs on this basis depends on conditions previously outlined; no definite figures can be given in any line.

For those who do not want to take the introductory risks incident to free-lance work, the salaried position is the thing to try for; and in casting about for a position certain common-sense principles must be considered. For instance, the artist-applicant is more likely to have steady and well-paying work if he engages in designing for some line of mercantile goods for which there is a staple public demand. Further, it is wise to get with some large, well-established concern, even though obliged to start on little or no salary, where opportunities for advancement are given to the ambitious and enterprising young artist. As has been previously stated, the young designer should make an intelligent choice of the line of work to which his training and circumstances best adapt him and then work himself up in that line. The pursuit of handicrafts design work will furnish one with a comfortable living; but it will not make one a millionaire. It is no get-rich-quick scheme or short cut to wealth, but a legitimate profession requiring hard and continuous effort.

46. Earnings of Industrial Designers.—If it were possible to make any kind of an estimate as to the average salaries paid by manufacturers and art-room managers to their designers employed on regular salary, it might be said that, if he is of any use at all, a designer should start at about $10 or $15 a week. In a very short time advances to $20 a week might come, if he increases his usefulness by endeavoring to improve his artistic and technical ability and become acquainted with the business policies of the company. If he continues to improve, he might advance to $30, $40, or even $50 a week, when he would be known as a high-grade man. If he receives as high as $75 a week, he must be a specialist, and can consider himself exceptionally well paid.

The most moderate salaries are paid to the novice in the tile, parquetry, and linoleum fields; beginning at about $10 or $15 a week. As the designer enters the wallpaper and carpet fields, salaries are higher—say $25 to $40 a week for good designers. In the work of stained-glass window designing opportunities are perhaps the best of all, for here, although the novice may start as low as $15 or $20 a week, it is possible for him to get as high as $75 a week if, in addition to his designing, he can also do glass painting. If he combines business and salesmanship with his designing his opportunities are good for earning even more than $75 a week.

TYPICAL EXPERIENCES IN OBTAINING POSITIONS

47. Advantage of Knowing How Others Succeed. When one has some new and strange task to perform, or is confronted by new conditions, he wants to know how some other beginner has acted under similar conditions. No two experiences of beginners endeavoring to obtain a position could possibly be alike, yet the citing of the experiences of a number of commercial designers who are now well established in their professions may be interesting and helpful. Although no one could expect to follow the exact procedure of the artists whose experiences are given, yet some of these experiences may serve to further emphasize the points of information and advice already given. It is hoped, also, that they may serve as a guide and an encouragement to some young applicants who are now passing through the stage of hunting a position or perhaps of apprentice service and to whom success seems slow in coming.

It is not easy to get a successful designer to say much of value about the struggles of his early days, the time when he started in the field of commercial art. These designers are liable to avoid the real issue by omitting important things and by unduly emphasizing those of little importance. Some will declare that their whole career, up until recent years, has been one long battle against starvation, and will give a series of hard-luck stories to illustrate how their own personal will power overcame their difficulties. Others will speak slightingly of the institutions where they actually received their art training, and will call themselves "self-trained" men. Still others will ridicule any attempt to classify or put on an accurate basis the matter of obtaining a position, and will speak of the whole thing as luck. All this is totally misleading and works harm on the impressionable mind of the novice. There is also a great deal of conceit and deception in such statements, for they are frequently used by a certain class of designers to cover up conditions in the earlier days of their careers which were not so rosy.

48. Fortunately, however, there are many serious-minded artists, now successful, who are willing to have it known by what means they have arrived at their present positions, if in that way aspiring young designers can be helped. It is the experiences of such artists that are given here. These artists were graduates of systematic training courses in commercial designing, just as are the students who read these pages, and their efforts to obtain positions are told in language that is plain and unmistakable, and uncolored by romantic untruths.

Mr. L., a graduate of a regular 4 years' collegiate course, studied 4 years more at an art school on a course in design. On seeking a position, many odd jobs at lettering, show-card writing work, etc., were offered him at salaries anywhere from $6 to $9 a week. He saw that such work would mean little advancement, so he tried through correspondence for a salaried position in several large cities, submitting examples of his work. After a personal interview with a tile manufacturer he was engaged as their designer. He secured a permanent stopping place in that city, returned to his native town to settle up his affairs there, packed his trunk and was all ready to start for his new position, when he received a telegram from the firm telling him not to come because their former designer had returned. After this setback he secured a position as a stained-glass designer in a Western city at a salary of $16 a week. After working there 3 years and learning the business he came East again. His salary with the new firm was increased to $25, then to $30, and later to $40 a week on account of his increased usefulness in doing the business correspondence for the firm and in soliciting contracts.

Miss S., trained in design work but with no commercial experience, simply submitted her art-school designs to a prominent manufacturer of silverware and was at once employed on the merits of her designs, because the manufacturer had judgment enough to see that her services would be useful to him.

Miss N. had a training in design and figure drawing. She established a small handicrafts shop in her own town, where she sold her own handicrafts designs and also that of others on commission. She also formed a class, to which she gave instruction in design and handicrafts work. She was energetic, had a pleasing personality, and was not averse to keeping her friends advised of her work, and what she had to sell, also doing much judicious advertising. She sold some clever designs to magazine publishers, but could not do justice to such work because she was obliged to submit them by mail. She also wrote and illustrated articles on artistic matters, and had no trouble in getting them accepted and published by magazines devoted to art. Later she became an instructor in an art school not far from her home town, at a very satisfactory salary.

Miss X., after taking a course in design, secured a position with an interior decorating firm. She began on a small salary, but, as she had good knowledge of historic styles, she was allowed to do original designing just as soon as she became familiar with the method of working with that firm. She later made an arrangement with them whereby she could work for them 6 months of each year, spending the other months at her home in a distant city. She took advantage of this long vacation to prepare many designs for wallpapers, textiles, etc., disposing of them to manufacturers when she returned to the city in the winter months. She now gives her entire time to independent work in designing.

Mr. C. had a general training in design. He first worked in the art department of the manufacturer of a well-known article of merchandise. Later he was employed as a designer of wall coverings and tapestries in an interior decorating establishment. Although not having a specialized training in the technicalities of this industry, he soon became acquainted with them by doing actual work in the studio.

Mr. F., a design graduate with a fair knowledge of historic styles and figure drawing, and much skill in producing harmonious and effective color arrangements, first secured employment as a designer for jig-saw puzzles. In the meantime he interviewed all the well-known interior decorators, showing examples of his work. Sometimes he was given courteous treatment and sometimes received little attention. He was familiar with the demands in the field of interior decorating work and, therefore, when an opening for a designer of tapestry presented itself, he was ready for it and got it. He did good work here for 2 years and then left to become a designer for a large and well-known company manufacturing silverware.

Many other typical experiences of young designers in their attempts to obtain positions could be enumerated; but those that have been cited are sufficient to serve as an inspiration and encouragement to the student about to seek a position as industrial designer.

PRACTICAL APPLICATION OF TRAINING

IMPORTANCE OF INDIVIDUAL EFFORT

49. Equipment Furnished the Student.—Doubtless the student has made it his custom, at the end of each subject of his Course, to pause and make a survey of what has been learned in that subject. Such a stock-taking process of his entire Course should now be conducted. When this is done it will be found that he has acquired an equipment for practical commercial work that can be secured from no other source.

Not only has a technical training, including drawing, designing, rendering, and the technical designing for handicrafts as well as industrial purposes been given, but also a business training, in which information and advice have been given as to selling drawings and obtaining a position. Beyond this point the art instructor cannot go; he has done all that any person is able and can be expected to do.

50. Student's Duty in Using This Equipment.—No training course of instruction in a technical line, nor information and advice on the proper marketing of such a training, can actually secure a position or a commission for the young artist. He must do that himself.

The graduate art student has only begun the carrying out of his duty to himself. He has received a practical art training that will serve as the foundation for some specific line in the field of commercial designing, and has been given practical advice as to where and how to apply this training commercially. It is now the designer's duty to take hold of his destiny from this point forward.

One may purchase an overcoat to keep himself warm, but unless the overcoat is used, it will of no service. Likewise, one may have purchased a scholarship and may have pursued a course in artistic design, but, unless he makes use of that training, he cannot consistently expect to receive any benefit therefrom. He cannot expect, from the mere fact that he has gone through a prescribed order of studies and has received a diploma, that his training will work in some patented automatic manner to bring him an income. His training is simply an outfit of tools by which he is to work out a successful career.

For this reason, the graduate art student who experiences difficulty at first in securing paying work or getting a position, cannot reasonably lay the blame for this state of affairs upon anybody except himself. It is his duty to acquaint himself with the available lines of commercial design work and how to enter them, and then to put this knowledge into actual practice. If he does not do so it is simply an evidence of indolence and lack of enterprise; with the result that his chances of securing a position will be small.

However, the student of this Course has a considerable advantage over the average art student in having been given information and advice, not obtainable elsewhere in print, that should enable him to eliminate the greenhorn stage. It will now require the exercise of only a reasonable amount of personal effort to make practical application of this information in securing a position or doing salable work.

FINAL WORD OF ADVICE

51. Appeal to Student to Apply His Training.—The experience in giving training to students in various applied-art subjects has been so extensive as to make the Schools acquainted with very many types of students, and their attitude toward their Course. It has been observed that many whose work on the individual subjects was of the highest quality, thus giving promise of assured successes in practical work, were timid and diffident when it came to actually making the effort to secure positions or commissions. They seemed to lack the courage to actually interview users of designs, as previously advised. The result was that their training was, on this account, of no practical use to them. Unfortunately, such

students would frequently, and very unjustly, place the blame
for their lack of success upon their Course of instruction or
their instructors, failing to see, or unwilling to see, that their
failure rested with themselves.

It is hoped that the student who has brought this Course to
a successful termination will step out with confidence and courage into the field of practical art work knowing that he is well
equipped to make a start in it.   He must not expect to secure
at once, however, the highest-grade position, or to do work up
to the standard of the well-known designers; that standard of
work comes only after years of practical experience.   But he has
the assurance that his training is sufficiently artistic and practical to enable him to get a start in the particular line he has
selected.   If his search for a position is carried on persistently
and intelligently, and interviews are tactfully arranged for and
held, eventually a position will be obtained.   The securing and
holding of subsequent positions will then be a simple matter.

52.   A Special Request.—The purpose of the Course has
been to give the student a training that, properly applied and
used, will secure for him an income; and this purpose is fulfilled in the case of such students as make the practical application.   Of these, many notify their instructors of their
successes in selling work or obtaining good positions, but there
is reason to believe that many others, for various reasons,
never tell their instructors of their successes.

All students are urged to remember that their instructors'
interest in them does not cease when they have completed their
Courses, but that this interest is extended also to the practical commercial work they do after graduating.   No matter
whether this practical work is merely a small free-lance commission or the securing of a desirable position at a good salary,
the student should tell his instructors about it, giving all the
details.

He must remember that his instructors are just as keenly
interested in his success as they were in his progress through the
Course, and want to learn of such success.   This will assure his
instructors that they have done their full duty to the student.

INDEX

NOTE.—In this Volume, each Section is complete in itself and has a number. This number is printed at the top of every page of the Section in the headline opposite the page number, and to distinguish the Section number from the page number, the Section number is preceded by a section mark (§). In order to find a reference, glance along the inside edges of the headlines until the desired Section number is found, then along the page numbers of that Section until the desired page is found. Thus, to find the reference "Brushes, §13, p8," turn to the Section marked §13, then to page 8 of that Section.

A

Acids, Etching with, §14, p39; §20, p26
  Stenciling with, §13, p17
Advantage of regular position, §21, p29
Advertising in trade papers, §21, p33
Advice, Final word of, §21, p47
  Value of professional, §21, p3
Affixing tesseræ to plan drawing, §16, p12
Agency, Artists', §21, p9
Air-brush work in colors, §14, p16
Amateur designs analyzed, §17, p37
American style, §20, p23
Antique glass, §20, p10
  style, §20, p23
Appeal to the student, An, §21, p47
Appearance of stencil-print, §13, p49
Applied faience, §16, p28
Applicant, Why, is rejected, §21, p38
Application of design principles, §18, p13
  of training, Practical, §21, p46
Applying gold to china, §15, p26
  the blocks to the fabric, §13, p56
Appointment, Making the, §21, p34
Approach, Methods of, §21, p32
Aptitude, §21, p30
Arbitrary motifs, Designs from, §13, pp31, 59; §14, p23; §15, p41
Arrangement, Basis of, §16, p6
  of wall surfaces, §19, p59
Arrangements, Diversity of, §19, p59
Article decorated, Shape of, §15, p36
  to be made, §14, pp19, 43
Articles for stenciling, Wood, leather, and metal, §13, p23
  suitable for leather work, §14, p19
  suitable for metal work, §14, p43
Artists' agency, §21, pp9, 32
  syndicate, §21, pp9, 32

289—38

Assembling the glass, §20, p35
Atomizer and dyes, Stenciling with, §13, p15
Avoiding discouragement, §21, p22
Axminster carpet, §18, pp5, 44
  carpet, Designing, §18, p46
  carpet, Manufacture of, §18, p44
  carpet, Patterns for, §18, p46
  carpet, Rendered design for, §18, p48
  carpet, Section of moquette, §18, p44
  carpet, Sizes of, §18, p46
  carpet, Specimen of, §18, p49
  carpet, Weave of chenille, §18, p45
  carpet, Weave of moquette, §18, p44
  Tapestry, §18, p50

B

Backgrounds in a window design, §20, p45
Badger brush, §20, p29
Base plate, §14, p33
Basis of arrangement, §16, p6
  of design, §16, p36
  of pattern arrangement, §16, p25
  of the design, §16, p28
  of the designs, §16, p18
Bathroom decoration with stencil, §13, p42
Bedrooms, Wallpaper for, §19, pp13, 14
Beginners, Painting outfits for, §15, p17
Bending and curving, §14, p40
  work, §14, p40
Block, Mash, §17, p26
  Wooden, §14, p33
  -print designing exercises, §13, p62
  -print, Principle of the, §13, p52
  -printing, Colors for, §13, p56
  -printing, Materials required for, §13, p52
  -printing on fabrics, §13, p56
  -printing, Suitable fabrics for, §13, p56
  prints and printing, §13, p52

Blocking in the pattern, §19, p16
    out design on squared paper, §18, p22
    out on squared paper, §18, pp35, 40, 46, 53
Blocks, Applying the, to the fabric, §13, p56
    Jig-saw method of making, §13, p53
    Outline, §17, p24
    Preparing printing, §17, p23
Body Brussels carpet, Specimen of, §18, p33
Brass, §14, p30
Brush and pigment, Stenciling with,
    §13, p12
    Badger, §20, p29
    Stippler, §20, p29
Brushes, §13, p8
    for china painting, §15, p12
Brussels carpet, §18, pp4, 6
    carpet, Characteristic weave of, §18, p8
    carpets, Designing, §18, p13
    carpet, Manufacture of, §18, p6
    carpet, Rendered design for, §18, p31
    carpet, Patterns for, §18, p14
    carpet, Specimen of body, §18, p33
    carpets, Sizes of, §18, p12
    Tapestry, §18, p50
    Wilton compared with, §18, p34
Building up a clientele, §21, p9
Bunsen burner, §14, p33
Burlap effects, §19, p23
Burning the leather, §14, p15
Burnishing brush, Glass, §15, p17
    gold, §15, p28
Burnt-leather work, §14, p14
Business cards, §21, p32
    cards and letters, §21, p7

                    C

Canvass, Personal, §21, p9
Cards and letters, Business, §21, p7
    Business, §21, p32
Care in outlining, Observing, §17, p34
    of kiln, §15, p34
Carpet, Axminster, §18, pp5, 44
    Brussels, §18, pp4, 6
    Characteristic weave of Brussels, §18, p8
    Characteristic weave of Wilton, §18, p33
    Cross-section of ingrain, §18, p39
    Cut-pile, §18, p33
    Design for definite kind of, §18, p13
    Designing Axminster, §18, p46
    -designing exercises, §18, p66
    Forms of tapestry, §18, p51
    Frames for Wilton, §18, p35
    Ingrain, §18, pp5, 38
    Kidderminster, §18, pp5, 38
    Manufacture of Axminster, §18, p44
    Manufacture of Brussels, §18, p6

Carpet, Manufacture of ingrain, §18, p38
    Manufacture of Kidderminster, §18, p38
    Manufacture of Wilton, §18, p33
    Patterns for Axminster, §18, p46
    Patterns for Brussels, §18, p14
    Planting for Wilton, §18, p35
    Printing tapestry, §18, p51
    Rendered design for Axminster, §18, p48
    Rendered design for Brussels, §18, p31
    Rendered design for ingrain, §18, p42
    Rendered design for Wilton, §18, p36
    Section of moquette Axminster, §18, p44
    Section of tapestry, §18, p50
    Sizes of Axminster, §18, p46
    Sizes of Wilton, §18, p35
    Specimen of Axminster, §18, p49
    Specimen of ingrain, §18, p42
    Specimen of tapestry, §18, p54
    Specimen of Wilton, §18, p36
    Specimens of body Brussels, §18, p33
    Tapestry, §18, p5
    Velvet, §18, p33
    Weave of moquette Axminster, §18, p44
    Weave of chenille Axminster, §18, p45
    Wilton, §18, pp4, 33
    Wood, §16, p34
Carpets, §18, p3
    and rugs, §21, p17
    Characteristics of tapestry, §18, p50
    Classification of, §18, p4
    Designing Brussels, §18, p13
    Designing ingrain, §18, p40
    Designing tapestry, §18, p53
    Designing Wilton, §18, p35
    General types of, §18, p4
    History of, §18, p4
    Manufacture of tapestry, §18, p50
    Patterns for ingrain, §18, p40
    Patterns for tapestry, §18, p53
    Patterns for Wilton, §18, p35
    Sizes of Brussels, §18, p12
    Sizes of ingrain, §18, p40
    Sizes of tapestry, §18, p53
    Tapestry, §18, p50
Cartoon, Preparing the stained-glass,
    §20, p62
Cartridge paper, §19, p23
Cathedral glass, §20, p11
    style, §20, p23
Cementing the window, §20, p39
Character of designs for hearth tiling,
    §16, p25
    of designs for wall tiling, §16, p25
    of luster colors, §15, p29

Characteristic weave of Brussels carpet,
§18, p8
weave of Wilton carpet, §18, p33
Characteristics of leather handicrafts,
§14, p1
of machine-made rugs, §18, p60
of metal handicrafts, §14, p1
of oriental rugs, §18, p56
of tapestry carpets, §18, p50
Charcoal kiln, The, §15, p32
Chasing, §14, p37
Materials and tools for, §14, p35
Outline, §14, p35
Chenille Axminster carpet, Weave of,
§18, p45
Children's bedrooms, Wallpaper for, §19,
p13
China, applying gold to, §15, p26
Coloring for, §15, p50
Color schemes for, §15, p50
colors, Examples of, §15, p51
colors, Palette for, §15, p15
crayons, §15, p5
decoration, §15, p2
decoration, Status of, §15, p1
decoration, Transfer-picture, §15, p3
-decoration designing exercises, §15, p75
Designing decoration for, §15, p36
Devices for stacking, §15, p33
Firing the, §15, p31
Gold painting on, §15, p25
Luster painting on, §15, p29
Methods of decorating, §15, p2
Methods of working on, §15, p18
painting like other painting, §15, p24
painting, Materials required for, §15, p4
Painting on, §15, p4
painting, Color theory applied to, §15, p50
Placing, in a kiln, §15, p34
Printing on, §15, p3
Stacking, in a kiln, §15, p34
surface, Tinting the, §15, p19
The firing of, §15, p31
Transferring design to, §15, p21
Chinaware, §15, p4
Classes of decorated, §15, p2
Chisel, §14, p32
Circular matter, §21, p32
City, Home town versus, §21, p30
Choice of line of handicrafts work, §13, p1
Choosing the proper field, §21, pp13, 28
Classes of decorated chinaware, §15, p2
of decorative leather work, §14, p5
of design motifs, §14, p45
of designs, §17, p29
of metal suitable for tooling, §14, p30

Classification of carpets, §18, p3
of hardwood floors, §16, p32
of linoleum, §17, p2
of oilcloth, §17, p22
of rugs, §18, p55
of tiles, §16, p3
Clientele, Building up a, §21, p9
Color blocks, §19, p3
in a window design, §20, p43
in oilcloth designs, §17, p28
pad, The, §13, p53
rollers, §19, p3
schemes for china, §15, p50
schemes, Trying out, §19, p17
theory applied to china painting, §15, p50
Colored glass, Composition of, §20, p10
leather work, §14, p16
Coloring and finishing, §14, p42
for china, §15, p50
for conventional designs, §15, p54
for figure subjects, §15, p58
for flesh, §15, p58
for flowers, §15, p55
Hints for, §15, p53
leather, §14, p2
sketches for painted windows, §20, p58
the design, §16, pp7, 18, 27, 29, 36; §18, p29
the sketches, §20, p54
Colors, §19, p6
Air-brush work in, §14, p16
available for cork tiles, §17, p5
Character of luster, §15, p29
Economy in use of, §17, p36
Examples of china, §15, p51
Finishing the metal in, §14, p42
for a planted design, §18, p27
for a solid-frame design, §18, p25
for block-printing, §13, p56
Forming the pattern in, §18, p9
Forming the pile in, §18, p9
in tubes, Moist, §15, p9
Luster, §15, p10
Making the sketch design in, §15, p60
Matt, §15, p10
of cork tiles, §17, p3
of encaustic floor tiles, §16, p5
of hearth tiles, §16, p24
of mosaic floor tiles, §16, p8
of wall tiles, §16, p24
Over-glaze, §15, p10
Palette for china, §15, p15
Powder, in vials, §15, p9
Preparing the, §15, p19
Scaled sketch design in, §13, p43
Spattering, §14, p16
Specimens of harmonious, §15, p51

Commercial art, China decoration in, §15, p1
product, Keeping in touch with, §17, pp5, 12
viewpoint, The, §21, p38
Composition applied to linoleum designing, §17, p20
of colored glass, §20, p10
of cork tiling, §17, p3
of floor oilcloth, §17, p23
of linoleum, §17, p10
of table oilcloth, §17, p43
of wall oilcloth, §17, p52
Considerations when designing rugs, §18, p62
Consistent style, Importance of a, §20, p45
Construction work, §14, p40
Conventional designs, Coloring for, §15, p54
Conventional repeating effects, §19, p24
Conventionalized motifs, Partly, §15, p45
motifs, Purely, §15, p44
motifs, Severely, §15, p44
versus naturalistic, §15, p40
Converting historic motif into stencil, §13, p40
Copper, §14, p30
Thickness of sheet, §14, p30
Varieties of sheet, §14, p30
Core, The, §20, p13
Cork-tile designs, Principles of, §17, p4
-tile patterns, Specimens of, §17, p6
tiles, Colors, §17, p3
tiles, Colors available for, §17, p5
tiles, Shapes of, §17, p3
tiles, Sizes of, §17, p3
tiling, §17, pp2, 3
tiling, Composition of, §17, p3
tiling, Designing, §17, p4
tiling, Laying, §17, p4
tiling, Manufacture of, §17, p3
tiling, Typical designs for, §17, p6
tiling, Use of, §17, p3
Corrosive liquids used on leather, §14, p17
Cost, Detail dependent on, §20, p49
Costumes in a window design, §20, p44
Crayons, China, §15, p5
Lithographers', §15, p5
Cross-section of ingrain carpet, §18, p39
Cups, Decorated, §15, p75
Curving, Bending and, §14, p40
Cut leather, Examples of, §14, p28
leather with tooled background, §14, p10
Cut-out leather work over silk, §14, p11
Cut pile carpet, §18, p33
Cutter, Sharpening the glass, §20, p22
The glass, §20, p18

Cutting difficult shapes, §20, p20
leather, §14, p2
Precautions in, §20, p21
simple shapes, §20, p18
tesseræ to shape, §16, p13
the glass, §20, p17
the leather, §14, p12
the patterns, §20, p14
the print block, Designing and, §13, p52
the stencil, Drawing and, §13, p3
the stencil, Tracing and, §13, p48
tool, The, §20, p18
Cylindrical cup, Full-size drawing for, §15, p68

D

Data, Securing preliminary, §20, p46
Dealers, Keeping in touch with, §19, p16
Decalcomania, §15, p3
Decorated china, Examples of, §15, p74
chinaware, Classes of, §15, p2
cups, §15, p75
Gothic period, §20, p6
plates, §15, p75
vases, §15, p75
Decorating china, Methods of, §15, p2
Decoration, China, §15, p2
for china, Designing, §15, p36
Glaze, §15, p3
Over-glaze, §15, p3
Planning, §20, p50
Transfer-picture china, §15, p3
Under-glaze, §15, p2
Decorations on walls, Stenciling, §13, p24
Decorative frieze effects, §19, p54
leather work, Classes of, §14, p5
Definite aim, Importance of, §21, p29
kind of carpet, Design for, §18, p13
Definition of leaded glass, §20, p10
of linoleum, §17, p2
of parquet flooring, §16, p33
of parquetry flooring, §16, p33
of stained glass, §20, p10
of term oilcloth, §17, p22
Della Robbia tile, §16, p31
Demand, Investigating the, §21, p5
Studying public, §21, p14
Design, Backgrounds in a window, §20, p45
Basis of the, §16, pp28, 36
Blocking out, on squared paper, §18, p22
Color in a window, §20, p43
Coloring the, §16, pp7, 18, 27, 29, 36; §18, p29
Colors for a solid-frame, §18, p25
Colors for a planted, §18, p27
Costumes in a window, §20, p44

Design, Drawing and painting the, §15, p60
Drawing the, §13, pp43, 59; §14, pp23, 45;
§19, p16
Figures in a window, §20, p44
for Axminster carpet, Rendered, §18, p48
for Brussels carpet, Rendered, §18, p31
for definite kind of carpet; §18, p13
for ingrain carpet, Rendered, §18, p42
for Wilton carpet, Rendered, §18, p36
from historic motifs, §13, p59
Making full-size, §13, p60
Making the, §16, pp29, 36; §17, p12
Making the full-size drawing or, §15, p66
Making the, in colors, §13, p59
Making the sketch, in colors, §15, p60
motifs, Classes of, §14, p45
Painting the, §15, p24
paper, Use of special, §16, p16
Perspective in a window, §20, p45
Planning the, §13, pp26, 58; §14, pp19, 43;
§15, p36; §19, p9
Preliminary sketch, §13, p25
Preparing the leather and the, §14,
pp10, 11
principles, Application of, §18, p13
Scaled sketch, in colors, §13, p43
Suitability of, to shape, §15, p36
Suitability of, to use, §15, p37
The leather and the, §14, p14
Ticking-in the, §18, p29
Tracing the, §14, pp27, 49; §15, p22
Tracing full-size, §13, p60
training, Marketing a, §21, p4
Transferring full-size, §13, p60
Transferring the, §14, pp8, 27, 35, 37, 38,
39; §15, p22
Transferring, to china, §15, p21
Transferring, to leather, §14, p6
Transferring, to metal, §14, p49
Transparency in a window, §20, p44
work, Requirements for practical, §16, p1
Designer making himself known, §21, p31
Things, must know, §21, p2
Designers, Earnings of handicrafts, §21, p40
Earnings of industrial, §21, p42
Experiences of handicrafts, §21, p25
Experiences of industrial, §21, p27
Reaching head, §21, p31
Salaries paid to, §21, p40
Designing and cutting the print block,
§13, p52
Axminster carpet, §18, p46
Brussels carpets, §18, p13
cork tiling, §17, p4
decoration for china, §15, p36
encaustic floor tiles, §16, p6

Designing exercises, Block-print, §13, p62
exercises, Carpet, §18, p66
exercises, China-decoration, §15, p75
exercises, Leaded-glass, §20, p65
exercises, Leather-work, §14, p52
exercises, Linoleum, §17, p59
exercises, Metal-work, §14, p52
exercises, Oilcloth, §17, p59
exercises, Parquetry, §16, p40
exercises, Rug, §18, p66
exercises, Stained-glass, §20, p65
exercises, Stencil, §13, p62
exercises, Tile, §16, p40
exercises, Wallpaper, §19, p65
faience tiles, §16, p28
Field of industrial, §21, p13
for definite rooms, §19, p11
floor oilcloth, §17, p27
floor oilcloths, Principles of, §17, p27
floors, Points for, §16, p37
Free-lance industrial, §21, p13
Handicrafts, §13, p1
hearth tiles, §16, p25
Industrial, §13, p1
ingrain carpets, §18, p40
inlaid linoleum, §17, p12
leaded glass, §20, p41
leather work, §14, p19
metal work, §14, p43
Mosaic tiling, §16, p16
of printed linoleum, §17, p20
parquetry, §16, p36
Principles of glass, §20, p41
Principles of wall-surface, §19, p9
print blocks, §13, p58
rugs, Considerations when, §18, p62
stained glass, §20, p41
stencils, §13, p26
table oilcloth, §17, p44
tapestry carpets, §18, p53
wall oilcloth, §17, p53
wallpaper, §19, p9
wall tiles, §16, p25
Wilton carpets, §18, p35
Designs, Amateur, analyzed, §17, p37
Basis of the, §16, p18
Character of, for hearth tiling, §16, p25
Character of, for wall tiling, §16, p25
Classes of, §17, p29
Color in oilcloth, §17, p28
Coloring for conventional, §15, p54
Display room for, §21, p7
Examples of mosaic floor, §16, p19
Examples of parquetry, §16, p38
Experiences in selling, §21, p25
Figure-subject, §15, p48

Designs for cork tiling, Typical, §17, p6
for inlaid linoleum, Typical, §17, p12
for printed linoleum, §17, p20
for table oilcloth, Typical, §17, p46
for wall oilcloth, Typical, §17, p56
from arbitrary motifs, §13, pp31, 59;
  §14, p23; §15, p41
from historic motifs, §13, p35; §14, p23
from plant-form motifs, §13, pp32, 59;
  §14, p23
Handicrafts, §21, p23
Importance of original, §14, p22
Industrial, §21, p24
Naturalistic floral, §15, p45
Necessity for original, §13, p20
not satisfactory, §21, p39
Portfolio of, §21, p7
Preparing the, §17, pp33, 45, 54
Prices paid for, §21, p23
Principles governing, §17, p44
Principles of cork-tile, §17, p4
Principles of wall-oilcloth, §17, p53
Producing salable, §17, p38
Reasons for failure to sell, §21, p12
Reasons why, are rejected, §21, p21
Selling, §21, pp4, 15
Selling, by mail, §21, p19
Sources of ideas for, §13, pp30, 59; §14,
  pp22, 44; §15, p41; §17, p29
Suggestions for obtaining, §18, p21
Typical floor-oilcloth, §17, p29
Where and how to sell, §21, p4
Desire to earn money, The, §21, p1
Detail dependent on cost, §20, p49
Details, Drawing the, §20, p52
possible, Fine, §17, p53
Developments, Importance of accurate,
  §15, p74
Devices for stacking china, §15, p33
Difficult shapes, Cutting, §20, p20
Dimensions, Laying out, §19, p16
Dining room decoration with stencil,
  §13, p42
room, Wallpaper for, §19, p12
Dips, Various, for metal, §14, p42
Discouragement, Avoiding, §21, p22·
Display rooms for designs, §21, p7
Disposition of materials, §15, p18
Diversity of arrangements, §19, p59
of styles, §19, p22
Dividers, Ring, §15, p6
Dividing reversed plan into sections,
  §16, p11
Drawing and cutting the stencil, §13, p3
and painting the design, §15, p60
for cylindrical cup, Full-size, §15, p68

Drawing for hemispherical cup, Full-size,
  §15, p71
Final, §19, p20
Full-scale reversed, §16, p9
Full-size, for plate, §15, p66
Glazier's, §20, p15
Laying glass on, §20, p34
Making the full-sized, §13, p46; §14, pp25,
  46; §15, p66
Pattern, §20, p15
room, The, §19, p12
sketches for painted windows, §20, p58
the design, §13, pp43, 59; §14, pp23, 45;
  §19, p16
the details, §20, p52
Drawings, Overstock of, §21, p39
Drill, Hand, §14, p34
Drop repeating pattern, The, §18, p16
Dull-glaze tile, §16, p31
-surface fabric, Patterns for, §17, p56
Dust needle, §15, p17
Duty, Extent of instructor's, §21, p1
Dyes for block-printing, §13, p56
Paints and, §13, p7
Pigments, etc., for wood-stenciling,
  §13, p22
Stenciling with atomizer and, §13, p15

E

Early Gothic period, §20, p5
Earnings of handicrafts designers, §21, p40
of industrial designers, §21, p42
Easel, Mounting glass on, §20, p27
Economy in use of colors, §17, p36
Effort, Importance of individual, §21, p46
Embossed leather work, §14, p8
tiles, §16, p23
Embroidery, Stenciling combined with,
  §13, p22
Enamel, §16, p27
Enameled tiles, §16, p22
Encaustic floor tiles, §16, pp3, 4
floor tiles, Colors of, §16, p5
floor tiles, Designing, §16, p6
floor tiles, Kinds of, §16, p4
floor tiles, Manufacture of, §16, p4
floor tiles, Sizes of, §16, p4
floor tiles, Use of, §16, p4
English style, §20, p23
Engraved leather, Plain tooled or, §14, p5
Equipment, Duty in using one's, §21, p46
furnished the student, §21, p46
of materials, A specimen, §13, p9
of useful materials, §14, p31
of useful tools, §14, p31
Erasing knives, Steel, §15, p17

Etching, §14, p39
Materials and tools for, §14, p39
with acids, §14, p39; §20, p26
Evolution of stained and leaded glass, §20, p2
Examples of china colors, §15, p51
of cut leather, §14, p28
of decorated china, §15, p74
of faience tiling, §16, p29
of leaded-glass sketches, §20, p56
of machine-made rugs, §18, p64
of mosaic floor designs, §16, p19
of oriental rugs, §18, p58
of painted-window sketches, §20, p60
of parquetry designs, §16, p38
of tooled leather, §14, p28
of tooled metal, §14, p50
of wallpapers, Typical, §19, p22
Exercises in block-print designing, §13, p62
Importance of, §21, p2
in designing carpets, §18, p66
in designing china decoration, §15, p75
in designing leather work, §14, p52
in designing leaded glass, §20, p65
in designing linoleum, §17, p59
in designing metal work, §14, p52
in designing oilcloth, §17, p59
in designing parquetry, §16, p40
in designing rugs, §18, p66
in designing stained glass, §20, p65
in designing stencil, §13, p62
in designing tiles, §16, p40
in designing wallpaper, §19, p65
Experiences of industrial designers, §21, p27
in obtaining positions, §21, p42
in selling designs, §21, p25
of handicrafts designers, §21, p25
of others, Knowing, §21, p25
Extent of instructor's duty, §21, p1

F

Fabric, Applying the blocks to the, §13, p56
Patterns for dull-surface, §17, p56
Patterns for glazed, §17, p58
Preparing the, for stenciling, §13, p12
Fabrics, Block-printing on, §13, p56
Principle of woven, §18, p6
Heavy, §18, p7
Stenciling on, §13, p11
suitable for block printing, §13, p56
suitable for stenciling, §13, p11
Faience, Applied, §16, p28
Meaning of term, §16, p27
tiles, §16, pp4, 27
tiles, Designing, §16, p28

Faience tiles, Manufacture and use of, §16, p27
tiling, Examples of, §16, p29
Failure to sell designs, Reasons for, §21, p12
False lead lines, Painting, §20, p27
Fancy glass, §20, p12
Feraghan rug, §18, p60
Field and borders, Patterns with, §17, p59
Choosing the proper, §21, pp13, 28
of industrial designing, §21, p13
Figure-subject designs, §15, p48
subjects, Coloring for, §15, p58
subjects in water color, §15, p64
work in mosaic, §16, p22
Figures in a window design, §20, p44
Final drawing, §19, p20
rendering, §19, p20
word of advice, §21, p47
Fine details possible, §17, p53
Finishing, Coloring and, §14, p42
the metal in colors, §14, p42
the window, §20, p39
Firing, §15, p25
gold, §15, p28
Length of time for, §15, p34
Necessity for, §20, p32
of china, The, §15, p31
ovens, §20, p32
the china, §15, p31
The first, §20, p32
the glass, §20, p32
The process of, §15, p34
First firing, The, §20, p32
use of window glass, §20, p2
Fitness, §21, p30
Salary versus, §21, p30
Fixing window in place, §20, p39
Flange, The, §20, p13
Flesh, Coloring for, §15, p58
Floor oilcloth, §17, pp22, 23
oilcloth, Composition of, §17, p23
oilcloth, Designing, §17, p27
-oilcloth designs, Typical, §17, p39
oilcloth, Manufacture of, §17, p23
-oilcloth patterns, Specimens of, §17, p39
oilcloth, Printing, §17, p23
oilcloth, Sizes of, §17, p23
oilcloths, Principles of designing, §17, p27
tiles, Encaustic, §16, p3
Flooring, Manufacture of parquetry, §16, p33
Parquet, §16, p32
Parquetry, §16, pp32, 33
Floors, Classification of hardwood, §16, p32
Hardwood, in patterns, §16, p32
Points for designing, §16, p37

Floral designs, Naturalistic, §15, p45
    patterns, Large, §17, p46
    studies in water color, §15, p61
    subjects in mosaic, §16, p19
Flowers, Coloring for, §15, p55
Fluxes, §15, p11
Follow-up letters, §21, p32
Form, Importance of, §20, p42
Forming the pattern in colors, §18, p9
    the pile in colors, §18, p9
Forms of tapestry carpet, §18, p51
Frames, §18, p8
    for Wilton carpet, §18, p35
Free-lance industrial designing, §21, p13
Frieze effects, Decorative, §19, p54
Full-scale reversed drawing, §16, p9
    selection of special tools, §14, p3
    -size design, Making, tracing, and trans-
        ferring, §13, p60
    -size drawing for cylindrical cup, §15, p68
    -size drawing or design, Making the,
        §15, p66
    -size drawing for hemispherical cup,
        §15, p71
    -size drawing for plate, §15, p66
    -size drawing, Making the, §13, p46;
        §14, pp25, 46
Furnishing names, Inadvisability of,
    §21, p20

                    G

Gas kiln, The oil and, §15, p32
Gauge and liner, Keramic, §15, p6
Gelatine tracing paper, §15, p7
General types of carpets, §18, p4
German style, §20, p23
Gilding leather, §14, p18
Glass, Antique, §20, p10
    Assembling the, §20, p35
    burnishing brush, §15, p17
    Cathedral, §20, p11
    Composition of colored, §20, p10
    cutter, Sharpening the, §20, p22
    cutter, The, §20, p18
    Cutting the, §20, p17
    designing, Principles of, §20, p41
    Evolution of stained and leaded, §20, p2
    Fancy, §20, p12
    Firing the, §20, p32
    First use of window, §20, p2
    Historic-period styles of, §20, p3
    Laying, on drawing, §20, p34
    Leading the, §20, p35
    Mounting, on easel, §20, p27
    Opalescent, §20, p11
    painting, Pigments for, §20, pp13, 23

Glass, Painting the, §20, p23
    Selecting the, §20, p17
    Stained and leaded, §20, p1
    staining, §20, p31
    Waxing up the, §20, p28
    White, §20, p12
    work, Materials for, §20, p10
Glaze, §16, p27
    decoration, §15, p2
Glazed fabric, Patterns for, §17, p58
    papers, Patterns for, §19, p58
    tiles, §16, p22
Glazier's drawing, §20, p15
Glazing the window, §20, p34
Gold, §15, p11
    Applying, to china, §15, p26
    Burnishing, §15, p28
    Firing, §15, p28
    Kinds of, §15, p20
    Liquid bright, §15, p20
    Methods of using, §15, p20
    Points to be observed in using, §15, p27
    painting on china, §15, p20
    Roman, §15, p20
Good coloring, Principles of, §15, p38
    design, Principles of, §15, p38
Gothic Revival period, §20, p7
Graphite paper, §15, p7
Grass-cloth effects, §19, p23
Ground-laying, §15, p20
Grounding oil, §15, p12
    Tinting and, §15, p19

                    H

Hall, The, §19, p12
Hallway, §13, p42
Hammer, §14, p32
Hammering up, §14, p41
Hand drill, §14, p34
    printing, §17, p26; §19, p7
Handicrafts designers, Earnings of, §21, p40
    designers, Experiences of, §21, p25
    designing, §13, p1
    Characteristics of leather, §14, p1
    Characteristics of metal, §14, p1
    designs, §21, p23
    work, Choice of line of, §13, p1
Hardwood floors, Classification of, §16, p32
    floors in patterns, §16, p32
Harmonious color combinations, §15, p52
    color contrasts, §15, p52
    colors, Specimens of, §15, p51
Head designers, Reaching, §21, p31
Heart of the lead, The, §20, p13
Hearth tiles, §16, pp4, 22
    tiles, Designing, §16, p25

Hearth tiles, Manufacture and use of, §16, p22
tiling, Character of designs for, §16, p25
Heavy fabrics, §18, p7
Hemispherical cup, Full-size drawing for, §15, p71
Hints for coloring, §15, p53
on leading, §20, p37
Historic motif, Converting, into stencil, §13, p40
motifs, Designs from, §13, pp35, 59; §14, p23
-period styles of glass, §20, p3
styles suited to certain rooms, §13, p41
History of carpets, §18, p4
Home stencil-decoration of walls, §13, p24
town versus city, §21, p30
How to obtain a position, §21, p28
others succeed, Knowing, §21, p42
to sell designs, Where and, §21, p4

I

Ideas for designs, Sources of, §13, p30; §14, pp22, 44; §15, p41; §17, p29
for motifs and repeats, §19, p14
Importance of original, §15, p41
Importance of accurate developments, §15, p74
of a consistent style, §20, p45
of definite aim, §21, p29
of experience, §21, p2
of form, §20, p42
of individual effort, §21, p46
of original designs, §14, pp22, 45
of original ideas, §15, p41
of self-advertising, §21, p15
Inadvisability of furnishing names, §21, p20
Individual effort, Importance of, §21, p46
Industrial designs, §21, p24
designers, Earnings of, §21, p42
designers, Experiences of, §21, p27
designing, §13, p1
designing, Field of, §21, p13
designing, Free-lance, §21, p13
Information needed, Special, §20, p48
Ingrain carpet, Manufacture of, §18, p38
carpet, §18, pp5, 38
carpet, Cross-section of, §18, p39
carpet, Rendered design for, §18, p42
carpet, Specimen of, §18, p42
carpets, Designing, §18, p40
carpets, Patterns for, §18, p40
carpets, Sizes of, §18, p40
paper, §19, p23
Initial salary, §21, p30
Inlaid linoleum, §17, pp2, 10

Inlaid linoleum, Designing, §17, p12
linoleum, Manufacture of, §17, p10
linoleum patterns, Specimens of, §17, p12
linoleum, Typical designs for, §17, p12
linoleum, Use of, §17, p10
motifs, Repeating pattern, §18, p14
Intaglio tiles, §16, p23
Interview, Advantages of personal, §21, p33
Preparing for the, §21, p34
Introductory practice in painting, §20, p24
Investigating the demand, §21, p5
Ironwork, §20, p13

J

Japanese method, Stenciling in the, §13, p21
Jig-saw method of making blocks, §13, p53
Joints, Soldering the, §20, p39

K

Keeping in touch with commercial product, §17, pp5, 12
in touch with dealers, §19, p16
in touch with manufacturers, §19, p16
Keramic gauge and liner, §15, p6
Kidderminster carpet, §18, pp5, 38
carpet, Manufacture of, §18, p38
Kiln and its use, The, §15, p31
Care and location of, §15, p34
Placing china in a, §15, p34
The charcoal, §15, p32
Kilns, §20, p32
Kirmanshah rug, §18, p59
Kitchen, The, §19, p13
Knife, Stopping, §20, p38
Knives, Steel erasing, §15, p17
Palette, §15, p16
Knowing experiences of others, §21, p25

L

Lapping stake, §14, p33
Large floral patterns, §17, p46
Laying cork tiling, §17, p4
glass on drawing, §20, p34
linoleum, §17, p11
mosaic floor tiling, §16, p8
out dimensions, §19, p16
out window shapes, §20, p48
parquetry, §16, p36
the mosaic, §16, p14
Lead lines, Painting false, §20, p27
lines, Putting in the, §20, p63
Leaded glass, Designing, §20, p41
-glass designing exercises, §20, p65
glass, Definition of, §20, p10
glass, Manufacture of, §20, p10
-glass sketches, Examples of, §20, p56

Leaded-glass windows, §20, p9
Leading, Hints on, §20, p37
   the glass, §20, p35
   -up the window, §20, p34
Leads, The, §20, p12
Leaf of the lead, The, §20, p13
Leather and the design, The, §14, p14
   articles for stenciling, §13, p23
   Burning the, §14, p15
   Coloring, §14, p2
   Corrosive liquids used on, §14, p17
   Cutting, §14, pp2, 12
   Examples of cut, §14, p28
   Examples of tooled, §14, p28
   Gilding, §14, p18
   handicrafts, Characteristics of, §14, p1
   Modeling the, §14, p8
   Mounting, over silk, §14, p12
   Painting, §14, p17
   Plain tooled or engraved, §14, p5
   Preparing the, §14, pp6, 8
   Preparing the, and the design, §14, pp10, 11
   suitable for tooling, §14, p2
   suitable for various purposes, §14, p2
   Transferring design to, §14, p6
   treatment, Kind of, §14, p21
   Tooling, §14, pp2, 8, 10
   Varnishing, §14, p17
   work, §14, p2
   work, Articles suitable for, §14, p19
   work, Classes of decorative, §14, p5
   work, Colored, §14, p16
   work, Cut out, over silk, §14, p11
   work, Designing, §14, p19
   -work designing exercises, §14, p52
   work, Embossed, §14, p8
   work, Repoussé, §14, p8
   work, Tools required for, §14, p3
Letters, Business cards and, §21, p7
   Follow-up, §21, p32
   Personal, §21, p32
Library decoration with stencil, §13, p42
   wallpaper, §19, p13
Limitations of wood cutting, §13, p58
Liner, Keramic gauge and, §15, p6
Lines, Plotting out the construction, §15, p21
Linoleum, §17, p2
   Classification and definition of, §17, p2
   Composition of, §17, p10
   designing exercises, §17, p59
   designing, Composition applied to, §17, p20
   Designing inlaid, §17, p12
   Designing of printed, §17, p20
Linoleum, Inlaid, §17, pp2, 10
   Laying, §17, p11
   Manufacture of inlaid, §17, p10
   Manufacture of printed, §17, p20
   nails, §17, p11
   patterns, Specimens of inlaid, §17, p12
   Printed, §17, pp2, 20
   Sizes of, §17, p10
   Typical designs for inlaid, §17, p12
   Use of inlaid, §17, p10
   Use of printed, §17, p20
Linoleums and oilcloths, §21, p16
Lithographers' crayons, §15, p5
Liquid bright gold, §15, pp11, 20
Living room, §13, p42
Location of kiln, §15, p34
Luster colors, §15, p10
   colors, Character of, §15, p29
   painting on china, §15, p29

M

Machine-made rugs, Characteristics of §18, p60
   -made rugs, Examples of, §18, p64
   -made rugs, Modern, §18, pp56, 60
   -made rugs, Sizes of, §18, p61
   printing, §17, p26; §19, p9
Making and using print blocks, §13, p52
   and using stencils, §13, p3
   full-size design, §13, p60
   the appointment, §21, p34
   the design, §16, pp29, 35; §17, p12
   the design in colors, §13, p59
   the full-sized drawing, §13, p46; §14, p46
   the sketch design in colors, §15, p60
   working drawings, §20, p13
Mallet, Wooden, §14, p34
Manufacture of Axminster carpet, §18, p44
   of Brussels carpet, §18, p6
   of cork tiling, §17, p3
   of encaustic floor tiles, §16, p4
   of faience tiles, §16, p27
   of floor oilcloth, §17, p23
   of hearth tiles, §16, p22
   of ingrain carpet, §18, p38
   of inlaid linoleum, §17, p10
   of Kidderminster carpet, §18, p38
   of leaded glass, §20, p10
   of mosaic tiles, §16, p8
   of parquetry flooring, §16, p33
   of printed linoleum, §17, p20
   of stained glass, §20, p10
   of table oilcloth, §17, p43
   of tapestry carpets, §18, p50
   of wall oilcloth, §17, p52
   of wall tiles, §16, p22

Manufacture of wallpapers, §19, p2
of Wilton carpet, §18, p33
Manufacturers, Keeping in touch with,
§19, p16
Reaching, §21, pp15, 31
Marketing a design training, §21, p4
Mash block, §17, p26
Materials and tools required, §14, p34
A specimen equipment of, §13, p9
Disposition of, §15, p18
for chasing, §14, p35
Equipment of useful, §14, p31
for etching, §14, p39
for glass work §20, p10
for piercing and sawing, §14, p37
for repoussé work, §14, p36
required for block-printing, §13, p52
required for china painting, §15, p4
required, The stencil and, §13, p3
Matt, §20, p28
burnish gold, §15, p11
colors, §15, p10
Matting, §20, p28
Medium and method of painting stencils,
§13, p26
and method of working, §15, p39
Metal articles for stenciling, §13, p23
Classes of, suitable for tooling, §14, p30
Examples of tooled, §14, p50
Finishing the, in colors, §14, p42
handicrafts, Characteristics of, §14, p1
in sheets, §14, p30
Tooling and piercing, §14, p30
Transferring design to, §14, p49
treatment, Kind of, §14, p44
Various dips for, §14, p42
work, §14, p30
work, Articles suitable for, §14, p43
work, Designing, §14, p43
-work designing exercises, §14, p52
work, Tools required for, §14, p31
Methods of approach, §21, p32
of decorating china, §15, p2
of self-advertising, §21, p6
of using gold, §15, p20
of weaving yarns, §18, p7
of working, Medium and, §15, p39
of working on china, §15, p18
of working on walls, §13, p24
Modeling the leather, §14, p8
Moist colors in tubes, §15, p9
Money, The desire to earn, §21, p1
Moquette Axminster carpet, Section of,
§18, p44
Axminster carpet, Weave of, §18, p44
Mosaic, Figure work in, §16, p22

Mosaic floor designs, Examples of, §16,
p19
floor tiles, §16, p8
floor tiling, Laying, §16, p8
Floral subjects in, §16, p19
Laying the, §16, p14
tiles, §16, p3
tiles, Manufacture and use of, §16, p8
tiling, Designing, §16, p16
Motif, Converting historic, into stencil,
§13, p40
Motifs and repeats, Ideas for, §19, p14
Classes of design, §14, p45
Designs from arbitrary, §13, pp31, 59;
§14, p23
Designs from historic, §13, pp35, 59;
§14, p23
Designs from plant-form, §13, pp32, 59;
§14, p23
Partly conventionalized, §15, p45
Purely conventionalized, §15, p44
Severely conventionalized, §15, p44
Mounting glass on easel, §20, p27
leather over silk, §14, p12
the sketches, §20, p61
Multi-symmetrical repeat, The, §18, p20

N

Names, Inadvisability of furnishing,
§21, 20
Naturalistic, Conventional versus, §15, p40
floral designs, §15, p45
repeating effects, §19, p31

O

Oatmeal paper, §19, p23
Objectionable personality, §21, p39
Observing care in outlining, §17, p34
public wants, §19, p15
Obtaining a position, §21, p28
positions, Experiences in, §21, p42
suggestions for designs, §18, p21
Oil and gas kiln, The, §15, p32
Oilcloth, §17, p22
Classification of, §17, p22
Composition of floor, §17, p23
Composition of table, §17, p43
Composition of wall, §17, p52
Definition of term, §17, p22
-designing exercises, §17, p59
Designing floor, §17, p27
Designing table, §17, p44
Designing wall, §17, p53
designs, Color in, §17, p28
Floor, §17, p22
Manufacture of floor, §17, p23

Oilcloth, Manufacture of table, §17, p43
  Manufacture of wall, §17, p52
  patterns, Specimens of table-, §17, p46
  Table, §17, pp22, 43
  Typical designs for table, §17, p46
  Wall, §17, pp22, 52
Oilcloths, Linoleums and, §21, p16
  Principles of designing floor, §17, p27
Oils, §15, p11
Opalescent glass, §20, p11
  style, §20, p23
Oriental rugs, §18, p56
  rugs, Characteristics of, §18, p56
  rugs, Examples of, §18, p58
Original designs, Importance of, §14, pp22, 45
  designs, Necessity for, §13, p30
  ideas, Importance of, §15, p41
Originality an essential, §17, p31
Outline blocks, §17, p24
  chasing, §14, p35
Outlines, Tooling the, §14, p7
  Trying, §20, p24
Outlining, Observing care in, §17, p34
  pens and ink, §15, p7
Ovens, Firing, §20, p32
Over-glaze colors, §15, p10
  -glaze decoration, §15, p3
Overstock of drawings, §21, p39

P

Painted tiles, §16, p23
  -window sketches, Examples of, §20, p60
  windows, Styles of, §20, p23
Painting and shading brushes, §15, p12
  China painting like other, §15, p24
  false lead lines, §20, p27
  Gold, on china, §15, p20
  Introductory practice in, §20, p24
  leather, §14, p17
  Luster, on china, §15, p29
  mediums, §15, p11
  Oil, §15, p11
  on china, §15, p4
  outfits for beginners, §15, p17
  Points for luster, §15, p29
  stencils, Medium and method of, §13, p26
  the design, §15, p24
  the design, Drawing and, §15, p60
  the glass, §20, p23
Paints and dyes, §13, p7
  for block-printing, §13, p56
Palette for china colors, §15, p15
  knives, §15, p16
Panel-and-crown effects, Plain, §19, p45
Paneling with wallpaper and wood, §19, p62

Paneling with wallpaper only, §19, p59
Parlor decoration with stencil, §13, p42
  Wallpaper for, §19, p12
Parquet flooring, §16, p32
  flooring, Definition of, §16, p33
Parquetry, §16, p32
  Designing, §16, p36
  designing exercises, §16, p40
  designs, Examples of, §16, p38
  flooring, §16, p32
  Laying, §16, p36
  patterns, §16, p35
  Tiles and, §21, p15
Partly conventionalized motifs, §15, p45
Pattern arrangement, Basis of, §16, p25
Pattern, Blocking in the, §19, p16
  drawing, §20, p15
  in colors, Forming the, §18, p9
  of isolated motifs, Repeating, §18, p14
  The drop repeating, §18, p16
Patterns, Cutting the, §20, p14
  for Axminster carpet, §18, p46
  for Brussels carpet, §18, p14
  for dull-surface fabric, §17, p56
  for glazed fabric, §17, p58
  for glazed papers, §19, p58
  for ingrain carpets, §18, p40
  for tapestry carpets, §18, p53
  for Wilton carpets, §18, p35
  Hardwood floors in, §16, p32
  Large floral, §17, p46
  Parquetry, §16, p35
  Small repeating, §17, p48
  Specimens of floor-oilcloth, §17, p39
  Specimens of table-oilcloth, §17, p46
  Specimens of wall-oilcloth, §17, p56
  Specimen wallpaper, §19, p22
  with field and borders, §17, p50
Pencil medium, §15, p5
Pens and ink, Outlining, §15, p7
Period of decadence, §20, p7
  style, §13, p35
Perpendicular Gothic period, §20, p6
Personal canvass, §21, p9
  interview, The, §21, p33
  interview, Advantages of, §21, p33
  letters, §21, p32
  solicitation, §21, p9
Personality, Objectionable, §21, p39
Perspective in a window design, §20, p45
Pigments, §15, p8
  dyes, etc., for wood-stenciling, §13, p22
  for glass painting, §20, pp13, 23
Piercing and sawing, Material and tools for, §14, p37

Piercing metal, Tooling and, §14, p30
Pile, Forming the, in colors, §18, p9
Placing china in a kiln, §15, p34
Plain panel-and-crown effects, §19, p45
-toned effects, §19, p23
tooled or engraved leather, §14, p5
Plan drawing, Affixing tesseræ to, §16, p12
Planishing, §14, p37
Planning decoration, §20, p50
the design, §13, pp26, 58; §14, pp19, 43;
§15, p36; §19, p9
Planted design, Colors for a, §18, p27
Plant-form motifs, Designs from, §13, pp32,
59; §14, p23
Planting, §18, p10
for Wilton carpet, §18, p35
Plate, Full-size drawing for, §15, p66
Plates, Decorated, §15, p75
Pliers, §14, p33
Plotting out the construction lines, §15, p21
Points for designing floors, §16, p37
for luster painting, §15, p29
Preparing the fabric for stenciling, §13, p12
the leather, §14, pp6, 8
the leather and the design, §14, pp10, 11
the sketches, §20, p46
Preliminary data, Securing, §20, p46
sketch design, §13, p25
trial sketches, §14, p45
Prices paid for designs, §21, p23
Principle of printing wallpaper, §19, p2
of the block print, §13, p52
of the stencil, §13, p3
of woven fabrics, §18, p6
Principles, Application of design, §18, p13
governing designs, §17, p44
governing linoleum designs, §17, p12
of cork-tile designs, §17, p4
of designing floor oilcloths, §17, p27
of glass designing, §20, p41
of good coloring, §15, p38
of good design, §15, p38
of wall-oilcloth designs, §17, p53
of wall-surface designing, §19, p9
Print blocks, Designing, §13, p58
blocks, Making and using, §13, p52
Purpose of block, §13, p58
Printed linoleum, §17, pp2, 20
linoleum, Designs for, §17, p20
linoleum, Manufacture of, §17, p20
tiles, §16, p23
Printing, Block prints and, §13, p52
blocks, Preparing, §17, p23
floor oilcloth, §17, p23
Hand, §17, p26; §19, p7
Machine, §17, p26; §19, p9

Printing on china, §15, p3
rollers, The, §17, p44
table oilcloth, §17, p44
tapestry carpet, §18, p51
wall oilcloth, §17, p53
wallpaper, Principle of, §19, p2
Precautions in cutting, §20, p21
Process of firing, The, §15, p34
Producing salable designs, §17, p38
Professional advice, Value of, §21, p3
stencil decoration of walls, §13, p25
Proper field, Choosing the, §21, p13
line, Selecting, §21, p5
position when working, §15, p18
Public demand, Studying, §21, p14
taste, Satisfying, §17, p32
wants, Observing, §19, p15
Punch, §14, p34
Purpose of block print, §13, p58
of stencil, §13, p26
of the window, §20, p42
Putting in the lead lines, §20, p63
Pyrography, §14, p14

R

Reaching head designers, §21, p31
manufacturers, §21, pp15, 31
Reasons for failure to sell designs, §21, p12
why designs are rejected, §21, p21
Reception room, §13, p42
Refiring, §15, p25; §20, p33
Regular position, Advantage of, §21, p29
Request, A special, §21, p48
Requirements for practical design work,
§16, p1
Removing paper, §16, p15
Renaissance period, §20, p6
Rendered design for Axminster carpet,
§18, p48
design for Brussels carpet, §18, p31
design for ingrain carpet, §18, p42
design for Wilton carpet, §18, p36
Rendering, Final, §19, p20
on squared paper, §18, pp35, 40, 46, 53
Repainting, §15, p25; §20, p33
Repeat, The multi-symmetrical, §18, p20
Repeats, Ideas for motifs and, §19, p14
Repeating effects, Conventional, §19, p24
effects, Naturalistic, §19, p31
pattern of isolated motifs, §18, p14
pattern, The drop, §18, p16
patterns, Small, §17, p48
Repoussé leather work, §14, p8
work, §14, p36
work, Materials for, §14, p36
work, Tools for, §14, p36

Restrictions, Technical, §20, p41
Reversed drawing, Full-scale, §16, p11
  plan, Dividing, into sections, §16, p11
Ring dividers, §15, p6
Riveting, §14, p41
Rollers, The printing, §17, p44
Roman gold, §15, p20
Rooms, Designing for definite, §19, p11
  Historic styles suited to certain, §13, p41
Rough-cast stake, §14, p34
Rubbing down, §16, p15
Rug-designing exercises, §18, p66
Rugs, §18, p55
  Carpets and, §21, p17
  Characteristics of Oriental, §18, p56
  Characteristics of machine-made, §18, p60
  Classification of, §18, p55
  Considerations when designing, §18, p62
  Examples of machine-made, §18, p64
  Examples of Oriental, §18, p58
  Feraghan, §18, p60
  Kirmanshah, §18, p59
  Sehna, §18, p59
  Meaning of term, §18, p55
  Modern machine-made, §18, p56
  Oriental, §18, p56
  Sizes of machine-made, §18, p61

S

Salable designs, Producing, §17, p38
Salaries paid to designers, §21, p40
Salary, Initial, §21, p30
  versus fitness, §21, p30
Satisfying public taste, §17, p32
Saw frame, §14, p34
Sawing and piercing, §14, pp37, 38
Saws, §14, p34
Scaled sketch design in colors, §13, p43
Schemes of wall arrangement, §19, p64
Scissors, Special pattern, §20, p16
Section of moquette Axminster carpet,
  §18, p44
  of tapestry carpet, §18, p50
Securing preliminary data, §20, p46
Sehna rug, §18, p59
Selecting proper line, §21, p5
  the glass, §20, p17
Self-advertising, Importance of, §21, p15
  -advertising, Methods and necessity of,
  §21, p6
Selling designs, §21, pp4, 15
  designs by mail, §21, p19
  designs, Experiences in, §21, p25
Services not needed, §21, p38
Setting the window in place, §20, p40
Severely conventionalized motifs, §15, p44

Shape of article decorated, §15, p36
  Suitability of design to, §15, p36
Shapes of cork tiles, §17, p3
  Cutting simple, §20, p18
Sharpening the glass cutter, §20, p22
Shears, §14, p32
Sheet brass, §14, p32
  copper, §14, p32
  copper, Thickness of, §14, p30
  copper, Varieties of, §14, p30
Sheets, Metal in, §14, p30
Silk, Cut-out leather work over, §14, p11
Silver, §14, p30
Simple assortment of tools, §14, p3
Situation of the window, §20, p42
Sizes of Axminster carpet, §18, p46
  of Brussels carpet, §18, p12
  of cork tiles, §17, p3
  of encaustic floor tiles, §16, p4
  of hearth tiles, §16, p24
  of ingrain carpets, §18, p40
  of floor oilcloth, §17, p23
  of linoleum, §17, p10
  of machine-made rugs, §18, p61
  of mosaic floor tiles, §16, p8
  of table oilcloth, §17, p43
  of tapestry carpet, §18, p53
  of wall oilcloth, §17, p52
  of wall tiles, §16, p24
  of Wilton carpet, §18, p35
  of wood strips, §16, p33
Sketch design in colors, Scaled, §13, p43
  design, Making the, in colors, §15, p60
  design, Preliminary, §13, p25
Sketches, Coloring the, §20, p54
  Examples of leaded-glass, §20, p56
  Examples of painted-window, §20, p60
  for painted windows, Drawing and color-
    ing, §20, p58
  Mounting the, §20, p61
  Preliminary trial, §14, pp23, 45
  Preparing the, §20, p46
  Submitting, to clients, §20, p61
Sleeping room decoration in stencil,
  §13, p42
Small repeating patterns, §17, p48
Smoothing stake, §14, p33
Soldering, §14, p41
  the joints, §20, p39
Solicitation, Personal, §21, p9
Solid-frame design, Colors for a, §18, p25
Sources of ideas for designs, §13, pp30, 59;
  §14, pp22, 44; §15, p41; §17, p29
Spattering in colors, §14, p16
Special information needed, §20, p46
  -pattern scissors, §20, p16

Special request, A, §21, p48
Specialized training, Necessity for, §17, p1; §18, p1; §19, p1; §20, p1
Specimen equipment of materials, A, §13, p9
of Axminster carpet, §18, p49
of body Brussels carpet, §18, p33
of ingrain carpet, §18, p42
of tapestry carpet, §18, p54
of Wilton carpet, §18, p36
wallpaper patterns, §19, p22
Specimens of cork-tile patterns, §17, p6
of floor-oilcloth patterns, §17, p39
of harmonious colors, §15, p51
of inlaid-linoleum patterns, §17, p12
of table-oilcloth patterns, §17, p46
of wall-oilcloth patterns, §17, p56
Squared paper, Blocking out and rendering design on, §18, pp22, 35, 40, 46, 53
Stacking china, Devices for, §15, p33
china in a kiln, §15, p34
Stained and leaded glass, §20, p1; §21, p18
and leaded glass, Evolution of, §20, p2
and leaded glass, Styles of, §20, p3
glass, Definition of, §20, p10
glass, Designing, §20, p41
-glass designing exercises, §20, p65
glass, Manufacture of, §20, p10
-glass windows, §20, p9
Staining, Glass, §20, p31
Stake, Lapping, §14, p33
Rough-cast, §14, p34
Smoothing, §14, p33
Status of china decoration, §15, p1
Steel erasing knives, §15, p16
Stencil and materials required, The, §13, p3
Converting historic motif into, §13, p40
-decoration of walls, Home, §13, p24
-decoration of walls, Professional, §13, p25
-designing exercises, §13, p62
Drawing and cutting the, §13, p3
Principle of the, §13, p3
print, Appearance of, §13, p49
Purpose of, §13, p26
Tracing and cutting the, §13, p48
Stenciling combined with embroidery, §13, p22
decorations on walls, §13, p24
in the Japanese method, §13, p21
on fabrics, §13, p11
Preparing the fabric for, §13, p12
Stencils and, §13, p3
with atomizer and dyes, §13, p15
Suitable fabrics for, §13, p11
with acids, §13, p17
with brush and pigment, §13, p12

Stenciling, Wood, leather, and metal articles for, §13, p23
Stencils and stenciling, §13, p3
Designing, §13, p26
Making and using, §13, p3
Medium and method of painting, §13, p26
Stippler brush, §20, p29
Stipplers, §15, p15
Stippling brushes, §15, p15
Stopping knife, §20, p38
Striking color combinations, §15, p52
Student, An appeal to the, §21, p47
Equipment furnished the, §21, p46
Studying public demand, §21, p14
Style, Importance of a consistent, §20, p45
Period, §13, p35
Styles, Diversity of, §19, p22
Historic, suited to certain rooms, §13, p41
of glass, Historic-period, §20, p3
of painted windows, §20, p23
of stained and leaded glass, §20, p3
Submitting sketches to clients, §20, p61
Suggestions for designs, Obtaining, §18, p21
Suitable fabrics for block printing, §13, p56
fabrics for stenciling, §13, p11
Suitability of design to shape, §15, p36
of design to use, §15, p37
Syndicate, Artists', §21, p9

T

Table oilcloth, §17, pp22, 43
oilcloth, Composition of, §17, p43
oilcloth, Designing, §17, p44
oilcloth, Manufacture of, §17, p43
oilcloth, Printing, §17, p44
oilcloth, Sizes of, §17, p43
oilcloth, Typical designs for, §17, p46
Tapestry Axminster, §18, p50
Brussels, §18, p50
carpet, §18, p5
carpet, Forms of, §18, p51
carpet, Printing, §18, p51
carpet, Section of, §18, p50
carpet, Specimen of, §18, p54
carpets, Characteristics of, §18, p50
carpets, Designing, §18, p53
carpets, Manufacture of, §18, p50
carpets, Patterns for, §18, p53
carpets, Sizes of, §18, p53
Technical restrictions, §20, p41
Tesserae, §16, p8
Affixing, to plan drawing, §16, p12
Cutting, to shape, §16, p13
Thickness of sheet copper, §14, p30
Things designer must know, §21, p2

Threads, Warp, §18, p7
  Weft, §18, p7
Ticking-in the design, §18, p29
Ties, or bridges, Necessity for, §13, p27
Tile, Della Robbia, §16, p31
  Dull-glaze, §16, p31
  -designing exercises, §16, p40
Tiles, §16, p3
  and parquetry, §21, p15
  Classification of, §16, p3
  Colors of encaustic floor, §16, p5
  Colors of mosaic floor, §16, p8
  Designing encaustic floor, §16, p6
  Designing faience, §16, p28
  Embossed, §16, p23
  Enameled, §16, p22
  Encaustic floor, §16, pp3, 4
  Faience, §16, pp4, 27
  Glazed, §16, p22
  Hearth, §16, pp4, 22
  Intaglio, §16, p23
  Kinds of encaustic floor, §16, p4
  Kinds of mosaic floor, §16, p8
  Manufacture and use of hearth, §16, p22
  Manufacture and use of wall, §16, p22
  Manufacture of encaustic floor, §16, p4
  Manufacture of faience, §16, p27
  Manufacture of mosaic, §16, p8
  Meaning of term, §16, p3
  Mosaic, §16, p3
  Mosaic floor, §16, p8
  Painted, §16, p23
  Printed, §16, p23
  Sizes and colors of wall, §16, p24
  Sizes and colors of hearth, §16, p24
  Sizes of encaustic floor, §16, p4
  Sizes of mosaic floor, §16, p8
  Use of encaustic floor, §16, p4
  Use of faience, §16, p27
  Use of mosaic, §16, p8
  Wall, §16, pp4, 22
Tiling, Designing mosaic, §16, p16
  Examples of faience, §16, p29
  Laying mosaic floor, §16, p8
Time for firing, Length of, §15, p34
Tinting and grounding, §15, p19
  the china surface, §15, p19
Tool, The cutting, §20, p18
Tooled background, Cut leather with, §14, p10
  leather, Examples of, §14, p28
  metal, Examples of, §14, p50
  or engraved leather, Plain, §14, p5
Tooling, §14, p35
  and piercing metal, §14, p30
  Classes of metal suitable for, §14, p30

Tooling leather, §14, p2
  Leather suitable for, §14, p2
  the leather, §14, pp8, 10
  the outlines, §14, p7
Tools, Equipment of useful, §14, p31
  for chasing, §14, p35
  for etching, §14, p39
  for piercing and sawing, §14, p37
  for repoussé work, §14, p36
  Full selection of special, §14, p3
  required for leather work, §14, p3
  required for metal work, §14, p31
  required, Materials and, §14, p34
  Simple assortment of, §14, p3
Tracing and cutting the stencil, §13, p48
  full-size design, §18, p60
  paper, Gelatine, §15, p7
  the design, §14, pp27, 49; §15, p22
Trade papers, Advertising in, §21, p33
Training, Necessity for specialized, §17, p1;
  §18, p1; §19, p1; §20, p1
  Practical application of, §21, p46
Transfer-picture china decoration, §15, p3
Transferring design to china, §15, p21
  design to leather, §14, p6
  design to metal, §14, p49
  full-size design, §13, p60
  the design, §14, pp8, 27, 35, 37, 38, 39;
  §15, p22
Transparency in a window design, §20, p44
Trial sketches, Preliminary, §14, pp23, 45
Trying out color schemes, §19, p17
  outlines, §20, p24
Tubes, Moist colors in, §15, p9
Turning over edges, §14, p40
Types of carpets, General, §18, p4

U

Under-glaze decoration, §15, p2
Use of colors, Economy in, §17, p36
  of cork tiling, §17, p3
  of encaustic floor tiles, §16, p4
  of faience tiles, §16, p27
  of hearth tiles, §16, p22
  of inlaid linoleum, §17, p10
  of mosaic tiles, p16, p8
  of parquetry flooring, §16, p33
  of printed linoleum, §17, p20
  of special design paper, §16, p16
  of wall tiles, §16, p22
  of window glass, First, §20, p2
Suitability of design to, §15, p37
Using one's equipment, Duty in, §21, p46
  print blocks, Making and, §13, p52
  stencils, Making and, §13, p3

V

Value of professional advice, §21, p3
Varieties of sheet copper, §14, p30
Various dips for metal, §14, p42
Varnishing leather, §14, p17
Vases, Decorated, §15, p75
Velvet carpet, §18, p33
Vertical-striped effects, §19, p39
Vials, Powder colors in, §15, p9

W

Wall arrangement, Schemes of, §19, p64
oilcloth, §17, pp22, 52
oilcloth, Composition of, §17, p52
oilcloth, Designing, §17, p53
-oilcloth designs, Principles of, §17, p53
oilcloth, Manufacture of, §17, p52
-oilcloth patterns, Specimens of, §17, p56
oilcloth, Printing, §17, p53
oilcloth, Sizes of, §17, p52
oilcloth, Typical designs for, §17, p56
-surface designing, Principles of, §19, p9
surfaces, Arrangement of, §19, p59
tiles, §16, pp4, 22
tiles, Designing, §16, p25
tiles, Manufacture and use of, §16, p22
tiling, Character of designs for, §16, p25
Wallpaper and wood, Paneling with, §19, p62
Designing, §19, p9
-designing exercises, §19, p65
only, Paneling with, §19, p59
patterns, Specimen, §19, p22
Principle of printing, §19, p2
Wallpapers, §19, p2; §21, p17
Manufacture of, §19, p2
Typical examples of, §19, p22
Warp threads, §18, p7
Water color, Figure subjects in, §15, p64
color, Flower studies in, §15, p61
Wax, §15, p7
Waxing up the glass, §20, p28
Weave of Brussels carpet, Characteristic, §18, p8
of chenille Axminster carpet, §18, p45
of moquette Axminster carpet, §18, p44
of Wilton carpet, Characteristic, §18, p33
Weaving yarns, Method of, §18, p7
Weft threads, §18, p7
Where and how to sell designs, §21, p4
Where to obtain a position, §21, p28
White glass, §20, p12
Why applicant is rejected, §21, p38
Wilton carpet, §18, pp4, 33
carpet, Characteristic weave of, §18, p33
carpet, Frames for, §18, p35
carpet, Manufacture of, §18, p33
carpet, Planting for, §18, p35
carpet, Rendered design for, §18, p36
carpet, Sizes of, §18, p35
carpet, Specimen of, §18, p36
carpets, Designing, §18, p35
carpets, Patterns for, §18, p35
compared with Brussels, §18, p34
Window, Cementing the, §20, p39
design, Backgrounds in a, §20, p45
design, Color in a, §20, p43
design, Figures in a, §20, p44
design, Costumes in a, §20, p44
design, Perspective in a, §20, p45
Purpose of the, §20, p42
design, Transparency in a, §20, p44
Finishing the, §20, p39
Fixing, in place, §20, p39
glass, First use of, §20, p2
Glazing the, §20, p34
Leading up, §20, p34
shapes, Laying out, §20, p48
Setting the, in place, §20, p40
Situation of the, §20, p42
Windows, Leaded-glass, §20, p9
Stained-glass, §20, p9
Styles of painted, §20, p23
Women's Exchange, §21, p8
Wood articles for stenciling, §13, p23
carpet, §16, p34
cutting, Limitations of, §13, p58
Paneling with wallpaper and, §19, p62
-stenciling, Pigments, dyes, etc., for, §13, p22
strips, Kinds of, §16, p33
strips, Sizes of, §16, p33
Wooden block, §14, p33
mallet, §14, p34
Word of advice, Final, §21, p47
Working drawings, Making, §20, p13
Woven fabrics, Principle of, §18, p6

Y

Yarns, Method of weaving, §18, p7

Lightning Source UK Ltd.
Milton Keynes UK
UKHW011350160219
337399UK00001B/32/P

9 781445 568416